UNVEILING SUFISM
FROM MANHATTAN TO MECCA

*William Rory Dickson and
Meena Sharify-Funk*

SHEFFIELD UK   BRISTOL CT

Published by Equinox Publishing Ltd.

UK: Office 415, The Workstation, 15 Paternoster Row, Sheffield, South Yorkshire, S1 2BX
USA: ISD, 70 Enterprise Drive, Bristol, CT 06010

www.equinoxpub.com

First published 2017

British Library Cataloguing-in-Publication Data
A catalogue record for this book is available from the British Library.

Library of Congress Cataloging-in-Publication Data
Names: Dickson, William Rory, 1979-, author. | Sharify-Funk, Meena, author.
Title: Unveiling Sufism : from Manhattan to Mecca / William Rory Dickson and
  Meena Sharify-Funk.
Description: Sheffield, UK ; Bristol, CT : Equinox Publishing Ltd., 2017.
Identifiers: LCCN 2016041928| ISBN 9781781792438 (hb) | ISBN 9781781792445
  (pb)
Subjects: LCSH: Sufism--History. | Sufism--Doctrines.
Classification: LCC BP188.5 .D53 2017 | DDC 297.4--dc23
LC record available at https://lccn.loc.gov/2016041928

ISBN: 978 1 78179 243 8   (hardback)
        978 1 78179 244 5   (paperback)

Typeset by CA Typesetting Ltd, www.publisherservices.co.uk
Printed and bound in the UK by Lightning Source UK Ltd., Milton Keynes and
Lightning Source Inc., La Vergne, TN

UNVEILING SUFISM

DEDICATION

As the authors of the book were working on an early version of the text some years ago, a child just out of his toddler years, approached them. He curiously enquired about the book and then suggested that they must "go beyond the earth". When asked to tell them more, he thoughtfully remarked that, "the universe has no end". When asked to say even more, he added, "You have no end".

This book is for you, Mikael.

CONTENTS

LIST OF FIGURES

PREFACE AND ACKNOWLEDGMENTS

Academic writing is by no means reducible to autobiography, yet it is undeniable that our life journeys have a profound impact on the truths we are prepared to discover. Personal experiences establish frames of reference that inform the tasks of research, meaning production, and composition, and shape our aspirations for the published word. Insofar as our journeys and experiences derive their content and richness from relationships and learning encounters, there is a very real sense in which a written work bears the imprint of many persons besides those officially listed as authors, and to all of them a debt of acknowledgement is owed.

For Meena Sharify-Funk, the story behind this book began over 20 years ago, in 1992, when her father, Majdeddin Sharifi-Hosseini, invited her to accompany him on a trip to Shiraz, Iran, the city of his birth and home to many of his ancestors. She is forever grateful for his Shirazi heart, for helping her to learn and seek the meaning of *del beh del ra dareh* ("between hearts there is no separation"), and for falling in love with Meena's Scandinavian American mother, Nancy Olga Sharify. Meena is eternally blessed by her mother's teaching, and steady example of what can be accomplished through hard work, fortitude, and compassion for others. She is also grateful to her brother Robert Hussein, and his example of intellectual curiosity and wonder as well as academic excellence.

The trip to Shiraz opened for Meena a world that had previously seemed very distant from her hometown of Greeley, Colorado and her undergraduate studies in Minnesota. In addition to hearing new stories about her late grandfather, Mohammed Hossein Sharifi-Hosseini, and his Sufi orientation and heritage, she came into a much deeper relationship with her extended Persian family, including her two dear uncles, Aladdin and Sadruddin Sharifi-Hosseini (both of whom she is indebted to for their loving kindness and for opening the heart of Shiraz to her). Shortly after the trip, the latter uncle, himself a professor of entomology, mailed her a package containing a most intriguing book, written entirely in Persian by a great-great-great grandfather during the 1800s. Folded into the centre of the book was a remarkable cosmological map drafted by yet another grandfather from six generations back. Although it would take years to begin to decipher the metaphysical content of this spiritual map, and to gain a firmer grasp of how this content synthesized centuries of Sufi thought about two arcs of the soul's journey through a multi-layered cosmos – an arc of emanation, and an arc of return – this mysterious centrepiece of the book captivated her attention and invited further explorations of Shiraz and its many saints, to whom she humbly bows. She also extends her love to all her Persian relatives including Badri and Parvaneh Sharifi-Hosseini; Faegheh, Cyroos, Arash and Scheherazad Pashootan; Homayoun, Mashid, and Shahir Khavari; Faredeh Dorafshan; and the Vahidi, Ahmadi, Samii, and Shahid-Salles families.

In 1994, Meena initiated graduate studies in Washington, DC, and met her mentor Abdul Aziz Said, a scholar of International Relations, Peace Studies, and Islamic Studies at the American University School of International Service. She is eternally grateful for his wise guidance, his unending support, and his teaching that "the whole world needs the whole world". Dr. Said opened many doors, including a door to studies in Arabic literature and Sufi philosophy at the University of Damascus in Syria, under the tutelage of Dr. Assad Ali, known by some as "a modern-day Ibn al-'Arabi". In Damascus, Meena was able to explore the linkages between her Persian heritage and Arabic literature influenced by Sufi thought. She is indebted to Dr. Ali for helping her pursue a research project on the Sufi intention within Arabic Literature. She also wants to thank from her Shirazi heart many souls in Damascus, including Da'ad, Awadis, Ramadan, Nada, Nuha and Suha, and many others, for their hospitality and for the invaluable assistance that she received during this sojourn. May the "Eternal City" find peace.

In 2001, Meena returned to American University to pursue doctoral studies as well as various related research and conference-convening projects. Along the way she gleaned further wisdom from Dr. Said as well as many other brilliant scholars and friends, including Shahabuddin Less, Elena Turner, Judy Barber, Hamil Tavernier, Ayub Ommayya, Seyyed Hossein Nasr, Mohammed Arkoun, Sulayman Nyang, Serif Mardin, Su'ad al-Hakim, Sachiko Murata, May Rihani, Fera Simone, Srimati Kamala, Carrie Trybulec, Yvonne Seng, Mohammed Abu-Nimer, Chaiwat Satha-Anand, Peter Mandaville, Armando Salvatore, Ayse Kadayifci, Maia Hallward Carter, Kiran Pervez, Lynn Kunkle and Margarita Pareja-Stoyell.

Soon, her journey turned northward, and shortly after completing her dissertation she secured a teaching position in the Religion and Culture Department at Wilfrid Laurier University in Waterloo, Ontario. Meena is indebted to all the Religion and Culture faculty for their friendship and collegiality, and in particular to Michel Desjardins whose infinite wisdom helped her to navigate the various aspects of professional academic life. Deep appreciation is also due to Jasmin Zine and other colleagues in the WLU Muslim Studies Option program and Darrol Bryant, Doris Jakobsh, Lorne Dawson and all the University of Waterloo's Religious Studies faculty.

For William Rory Dickson, his path to the book began with his discovery of mystical traditions in his late teens. Although it was not a subject that most of his peers in Alberta, Canada, were interested in at the time, this discovery launched an enduring passion for the world's various paths of spiritual transformation. After undergraduate studies, first in Camrose and Calgary, Alberta, and then in Montreal, Quebec, Rory's interest in contemplative traditions in general, and in Islam in particular, took shape with an MA and PhD in Religious Studies at Wilfrid Laurier University and the University of Waterloo. There he met Meena Sharify-Funk, who, as his doctoral supervisor and mentor, inspired him to study the Arabic language, travel to Damascus, Syria (where Rory remains grateful to Kinan Houssain and Dr. Assad Ali for their kindness and inspiration), and pursue research on contemporary Sufism. Rory could not, despite his best efforts, do enough to thank Meena for her inestimable role in his formation as a scholar and a person, and for including him as a part of her wonderful family. Professors Barry Stephenson, Kay Koppedrayer, Ron Grimes, Peter Erb, and Janet McLellan offered rich graduate courses that shaped Rory's understanding of religion and his approach to studying the subject. The exceptional guidance and expertise of doctoral committee members Michel Desjardins and Carol Duncan further helped shape Rory's theoretical and methodological approach, as well as his writing.

Under Meena's rich, inspired supervision, Rory's PhD research involved studying trends in contemporary Sufism, which included meeting with and interviewing Sufi leaders in the United States and Canada. The time spent with Sufi teachers, often staying at their centres, profoundly affected Rory's understanding of the Sufi tradition, putting "flesh" on the "bones" of academic reading on the subject. Here Rory would like to thank Tevfik Aydoner, Zia Inayat Khan, Seyyed Hossein Nasr, Jonathan Granoff, Michael Green, Robert Frager, Kabir Helminski, Hisham Kabbani, Fariha Friedrich, and Ahmad Tijani Ben Omar, all for sharing their time and insights, and Yannis Toussulis for acting as a continuing and incisive dialogue partner. Rory further met with Llewellyn Vaughan-Lee during doctoral research and has continued to meet with him in regards to more recent research on his Golden Sufi Centre. Rory would like to thank Vaughan-Lee for his time and assistance with Rory's research, and for graciously agreeing to share his insightful reflections on earlier drafts of this project.

Scholars do not work in isolation, but are nurtured, supported, and sustained by family, friends, and colleagues. Rory often wonders at his amazing good fortune to have been born to parents Bev and Kevin Dickson, whose unfailing support, good cheer, and encouragement have had an incalculably positive effect on his life and work, and he is profoundly grateful to them. Rory is further grateful to his wonderful grandmothers Arline Lozensky and Janice Dickson, and to his late grandfathers Michael Lozensky and Bill Dickson, whose legacies continue to inspire him. Rory's brother Rhett Dickson and his wife Katie Wattie motivate him to try (but not quite) keep up with them in living life to the fullest. Rory is grateful for the friendship of Brad Benner, Ryan McLeod, Adam Stewart, Amarnath Amarasingam, Andre Furlong, Kathryn Jones and Tyler Harris, Peter McCullough, Zabeen Khamisa, Joel Fink, Naniece Ibrahim, Randi Anderson, and Bridget Nordquist. Special thanks go to Rachel Brown and Marc Kellerman for including Rory in their family as godfather to their son Eli, for adopting Rory's parents in Victoria, and to Rachel for being a true sister (both in terms of affection and friendly rivalry). Rory is grateful to senior colleagues and department chairs who have encouraged his research work, including Greg Peterson, and the late April Brooks at South Dakota State University, and Jane Barter and Carlos Colorado at the University of Winnipeg. A shout out goes to Ted Malcolmson for intrepid, generous assistance in teaching and grading in the Winter and Spring Semesters of 2016.

Both Meena and Rory would like to thank senior fellow Mirabai Bush and former executive director Daniel Barbezat of the Centre for the Contemplative Mind in Society for a grant to develop a course on Islamic mysticism. As Meena and her then graduate student Rory began working on developing the project, the idea of this introductory text that could be used for such a course emerged. Additionally, throughout the process of developing the text, we had the pleasure of working with Janet Joyce, Valerie Hall, Sarah Lee and Norma Beavers at Equinox, and we would like to thank them for their help in bringing this work to light. Janet kindly saw the potential of the book at the proposal stage and encouraged its development, while Valerie has been supportive of the project and all the numerous questions we posed for her. We would also like to thank the amazing artists and scholars who allowed us to include their beautiful artwork and photography: Robert Lentz, Murray Schafer, Michael Green, Eric Ross, Nuria Garcia Masip, Hassan Massoudy and Laleh Bakhtiar.

The authors would very much like to thank Nathan C. Funk, for his unwavering support through endless conversations, proofreading, wordsmithing, and discussing key themes of the book. This book simply would not have been possible without his consistent and appreciated patience and engagement. A debt of gratitude is also owed to Jan and Richard Potter for helping to show the way, and to Jan Potter specifically for offering editorial skills as well as invaluable insights and suggestions. Also, Elysia Guzik gifted the authors her meticulous attention to detail and brilliant copyediting skills, playing a paramount role in bringing the book to completion. The authors would further like to thank Sahir Dewji, Ahwaz Chagani, Nurdin Dhanani, and Farouq Manji for their kind assistance in organizing book launch events for this work. Finally, Meena and Rory would like to acknowledge students and friends who have contributed to this book, Deborah Birkett, Munira Haddad, Zahra Ludin, and Merin Shobhana Xavier. Special thanks go to Stephanie McCabe and her Irish heart, who was a key part of early conversations on the structure of the book, helping the authors to conceive of a multidimensional approach to Sufism.

Ultimately, we are unable to express enough gratitude to all those who have helped us along our path, and in the development of this book. Its faults and limitations are truly our own.

INTRODUCTION

In the market, in the cloister – only God I saw.
In the valley and on the mountain – only God I saw.

Him I have seen beside me oft in tribulation;
In favour and in fortune – only God I saw.

In prayer and fasting, in praise and contemplation,
In the religion of the Prophet – only God I saw.

Neither soul nor body, accident nor substance,
Qualities nor causes – only God I saw.

I opened mine eyes and by the light of his face around me
In all the eye discovered – only God I saw.

Like a candle I was melting in his fire:
Amidst the flames outflashing – only God I saw.

Myself with mine own eyes I saw most clearly,
But when I looked with God's eyes – only God I saw.

I passed away into nothingness, I vanished,
And lo, I was the All-living – only God I saw.
(Baba Kuhi in Arberry 1960: 81–82)

The above poem is from one of the oldest collections of Persian Sufi poetry still extant, by Shaykh Abu 'Abdullah Mohammad ibn 'Abdallah ibn 'Ubaydallah Bakuya Shirazi (d. 1037), popularly known as Baba Kuhi or "Father of the Mountain". He was born in Shiraz in Southern Iran, the famous city of saints and scholars, poets and philosophers. Shiraz was a city renowned as the *dar al-'ilm*, the "House of Knowledge", for it possessed a rich heritage of theologians, Sufis, calligraphers, and scientists.

Hailing from Shiraz, Baba Kuhi travelled far and wide seeking knowledge. He met some of the leading Sufis of his time, even studying under one of the disciples of the famous Sufi martyr of Baghdad, Mansur al-Hallaj (d. 922). After years on the road, he returned to his native Shiraz where he took up residence in a cave in a mountain north of the city, now named Baba Kuhi after him. The cave soon became a site for pilgrimage, vigil, and prayer. According to a popular legend (of which there are a number of versions), a young Shams al-Din Hafiz (d. 1326) working as a humble baker, caught a glimpse of an aristocratic girl and fell madly in love with her.

Knowing that she was beyond his reach, yet longing unceasingly, he sought a way out. Hafiz recalled the "promise of Baba Kuhi", that if someone spent 40 nights awake at his tomb on the mountain, the Sufi saint of the mountain would grant that person's wish. Hafiz struggled through 40 gruelling days of work for the bakery, with each night passed in wakefulness at the saint's tomb. Finally, after the 40th night, he encountered the archangel Gabriel. Gabriel asked Hafiz what he desired, and Hafiz, so struck by the angel's beauty, could only think of how much more beautiful God must be, and instead of invoking the girl that had taken his heart, he said that he wanted only God. After returning to town he found himself endowed with the gift of poetry, and was guided toward a Sufi teacher, to whom he would become a disciple for the next 40 years. Thenceforth Hafiz travelled the Sufi path to God and became one of Persia's most celebrated poets, read throughout the Muslim world and later beloved by Western readers.

Until recently, there lived in Baba Kuhi's tomb a local hermit who was himself called Baba Kuhi. The living Baba Kuhi resided in a small room built into the mountain, and would receive pilgrims who would climb the mountain to pay homage to both the original Baba Kuhi and his current representative. Some families would have their children make the rather arduous hike up to Baba Kuhi every Friday morning to bring him food and fruit, the weekly journey being a part of their moral and religious formation. In response, Baba Kuhi would recite from the Qur'ān (holy book for Muslims) and from the poetry of Hafiz. If many visitors arrived at the same time, Baba Kuhi would simply say, "when you have unexpected guests you just add more water to the pot". At times Baba Kuhi would have to keep a low profile to avoid intimidation by local authorities, who were not always friendly to Sufis. Eventually, one cold winter night the last Baba Kuhi passed away, with some speculating that locals had no longer been checking on him or bringing him food as they once did. In recent years the local government has built a shrine complex at the site, and the space has become a more popular destination for those seeking refuge from the bustle of modern urban life. Families with children and the elderly have picnics there; fashionably-dressed youth hold singing and story telling parties; tourists go seeking a beautiful view of Shiraz; while others find solace in prayer.

The story of Baba Kuhi and his tomb atop a small mountain near Shiraz conveys the rich legacy of Sufism within many traditional Islamic societies. Baba Kuhi's poem draws upon a range of imagery to express one of Sufism's central metaphysical claims, that amidst the varied landscapes, systems of belief, fortunes and misfortunes one encounters in the world, only God truly exists, all else having a relative, temporary, and ultimately illusory status. The legend of young Hafiz's vigil at Baba Kuhi's tomb highlights the inestimable significance of tomb-shrines in Muslim societies historically, as sites of seeking, prayer, vigil, spiritual experience, and artistic inspiration. The continuing importance of Baba Kuhi's site shows how until recently, for many Muslims, paying homage to Sufis and making pilgrimage to Sufi shrines was understood to be an integral part of Muslim devotion. The fact that these traditions are in some cases disappearing reflects a shift found in a variety of Muslim contexts, where Sufi traditions are being either forgotten or in some cases actively erased. As the most recent Baba Kuhi had to avoid official harassment, we can see that Sufism is not always something favoured by political elites.

Baba Kuhi (centre) with author's uncle, Aladin Sharifi-Hosseini (right) and Dr. Dorafshan (left).

THE STRUCTURE OF THE BOOK

As illustrated above, Sufism is a multidimensional phenomenon. To introduce Sufism's many dimensions, we have divided each chapter in this work into four thematic sections: (1) Politics and Power, (2) Philosophical Principles and Practices, (3) Arts and Culture, and 4) Overview of Historical Developments. Sufism has informed all levels of Islamic culture and society, and dividing chapters into these four broad categories allows us to highlight some of the ways in which Sufism has influenced Muslim politics, philosophy, metaphysics, art, and culture in each historical period. With each category we illustrate the relevant issues through detailed case studies, whether of a particular Sufi figure, place, artistic expression, or philosophical view. This allows the reader to develop a richly contextualized appreciation of Sufism. We seek to avoid reducing Sufism to a private mystical experience divorced from socio-political expression, and present historical figures in dynamic relation to one another and to the major events and movements of an era.

In contrast to most introductory texts on Sufism, we begin not with the historical past, but with the contemporary present. We begin with the diversity of lived Sufism in North America today. We begin with the here and now. Starting with Sufism as it is lived today in North America, with each chapter we unveil the complexities of Sufism as we move deeper through time and space, journeying through a variety of historical, political, and cultural contexts, further delving into the past, and closer to the origin of Sufism. This geneological framework enables the reader to understand the patterns of connection between contemporary manifestations of Sufism and past realities. From the bustling metropolis of twenty-first century Manhattan, we move back to colonial Algeria, through medieval Delhi and Istanbul, back to Baghdad and ultimately Mecca – the birthplace of Islam and its mystical tradition. Of course, there are significant limitations inherent in any summative work, and as it is impossible to provide a comprehensive history of such a rich and varied subject, we have highlighted particular examples to suggest broader patterns. There is a multitude of examples that could have been chosen, though we have selected ones that should offer doorways for the reader to develop a deeper understanding of the subject as a whole.

We use the term "unveiling" in the title of this book with due awareness of the often clichéd manner in which the term has been employed in discussing subjects related to Islam and Muslim women in particular, a usage rooted in Orientalist tropes of exotification. However, we use the term in a specific sense, invoking the Arabic word *kashf*. Derived from the tri-lateral root *ka-sha-fa*, the word *kashf* can be translated as "unveiling", but has further connotations of searching, bringing to light, disclosing, discovering, exploring, and revealing what is hidden. Within the context of Islam's mystical or contemplative traditions, the word *kashf* is a technical term referring to mystical knowledge, the knowledge of the unseen that God "unveils" or reveals to the seeker.

Also in this book, we integrate accounts of women's participation in shaping the Sufi tradition historically and today. Feminist scholars have long noted the erasure of women from history, and have struggled to re-write women back into the larger story of humanity. Islamic history is no exception, and the historically critical roles played by women remain in need of attention. In the present text we do not devote a separate chapter to Sufi women, but do address the absence of women in such histories by integrating stories of Sufi women throughout the text, as they naturally arise in discussions of Sufi thought and practice. The contribution of women to Sufism is important and cannot be neglected lest an inadequate treatment of the subject as a whole result. The influence of Sufi metaphysician Ibn al-'Arabi

(d. 1240) for example, cannot be adequately discussed without noting his female Sufi teachers, nor can Sufism's theology of love be understood without an appreciation of the great female saint Rabi'a al-'Adawiyya's (d. 801) foundational role in its development. In the current context, there has been a notable rise of female Sufi leaders in both North America (Fariha al-Jerrahi, for example) and in the Middle East (Nur Artiran and Cemalnur Sargut).

In Chapter 1, we explore Sufism in twentieth century and twenty-first century North America. We begin painting a picture of the political climate within which contemporary Sufis operate, in exploring Sufism in post-9/11 Manhattan. Sufis frequently find themselves at the intersection of a variety of political pressures, including growing anti-Muslim sentiment among Americans, and growing anti-Sufi movements among Muslims. We then shift from contemporary politics, to discuss the different interpretive tendencies emerging among Sufi communities in North America, including universalist tendencies that understand Sufism as something not limited to Islam, to more traditionalist perspectives that assert Sufism's necessary connection to Islamic practices and laws. In order to shed light on Sufism's remarkable influence on North American artists, we look at the thirteenth century Sufi personality, Jalal al-Din Rumi (d. 1273), whose immensely popular poetry has inspired a variety of cultural expressions, from restaurants, to visual art, yoga, social activism, dance, and music. We conclude with a brief mapping of Sufism's historical development throughout the twentieth century, charting the lives and influences of Sufi personalities, who would shape distinct trends, including more universalist approaches to Sufism, and those more closely affiliated with Muslim identity and ritual life.

Understanding the contemporary complexity of Sufism's place in North America, and indeed around the world, is possible only if we understand how that place has been shaped by the global power shifts, conflicts, and migrations of the past three centuries, during a period known as the colonial era. The reverberations of this era continue to undergird contemporary patterns, such as the Western fascination with Sufism, and opposition to Sufism among some Muslims. Chapter 2 allows us to make sense of these contemporary dynamics. Politically, Sufis such as 'Abd al-Qadir al-Jaza'iri (d. 1883) organized military resistance to growing European dominance of the Muslim world. Despite being at the forefront of Islamic resistance and revival movements, Sufis like Ahmad al-'Alawi (d. 1934) were soon facing anti-Sufi reformist movements, having to justify their place within Islam in unprecedented ways. Just as Sufism was being contested among Muslims however, Western literary figures like Johann Wolfgang van Goethe (d. 1832) and Ralph Waldo Emerson (d. 1882) were being drawn to Sufism's rich poetic traditions. The availability of Sufi poetry was in many cases a direct result of the access European colonial officials had to the classical Sufi literary canon. However, their presentation of Sufism largely situated it as something apart from Islam. This separation would have implications for how Sufism was perceived by Muslims and Westerners during this period and ultimately into the twentieth and twenty-first centuries.

The diversity of contemporary Sufism and its dynamism during the colonial era can be traced to shared roots, which we explore in Chapter 3, considering Sufism's role during the height of the Muslim "Gunpowder" empires between the fifteenth and eighteenth centuries: the Ottoman, Safavid, and Mughal dynasties. In terms of politics and power, this chapter delves into the close relations some Sufis had with Muslim dynasties. The Safavid political dynasty itself emerged out of a Sufi order, while Sufi orders were integral to the social and political structures of Ottoman life. In Mughal India, Sufism was closely associated both with efforts to dissolve boundaries between Muslims and Hindus, and with movements to reassert the superiority of Islam and to entrench the boundaries between Muslims and non-Muslims. In contrast to Sufism's relationship with imperial elites, we discuss the wandering mendicants of Islam, the dervishes, representing a counter-cultural Sufism that rejected social norms and conventions. Regardless of their position in society, Muslims in general during this period congregated in Sufi shrines, seeking the blessings of the saints. The Sufi shrine then brought together all elements of Muslim society, being honoured by imperial courts, venerated by dervishes, and respected as focal points of local devotion. As we illustrate, in contrast to the contemporary period, Sufism during this era was integral to almost every facet of life in Muslim societies, infusing government, commerce, and industry as well as the arts and sciences.

Moving deeper into history, in Chapter 4, we consider those Sufis who integrated Islamic law, theology and philosophy with the aesthetics and practices of Sufism to forge a holistic paradigm in the medieval era. It was between the eleventh and thirteenth centuries that Sufism crystalized as a comprehensive worldview, one that would define Islam for centuries to follow, shaping the culture of Muslim societies and empires. The great synthesizers of Sufi thought, figures such as Muhyi al-Din Ibn al-'Arabi (d. 1240) and Abu Hamid al-Ghazali (d. 1111), played paramount roles in drawing the outlines of classical Sufism. Some Sufi scholars like al-Ghazali worked within government institutions, seeking to reconcile Sufism with both Islamic jurisprudence and the political powers of his day. Philosophically, Ibn al-'Arabi articulated a metaphysics of oneness alongside a conception of human perfectibility, leading to a cosmology of unity and sainthood. Socially, Sufism was institutionalized during this period as a series of religious orders, four of which will be explored in this chapter (the Shadhili, Qadiri, Naqshbandi, and Chishti orders), each representing a different cultural region within Islamic civilization. With Sufism's institutionalization in a system of orders, Sufi practices became more codified, with each order developing its own particular forms of devotion, meditation, and contemplation. We see during this time the development of a sound mysticism, as Sufi devotion was integrated with musical traditions, and Sufi chanting coordinated with breath and body, producing spiritual practices of song, dance, and ecstasy.

In Chapter 5, we trace the formation of Sufism in the early period of Islam, from the eighth to the tenth centuries. Islamic spirituality, like law and theology, was being formulated during this period. It was hence subject to conflicts over the nature of God, the Qur'ān, and the ideal Muslim self and society, conflicts that affected all aspects of the emergent Islamic civilization. Proto-Sufis emerge as exponents of the Qur'ān's hidden meaning, rejecters of the newfound wealth and worldly status of early Islamic empires, and proponents of relating to God not simply as a law-giver and lord, but also as an intimate friend and lover. Seminal figures of this era include Hasan al-Basri (d. 728) and Rabi'a the great female Sufi and representative of the path of divine love. Sufis drew controversy for their claims of intimacy and unity with God, most notably culminating in the death of Sufism's famous "martyr of love" al-Hallaj. Also, in this period Sufism began to be understood as a distinctive science within Islam due in large part to the efforts of Sufi biographers like Abu al-Qasim al-Qushayri (d. 1074) to document the principles and practices of Sufism. Sufis would further embrace the structure and themes of pre-Islamic poetry, using its imagery of loss, longing, and the journey to find the beloved, to represent the spiritual search for God.

In Chapter 6, we conclude our journey back through history to consider Sufism's origin during the seventh and eighth centuries. The many principles and practices of Sufism explored in the book can be traced back to the Qur'ān, the revelatory experience of the Prophet Muhammad. To understand the roots of Sufi hermeneutics and concepts such as *kashf*, we take a closer look at the interpretive approach of Ja'far al-Sadiq, one of Islam's early polymaths and mystics. His suggestion that *kashf* revealed deeper layers of meaning in the Qur'ān would shape Sufi approaches to the text thereafter. We further consider those verses of the Qur'ān and sayings of the Prophet Muhammad that have shaped later Sufism. Sufi understandings of the Qur'ān were controversial, and their claim to have access to the Qur'ān's deeper meanings was contested by scholars who rejected the possibility of esoteric interpretation. This started a debate that continues to this day among Muslims over how to understand the Qur'ān. We then explore Muhammad's life and spiritual practices, which are exemplary for Sufis, and further consider the Prophet's metaphysical status and meaning for Sufi practitioners. Attention will also be given to Sufi use of Qur'ānic calligraphy to beautify expression of the Divine word, and to the development of Sufi thought about the mystical significance of Arabic letters. Finally, we consider Sufism in the larger world historical context. Although Sufism may not have originated outside of Islam, it has undoubtedly integrated various mystical and philosophical systems prevalent in the Near East. As such, we look at the influence of some of these, including Christian mysticism, Neoplatonism, Hermeticism, and Zoroastrianism.

DEFINING SUFISM

But what is Sufism? Who is a Sufi? The English word "Sufism" is derived from the Arabic term *tasawwuf*. To define *tasawwuf*, there is arguably no better place to start than with the first comprehensive treatise on Sufism written in Persian, the *Kashf al-Mahjub*, or "Unveiling the Mystery". The discussion of Sufism in the work remains paradigmatic, and many contemporary definitions of Sufism refer back to this work. The author 'Ali al-Hujwiri (d. 1073) was renowned for the eloquence of his Persian. In the *Kashf* al-Hujwiri documents the origin and development of Sufism. He summarizes theories on the etymological origin of the word *tasawwuf*, relating that some consider the term to be derived from the Arabic word for wool, *suf*, as early Sufis wore wool as a sign of renunciation. Others say the word comes from *safa*, meaning purity. Some connect *tasawwuf* to the Greek word for wisdom, *sophia*. Al-Hujwiri however, does not consider any of these theories to be certain, and concludes that no one can determine the origin of the name with any finality. Instead, he proposes a definition of a Sufi that tells us something about a Sufi's purpose: a Sufi is defined as "he that is absorbed in the Beloved and has abandoned all else" (Nicholson 1990: 30). Unlike the English word, which, with the suffix "ism", indicates an ideology or doctrine, *tasawwuf* is a verbal noun that refers to a process, the process of becoming a Sufi (Ernst 1997: 21). At its most basic then, Sufism is a process of becoming, or as al-Hujwiri suggests, the process of becoming absorbed in the Beloved or God.

This process of becoming is the culmination of many principles and practices, which early Sufi biographers like al-Hujwiri and al-Qushayri collected and recorded. Some of these include developing a keen sense of etiquette, renouncing attachment to the world, engaging in repentance, refining one's morals and practising virtues, trusting in God, gaining hidden knowledge, and longing for as well as experiencing Divine love. Early Sufi definitions of Sufism often highlight these principles, as the definitions have a pedagogical purpose for Sufi aspirants. For example, Abu-Sa'id ibn Abi al-Khayr (d. 1049) said, "Sufism is this: Whatever you have in your mind – forget it; whatever you have in your hand – give it; whatever is to be your fate –face it!" 'Abd al-Rahman Jami (d. 1492) relates that, "A seeker went to ask a sage guidance on the Sufi way. The sage counselled, 'If you have never trodden the path of love, go away and fall in love, then come back and see us'". According to 'Amr ibn 'Uthman al-Makki (d. 909), "The Sufi acts according to whatever is most fitting to the moment". Paradoxically, Abu Yazid al-Bistami (d. 874) says that, "the thing we tell of can never be found by seeking, yet only seekers find it" (Fadiman and Frager 1997: 36–39). Abu al-Qasim al-Junayd (d. 910) relates that, "Sufism means that God causes you to die to yourself and gives you life in Him" (al-Qushayri 1990: 302), reflecting al-Hujwiri's understanding that "The Sufi is absent from himself and present with God" (Fadiman and Frager 1997: 36).

Historically, this path of moral development, renunciation, knowledge, and love, was traced to the Qur'ān and teachings of the Prophet Muhammad. Sufis believe that, based on the Qur'ān, the Prophet shared with his closest companions, like 'Ali ibn Abi Talib (d. 661) and Abu Bakr (d. 634), these principles of moral and spiritual transformation. As this transmission of spiritual transformation took place from master to disciple over generations, the various doctrines and practices associated with it became increasingly codified, and the term *tasawwuf* was developed to refer to those Muslims who focused on drawing closer to God by practicing these teachings. Once the term *tasawwuf* had a cultural currency however, those claiming to be Sufis for social status began to emerge. To distinguish genuine Sufis from the imposters, Sufis began to increasingly emphasize the importance of having a *silsila* or chain of transmission, naming their own master, and the masters before him or her going back to the Prophet. As we will see in the first chapter, this *silsila,* this chain of transmission of spiritual blessing so central to Sufism, continues to be passed on through generations from master to disciple, even in contemporary Manhattan.

1

THE MANY FACES OF CONTEMPORARY SUFISM IN NORTH AMERICA

Nestled among the taverns and lofts of Tribeca is the Masjid al-Farah, a small mosque in a non-descript white building. The Masjid al-Farah, which means the "mosque of joy", is home to the Nur-Ashki Jerrahis in Manhattan. The Nur-Ashki Jerrahis are a Sufi order with roots going back to Ottoman Istanbul, where Pir Nur al-Din al-Jerrahi (d. 1721) established the Jerrahi branch of the Halveti order in 1704. The mosque is well-known for its liberal and laid back atmosphere, drawing people from all faiths and orientations. Muzaffer Ozak, a large, gregarious and charismatic Jerrahi Sufi teacher from Turkey, began visiting the United States in 1978. In 1980 some of his students offered Ozak a property on Mercer Street to use as a mosque for the growing community of American seekers. Soon after the mosque's opening, an American religious studies scholar and convert to Islam, Lex Hixon, began leading *dhikr* sessions there every Thursday night. *Dhikr* is an important practice for Sufis which literally means "remembrance". The Qur'ān commands Muslims to perform *dhikrullah*, the "remembrance of God", and Sufis in particular seek to integrate the remembrance of God with each moment of life. Sufis have developed their own unique ritual practices to remember God, usually involving the collective chanting of some of God's Names mentioned in the Qur'ān. It was sessions of this collective *dhikr* that Hixon began leading at the newly established mosque in the heart of America's bustling cultural capital, Manhattan.

In 1980, Ozak formally authorized Hixon to act as a teacher within the Jerrahi order. In his work, *Atom from the Sun of Knowledge*, Hixon describes how he knelt beside Ozak in their New York City mosque: "After placing his magnificent green and gold turban upon my head, the Grand Shaykh opened his palms and offered this supplication: 'May whatever has come into me from Allah and from the Prophet of Allah now enter into him'" (Hixon 1993: v). In Sufism, a *shaykh* or *shaykha* (feminine) is an honorific term given to a spiritual guide. Sometimes the head of a Sufi order is called a "Grand Shaykh" (as Hixon describes Ozak here). When Ozak authorized Hixon as a teacher within the Jerrahi order, he was transmitting the lineage of the order, a lineage of spiritual authority and blessing traced back to the Prophet Muhammad and finally to Allah (the Arabic name for God). In

Figure 1.1: *Dhikr* at the Masjid al-Farah in Manhattan, New York.[1]

Arabic, a Sufi lineage is known as a *silsila*. Sufis believe that the blessing of the *silsila*, a blessing known in Arabic as *baraka*, has the power to spiritually transform those who encounter it, as the lineage's *baraka* ultimately comes from God.

Hixon – or, as he was known to his students, Shaykh Nur al-Jerrahi – wanted to foster a particularly American form of Sufism. He welcomed people from all religious backgrounds to join the Jerrahi order and attend *dhikr* sessions at the Masjid al-Farah. He believed that America's culture of pluralism and democracy created a framework within which Sufism could expand its borders to include all, regardless of their religious affiliation. Traditionally, the majority of Sufi teachers have considered the practice of Islam as foundational to Sufism, without which the seeker cannot progress beyond the initial stages of the path. In contrast, Hixon wanted seekers to feel free to adopt only those Islamic practices with which they were comfortable, or to retain their other religious commitments. He himself lived something of a plural spiritual path. Besides his practice as a Muslim Sufi *shaykh*, Hixon practiced Zen Buddhism and studied Orthodox Christianity at St. Vladimir's Seminary in Crestwood, New York. Testifying to his active presence on the "spiritual scene" of the 1970s and 80s, the famous Beat poet Allen Ginsberg (d. 1997) described Hixon as "a pioneer in the spiritual renaissance in America" (Gooch 2002: 345).

1. The leader of the Nur-Ashki Jerrahis, Shaykha Fariha, leads a dhikr session with her students at the Masjid al-Farah, Manhattan, New York.

Besides emphasizing the possibilities for pluralism within the practice of Sufism, Hixon advocated for women to take on more active roles in leading the Jerrahi order. He believed that women were often better suited to Sufism, a path of devotion, love, and surrender. A fellow student of Ozak's, Fariha Friedrich, began offering guidance to women in the order. Born Philipa de Menil, Friedrich grew up in a wealthy Texan family known for its association with Schlumberger Ltd., the giant oilfield service company. Like Hixon, Ozak formally authorized Friedrich to act as a *shaykha* in the Jerrahi order. When Hixon died in 1995, she inherited the leadership of Nur Ashki Jerrahis. Although there have been different roles for female Sufi personalities in Sufism's past, women have not usually functioned as the head of a Sufi order. Under Friedrich's leadership, the Nur-Ashki Jerrahi Sufi order "promotes gender equality and women's participation and empowerment at all levels" (2009: 174). Friedrich's leadership has also extended to fulfilling roles in Islam usually reserved for men. In particular, she has acted as an *imam*, or prayer leader, leading both men and women in the *salat*, the daily ritual prayer practiced by Muslims. Women frequently lead other women in prayer, but most Muslims believe that only a man can lead both men and women as an *imam*. Notably in 2005, a Muslim feminist scholar, Amina Wadud, led both women and men in the weekly Friday prayer in Manhattan, requiring police protection due to anonymous threats and protests outside. The prayer was held in the Synod House of the Cathedral of St. John the Divine, after three local mosques and an art gallery refused to host the event due to security concerns. In contrast, Friedrich has been low key about her own prayer leading, neither acting in this capacity at all times, nor publicizing her role in this regard. Perhaps the perception in some Muslim quarters that Sufism is marginal to mainstream Islam has helped Friedrich avoid the larger controversy that Wadud faced in 2005.

Hixon and Friedrich have worked to develop an authentically American Sufism, one not only at home in Manhattan, but also comfortable with contemporary American values and lifestyles. The approach taken by Freidrich and Hixon to adapt Sufi practice in North America is not the only one however; in what follows we will see some of the diverse ways in which contemporary Sufis understand their own tradition. We begin first with the question of politics, and how Sufis in North America, particularly those grounded in Islamic identity and practice, have engaged with the often contentious politics of being Muslim in the West, especially in the late twentieth and twenty-first centuries. As we will see, Muslim Sufis have struggled to uphold the legitimacy of Islam as a peaceful, integral part of North American society, against powerful anti-Islamic movements, while simultaneously defending the legitimacy of Sufism as an integral aspect of Islam, against a growing anti-Sufi movement among Muslims. In the next section of this chapter we explore this complexity of what it means to be

Sufi in relation to Islam and all its diverse manifestations in North America. Following that, we delve into the contemporary Western popularity of the famous Sufi poet Jalal al-Din Rumi (d. 1273). Having inspired various artists, social activists, and cultural creatives in North America, Rumi has become something of an icon, but at what cost? We then conclude the chapter by uncovering some of the history underlying contemporary Sufi expressions, outlining the historical trajectory of Sufism's unfolding presence in North America beginning in the early twentieth century.

CONTEMPORARY SUFISM AND THE POLITICAL IN NORTH AMERICA

As will be explored throughout this book, Sufis have taken a range of approaches to politics and power throughout history. Some have been involved with government, acting as advisors and allies to the powers that be, whereas other Sufis have distanced themselves from politics, seeing its potential for corruption and the abuse of power. Still others have actively opposed government systems as unjust, engaging in forms of resistance. As human beings embedded in historical, social, and political contexts, Sufis, like others, have made diverse choices on how to relate to systems of power and authority, and North American Sufis in many ways perpetuate this range of approaches.

In 2010, the *imam* of the Masjid al-Farah, Feisal Abdul Rauf, would find himself at the centre of one of the most controversial political issues in America that year: the "Ground Zero Mosque" affair. Abdul Rauf grew up following his father, a Sunni Egyptian cleric, around the world from Kuwait to Malaysia and then to Washington, DC. Finally settling in New York, his father led a mosque on West 72nd Street, working with a small congregation there. Following university, Abdul Rauf began seeking a deeper spiritual foundation for his life and explored Sufism. Friends kept inviting him to the Masjid al-Farah and finally in 1983 he went, feeling an instant connection to the place. Muzaffer Ozak soon asked Abdul Rauf to be the *imam* of the Masjid al-Farah. Abdul Rauf would remain the *imam* of the mosque until 2009, establishing himself in the local community and working to build bridges between Muslims and others.

Abdul Rauf has devoted much of his life to bridging the gap between Islam and the West. He has worked with the National Inter-religious Initiative for Peace, is a member of the board of trustees of the Interfaith Centre of New York and has lectured at the New York Seminary, which trains interfaith ministers (Gooch 2002: 354). In 1997, he founded the American Sufi Muslim Association, which was later renamed the American Society for Muslim Advancement (ASMA) to foster a deeper awareness of America's Islamic heritage and better connect Muslims with mainstream American society. In 2004, Rauf created the Cordoba Initiative: "A multi-national, multi-faith organization dedicated to… building trust among people of all cultures and faith traditions" (Cordoba 2016). Following the attacks of 9/11, which happened just 12 blocks from the Masjid al-Farah, Abdul Rauf sought "a new vision for Muslims and the West" and published *What's Right with Islam is What's Right with America* (2004) to show the ways in which the core values of Islam and the core principles of the United States overlap. Then, in 2010, he began work on a long-time goal to build a community centre and mosque through the Cordoba Initiative in lower Manhattan. Although finding affordable property for sale in the area was a challenge, eventually Abdul Rauf secured a property – one that happened to be a few blocks from where the World Trade Center's twin towers had stood. His project had the dual purpose of establishing a mosque to meet the religious needs of the growing Muslim community in the area, and of creating a community and recreation centre, akin to the YMCAs found in most American cities. Although news of the centre's development was initially welcomed by city officials and media outlets, Pamela Geller, a conservative blogger and activist, condemned Abdul Rauf's centre as an example of Islamic triumphalism, as a mosque purposefully and maliciously built at "ground zero" to signal Islam's dominance and conquest (pamelageller. com). As the story was picked up by national news outlets in the summer of 2010, Abdul Rauf was thrust into the centre of a media firestorm, and was characterized on various occasions as a radical aligned with extremism, and with connections to terrorist organizations. Protests were organized at the site of the proposed mosque and community centre, and the controversy set off a national debate over religious freedom, sensitivity to the victims of 9/11, and Islam's place in America.

Interestingly, lower Manhattan near the site of the World Trade Center had long been known as "Little Syria", a section of the city home to Lebanese and Syrians, both Christian and Muslim, who left the Ottoman province of Sham (Syria or the Levant) to build new lives as traders, peddlers, and shop owners in the New World. Starting in the 1880s these immigrants built businesses and communities in New York, with almost 100,000 settling in America in the late nineteenth and early twentieth centuries. Within decades Arabs built almost 300 businesses and community organizations in lower Manhattan, and even established the first Arabic language newspaper in North America, *Kawkab Amirka*, in 1892. Little Syria was also home to a mosque that reportedly was open from the early 1900s until the 1950s, just a short walk from the site of the World Trade Center (Brait and Gajanan 2015).

Although Islam has been a part of America's diverse cultural fabric for some time, in many respects, the debate over Islam in America has only grown in range and intensity, with voices of suspicion and hostility toward

Muslims gaining ground, in what some have referred to as a larger problem of Islamophobia. The rhetoric of political presidential candidates during the 2015–2016 primary season was notable for the frequency of references made to the danger Muslims and Islam posed to America, and the need for in some cases banning Muslims from government positions or even from entering the country (Donald Trump's campaign press release in December 2015 being the most notable example here). This rhetoric corresponds with a documented rise in hate crimes and discrimination against Muslims, and the significant growth in efforts to prevent the construction of mosques. According to the American Civil Liberties Union (ACLU) there were nine cases of conflict over mosques between 2005–2007, and 89 cases between 2010–2012.

This growing controversy surrounding the place of Islam and Muslims in America is important to highlight as it illustrates quite well the complex political and cultural negotiations Muslims face in establishing themselves as an integral part of the American mosaic. Will Herberg, in his work *Protestant, Catholic, Jew*, notes that Americans developed a sense of a "triple melting-pot" in the twentieth century, whereby Protestant and Catholic Christianity, along with Judaism, became acceptable as respectable religions in America, integral to its public, political life (Herberg 1955). As the "Ground Zero Mosque" controversy, political rhetoric, and the continuing issues Muslims face in building mosques illustrate so clearly, Islam remains outside of this circle of acceptability. Although Abdul Rauf has an extensive record of interfaith dialogue and intercultural bridge building and has been the *imam* of a remarkably open and progressive mosque for over two decades, in a post-9/11 America, suspicions were easily cast over him as something of a Trojan horse for al-Qaeda style extremism. Interestingly, very little commentary was available in the media on the nature of Abdul Rauf's religiosity, including his Sufi orientation. This is somewhat surprising as American media, think tanks, and commentators have, since 9/11, increasingly suggested that Sufism can act as an "antidote" to Islamic extremism. In 2007, the Rand Corporation suggested that Sufis were "natural allies of the West" (Rand 2007) and in 2009 *TIME* magazine asked, "Can Sufism Diffuse Terrorism?" (Tharoor 2009).

Despite the growing sense in Europe and North America that Sufis are "good" Muslims, or allies against extremists, Abdul Rauf's Sufism did not alleviate accusations of extremism in 2010. For many it seems, Islam is a singular, opaque category that permits little in the way of internal diversity. With the "Ground Zero Mosque" controversy, the nuances and diversity within Islam were obscured as a liberal Sufi *imam* was, for many Americans, indistinguishable from the most extreme kinds of militancy. Although Sufis are often perceived as allies, as Muslims they are not immune to the suspicions cast on the whole community due to the actions of a few.

Other Sufis, however, have utilized the perception of themselves as "good" Muslims to ally with the American government in combating terrorism and militant political ideologies among Muslims. Hisham Kabbani of the Naqshbandiyya-Nazimiyya (formerly the Naqshbandi-Haqqani) Sufi order has been particularly active in this respect. Hailing from a prominent family of Muslim businessmen and theologians in Lebanon, Kabbani moved to America in 1989 where he established a branch of the Naqshbandiyya-Nazimiyya order. During the past 20 years this order has become one of the more politically active Sufi organizations in America. Under Kabbani's leadership, the Naqshbandiyya-Nazimiyya Order has established centres in Washington, DC, New York, Michigan, and California. Kabbani has participated in numerous national political events, including White House receptions with former Presidents Bill Clinton and George W. Bush. The Naqshbandiyya-Nazimiyya order actively campaigned to increase the number of Muslim chaplains in the military and to have the US postal service issue a commemorative Ramadan stamp (Damrel 2006: 119).

Kabbani is in many respects a traditional Sunni Muslim *shaykh*. He wears a robe, turban, and writes about Islamic law and theology. He is a vocal representative of the classical Islamic-Sufi tradition prevalent in earlier centuries of Islamic history. Due to his traditional appearance and orientation, some may not initially think of him as one of the Sufi teachers most outspoken against extremism amongst Muslims. And yet Kabbani has conscientiously devoted much of his energy to combating what he calls "Wahhabism", referring to the somewhat puritan, exclusivist, and strongly anti-Sufi trend in Islam traceable to the teachings of Muhammad Ibn 'Abd al-Wahhab (d. 1792). In the following chapter, we will discuss in more depth Ibn 'Abd al-Wahhab's role in reviving anti-Sufi movements in Islam during the colonial period, and how his movement would have implications for Sufism's place in Islam in the twentieth and twenty-first centuries. His teachings remain popular, inspiring a range of interpretations. Some present-day followers of Ibn 'Abd al-Wahhab's teachings have combined his puritan theology with militant activism, participating in groups such as al-Qaeda.

Various militant organizations affiliated with al-Qaeda (or sharing the broad outlines of its ideology), have attacked Sufis and destroyed Sufi shrines, often centuries old sites that Muslims hold sacred to this day. In contrast, they see these shrines as idolatrous corruptions of Islam, and generally view Sufism as a dangerous, false teaching of which Islam must be purified. In 2010, for example, the Pakistani Taliban carried out a dual suicide bombing at the shrine of the famous Sufi master and author 'Ali al-Hujwiri, whose foundational treatise on Sufism we discussed in the introduction. Thousands had gathered at the shrine for a festival of song, dance, and devotion. Forty-two Muslims were killed and almost 200 injured during the bombings at the revered site in Lahore, Pakistan. In 2012, al-Qaeda-affiliated militias in Mali destroyed numerous Sufi shrines in the ancient centre of Islam in West Africa, Timbuktu. In 2014, members of the Islamic State in Iraq and Syria (ISIS) bulldozed the shrine of the famous Sufi saint Ahmed al-Rifa'i (d. 1182) near Talal Afar in Northern Iraq. These are just a few of many examples of shrine destruction in the twenty-first century.

In order to combat such anti-Sufi perspectives among Muslims and offer some new, more Sufi-oriented representation of the American Muslim community, Kabbani established the Islamic Supreme Council of America in 1991 and opened an office of the organization in Washington, DC, in 1998 (Curtiss 1999: 101). In January 1999 Kabbani was the keynote speaker at the State Department's public forum, entitled, "The Evolution of Extremism: A Viable Threat to US National Security". Kabbani warned the State Department that extremists were in control of the majority of mosques in America and that a significant terrorist attack was imminent. He further stated that extremist ideology had infiltrated Muslim student organizations across American campuses (Damrel 2006: 120). Kabbani's statements to the American government drew widespread condemnation from national Muslim organizations, as they were seen to bring even more suspicion upon a community already feeling the pressure of a larger cultural hostility and governmental scrutiny.

This public antagonism between Kabbani's and other Muslim organizations can be understood within the context of Muslim-American experience and in terms of religious authority. Muslims living in America – especially since the Islamic revolution in Iran (1979) and the first Gulf War (1991) – have often felt "othered" by mainstream America, singled out as being a dangerous, alien presence (Dickson 2014: 412). This feeling among Muslims is exacerbated by a growing public discourse that depicts them as a potential fifth column of un-American subversion, or as an alien threat to "Judeo-Christian" and secular values. It is critical that we keep in mind this element of the American socio-political context, as it tells us much about why most North American Muslim organizations condemned Kabbani's remarks to the State department in 1999, even if those remarks contained an element of truth about contemporary Muslims' struggle with extremist ideology.

Second, Kabbani's conflict with other Muslim organizations was the result of his attempt to establish his branch of the Naqshbandiyya-Nazimiyya Sufi order as representative of the American Muslim community more broadly (Dickson 2014: 413). American Muslims form a remarkably diverse community made up of different cultural and theological groups, and it is fair to say that communal leadership, especially at the national level, is contested: no one organization speaks for Muslims in America, though at times various organizations or religious groups try to. To further raise the prominence of Sufism as a legitimate representative of authentic Sunni Islamic teachings,

Naqshbandiyya-Nazimiyya literature and websites claim to present true Islam while denouncing the heretical deviations of Muslim extremists (who also claim to represent true Islamic teachings). In a sense, Kabbani's efforts are part of a broader Sufi counter attack against a variety of anti-Sufi movements that have emerged since the colonial era, movements that will be explored in more detail in the following chapter. These movements have been denouncing Sufism since the late eighteenth century as a corrupt, decadent, un-Islamic spiritualism that Muslims need to abandon (Voll 1999: 517).

With the concerted opposition to Kabbani following his warning at the State Department, Kabbani found himself somewhat vindicated after the attacks of 9/11, as his warning about the dangers of extremism and terrorism within the Muslim community seemed tragically prescient. Since this time Kabbani has continued to work closely with governments around the world to counter extremist movements. Kabbani's approach in fact represents a long tradition of Sufi alliance with state power. Kabbani has told his followers that, "If you obey those who are in authority, you will be happy, or else you are in problems, and Allah created us to be happy, not to have problems" (Barret 2007: 210). This view is rooted in a long tradition of pragmatism in regards to authority in the Islamic tradition – namely, that in most cases, it is better to accept than challenge it. As an early and striking example of this tradition, Malik ibn Anas (d. 796), the founder of one of Sunni Islam's four schools of law (the *Maliki* school), is reported to have said, "one hour of anarchy is worse than sixty years of tyranny" (Ahmed 2007: 6). In particular, Sufis have frequently chosen political pragmatism over idealism as the best means by which to secure law, order, and a stable environment for spiritual practice. As we will explore in Chapter 4, the famous Sufi polymath Abu Hamid al-Ghazali (d. 1111) influentially argued that Muslims should submit to political authorities, even if they have gained power through force of arms alone. Earlier, as will be elaborated upon in Chapter 5, one of Sufism's forefathers, Abu al-Qasim al-Junayd (d. 910), counselled that Sufis should maintain a strict public discretion, keeping their experiences and metaphysical doctrines quiet, while ensuring conformity to the norms of Muslim religious and political authorities.

Anti-Sufism in North America: The Erasure of Sufism from Islam

The past decade has seen extremist Muslim militias engage in an increasingly systematic destruction of Sufi sites. From Somalia, Mali, Tunisia, Libya and Egypt in Africa, to Syria and Iraq in the Middle East, and to Pakistan in South Asia, across much of the geography of traditional Islamic civilization, Muslims are destroying the resting places of Sufi saints. Each bulldozing or dynamiting of a local site that had been sacred to Muslims for centuries signals a larger cultural purging that is taking place. Whether the desecration of the grave of Ahmad Zarruq (d. 1493) in Libya in 2012, the destruction of a number of Sufi shrines in Mali that same year, or the bulldozing of Ahmad al-Rifaʻi's tomb in Iraq in 2014, groups affiliated with al-Qaeda, the Taliban, and the Islamic State have sought to purify the lands they control of anything they deem to be an idolatrous veneration of people and places. The young fighters carrying out such acts, even with just pick axes and Kalashnikovs, see it as their religious duty to attack and destroy Sufi shrines, sites where they believe saints are worshipped alongside God. For them, purging Muslim societies of such sites will help restore the pure, powerful Islam of the first generations of Muslims (the *Salaf*), paving the way for a revived Islamic society, a society once again prominent on the world stage.

In the twentieth century, Sufis became caught up in the debates over how best to practice and preserve Islam in the modern world. The widespread collapse of traditional Muslim political and religious institutions in the colonial era (particularly in the nineteenth and early twentieth centuries) created a vacuum of religious authority for Muslims. This vacuum has been filled by competing voices vying to define what exactly Islam is and what an Islamic society should look like. As modernizing states in the Muslim world competed with Islamic revivalist groups to lay claim to Islamic symbols in the mid-twentieth century, Sufis have come under increasing pressure. The religious and political legitimacy of Sufis have been challenged by modernizing reformers who see Sufis as backwards, superstitious remnants of Islam's old, decadent order, and by revivalists who believe that Sufism is a corruption of "pure" Islamic teachings.

In particular, anti-Sufi perspectives have gained a powerful impetus in the last fifty years, with significant assistance from Saudi Arabia-based funding. Ibn ʻAbd al-Wahhab's anti-Sufi theology returned to power in Arabia in the early twentieth century, with the founding of the Saudi Arabian kingdom in 1932. With the discovery of vast oil reserves in the Arabian Peninsula in the 1930s, and the resulting accumulation of oil wealth, the Saudi state and private organizations have exported Ibn ʻAbd al-Wahhab's call to purify Islam of Sufi innovations throughout the world, in many ways fundamentally altering the religious landscape of Islam. It is important to point out that contemporary Wahhabi Muslims reject the term "Wahhabi", and tend to self-describe as "Salafi", in reference to their claim of restoring the pure Islam of the righteous early generations of Islam, the *Salaf al-Salih*.

This dissemination of Wahhabi / Salafi thought in the latter half of the twentieth century has occurred through a variety of channels, including Saudi support of a large number of universities, forms of television and internet media, publishing houses, conferences, mosques, and charities around the world, including in North America. This has meant a very real marginalization of Sufis in Muslim communities in North America. Around the world, Sufism is being erased from Muslim cultural memory, excised from the body it was an integral part of for so long.

This influence of foreign, anti-Sufi funding on mosque administrations, national organizations, and annual conventions in North America helped create an environment in which Sufism was generally understood to be something inauthentic and corrupt. It follows that many Muslims in North America have come to understand Sufism in this way, seeing it as something un-Islamic. Following the discovery of the predominantly Saudi origin of the 9/11 hijackers however, Saudi charities, religious organizations, and Wahhabism in general drew scrutiny from American intelligence agencies and media commentators. Both the United States government and the Muslim community itself pursued a crackdown on militancy. This crackdown however allowed for other Muslim perspectives to gain public voice and recognition. Whereas before 9/11 Salafi and Islamist views were often assumed as normative throughout the various strata of the Muslim community's infrastructure in North America, the atmosphere shifted after 2001, as these views were implicated in the attacks. A new willingness to consider other perspectives emerged. Sufi claims to a traditional, orthodox, balanced, spiritual, and open-minded Islam suddenly gained increasing appeal amongst many Muslims in North America (Dickson 2015: 47).

Alongside more traditional perspectives, like Kabbani's, that have risen to prominence in the post-9/11 environment, movements for a "Progressive Islam" have taken root in the United States, primarily among Muslim academics and activists. Omid Safi edited an influential collection of essays entitled, *Progressive Muslims: On Justice, Gender, and Pluralism* (2003). Many of the work's authors have either been influenced by Sufism or have been galvanized by the spread of anti-Sufi theologies such as Wahhabism. Safi notes in the introduction that "progressive Muslims need to problematize, resist, and finally replace the lifeless, narrow, exclusivist, and oppressive ideology that Wahhabism poses to Islam" (Safi 2003: 8). Many progressive Muslims see Sufism as an integral part of any Islam that seeks to recover and develop Muslim traditions of humanism, justice, and dialogue. Safi writes that, "As much as any group of Muslims, the Sufis have attempted to cultivate this interpersonal ethic at a communal level" (2003: 14). Safi here is referring to the Sufi emphasis on *adab* or considerate, refined behaviour toward others. There is a famous Sufi saying that, "all of Sufism is *adab*", emphasizing the central role kindness, manners, and consideration of others play on the Sufi path. Progressive Muslims briefly came together to form the Progressive Muslim Union of North America (PMUNA) in 2004 (GhaneaBassiri 2010: 358). Although it dissolved in 2006, activists and scholars involved with PMUNA continue to pursue an agenda of liberalizing Muslim discourse on women, same-sex relationships, social justice, and relations with non-Muslims (Dickson 2015: 49). They have in some cases created new sorts of mosques led by women, open to people of all gender and sexual identities.

Many contemporary Sufis work to develop international networks devoted to peace building, conflict resolution, and interfaith understanding. For example, Jonathan Granoff, or Ahamad Muhaiyaddeen, is a long-time student of Bawa Muhaiyaddeen's, having met the Sri Lankan Sufi teacher in the early 1970s after he settled in Philadelphia. Granoff is also president of the Global Security Institute, headquartered in Philadelphia, with offices in New York, Washington, DC and New Zealand. The Institute's stated aim is to establish security for all peoples through the elimination of nuclear weapons.

Granoff is an attorney and expert on international law regarding nuclear non-proliferation. He is the vice President of the NGO Committee on Disarmament, Peace, and Security at the United Nations, and is also a senior advisor to the Nobel Laureate Peace Summit. Much of his work involves meeting with world leaders and diplomats to encourage them to sign onto and adhere to international conventions on the non-proliferation, reduction, and eventual elimination of nuclear weapons.

He has worked with such international figures as the Dalai Lama, Kofi Annan and Bill Clinton, and celebrities including Angelina Jolie, Michael Douglas, and George Clooney. Granoff understands his career as a nuclear non-proliferation lawyer-activist was simply his way of practicing Sufism in the contemporary world. In a sense, Granoff himself acts as a bridge between the world of international politics and traditional Sufi Muslim practice. On the one hand, Granoff dresses in traditional dervish clothing (a white cap and gown), praying at a celebration of the Prophet Muhammad's birthday, with the many turban-wearing attendees shouting reverently, *"Allahu akbar"* or, "God is the greatest". On the other hand, Granoff has been interviewed by his friend Deepak Chopra (a popular author on spirituality), about the danger posed to life and the planet by nuclear weapons. These two examples illustrate his spirituality as a Muslim Sufi, and his international activism against nuclear weapons. Granoff reflected on Sufism's global, political relevance as follows:

> Sufism is premised on the unity of the human family without divisions. To treat all lives as sacred and all human beings as equal. These are very powerful and needed principles for a globalized world. You cannot protect the oceans if one country can dump under their flag of convenience. So we need global regimes to protect the very oceans that the systems of life on the planet depend upon. And legal regimes have to depend on ethical foundations. Sources for universal ethical foundations that bring people together on a global level have enormous relevance in today's world, and they're really needed. I'm not saying Sufism is the *only* source for this, but it's certainly *a* source (Dickson 2010).

Even Granoff's teacher, Bawa Muhaiyaddeen, intervened in Islam's political discourse during the Iranian revolution in the late 1970s and early 1980s. Especially in response to the Iranian hostage crisis, Bawa Muhaiyaddeen wrote a book intending to contrast authentic, peaceful Islam, from that being touted by Iranian revolutionaries like the Ayatollah Khomenei (d. 1989).

Regardless of their political orientation, Sufis in North America are in a sense politically significant by simply making their voices heard in the public sphere. Sufism is often left completely out of contemporary public debates about the nature of Islam, debates that increasingly play out on news programs, in popular books, and on blogs and websites. As a consequence, Islam's rich tradition of spirituality remains virtually unknown to many North Americans, who are far more familiar with sensationalized debates about suicide bombing, the oppression of women, and Islamic law. Islam becomes, in the minds of many, associated more with political conflict and violence rather than spirituality, philosophy, and love poetry. This tends to feed into the widespread misperception that Islam is better thought of as a political ideology, rather than a tradition of spirituality and metaphysics expressed throughout a diverse cultural heritage. Conservative American activists who oppose what they call the "Islamization" of America have in recent years launched a campaign against what they see as the dangers posed by political Islam. Some have even suggested that Islam is not a religion at all, but a collectivist, totalitarian ideology. Strangely, some of the most vocal Muslims in favour of an "Islamic state" agree with such anti-Islamic activists, proposing that Islam is a political ideology first and foremost. Activists on both sides of the debate ironically come together in over-emphasizing Islam's political and legalistic elements to the detriment of its spirituality and culture. Although Sufism has been interwoven with the politics of Islam historically, Sufis are well placed to point out what is missed in much public discourse on Islam today: namely Islam's ancient tradition of spirituality and rich heritage of art and culture, the history of which has been largely erased from memory. Simply pointing out the ubiquitous role of Sufism in Islamic history and its influence on Islamic culture can go a long way towards countering reductionistic depictions of Islam as an ideology or political movement.

As we will find in the following section, it is interesting to see how Sufis themselves differ on the nature of the relationship between Islam and Sufism. For some, Sufism is the spiritual essence of Islam, the fruit of a devout and committed Muslim life. For others, Sufism is a path of transformation that can take on a variety of forms to meet the needs of people in different times and places: Sufism may function both within and without the practice of Islamic law and ritual.

ISLAMIC, UNIVERSAL, OR BOTH? INTERPRETIVE DIVERSITY WITHIN CONTEMPORARY SUFISM

In the century since its arrival on North American shores, Sufism has grown into a remarkably diverse tradition. Its diversity has raised some interesting philosophical issues on the nature of the tradition, particularly in its relation to Islam. Jay Kinney, in his introduction to *Gnosis* magazine's issue on Sufism (1994), describes the "Sufi Conundrum". Kinney recalls first encountering "Sufi dancing" in the early 1970s in San Francisco's counterculture scene, as the purview of the area's hippies. Years later, he read some of Idries Shah's (d. 1996) popular works on the subject. In his introduction to *The Sufis*, Robert Graves (d. 1985) suggests that Sufism is "an ancient spiritual freemasonry whose origins have never been traced or dated" (Shah 1964: vii). Kinney would later meet traditional Sufis from the Middle East who seemed "*very* Islamic" in comparison to the Sufi dancers of the Bay Area. He was confused as to the nature of Sufism: Was Sufism a part of Islam or beyond any religion? Was it the purview of hippies or Islamic preachers? "What, in short, was going on?", he asks (Kinney 1994: 10).

The best answer might just be "all of the above". Sufism takes on a wide variety of shapes in North America, many of which do not fit with common expectations of what a traditional Sufi order should look like. All Sufi lineages without exception trace their lineage to the Prophet Muhammad and utilize some aspects of classical Sufi terminology rooted in the Qur'ān and *hadith* (reports about what the Prophet Muhammad said, did, or remained silent on). In this sense all of the varieties of Sufism in North America can be described as Islamic. And yet contemporary Sufi teachers differ quite markedly when it comes to the questions of whether or not one needs to be a Muslim to practice Sufism, and whether Sufism can be legitimately taught in non-Islamic forms.

Seyyed Hossein Nasr is a Senior Professor of Islamic Studies at George Washington University and a prominent leader of the Maryamiyya Sufi order. The order is a branch of the 'Alawi order, originating in Algeria, but transmitted to Europe and North America by Swiss author and mystic Frithjof Schuon (d. 1998). Schuon is one of the founders of a philosophy known as Traditionalism, which suggests that the world's religions are traditions that encapsulate the same ancient metaphysical truths in different ways. (We will discuss Traditionalism, Schuon, the Maryamiyya, and the 'Alawi order in more depth in Chapter 2.) Nasr describes Sufism as the "heart of Islam", or the esoteric/inward dimension of the Islamic revelation. In his view, to attempt to practice Sufism outside of Islam is to try to get at the fruit of the Islamic revelation without the tree. For Nasr, the "fruit" of Sufi spirituality grows from the "tree" of the Qur'ān, Muhammad, and a life of Islamic practice. He explains:

> Sufism is the crystallization of the inner teachings of Islam. The Islamic revelation had an aspect having to do with law, the laws of society, with human interactions in the world, with the external world, and also the world of nature. It had an aspect that had to do with the inner life, with spiritual perfection, with the inner meaning of things including the Qur'ān itself. This crystallized into what we call Islamic esotericism: into primarily Sufism, though some of this is also to be found in early Twelver Imami Shi'ism and also in later Twelver Imami Shi'ism and in Ismailism. Sufism, you might say for the sake of simplicity, is the inward or esoteric or mystical aspect of the Islamic tradition (Dickson 2015: 170).

Hence for Nasr there can be no Sufism outside of Islam: those who claim to practice non-Islamic Sufism are simply fooling themselves, engaging in what Nasr calls "pseudo-Sufism". Nasr's Sufi practice and teaching coincide with his life-long devotion to Islamic scholarship. Most recently, in collaboration with a number of editors, Nasr published *The Study Qur'ān* in 2015, a landmark in Islamic studies which makes available for the first time in English, a translation of the Qur'ān that includes a range of classical commentaries, some of which were written by famous Sufi figures (i.e. 'Abd al-Razzaq al-Kashani, d. 1329).

Nasr is not alone in his perspective, and many traditionally-oriented Sufi teachers reject streams of Sufism that do not require adherence to Islamic law and practice. This understanding of Islam and Sufism that holds the two as coeval is sometimes conveyed through the traditional three-fold breakdown of the Sufi path: *shari'a*, *tariqa*, and *haqiqa*. One begins the spiritual path with the *shari'a*, or Islamic law. One carefully observes the moral boundaries set up by Islamic law, and fulfils its ritual requirements: praying five times a day, giving charity annually, fasting during Ramadan, and making the pilgrimage to Mecca if possible. This moral, ritual observance is believed to establish the necessary equilibrium, humility, and submission to God without which one cannot delve deeper into spiritual matters. Once the foundation of *shari'a* is established, the seeker can then pursue the *tariqa* – the "way" or "path" offered by a particular Sufi teacher and lineage. This "way" builds upon the first stage with the addition of the particular rituals of the Sufi lineage one is a part of, the particular kind of *dhikr* the order specializes in, or the *dhikr* that one is assigned by one's teacher. Following this path takes one to *haqiqa*, an Arabic word meaning "truth" or "reality" itself: hence this three-fold breakdown of Sufism can be summarized in English as law, path, and truth. The important point from this perspective, is that without the *shari'a* one cannot encounter *haqiqa*: the rules and rites of Islam are an integral part of the path to spiritual perfection and realization. Sufism then is the deepening of Islamic practice and the cultivation of its spiritual fruit.

Understanding Sufism as the perfection of Islam has classically been illustrated with reference to the *hadith* of the Angel Gabriel. Narrated in the Sahih Muslim collection of *hadith*, the *hadith* of Gabriel is also the second *hadith* in Yahya Ibn Sharaf al-Nawawi's (d. 1277) famous collection *Forty Hadith*. In the *hadith*, 'Umar Ibn al-Khattab (d. 644), a close companion of Muhammad's, relates that a man appeared to Muhammad and a group of his followers, a man whose "clothes were exceedingly white and whose hair was exceedingly black", someone not seen before. The individual proceeds to question the Prophet on the nature of Islam, *iman* (faith), and *ihsan* (doing what is beautiful). The Prophet responds that Islam is the five pillars of practice (the statement of faith, prayer, fasting, annual charity, and the pilgrimage to Mecca), *iman* is the six tenets of belief (God, his Angels, his Scriptures, his Messengers, the day of judgment, and divine predestination), and that *ihsan* is to worship God as though you see Him. Sufis have traditionally situated Sufism as that aspect of religion that addresses *ihsan*, the advanced or highest level of practice, dealing with awareness of God, and excellence and beauty in character. *Ihsan* then, is the perfection of both Islam and *iman*, and cannot be conceived of apart from them, nor can Islam and *iman* be complete without *ihsan*.

Although Sufi teachers disagree themselves over the acceptable forms that Sufism can take, it is important to acknowledge the reality of this disagreement and the diversity within Sufism that it has led to. Sufism does in fact take on a wide variety of forms depending on the particular order or teacher who transmits it, some emphasizing Islamic religiosity while others downplay this considerably. While North American Sufi teachers tend to agree that Sufism is an ancient mystical tradition traceable to the earliest times, a tradition that has existed in a variety of contexts, in all cases involving the transformation of the human soul, some of these teachers believe that the transformation of the soul, or the encounter with *haqiqa*, does not require the *shari'a,* as conventionally understood in relation to Islamic jurisprudence, or adopting Muslim identity and practice. For those who take this trans-religious approach to Sufism, an approach that is sometimes labelled "universal Sufism", one may or may not be a Muslim, but regardless of one's religious affiliation one can fully engage with a master within a Sufi lineage, and as a result can be transformed by Sufi teachings.

A notable example of this approach is found in the Golden Sufi Center, a meditation centre and collection of retreat homes in the hills of Marin County, California. Golden Sufi Center is located near Tomales Bay, surrounded by an ecological reserve and state park. The landscape, with its lagoon, wooded hills, and periods of intense fog, is beautiful and dramatic. Although some have jokingly referred to "California Sufism" as a sort of New Age approach to Sufism marked by shallowness and a lack of seriousness, the Golden Sufi Center could not be further from this stereotype. Llewellyn Vaughan-Lee is a prolific author and leader of the Center. It is a branch of the Naqshbandi-Mujaddidi order, an Indian Sufi order renowned for its emphasis on Islamic law and its serious spiritual sobriety. In contrast to the order's orthodox roots however, Vaughan-Lee describes his particular branch of the order as "non-Islamic". The absence of Islamic practice in the order is not something that Vaughan-Lee developed himself. His predecessor in the order, Irina Tweedie (d. 1999), was taught by Radha Mohan Lal (d. 1966), a Hindu Sufi teacher in India. Ahmed Khan (d. 1907), Lal's Muslim Sufi teacher, counselled him to remain with the Hindu religion of his birth. Khan said that Lal did not need to convert to Islam to follow the path to truth. In Khan's approach, *haqiqa* did not require *shari'a*, at least not as it is traditionally conceived.

Vaughan-Lee describes the approach of his order as "formless", noting that it was transmitted without ritual or rule because this suits some people

(Dickson 2015: 187). Vaughan-Lee does not suggest that approaches to Sufism based more on religious practice are misguided, but simply that different approaches suit different mentalities. He continues to teach from early Sufi manuals, and requires the same commitment to the *shaykh*, lineage, and meditation practice as found in more traditionally-oriented orders. One could argue that the deep structure of the order closely resembles other, more Islamically-oriented Sufi orders, but that its presentation contrasts markedly with them. On this issue, Vaughan-Lee shares:

> I regard the Sufi teachings within Islam of being of tremendous benefit to the contemporary seeker, which is why I have written a number of books and articles relating spiritual/mystical experiences – for example annihilation (*fana'*), or the stages of the journey (*maqamat*) – to their roots within Islamic Sufi literature. This literature provides us with the most detailed understanding of the transformation of the heart and the inner spiritual journey of the mystic – for example the detailed description of the chambers of the heart, or the valleys of the quest, that belong to the path of love. But as one Sufi said, 'Why listen to second hand reports when you can hear the Beloved speak Himself'. What matters on the mystical path are direct inner experiences [*kashf*], and these experiences do not require the outer form of any religion (Vaughan-Lee, email message to author, 11th November 2014).

The different approaches to Sufism represented by Nasr and Vaughan-Lee can in part be conceived of as different understandings of the degree to which Sufism can be adapted to suit different times, places, and people. For Nasr, the classical form that Sufism crystalized into during the medieval period represents a manifestation of the Islamic revelation that should be preserved as much as possible, with only very minor changes in form desirable as Sufism moves from one cultural context to another. For others like Vaughan-Lee however, Sufism is a spiritual essence that can take a variety of forms depending on the needs of people in different places. These forms may contrast sharply with traditional Islamic forms, though the essence is thought to remain the same.

Perhaps representing a middle position between those of Nasr and Vaughan-Lee, Yannis Toussulis is a psychologist and professor based also in California. He is primarily associated with the Malamati-Naqshbandi lineage of the nineteenth century Sufi reformer Pir Nur al-Arabi (d. 1888). Like Nasr, Toussulis indicated that there could be no Sufism without Islam. And yet he suggests that Islam has a wider meaning beyond conventional religious practice, and notes that some Muslims may not consider Sufis orthodox:

> 'Islam' or Islamic traditions vary greatly. One could say, on the one hand, that Sufism is the very essence of Islam. On the other hand, it might appear that Sufis do not adhere to what others believe is required of a Muslim. It is a matter of perspective... After all, the word 'Islam', itself,

means to surrender. In a narrower sense, Sufism is the particular form of mysticism that evolved through a direct interface with the traditions of philosophy, worship, and practices that are associated with the formal religion of Islam. The forms that Sufism takes, however, vary over time – and this has always been the case (Dickson 2015: 182–83).

Toussulis maintains Sufism's relation to the basic meaning of Islam (surrender), and further acknowledges that Sufism is particularly related to Islamic civilization, being in a sense the Islamic form of mysticism. And yet he maintains that Islam is an inherently dynamic tradition that changes over time, and as such takes on a variety of forms, not all of which correspond to what is considered orthodox.

In his work, *Sufism and the Way of Blame: Hidden Sources of a Sacred Psychology* (2010), Toussulis seeks to critique the Traditionalist perspective of which Nasr is a representative. Toussulis argues that the Traditionalist insistence that Sufism is the inner aspect of Islamic orthodoxy, fails to account for the ways in which Sufism integrated elements of non-Islamic traditions present in the Near East during its formative period. He suggests that Traditionalists, in seeking "hyper-coherence", have glossed over the very real tensions between jurists and Sufis throughout Islamic history, downplaying the diversity of forms Sufism has historically taken, not all of which have been acceptable to Islam's jurists and theologians (Toussulis 2010: 31–36).

Although we can see that contemporary teachers of Sufism in North America have different perspectives on the diverse ways in which Sufism is presented, the diversity within the tradition is a fact: Sufism is taught and practiced in North America in a variety of ways, some of which are inseparable from a devout Muslim life, whereas others may appear to have very little outward connection to Islamic traditions.

Contemporary Sufi Female Leaders

Camille Adams Helminski (b. 1951) is Co-Director of The Threshold Society, a branch of the Mevlevi order based in the United States. She also is a faculty member at Spiritual Paths Foundation (which advocates for peace and interfaith understanding through contemplative practice), a mentor at Snowmass Interspiritual Dialogue, and spiritual leader at WISE (Women's Initiative in Islamic Spirituality and Equality). She co-founded The Threshold Society with her husband, Kabir Edmund Helminski (m. 1974) in 1985, four years after they co-founded Threshold Books. The organization is associated with teachers from Sufi orders in Turkey, Iran, Syria, and India who balance classical traditions with contemporary spiritual needs. Helminski holds a Bachelor of Arts from Smith College and an honorary doctorate in Arabic from the University of Damascus. She has written extensively, including collaborations with Kabir Helminski (e.g. *Rumi Daylight: A Daybook of Spiritual Guidance* [1999], *The Rumi Collection* [1998], *The Pocket Rumi* [2000]), individual works (*Women of Sufism: A Hidden Treasure* [2003]) and translations (e.g. *Awakened Dreams* [1999]). Helminski is the first woman to translate substantial selections of the Qur'ān into English, in *The Light of Dawn: Daily Readings from the Holy Qur'ān* (2000). For more information about The Threshold Society, visit their website: www.sufism.org or Twitter @thresholdsoc.

Nur Artiran is a current master (*shaykha*) of the Mevlevi order founded by Jalal ad-Din Rumi, having succeeded her teacher, Şefik Can (d. 2005). Daniel Dyer, writing about his trip to the Şefik Can Foundation in September 2013 which was led by Kabir Helminski and Camille Adams Helminski, described Nur Artiran as "one of Turkey's most respected spiritual teachers" (Dyer 2013). She is the President of the Şefik Can International Mevlana Education and Culture Foundation (based in Istanbul), and a board member of the Universal Sufi Council (based in Wassenaar, the Netherlands). Fascinated with mysticism since she was a child, Nur Artiran has written scholarly articles (Artiran 2010) and contributed to Şefik Can's book, *Cevâhir-i Mesneviyye* (2001). She has also presented at local and international conferences (e.g. Zenith Institute Sufi Summer Camp, International 'Alawiyya Sufi Association, International Congress of Turkish Culture), and on radio and television programs.

Cemalnur Sargut (b. 1952) is a prominent Sufi teacher of the Rifa'i-Jerrahi order. She earned a Bachelor of Science in Chemical Engineering and taught chemistry for two decades. She also received her religious education from Samiha Ayverdi (d. 1993, founder, Turkish Women's Cultural Association), who encouraged her to give lessons on Rumi's famous work the *Masnavi* and whom she succeeded as the association's current President. Sargut publishes works on Sufism and Quranic commentary compilations (which include the writings of famous Sufi figures from the classical tradition). A list of her selected works can be found in her biography (www.cemalnur.org). In addition to her writings, Sargut gives spiritual lectures on Rumi's *Masnavi* and Ibn al-'Arabi's (d. 1240) *Fusus al-Hikam*. Her lecture at the Baraka Institute can be found at: www.onbeing.org. She has led groups of well-educated women followers to take part in Rumi Festival in Chapel Hill, North Carolina. She sees Sufism as a "common language" that people of various cultural and religious backgrounds can share. To further this humanistic vision of Sufism, Sargut has established chairs of Islamic studies at the University of North Carolina, Chapel Hill, and at Peking University, Beijing. Additionally in March 2017 the Kenan Rifai Centre of Sufi Studies was inaugurated at Kyoto University in Japan.

Fatima al-Yashrutiyya (d. 1978) was the daughter of Shadhili Shaykh Nur al-Din al-Yashruti (d. 1899). She was raised in her father's Sufi centre or *zawiyya* (which was originally in Acre, Palestine, and well-established in Syria, Palestine, and Jordan) and educated in theology, jurisprudence, and Sufism. In 1954, Fatima al-Yashrutiyya completed an account of her father's life and teachings in *Rihla ila al-Haqq* (A Journey Toward the Truth). She wrote three other books, namely, *Masirati fi Tariq al-Haqq* (My Journey on the Path of the Truth), *Mawahib al-Haqq* (Gifts of the Truth), and *Nafahat al-Haqq* (Breaths of the Truth). According to Leslie Cadavid, her "most important" works are *Rihla ila al-Haqq* and *Masirati fi Tariq al-Haqq*, "which contains her autobiography as well as descriptions of many members of her family" (Cadavid 2007: 176). Fatima al-Yashrutiyya was active in the revivalist pan-Islamic movement that began in the nineteenth century, and carried the order's blessing to initiate others into the order following her father's death. As Cadavid suggests, "the fact that so many scholars from both East and West came to visit Fatima al-Yashrutiyya during her lifetime demonstrates the importance of her position in the world of Islam and Sufism".

Alongside questions of Sufism's relation to Islamic practice, Sufi teachers in North America differ over the nature of women's roles within Sufi orders. As illustrated throughout this text, Sufi female personalities were influential in the development of the various aspects of the Sufi tradition, from developing its principles and practices, to transmitting knowledge, and being recognized as saints, spiritual teachers, and authorities. In North America, women continue to play important roles in the tradition's development and in some cases have even extended these roles beyond traditional boundaries. Sufi teachers within the Mevlevi order in North America, have taught women the traditional Mevlevi whirling ritual (the *sema*), previously the exclusive preserve of men. A Mevlevi master from Istanbul, Suleyman Loras (d. 1985), first authorized women to participate in the traditional Mevlevi "whirling ritual", which itself has become an iconic symbol of Sufism. Two of his students, Kabir and Camille Helminski, were initiated into the Mevlevi order in 1980. In 1990 Kabir was designated as one of the first Mevlevi *shaykhs* in North America by the head of the Mevlevi order in Istanbul. Kabir and Camille established the Threshold Society to transmit Mevlevi teachings, now with branches in six countries, with approximately 200 active members. Continuing the trajectory established by Loras, the Helminskis have maintained elements of traditional Mevlevi Sufism while adapting others to better fit with North American norms. Women and men are both taught the whirling practice, and some of the gender divisions found in more traditional contexts are not maintained.

Besides their role as teachers of Sufism, the Helminskis have been instrumental in sharing the works of their order's founder, Rumi, with an English-speaking audience. In what follows, we take a closer look at the ways in which this thirteenth century Persian poet and spiritual master has influenced cultural creatives in North America, from poets, to musicians, choreographers, activists, and restaurateurs.

RUMI: THE MAKING OF A CONTEMPORARY ICON IN NORTH AMERICA

As we will see throughout this book, Sufi poetry has long been one of the most popular means of communicating the otherwise incommunicable experiences that form the heart of the Sufi path. In North America, Sufi poetry has acted as a sort of underground river of inspiration for artists and authors since the nineteenth century. As we explore further in the second chapter, Ralph Waldo Emerson (d. 1882) would offer many nineteenth century Americans their first exposure to Persian Sufi poetry, notably that of Hafiz (d. 1390) and Sa'di (d. 1291) (Rishmawi 1995: 147). Emerson's transmission of Persian Sufi poetry in the nineteenth century prefigured the immense popularity of this poetry during the latter part of the twentieth century, when a proliferation of translations of the thirteenth Century Persian Sufi master, Jalal al-Din Rumi would seep into the cultural, artistic grooves of the North American cultural landscape. Rumi's significance for both Sufism and Persian literature is difficult to overestimate, and hence it is perhaps no surprise that Rumi's poetry has had such a powerful impact in North America.

Figure 1.2: Jalal al-Din Rumi holding a tablet with the Arabic word for "Truth" or "Reality", done in the traditional Orthodox Christian iconographic style.[2]

2. Robert Lentz is a Franciscan friar in the United States, and an artist who creates traditional-style icons of various classical and contemporary religious and political leaders. His work is featured at www.trinitystores.com

The Life and Transformation of Rumi

Who was this medieval Sufi poet that would have such a profound effect on North American culture? Jalal al-Din Rumi was born in 1203 in Balkh (present-day Afghanistan). His father was Baha al-Din Walad (d. 1231), a Muslim preacher, theologian, and mystic. Although by day Walad was a scholar, his diaries revealed that, by night, he penned mystical accounts of his intimate relationship with God, the Beloved. Rumi's eventual outpouring of poetry on Divine Love then can be traced to his father's own spiritual preoccupation.

Around 1215 or 1220, Rumi's father took his family West, likely sensing the growing threat posed by the Mongols. The Mongols would indeed soon invade central Muslim lands, before sacking Baghdad in 1258, marking the end of the 'Abbasid era. Thenceforth, Muslim societies struggled to regain their footing. Although Rumi's father could not have known it at the time, his son's teaching would play a critical role in shaping the contours of the post-Mongol Islamic tradition.

Rumi's family lived in Damascus for a short period before settling in Konya, in the Anatolian peninsula (present-day Turkey). Rumi married at 18 and when his father died in 1231 he took over his position at the local *madrasa* (Islamic religious school), teaching Islamic law and theology. Rumi's immersion in the traditional Islamic sciences is apparent in the ease with which he references the Qur'ān and Prophetic traditions in his poetry (Schimmel 2001: 13).

At this point in his life, Rumi showed little inclination towards the mystical. We cannot know whether or not he was familiar with his father's own rather secretive love mysticism. However, one year after his father's death, one of his father's disciples, Burhan al-Din Muhaqqiq, arrived in Konya and soon began teaching Rumi the works of his father as well as the mystical poetry of Hakim Sana'i (d. 1131). Sana'i was a court poet in Ghazna (present-day Afghanistan) who became a renowned Sufi author. He was the first to use the form of *mathnawi*, which contains rhyming couplets in Persian that offer a nonlinear mixture of parables, stories, and aphorisms. Sana'i used this literary form to express Sufi teachings, a pattern that Rumi would follow to perfection. Despite being an unrivalled wordsmith, Rumi would always emphasize that words were a veil, suggesting that seekers look for the underlying meaning and essence.

Rumi spent the 1230s and 40s living the life of a religious scholar and family man. He was a respectable, uncontroversial member of the upper-middle class in Konya. Then in October 1244, Rumi met a wandering mystic who would forever change the course of his life and who was to become the inspiration for his great works of poetry: Shams of Tabriz. We cannot likely overstate the effect that Shams had on Rumi. Unlike Rumi, Shams was a dervish, a wild, mendicant mystic, who paid no mind to the social conventions of the cultural elite. Shams was known to speak the truth regardless of how awkward its intrusion might have been deemed by those not given to such blatant expressions of "things as they are". He was fiery, intense, and passionate. He was the spark that would set Rumi aflame with music, dance, poetry, and spiritual intoxication. In his *Divan-i Shams-i Tabriz*, Rumi writes:

On account of you there is wind in my head and my whiskers.
Who wouldn't be drunk with pride from such good fortune?

Every moment, to spite sobriety
I drink a thousand goblets, without any cup or vessel.

Birds of the sky, the Godly falcons,
I capture from thin air, without trap or craft.

Birds of wonder grow from the palm of my hand.
I am exultant, wine seething from my teeth

(Anvar 2002: 31)

As we can see in the above passage, Rumi, like many Sufi poets before him, utilized the symbolism of wine and drunkenness to represent the ecstatic quality of God's love. The various terminology associated with wine culture, such as the tavern, the goblet, the tavern owner or wine bearer, intoxication, addiction and desire, all were used by Sufi poets to express the sublime love between the seeker and God, and the ways in which the wine of God's love takes the seeker beyond the rational mind, a state of being symbolized by the loss of mind associated with drunkenness. The Sufi master was often portrayed as the tavern owner or bar tender, pouring the love of God into the disciple's cup.

After their initial encounter Shams and Rumi spent days and even months together, two kindred spirits. Rumi's friends and family were not pleased with these new developments, as the man who they previously knew as a sober religious teacher, father, and husband, was now associating with a strange, wandering Sufi and neglecting everything else in the process. For his part, Shams made no effort to endear himself to the people of Konya, or Rumi's friends and family, and his fiery personality likely engendered their hostility. Shams, like the meaning of his name ("the Sun") refused to let people sleep in delusion, but sought to awaken them whenever possible. Sensing the growing hostility and even danger to his person, Shams disappeared as suddenly as he had arrived. Rumi was heartbroken. The companion who set his heart ablaze with mystical insight and the love of God was gone, and he was stricken with grief. However, his suffering proved to be the catalyst for his creativity. He began to compose verses of poetry, to express his longing and separation. He started attending musical concerts, and danced.

Rumi sought out Shams, writing letters, seeking his whereabouts, all in vain. Finally, Rumi heard word that Shams had been sighted in Damascus. He sent his son, Sultan Walad, there to bring Shams back to Konya. This time Rumi insisted Shams stay at his home. He arranged a marriage between a girl raised in his home to Shams, and the two men resumed their hours of deep conversation and shared presence. Again however, jealousy arose among Rumi's people, as Rumi's time was monopolized by Shams once more. Some accounts indicate that Rumi's younger son, 'Ala' al-Din deemed Shams an unwelcome intruder, and, as a result, secretly had him murdered and thrown into a well. Other accounts suggest that Shams was simply aware of the problems his presence was creating for Rumi, and disappeared of his own accord one day, leaving again for Syria. We may never know what exactly happened to Shams, but what is certain is that he left Rumi's life for good, with the result that Rumi was heartbroken and left looking for the spiritual spark that once ignited his life so powerfully.

Rumi journeyed to Syria to find Shams, but to no avail. Out of the depths of his despair however, arose a great discovery. While on the road to the Damascus, looking for Shams, Rumi "found Shams in himself, radiant as the moon".

> Since I am he, what need to seek?
> I am the same as he, his essence speaks!
> Indeed I sought my own self, that is sure,
> Fermenting in the vat, just like the must (Schimmel 1992: 19)

Rumi had finally experienced the complete annihilation of the self (*fana'*) in the Beloved; he had become one with the spirit he loved, and realized that what he sought from the very beginning was within him all along.

"Rumimania": Poetry and Popular Culture

Rumi's poetics of love and longing would capture the imagination of North American seekers of a life-affirming spirituality, and would act as a creative catalyst for a variety of artists in North America. While Sufi personalities and practices of various forms have been introduced and interwoven into the fabric of contemporary North America, in recent years Rumi has become Sufism's icon, a figure that functions to outwardly unify the tradition in the popular imagination. Since the 1800s, every century of Western readers has had a prominent and renowned Persian poet to call its own: "In 1800 it was Hafiz, in 1900 it was Omar Khayyam, and in 2000 it is Rumi" (Axworthy 2010: 115–16). The waves of admiration and esteem for these poets have not simply been due to their mastery of the word, but also due to the ways in which their ideas could be reconciled with the prevalent sensibilities of the time: "Hafiz was interpreted to fit with the mood of Romanticism, Omar Khayyam with the aesthetic movement" and Rumi to suit contemporary ideas of spiritual oneness and universality (Axworthy 2010: 116). Rumi's poetry transcends culture, religion, and history. Indeed, much of his poetry notes the confusion wrought in people by differences in language and religion, when the reality underlying them is one. Rumi writes:

> The conflicts among men stem from names
> Trace back the meaning and achieve accord
>
> (Lewis 2000: 405)

> Whether you are Arab or Greek or Turk –
> Learn the language without words!
>
> (Schimmel 1992: 44)

> Every prophet, every saint has his path
> but as they return to God, all are one.
>
> (Lewis 2000: 406)

Love's folk live beyond religious borders
The community and creed of lovers is one: God.

(Lewis 2000: 406)

Although Rumi's success in North America is no doubt related to the appeal of his message, he has had assistance in achieving his current reputation. In 2002, *TIME* magazine suggested that translator and poet Coleman Barks had effectively created an "American Rumi", whose words were now able to transcend time and space and communicate directly to the Westernized reader (Tompkins 2002). Barks has taken Rumi's poems and situated them in a form that contemporary North American readers are able to approach with ease. Discussing this process Barks articulated, "'I try to feel what spiritual information is trying to come through Rumi's images and then I try to put that into an American free-verse poem in the tradition of Walt Whitman and many others'" (Simon 2013). Barks does not read or speak Persian (the language that Rumi wrote in), so in order to develop his distinctive interpretations he instead attempts to relay the spirit of the poetry based on literal translations he has received from others. It is a unique and sometimes criticized approach, but his variety of publications have nonetheless successfully introduced many in the West to the beauty and profundity of Rumi's works. In 1995, Barks released his text entitled, *The Essential Rumi*. Today, it is the bestselling English version of Rumi's poetry, and on Amazon.com's 20 all-time bestselling books of poetry, coming in only after the likes of Edgar Allan Poe, Shakespeare, and Homer.

Rumi's contemporary rise to fame has also been inspired by groups like the United Nations Educational, Scientific and Cultural Organization (UNESCO). In 2005, they named the "Mevlevi Sema Ceremony" as one of the Masterpieces of the Oral and Intangible Heritage of Humanity and in 2007, declared it the "International Year of Rumi" in commemoration of the 800th anniversary of his birth. Under the auspices of UNESCO, cultural events were organized around the world. A three-day conference was held in Tehran, Iran, exploring Rumi's poetry and its relevance today. Celebrations of Rumi's birth were held in Afghanistan, where Rumi was born, and in Turkey, where he lived most of his life and is now buried. However, events were organized not just in countries where Rumi lived or where his poetry is a part of the literary canon, but around the globe. A performance of the whirling dervishes accompanied by Turkish classical music and recitations of Rumi's poetry was held in Toronto, Canada, in 2007, exemplary of the kind of events that happened throughout the world that year.

Rumi's stardom has not been unaffected by commercial forces. The marketplace has had a profound effect on contemporary spirituality, sanctioning and solidifying Rumi's rise to fame in present-day North America. This spiritual market is designed to take appealing practices, figures and ideas associated with ancient religious traditions and market them as remedies to contemporary ailments and anxieties. Dedicated conversion to a particular practice or system is no longer a requirement. Instead of regularly attending a religious gathering or communal service to access spiritual guidance, one simply goes to one's local shopping mall or online store to purchase a book, movie or album of popular spiritual remedies that suit one's needs. The most prevalent examples of this in North America are related to Buddhism: simply think of the decorative Buddha statues one can purchase for your home or garden, or the inspirational messages from the Dalai Lama posted on social media. Sufism however, has not been exempt from this development (Carrette and King 2004: 1–6).

Perhaps unsurprisingly then, today you can find *The Complete Idiot's Guide to Rumi Meditation* (2008), or a CD developed by spiritual guru Deepak Chopra of Rumi's poetry. On this album celebrities such as Demi Moore and Madonna recite Rumi's poetic words to the listener in a way that is said to create a "sincere and potent" spiritual experience. For the more creative seekers, you can also purchase temporary tattoos of Rumi's works that may be "Temporary on the skin" but according to the website, "Indelible on the Soul" (Conscious Ink 2016). Additionally, there are upwards of 50 Rumi-related smartphone apps available, including *Rumi* and *Daily Rumi*. Even Hollywood has embraced Rumi. In 2016, controversy emerged over news that a film on Rumi being produced had cast Leonardo DiCaprio as Rumi. Regardless, this form of spiritual marketing and pop culture representation has no doubt been a contributing dynamic in bringing increased attention and accessibility to Rumi in North America.

In spite of its success, there have been mixed evaluations concerning this process and the way Sufism has been advertised. Scholars have argued that the development of an overarching and positive image of Sufism, particularly through one figure, though in one respect welcome, is in another respect profoundly restrictive, and can even end up recycling Orientalist tropes that falsely separate Islam and spirituality. It has been argued that the spiritual market succeeds precisely because it distances the marketable product from traditional religious organizations (Carrette and King 2005: 125). Even Coleman Barks, a figure who has at the very least financially benefitted from this upsurge of popularity, feels he has sold too many books and that this market misunderstands Rumi's true intent. In the preface to *Rumi: The Book of Love*, he warns:

> Rumi translations have no business cresting in a wave of over half a million. It's like selling picnic tickets to an unmarked minefield… I once told a greeting card company that wanted to put Rumi verses on a card, 'Rumi's poetry wants to dissolve the lovers. Annihilation is the point'. There was a long silence on the other end (Barks 2009: xv).

Rumi and Contemporary Art Forms in North America

In spite of the controversy and debates surrounding the marketing of Sufism and Rumi, in the realm of arts and culture in particular, the effects of this process have been palpable. From fine art to choreography, and from human rights campaigns to restaurants, Rumi's words and ideas have resonated and manifested in ways that Rumi would have never predicted. The desire for Rumi in North America has developed a variety of roles for the "up and coming" mystic. Being that his words preach ideas of oneness and the fluidity of borders and boundaries, his work has become a lens through which artists from various fields have been able to contextualize their ideas.

Robin Becker, for instance, is a choreographer based in Manhattan. Her internationally recognized dance company is directly inspired by the works and rituals established by Rumi. Reading through Becker's repertory, Rumi's influence is clear. Themes of "acceptance", "longing for union", "meeting and returning", and "interconnectedness" dominate in her artistry. Many of her pieces are also improvised, reflective of the various ways Rumi's work can be absorbed and comprehended by individual readers and audience members. As Becker stated, "the most extraordinary part of [Rumi's] popularity comes from his complexity... There's so many ways to interpret the relationship with the Beloved: as a friendship, romance, or spiritual union" (Sims 2010). As mentioned, Becker has not simply been inspired by Rumi's words, but also the rituals of movement he developed, including the *sema* ceremony. One of her pieces, entitled, *Galaxies*, consists of "eleven dancers spiralling as stars drawn together like gravity culminating in the Sufi practice of whirling. Becker has had a life-long passion to use dance as a 'tool for transformation' and Rumi has become an influential channel through which her passion manifests" (Robin Becker Dance 2014).

Rumi's presence is further found among architects and musicians. Iranian-American architect E. Nader Khalili (d. 2008) established the California Institute of Earth, Art and Architecture (Cal-Earth) in 1991. This non-profit research organization was designed to develop effective and viable ceramic houses that would support the poor and displaced in an environmentally safe and sustainable way. Khalili believed that every man and woman should be able to "heal and shelter themselves" while simultaneously believing that, "the only way the world's poor could ever afford a home was to build with earth and fire" (Lewis 2000: 606). Under Khalili's leadership several successful prototypes were developed including "Rumi Dome of Lights", "Eco-Dome" and "Earth One". According to the Cal-Earth website, "the prototypes are significant because they realize a powerful idea at the service of humanity. Such an idea is carried in the mind and the architecture is repeatable universally" (Cal-Earth 2014).

Murray Schafer, who has been touted as one of Canada's "most original musical minds" (Tresham 2013) has also been deeply inspired by the works of Rumi, using his ideas and poetry to create some of his most dynamic compositions. In 1970, he developed two works: *Divan i Shams i Tabriz* and *Music for the Morning of the World* – both directly inspired by Rumi's works. *Music for the Morning of the World* consists of a soloist reciting a mixture of poems and discourses by Rumi. The piece begins with the smothering of the lights so the room is engulfed in darkness. Afterwards the soloist lights a single candle that produces the only illumination for the entire performance until the conclusion, when it is extinguished. Schafer has said the piece is, "contemplative with ecstatic outbursts", with the transitional lighting offering "a mood of spiritual transcendence, appropriate to the Rumi text" (Schafer 2012: 38–39).

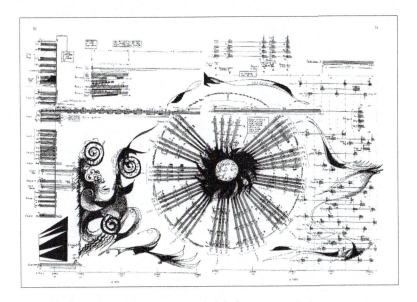

Figure 1.3: *Divan i Shams i Tabriz* by Murray Schafer.

Schafer is not alone in his admiration for Rumi, other well-known musicians including Philip Glass, Loreena McKennitt, Tom Ries of the Rolling Stones, and various indie bands such as *mewithoutYou* have also infused Rumi into their compositions and musical developments. Aaron Weise, the lead singer of *mewithoutYou*, has stated that Rumi's words have been a source of support for him throughout his life and career and often allowed him to reconcile despair with happiness. As Weise stated in an interview with *What the Glass Contains*, "Rumi has been really encouraging to me. Very loving. Very tenderhearted… There is no sorrow in there, no heaviness. Even if he does deal with heavy issues, he always brings a sweetness to it" (2012).

The culinary arts have also been impacted by Rumi's increased popularity and exposure in North America. The lively streets of Montreal offer a particularly unique Rumi-inspired culinary experience, aptly named, *Restaurant Rumi*. This distinctive manifestation of Rumi's philosophy offers Iranian, Turkish, North African, Moroccan, and Afghani food in a Pakistani, Indian, Turkish and Moroccan décor. The owners named the restaurant after Rumi because they were inspired by his ideas regarding the interconnection of all beings. They wanted their restaurant to be a place where people could eat, drink and celebrate collectively in spite of what differences they have between them. Rumi inspired these owners to prioritize a peaceful eating experience – not simply through organic food and serene surroundings, but also by ensuring the positive nature of those creating and presenting the food. It is important to these owners that the people creating the food are clean not only physically but also spiritually. *Rumi Restaurant* is just one of a number of examples around the world of Rumi-themed cafes and restaurants.

Figure 1.4: Rumi Restaurant in Montreal, QC, Canada.

In addition to becoming influential in the North American art scene, Rumi has also become an icon for various social and political movements. Unsurprising is Rumi's contribution and influence on various interfaith movements. For these groups, he is an ideal icon due to his unwavering belief in the unity of all people across borders of culture, gender, or race. *Rumi Forum* is one of these initiatives. With chapters in Delaware, Kentucky, Maryland, Virginia and North Carolina, *Rumi Forum* was developed in 1999 with a mission to nurture interfaith and intercultural dialogue. The community has developed two main centres: Center for Policy Studies and Center for Interfaith and Intercultural Dialogue. The Forum was inspired by Rumi's message:

Figure 1.5: Rumi's House of Kabob in Greeley, CO, USA.

> Come, whoever you are, come,
> Wanderer, worshiper, lover of leaving. It doesn't matter.
> Ours is not a caravan of despair.
> Come, even if you have broken your vows a thousand times.
> Come, yet again, come, come.

It works on a global scale to promote peace, dialogue, mutual respect and universal well-being. A variety of other interfaith and intercultural groups can be found that have been inspired by Rumi, including the *One Through Love* project, *Rumi Intercultural Dialogue Club*, and *Rumi Club for Interfaith Dialogue* (Rumi Forum 2014).

Rumi has also become an icon for the Lesbian, Gay, Bisexual, Transgender and Queer (LGBTQ) rights movement. In 2010 the Gay Straight Alliance (GSA) named Rumi as a Gay Icon along with individuals like Cynthia Nixon, Rufus Wainwright and Jane Lynch. The Gay, Lesbian, Bisexual, Transgender and Queer Culture online Encyclopaedia has an entire article dedicated to Rumi, and famous gay rights authors like Robert Duncan and Edmund White have written pieces inspired by Rumi's words. Duncan dedicated his piece, *Circulations of the Song*, to his partner Jesse Collins, and the poem was later published in the gay rights magazine *The Advocate* (Lewis 2000: 584). Whether in the realms of the political, the culinary, or the arts, Rumi's poetry is a remarkable example of Sufism's cultural reach in North America.

A BRIEF HISTORY OF SUFISM IN NORTH AMERICA

Besides the wide-ranging cultural influences described above, Sufism's presence in North America has, for over a century, included the concerted practice of Sufism as a path of spiritual transformation. The roots of North American interest in Sufism as a mystical way can be traced back to the late nineteenth century's "Occult Revival", which saw a passion for all things "mystical", "esoteric", "transcendental", and "Eastern" take hold. The proliferation of Helena Blavatsky (d. 1891) and Henry Steel Olcott's (d. 1907) Theosophical Society in North America illustrates well the extent to which North Americans were developing an interest in the metaphysical teachings of religions like Buddhism and Hinduism. However, these teachings were to a large degree extracted from their traditional communal contexts and presented as forms of a universal mysticism accessible to all, regardless of religious affiliation. Swami Vivekananda (d. 1902), for instance, presented Vedanta as the mystical essence of Hinduism, something North Americans could engage in regardless of their religious backgrounds. His wildly popular reception at the World's Parliament of Religions at the Chicago World Fair in 1891 indicates the appeal that such presentations of mystical teachings had for North Americans. It is not necessarily surprising then, that the first sort of Sufism to be taught directly to North Americans would take a universalistic form.

Sufism's "First Wave" in North America: Hazrat Inayat Khan's Universal Sufism

The establishment of Sufism as a sustainable practice in North America really began with the arrival of an acclaimed Indian musician and his brothers in Manhattan in 1910. Traveling by ship from India, the court musician and Sufi master, Hazrat Inayat Khan (d. 1927), sought to bring the universal message of Sufism from the shrines and mosques of India to the skyscrapers of America. Inayat Khan's *murshid* (teacher), Mohammed Abu Hashim Madani (d. 1907), asked him to go to the West to harmonize the East and the West through his music. Between 1910 and 1926 Inayat Khan travelled throughout North America and Europe giving talks, musical concerts, and establishing his Sufi Order of the West, which would remain the only visible form of Sufism available in North America until the 1960s (Genn 2007: 257). Inayat Khan was the central figure in what Jay Kinney and Gisela Webb have called Sufism's "First Wave" in the first half of the twentieth century (Webb 2006: 87).

Inayat Khan called his message "the Sufi Message"; it was a universal message that built upon traditional Sufism but included what his son and successor Pir Vilayat Inayat Khan often called "a new dispensation", a new vision for humanity. Pir Vilayat quoted his father: "Why should the Message have been fostered by Sufism rather than any other group? Because it has traditionally been the cross-roads of esoteric orders, and we are living in the age of unity, of convergence of ideals and ideas". Inayat Khan stated: "the Message far exceeds the bounds of traditional Sufism" (Inayat Khan 1978: 425).

Inayat Khan was born into a family of talented and accomplished Indian musicians in 1882. He grew up in an environment of openness to new ideas and different religious beliefs. His later efforts to harmonize East and West through the teaching of Sufism were foreshadowed by the Maharaja of Baroda, Sayaji Rao Gaekwad III (d. 1939), who stated that India must "teach philosophy to the West and learn its science, to impart purity of life to Europe and attain to her loftier political ideal, to inculcate spirituality to the American mind and acquire the business ways of her merchants" (Witteveen 2013: 19).

Studying under his grandfather, Inayat Khan himself became a renowned court musician while still a teenager, winning the appreciation of a local Muslim king, the Nizam of Hyderabad. As we will see in Chapter 4, although music has been at times prohibited by Muslim scholars, many Sufis have long understood music to have profound spiritual value. Inayat Khan soon left court life to embark on a spiritual search, being increasingly drawn to meditation. In what follows, he describes the ways in which his musical studies informed his spirituality and philosophy:

> I had composed songs; I sang and played the vina; and practicing this music I arrived at a stage where I touched the Music of the Spheres. Then every soul became for me a musical note, and all life became music. Inspired by it I spoke to the people, and those who were attracted by my words listened to them, instead of listening to my songs. Now, if I do anything, it is to tune souls instead of instruments; to harmonize people instead of notes. If there is anything in my philosophy, it is the law of harmony: that one must put oneself in harmony with oneself and with others. I have found in every word a certain musical value, a melody in every thought, harmony in every feeling; and I have tried to interpret the same thing, with clear and simple words, to those who used to listen to my music. I played the vina until my heart turned into this very instrument; then I offered this instrument to the divine Musician, the only musician existing. Since then I have become His flute; and when He chooses, He plays His music. The people give me credit for this music, which in reality is not due to me but to the Musician who plays on His own instrument (wahiddudin.net).

Inayat Khan's Sufi training took place within the Chishti order, a Sufi order brought to Ajmer, India, by Khwaja Mu'in al-Din Chishti (d. 1236) and known for its embrace of South Asian Hindu culture, and its openness to non-Muslims. Chishti teachers accepted disciples regardless of their religious background, and Chishti practices incorporated visible elements of Hindu practice.

Figure 1.6: Hazrat Inayat Khan pictured with the vina, the instrument that he would describe his heart becoming one with.

Inayat Khan's pioneering mission was to teach Sufism in a culture almost completely unfamiliar with it. With this new context in mind, he presented Sufism as a practice little connected with outward aspects of Islam. He found that Europeans and Americans were not really interested in adopting Islam, a religion which they tended to perceive rather negatively. Many Westerners however had been exposed to Theosophical ideas, and had come to believe that what the world needed was a new mystical approach that transcended religious and cultural borders. Islamic practices such as the traditional five-times daily prayer, or adherence to Islamic law, were not taught by Inayat Khan to his students, and they were not expected to convert to Islam. He did, however, give his students traditional Sufi spiritual practices (such as *dhikr*) as well as several prayers in the English language that he developed; he suggested that a specific prayer (*Saum*) be said in the morning, another (*Salat)* at noon, and another (*Khatum*) at night as a way of attuning to God. He believed mysticism, with the goal of the realization of God, was the essence of all religion, philosophy, and science. To express this universality in practice, Inayat Khan developed the Universal Worship service, in which a candle was lit for each of the world's religions and a brief passage of each religion's scripture was recited. Inayat Khan attracted middle and upper class Europeans and Americans seeking a non-dogmatic spirituality that fit with modern life, transcending religious divisions and cultural provincialism.

Inayat Khan put forth a vision of universal human spiritual development, the oneness of all religions, and universal brotherhood. This vision is embodied in the three "objects" of his Sufi Order:

1. To realize and spread the knowledge of unity, the religion of love and wisdom, so that the variety of faiths and beliefs may of themselves cease to exist, the human heart may overflow with love and all hatred caused by distinctions and differences may be rooted out.
2. To discover the light and power latent in man, the secret of all religion, the power of mysticism and the essence of philosophy, without interfering with customs or belief.
3. To help bring the world's two opposite poles, East and West, close together by the interchange of thoughts and ideas, that the universal brotherhood may form of itself, and man may meet man beyond the narrow national and racial boundaries (Graham 2001: 141–42).

Inayat Khan focused on those elements of Sufism that transcended the particularity of a given religion or cultural context. His focus fit well with the religious universalism prominent in the West at the time, much of which was framed by Theosophical teachings and Transcendentalism, among other strains of nineteenth century spirituality. Inayat Khan presented his teaching in increasingly universal terms, speaking of "the Sufi Message", and finally just "the Message". Many of Inayat Khan's senior students were also involved in Theosophical circles, and, in accord with Theosophical teachings, were awaiting the arrival of a "World-Teacher", one who would unite humanity and foster "a New Age" of enlightenment and spirituality (Inayat Khan 2006: 264). Towards the end of his life many within the Sufi Order began to see Inayat Khan as not simply a Sufi master but as a world-teacher and prophetic figure, one sent with the message urgently needed to bring humanity together. Inayat Khan never publicly claimed this status, though he did privately confirm some of their impressions that he was a teacher of world import bearing the "Message of the time" (Inayat Khan 2006: 147).

Figure 1.7: Unveiling of the statue of Noor Inayat Khan in London, England.[3]

Noor Inayat Khan

In 1949 Noor Inayat Khan was posthumously awarded the George Cross for her display of courage and bravery during World War II. Though it may seem extraordinary that the daughter of Hazrat Inayat Khan, an adamant proponent of nonviolence and the ideals of universal brotherhood would win a medal for her work with the Allies, her participation in the War was directly correlated to the ethics and ideals passed down by her well-known Sufi father.

Born 2nd January 1914 in Moscow, Noor Inayat Khan and her family settled in Paris in the spring of 1920. Noor's father travelled extensively during her youth and died in Delhi when Noor was only 13, leaving Noor to care for her grieving mother and three younger siblings in France. Though Hazrat Inayat Khan passed early in Noor's life, his Sufi ideas regarding the collective human spirit and the oneness of all religions remained a consistent source of encouragement and guidance for her and her siblings.

Prior to the war, Noor attended the École Normale de Musique de Paris. She had inherited much of her father's talent and excelled in many musical endeavours, often playing for her father's followers at their home and composing her own works (Basu 2008: 732). Noor also took a profound interest in Child Psychology, pursuing related studies in 1932 at the Sorbonne University in Paris. Around this time Noor also started

---

3.   On November 8th, 2012, a commemorative statue of Noor Inayat Khan, daughter of Inayat Khan, was unveiled by Princess Anne, the Princess Royal and daughter of Queen Elizabeth II, in Gordon Square in London. It stands near the house in which Noor and her family lived.

writing Sufi children's stories for the *Sunday Figaro*, a French newspaper published in Paris. As Shrabani Basu, author of *Spy Princess: The Life of Noor Inayat Khan* articulates, "Her stories – usually about magical creatures and nature – were greatly appreciated by the paper. Noor had an endearing style that immediately drew in young readers" (Basu 2008: 850–62).

In spite of Noor's increasing success in her studies and career, the burgeoning threat of the Nazis in France had become impossible to overlook. Of course, the ideology of Nazism was entirely antithetical to the Sufi principles Noor had been raised under and continued to practice. Although she understood Nazism as a practice that required swift intervention, joining the war effort held its own complications. As Basu conveys, as Sufis, both Noor and her siblings had been raised to believe in the superiority of non-violence. Unfortunately, seeing the severity of Nazism at their doorstep, they questioned their personal culpability in the disorder if they continued on the path of non-violent action and allowed the Nazis to carry on without meaningful resistance. Viliyat, Noor's brother asked her, "If an armed Nazi comes to your house and takes twenty hostages and wants to exterminate them, would you not be a accomplice in these deaths, if you had the opportunity to kill him … but did not do so because of your belief in non-violence?" (Basu 2008, loc. 927). After sincere and earnest questioning, Noor and her brother decided that the only way to effectively halt the actions of the Nazis was by joining the war effort.

In 1940 both Noor and her brother moved their family to London, in November of that year Noor joined the Women's Auxiliary Air Force (WAAF). Noor, who was registered as Nora, was trained in wireless operations along with 40 other women, "becoming the first batch of WAAFs to be trained as radio operators" (Basu 2008: 1054). After training diligently with WAAF and taking on different posts through the years, on 21st October 1942 the Special Operations Executive (SOE) wrote to Noor suggesting she be called for an interview due to her proficiency in both English and French (Basu 2008: 1216). The interview was designed to find individuals best suited to become part of Churchill's special force of secret agents against Fascism. While most interviewees had three interviews, Noor was accepted after only one (Basu 2008: 1367).

After significant training for SOE, including the use of powerful weapons, in 1943 with the codename Madeleine, Noor became the first female radio operator sent to work in Nazi-occupied France. It was only ten days after her arrival in Paris that her first act of bravery was required. The Gestapo had developed methods to locate allied radio operators including listening machines and the utilization of random searches. The random searches were particularly problematic as radio operators were required to wear their radios on them at all times (Atwood 2011: 172). Due to these measures, ten days after Noor arrived the Gestapo had located and exposed the names and addresses of various French Resistance members and began rounding them up for arrest (Atwood 2011: 173). Although the SOE had developed plans to rescue Noor from immanent danger, she refused to leave occupied France, knowing that this would cease all outgoing information to London and negatively effect the program. Noor's personal decision to stay in France resulted in celebrated achievements for Britain.

Between July and October 1943, Noor sent and received messages that helped 30 allied airmen escape, arranged for four agents to obtain false identity papers, pinpointed exact positions for airplane drops, helped obtain weapons and money for members of the French resistance, and communicated the exact spot where the Nazis were hiding a supply of torpedoes (Atwood 2011: 173).

In spite of her long list of brave accomplishments and rapid and skilful transmitting skills, Noor was ultimately captured. Even under intense interrogation while captured, Noor refused to offer any information to the Gestapo. As a result, she was transferred from the headquarters in France, to Pforzheim, a high security prison in Germany. Here, Noor was kept in atrocious conditions and tortured. For ten months in isolation, Noor was given limited food, her hands and feet were chained and she was unable to feed or clean herself (Basu 2011: loc. 3530). In spite of the dreadful circumstances Noor maintained her unwavering loyalty to Britain and her fellow dispatchers. According to two Gestapo agents Goetz and Kieffer, her capture was effectively futile. Both Goetz and Kieffer wrote in sworn statements that, "no arrests were made as a result of Noor's capture and she revealed nothing" (Basu 2008: 3388).

On 11th September 1944 Noor was transferred to Dachau concentration camp, it was here on 12th September that she and two other British agents were shot and burned for their work (Atwood 2011: 175). Noor's last word, kneeling in front of the firing squad was, "liberté".

Seventy years later, visitors can find a plaque at Dachau that commemorates the sacrifice of Noor and those who were executed with her. Basu also articulates that commemorations for Noor can be found in the Remembrance Hall located in the Museum in Dachau, St. Paul's Church in Knightsbridge, the Memorial Gates to the Commonwealth in London, the agricultural school in Gringnon where she began transmitting, and at her childhood home in Suresnes (Basu 2008: 4117). On 8th November 2012 a commemorative statue was also placed in Gordon Square in London. It stands near the house in which Noor and her family lived and was unveiled by Anne, The Princess Royal. Princess Anne stated that she hoped the statue would force people to ask, "Who was she? Why is she here? And what can we achieve in her memory?" (Wilkes 2012). Her cousin, who also attended the event stated, "I remember her as a very refined girl who believed in freedom as a spiritual condition. Later I think she decided freedom had to be a political and social experience too" (Wilkes 2012). A movie by Paramount Films about the life of Noor entitled, *Enemy of the Reich: The Noor Inayat Khan Story*, was released in February 2014.

Inayat Khan's universal Sufi Order originally consisted of three primary activities: the Esoteric School, Universal Worship, and Universal Brotherhood. The Esoteric School was established as the program of spiritual training at the heart of the Sufi Movement, in which the aspirant (*mureed*) enters into a direct relationship with the spiritual guide (*murshid*). The Esoteric School was established as the spiritual core of the Sufi Movement, while the Universal Worship was developed as the movement's religious framework.

It began in 1921 as the Church of the All, inspired by the League of Nations and the model of pluralism and universal cooperation it represented. The Church was an expression of Inayat Khan's sense of the pressing need for people to move beyond ethnic and religious differences and come together in a spirit of global unity and peace (Dickson 2015: 77–78).

The current head of The Universal Worship, Shahabuddin David Less, in addition to working with members to develop advanced training programs for *cherags* (persons who lead the Universal Worship services), is working internationally to build peace initiatives. A notable example is the Abrahamic Reunion group, which has for several years brought together members of four religions in the Israel/Palestine area: Islam, Judaism, Christianity, and the Druze religion. In the face of serious opposition and threats, these men and women meet regularly and hold monthly communal dinners where they eat, sing, and pray together. Their goal is to build mutual understanding and trust and to model the reality that this is possible in the current challenging political climate. Members of the group made presentations at the 2015 Parliament of World Religions in Salt Lake City and subsequently toured North America to speak about their work and encourage support of such efforts. One associate, Ghassan Manasra of Nazareth, is currently facilitating interfaith study groups through Shahabuddin David Less' centre, Rising Tide International, in Sarasota, Florida.

This same desire was behind the development of Kinship, first known as Universal Brotherhood, the third of the beginning three elements of the Sufi Movement. The purpose of Universal Brotherhood was to foster a sense of global unity, overcoming the opposition of East and West, and transcending divisions based on culture, ethnicity, or religion. Whereas the Esoteric School was a continuation of the Sufi lineage Inayat Khan inherited, the Universal Worship and Brotherhood were developed by Inayat Khan for his Western students, both of which were based on the hope of furthering humanity's "spiritual evolution" towards a new age of human oneness and spiritual harmony (Dickson 2015: 78).

The Use of Wasifas, Dhikr and Other Practices in the Spiritual Development Process

Inayat Khan and his successor, Vilayat Khan, carefully mentored their *mureeds* (students) in their spiritual development process. For Vilayat Khan, this involved in-depth personal interviews (often called *darshan*, a Hindu term describing a mystical seeing or experience of the divine) at least once each year, and students generally attended a minimum of one intensive retreat each year, either group retreats or individually guided retreats. Experienced senior teachers in the Order were (and continue to be) available to guide many students as well. The central transformative practices for *mureeds* are individually assigned *wasifas* (similar to the concept of mantras) and various forms of the *dhikr*. In addition, students are expected to practice concentration, contemplation, and meditation daily, as appropriate for their levels of advancement.

The *wasifas,* selected for each individual *mureed* by the teacher from the Beautiful 99 Names of God, are seen as sacred qualities of God, which also exist latent in the individual. By repeating one's *wasifa* prayerfully the suggested number of times each day, the student begins to realize the existence of the divine quality in his or her own being. As the quality comes alive within, the student gradually experiences increased self-effacement in the divine (*fana'*). Paradoxically, the student also experiences enhanced efficacy in his or her life in the world, as the quality transforms one's capacity to live a meaningful life. Often the repetition of the *wasifa* aloud is followed by the practice of the *wasifa* on the breath (*fikr),* and then the silent absorption in the quality (*fikr-as-sirr).* The *wasifa* as assigned to the student by the teacher conveys *baraka,* the grace and power transferred through the *silsila* (chain of teachers) from teacher to student. *Wasifas* selected from a book by a student are not considered to contain such *baraka. Mureeds* who live near a Sufi centre also may participate in the group practice of *wasifas* and *dhikr,* commonly at weekly meetings. Such centres usually also offer regular Universal Worship services, Healing Order services, and often the Dances of Universal Peace. In addition, most centres also offer sessions where Sufi writings are read and contemplated.

"Second" and "Third Wave" Sufism: Literature, Dance, and Sacred Space

Although Inayat Khan's universal Sufi message resonated with cultural elites in Europe and North America, Sufism would not gain a more popular profile until the 1960s. The 1960s are frequently eulogized as an era of social and cultural change, dynamism, and conflict. Indeed, the post-war cultural consensus of mainstream North American society gave way in that decade as young people questioned the legitimacy of their society's political institutions, social norms, and religious values. The civil rights, feminist, and anti-war movements galvanized a generation of young people and irreversibly changed the cultural landscape. North Americans were thirsting for religious alternatives. Many turned to the mystical traditions of India and East Asia.

One of the traditions that drew increasing interest at this time, alongside Zen and yoga, was Sufism. In the 1960s, an enigmatic Afghani-British author named Idries Shah became a bestselling author, introducing Sufism to a wider readership on both sides of the Atlantic, with books like *The Sufis* (1964) and *The Way of the Sufi* (1968). Shah was born in India in 1924 to Afghani businessman and noble Iqbal Ali Shah (d. 1969) and his Scottish wife, Elizabeth Louise Mackenzie (d. 1960) (Dickson 2015: 89). Growing up in England, in 1963 he emerged as a representative of Sufism, or what Shah simply referred to as "the Tradition". Like Inayat Khan, Shah taught a Sufism not necessarily connected to Islam. In response to the question, "is Sufism the interior meaning of Islam?", Shah wrote that, "Sufism is the knowledge whereby man can realize himself and attain permanency. Sufis can teach in any vehicle, whatever its names. Religious vehicles have throughout history taken various names" (Shah 1968: 312). Shah is also largely responsible for introducing Western audiences to the tales and jokes of Mulla Nasruddin, a hapless figure found in folk tales across much of the Muslim world, tales sometimes used by Sufis as teaching devices. Perhaps the most well-known representative of the phenomenon of the "holy fool" in Islam, the Mulla Nasruddin stories were beloved by Muslims from a variety of ethnicities and cultures (as we will discuss further in Chapter 3).

Shah claimed to represent of a secret branch of the Naqshbandi Order, and some of his followers described him as "Grand Sheikh of the Sufis" (Shah 1964: xx). However, he did not establish an order himself. He published books on Sufism, taught a small number of students, and organized some of his teaching activities through the Institute of Cultural Research, founded in 1965. He was critical of the major orders as institutions that had outlived their spiritual vitality. For Shah, most major Sufi orders had become stagnant, dogmatic systems out of sync with the times. According to him, the form Sufi teaching took has always been dictated by the peculiar needs of time and place, and it is constantly adapting its form as the world changes. Outdated forms can act as obstacles to understanding, rather than vehicles of it, being tailored for different people in a different time (Dickson 2015: 90).

On the ground, Sufism became associated with a growing trend amongst the hippies in the 1960s: the "Sufi Dancing" (the Dances of Universal Peace) of Samuel Lewis, or "Sufi Sam", as he was known to the youth of the San Francisco Bay Area. Lewis became a student of Hazrat Inayat Khan's in 1923 in San Francisco. Following Inayat Khan's death in 1927, Lewis became the chief assistant to Murshida Rabia Martin (d. 1947), who had been appointed previously as a representative of the Sufi Movement in Fairfax, California. During the 1960s he travelled widely on pilgrimage to Egypt, Pakistan, and India, where he connected with numerous Sufis and continued to pursue his mission of promoting world peace through discussions on horticulture practices. He was recognized as a *murshid* (spiritual teacher) and given a robe by Pir Barkat Ali in Pakistan in 1962 (Lewis 2013).

In 1967, while recovering in hospital from food poisoning, Lewis reported hearing the voice of God say to him, "I make you Spiritual Teacher of the hippies" (Meyer 2001: 425). He began holding classes in his home in the Mission district of San Francisco, attended by throngs of young people curious about spirituality, often following psychedelic experiences. Lewis's classes included readings from different religious scriptures, Zen stories, and Hindu mantras. As Sufi Sam Lewis's dances resonated with the spirit of the times. The Sufi Dances were often accompanied by Lewis's Sufi Choir, which became a frequent presence in San Francisco's cultural scene, performing with *The Grateful Dead* and at Governor Jerry Brown's prayer breakfast. The dances were mostly "folk circle dances" combined with chanting, usually "Allah, Allah", or "Om Sri Ram Jai Ram Jai Jai Ram". The dances frequently came to Lewis in dreams and invoked the names of God and sacred phrases from many spiritual traditions. In 1970, Lewis founded the Sufi Islamia Ruhaniat Society, but he died shortly after in 1971 (Dickson 2015: 93).

With Sufism's "third wave" we find the establishment of more traditional, Islamically-oriented Sufi orders in North America, such as the Mevlevi, Jerrahi, Shadhili, and Naqshbandi Sufi orders. Unlike more publicly prominent Hindu and Buddhist teachers, whose popular books, public profiles, and numerous meditation centres made these forms of "Eastern spirituality" well-known to North Americans, Sufi teachers arriving during this period tended to be less noticed by the cultural mainstream. Sufi teachers like Bawa Muhaiyaddeen, Sulaiyman Loras, Muzaffer Ozak and Frithjof Schuon all arrived during this period. Most of these Sufi teachers continued to emphasize the universality of Sufism. They remained grounded, however, in some form of Islamic practice and tended to take a more traditional approach to the Sufi path.

If Lewis's death in 1971 can be thought of as marking the end of Sufism's second wave, its third wave can be considered to begin in October of that year, with Bawa Muhaiyadeen's arrival in Philadelphia from Sri Lanka. Bawa first came to America at the request of two Americans who had been in correspondence with him. He was sought both as a spiritual teacher, and as someone who might contribute to easing racial tensions in Philadelphia. In one of west Philadelphia's row houses, Bawa began teaching a small circle of South Asian immigrants, African-Americans, and hippie American seekers. In these early years, Bawa was referred to as a guru rather than a Muslim or Sufi. The small circle of seekers who gathered around him referred to themselves as the "Guru Bawa Muhaiyaddeen Fellowship" (Dickson 2015: 94–95).

During his early years in America, Bawa gave discourses two or three times daily at the Philadelphia house, and many Fellowship members – including young seekers emerging from the counterculture – decided to move to Philadelphia to be with their spiritual teacher, where "the early members lived in the house itself, sleeping on the floor in sleeping bags until they were able to move out on their own" (Snyder 2003: 31). Although many of the young seekers who visited Bawa were actively looking for mystical rituals and symbols of identity and belonging, Bawa downplayed these as unnecessary. In the *Guidebook* (1976), Bawa instead asked his students not to alter any aspect of their personal lives for God, not to grow long hair or a beard for God, or wear a robe or gown, as "such symbols are unnecessary for Him" (Snyder 2003: 48).

Bawa taught his students to constantly remember God and to live God's qualities in their lives, and yet they did not associate Bawa and his teachings with Islam. Seekers were drawn to him as a wise teacher and spiritual guru who accepted all without distinction. However, over time, Bawa taught his students elements of Islamic practice. In 1976, Bawa introduced a morning *dhikr* practice that consisted of ablutions, the recitation of short chapters form the Qur'ān and the first part of the Islamic statement of faith, *La ilaha illa Allah* (There is no god but God), and then exchanging Islamic greetings of peace following the practice (Dickson 2015: 96). In the early 1980s, as some of his students began to practice the Islamic daily prayer, *salat*, Bawa said they could teach the practice to others who were interested in it. Eventually he would appoint an *imam* to lead the community in prayer five times daily. He ensured that the prayer was performed according to the guidelines of Islamic law, so that Muslims from outside the Fellowship would be comfortable praying at the mosque (Dickson 2015: 96).

Bawa gradually introduced elements of Islamic ritual life into his teaching, but like many other Sufi teachers in North America, he did not have a narrow or exclusivistic understanding of Islam. He continued to affirm the validity of other traditions and emphasized the universality of God's love for all humanity, regardless of religion, race, or station in life. Bawa taught Islam as "a state of unity and trust in God, an inculcation of the qualities of God, a disregarding of 'distinctions' of race, case, and religion" (Webb 2006: 93). In 1982, Bawa began discussing building a mosque in Philadelphia. Like the mosque he built in Jaffna, Sri Lanka, the Philadelphia mosque was, according to Bawa's specification, to be a house of God open to people of all faiths, though Muslim prayer times were to be respected. The mosque was completed in 1984. Despite its inclusive orientation, building the mosque posed the question of the Fellowship's identity more poignantly than the previous introductions of Islamic practice. Some of Bawa's students left during the mid-1980s with the construction of the mosque, but the majority stayed on, and a variety of perspectives on Bawa's teachings and Islam began to form within the Fellowship, some more grounded in Islamic ritual and law, and others with a more formless understanding (Dickson 2015: 97).

Following Bawa's death in 1986, his followers built a tomb-shrine or *mazar* for him on the group's farm in Chester County. The shrine outside of Philadelphia would become North America's first major Sufi shrine. Although initially built as a memorial space for Fellowship members, by the early 2000s, it had become a site of pilgrimage for South Asian Muslims in particular, who were able to replicate shrine festivals and rituals common to South Asian forms of Islam, otherwise unavailable in North America. Fellowship members are largely embracing their emerging role as shrine-keepers for a pilgrimage site of growing importance to Muslims in North America.

Figure 1.8: The *Mazar* of Bawa Muhaiyaddeen.[4]

Over time, the Bawa Muhaiyaddeen Fellowship came to include a variety of different approaches to Sufism, some connected with Islamic identity and ritual and others less so. This interpretive diversity within the Fellowship exemplifies a broader trend in North American Sufism as it develops into the twenty-first century. We see some Sufi seekers relate to the tradition as a universal message of harmony and transformation, one possibly but not necessarily connected to a particular religious identity and practice. We find others, born or becoming Muslim, understanding the rituals of Islam as an ancient set of spiritual technologies that open doorways to a deeper knowledge of reality. For them, Sufism and Islam are two terms for a singular reality grounded in Islamic scriptures and the example of the Prophet Muhammad. These two trends of course represent two points on a wider spectrum, where individuals in these various groups constantly negotiate their relationship to religious form and spiritual essence. This diversity of approach among practitioners will shape the directions Sufism takes in the next century.

4.   This photo is by Michael Green, a student of Bawa Muhaiyaddeen, and a musician, artist, and author. He has collaborated with Coleman Barks to produce illustrated books on Rumi's poetry, and produces a variety of visual art integrating spiritual themes. His work is featured at http://michaelgreenarts.com

As we will discover in the following chapter however, questions over Sufism's nature and its relation to Islamic identity and practice do not emerge from a vacuum. Sufism's comfortable place in Islam was seriously challenged in the eighteenth and nineteenth centuries, during a tumultuous era marked by the growing European political, economic, military, and cultural domination of the Muslim world. The colonial period was one in which Muslims were forced to confront the limitations of medieval formulations of Islam, in the face of Europe's prominence on the world stage, and conquest of their own societies. In many cases, Muslim reformers associated Sufis with medieval superstition, introversion, and corruption, allowing for a cultural decadence in Islamic societies that facilitated their failure to keep abreast of modern developments. Sufis responded to European domination and Muslim opposition in a rich variety of ways, ranging from military resistance in the face of modern military force, to establishing their own Islamic revival and reform movements.

Discussion Questions:

1. After reading this chapter, how might you define Sufism?
2. What is contemporary Sufism's relationship to Islam?
3. How does Sufism play a role in contemporary political debates about Islam?
4. Why has Rumi's poetic form of Sufism inspired such a variety of artists and cultural creatives?
5. What does the history of Sufism in North America tell us about the dynamics of adapting a religious tradition in a new context?

Further Reading:

Dickson, W. R. (2015). *Living Sufism in North America: Between Tradition and Transformation.* Albany, NY: State University of New York.

Hahn, L. E., Auxier, R. E., and Stone, L. W., Jr. (eds.) (2001). *The Philosophy of Seyyed Hossein Nasr.* Peru, IL: Open Court.

Hermansen, M. (1996). "In the Garden of American Sufi Movements: Hybrids and Perennials". In: *New Trends and Developments in the World of Islam*, ed. Peter B. Clarke, 155–78. London: Luzac.

Inayat Khan, H. (1999). *The Heart of Sufism: Essential Writings of Hazrat Inayat Khan.* Boston, MA: Shambhala.

Malik, J., and Hinnells, J. (eds.) (2006). *Sufism in the West.* New York: Routledge.

Vaughan-Lee, L. (1998). *Catching the Thread: Sufism, Dreamwork, and Jungian Psychology.* Inverness, CA: The Golden Sufi Centre.

Wuthnow, R. (1998). *After Heaven: Spirituality in America Since the 1950s.* Berkeley, CA: University of California Press.

2

WARRIORS, PHILOSOPHERS, AND POETS: SUFIS IN THE AGE OF COLONIZATION

In the heart of North America we find the town of Elkader, in north-eastern Iowa. Surrounded by cornfields and dairy farms, far from places like Manhattan, the multicultural metropoles of the coasts, Elkader is the only town in America named after a Sufi saint – namely, 'Abd al-Qadir al-Jaza'iri (d. 1883). During the height of 'Abd al-Qadir's fame, in the midst of the colonial era, 'Abd al-Qadir (or el-Kader) "struck many different chords with Americans, Europeans and Arabs: freedom fighter, chivalrous enemy, holy man, scholar and philosopher-statesman" (Kiser 2008: ix). Thousands of Americans read about 'Abd al-Qadir's heroic exploits in popular magazines like *Litell's Living Age*. Like many Americans, the founders of Elkader were deeply moved by tales of the Algerian *shaykh's* courage, nobility, martial skill, and kindness. His resistance to French colonial domination resonated with the American cultural memory of fighting off the British, while his unfailing protection of Christians under threat and humanitarian care for French prisoners of war made him a beloved symbol of chivalry across the world. 'Abd al-Qadir was a hero not only to Algerians, Arabs, and Muslims, but a hero to Americans, British, and even the French, whom he fought for decades. The following excerpt from a statement from Elkader High school's Class of 1915 illustrates the depth of American admiration for this Arab mystic and resistance fighter:

> Such is the history of the man for whom our town is named. A scholar, a philosopher, a lover of liberty; a champion of his religion, a born leader of men, a great solider, a capable administrator, a pervasive orator, a chivalrous opponent; the selection was well made, and with those pioneers of seventy years ago, we do honour the Sheik (Kiser 2008: xiii).

'Abd al-Qadir's tumultuous life and resistance to the colonization of his country neatly encapsulates the dynamics of an era of crisis and contestation for Muslims and Sufis, where the integrity of Islamic civilization itself was challenged in ways unprecedented in the history of Islam. This era is usually thought to begin in the eighteenth century, transitioning to the post-colonial period in the middle of the twentieth century. In many respects, the later twentieth and early twenty-first centuries continue along trajectories formed during the colonial period.

In this chapter, we first look at how Sufis resisted European invasions, before they faced defeat and eventual cooption into colonial regimes. This opened up Sufis to critique from newly emerging Muslim reformist movements, the leaders of which believed that Muslims needed to abandon Sufism to revive their societies in the face of European domination. This pattern of Sufi resistance, defeat, cooption, and critique, is illustrated first by 'Abd al-Qadir, who organized some of the most effective resistance to French rule in Algeria, before eventually accepting surrender and exile as inevitable. The consequent emergence of Muslim reformist movements and their critique of Sufism is then illustrated by Ahmad al-'Alawi (d. 1934), a famous Algerian Sufi master who felt compelled to respond to the increasingly prominent attacks on Sufism penned by anti-Sufi reformist intellectuals, utilizing the emergent print culture of the Middle East.

'Abd al-Qadir and al-'Alawi are helpful to consider in the second section of this chapter as well, as they not only engaged in the political debates of their day, but wrote on and attempted to live Sufi metaphysics. For 'Abd al-Qadir, his engagement with Sufi thought fostered a worldview that allowed him to see holiness in other religions like Christianity, and in the representatives of that faith. His renowned chivalry and respect for non-Muslims was directly linked to the classical Sufi philosophy of unity and pluralism he studied, taught, and wrote about. For al-'Alawi, his response to anti-Sufi critiques was grounded in a mystical understanding of the sacred sources of Islam as the oceanic well springs of Sufi thought and practice. Al-'Alawi would further play a role in shaping a Western philosophical and mystical school of thought known as Traditionalism.

Interestingly, just as many Muslims were turning against Sufism, Westerners were beginning to discover its literary riches, a discovery that we explore in the chapter's third section. From Goethe to Emerson, Western literary figures became entranced with classical Sufism's effervescent poetic tradition. This discovery of literary Sufism was facilitated by the access to Middle Eastern and South Asian texts that colonial domination offered. Colonial officials and scholars soon separated Sufism from Islam, seeing in its sophisticated poetry and philosophy something that in their minds had to originate with Greeks, Persians, or Indians, rather than Arabs. The final section of this chapter provides an historical overview of this complex era of revival and reform, which saw movements – both Sufi and anti-Sufi – emerge across Muslim societies, from North Africa to Central, South and Southeast Asia.

SUFISM AND THE POLITICS OF COLONIAL RESISTANCE

Too often in the West we suffer from an historical amnesia (wilful or otherwise) when it comes to the colonial period. Only really coming to a close after the Second World War (and arguably continuing to the present day in other forms, sometimes referred to as "neo-colonialism"), the era of colonization saw Western European states achieve an unprecedented dominance of the globe. The material power and technological advances unlocked by the Industrial Revolution and modern capitalism gave Western European states like Britain and France an exponential advantage over non-Western states. Not only did the British, French, and other European powers gain control of African, Middle Eastern, Asian, and South Asian countries during this period, but they attempted in many cases to remake these non-Western societies in their own image, instituting Western modes of government, law, economic production, and education.

Beginning in the late seventeenth century, the three largest Muslim states – the Ottoman, Safavid, and Mughal Empires – found themselves increasingly cornered by Europe's growing influence. Although these empires, to varying degrees, attempted administrative reform along European lines, they could not sustain themselves in light of Europe's rapid technological, military, and economic advance. European colonial powers like Britain, Holland, Russia, and France made extensive political and economic inroads into much of the Muslim world in the eighteenth century. By the mid-1700s, the British East India Company became the *de facto* ruler of Bengal. More shockingly for Muslims, Napoleon Bonaparte (d. 1821) successfully invaded Egypt in 1798, bringing European rule to the heart of Islamic civilization. As the economies of Muslim empires became increasingly tied to Europe's rapidly expanding system of capital, Western influences began to penetrate Muslim societies in the form of manufactured goods, military technology, and mass media. Muslim lands were drawn into the orbit of European rule, and new forms of administration, education, and cultural values took hold. Such influences began to largely restructure Muslim societies from the top down, as more and more Muslim states fell under the direct rule of European colonial powers.

Sufism's Warrior-Philosopher: Amir 'Abd al-Qadir

'Abd al-Qadir was born in 1807 in western Algeria. He came from a noble family that traced its descent to the Prophet Muhammad (Kiser 2008: 10). The family had become associated with the Qadiri Sufi order in recent generations. He was named after the order's founder, 'Abd al-Qadir al-Jilani (d. 1166) – both the founder and the order will be discussed at length in Chapter 4. The village where 'Abd al-Qadir was born, al-Qaytana, was established by his grandfather Mustafa, who built a Qadiri lodge on the site in 1791, including a mosque, school, hostel for travellers and refuge for the poor (Abun-Nasr 1987: 203). Mustafa's success in promoting the Qadiri order in the region is evidenced by the fact that, by the time of his death, even the Ottoman governor of Western Algeria had become a follower of his (Abun-Nasr 1987: 203).

Figure 2.1: Amir 'Abd al-Qadir in traditional Algerian clothing with French medals.

'Abd al-Qadir was given a thorough education, first in the basics of Islam and the Qur'ān by his mother, Lalla Zahra, a woman renowned for her piety and wisdom, and someone whom he would keep by his side all of her life. Later, under the tutelage of a local judge, he studied classic works of Islamic law, philosophy, pharmacology, and veterinary medicine. Besides his scholastic education, coming from a family of Sufis, he was raised with a keen sense of *adab*, the importance of good manners, respectful behaviour, and maintaining the *Sunnah* of the Prophet Muhammad in all of one's actions. As he came of age, 'Abd al-Qadir would receive *ijazas* or permissions to teach Sufi spirituality from eminent Qadiri leaders in Baghdad.

'Abd al-Qadir's young life, drawn out between religious study and developing his horsemanship, certainly had something of the idyllic in its simplicity. However, the clouds of war gathered as a post-Napoleonic French Empire set its sights on Algeria. Having lost colonies in America, some in the French administration saw North Africa as a site where the French could recover imperial glory, material resources, and regional influence. The French started the invasion of Algeria in May 1830 and within two months had occupied Algiers and other vital coastal areas (Abun-Nasr 1987: 204).

The invasion continued, and with the unmatched force of modern military technology, the French took over eastern Algeria and destroyed Ottoman rule in the west, creating an anarchic situation in the region.

Those in western Algeria were left without effective governance, and as a result, in 1832 the chiefs of the seven main tribes of the region asked 'Abd al-Qadir's father, Muhyi al-Din (also a *shaykh* of the Qadiri order), to be their sultan and help them fight the French invasion. Being too old, he suggested his son, 'Abd al-Qadir (now only age 24), to lead them in his place. Already with an established reputation for piety and courage under fire, 'Abd al-Qadir proved to be a popular choice.

In a large, moving inauguration ceremony, 10,000 horsemen of the seven tribes formed a crescent around a single black tent near an ash tree on the Plain of Ghriss. As the sun rose, 'Abd al-Qadir rode to the tent, greeted by drums, flutes, and rifle fire into the air. His father presented 'Abd al-Qadir to the tribes, with his first words as sultan expressing his intent to rule by Islam and to fight the French: "I will recognize no other law than the Qur'ān. There is no liberty except through defending the faith. Paradise is found in the shadow of the sword" (Kiser 2008: 50). Once he was installed as sultan in Mascara, Jewish and Christian leaders also came to pay their respects to 'Abd al-Qadir. He lived up to his first words, banning gambling, drinking, smoking, and prostitution in lands he ruled, and engaging in an effective campaign of *jihad*, or religiously-sanctioned warfare, against the French.

"Over the next fifteen years ['Abd al-Qadir] united the people of Algeria in sustained resistance movement against the French occupation… It is no exaggeration to say he was a legend in his own lifetime – in the West and the Arab world alike" (Rogan 2011: 115). His charisma, integrity, and renowned leadership increasingly drew the admiration of his enemies. Even the famous French literary figure Victor Hugo (d. 1885) praised 'Abd al Qadir, referring to him as, "le beau soldat, le beau pretre" or "the handsome soldier, the handsome priest" (Rogan 2011: 116). His most stalwart opponents in the French military respected him as a brilliant military strategist and remarkably effective administrator, calling him a "genius". To his followers however, 'Abd al-Qadir was known as the "Commander of the Faithful" or *Amir al-Mumineen*. He was often referred to simply as the Amir.

Until his capture in 1847, 'Abd al-Qadir alternated between periods of fighting the French and maintaining alliances with them. Soundly defeating French forces in an ambush at the Machta River in 1835, the Amir earned a reputation as an effective tactician. For some Algerians however, he was too eager to wage *jihad* against the non-Muslim French. And yet for others he was seen as far too willing to compromise and share rule with them. When he was dealing with French leaders who were willing to foster alliances, 'Abd al-Qadir proved amenable to forming and abiding by peace treaties. In 1841 however, General Bugeaud (d. 1849), who had previously signed a peace treaty with 'Abd al-Qadir, returned to Algeria with the express goal of completing the conquest and establishing permanent French colonies: he insisted that if the war in Algeria was to be won, it would be with the "gloves off". The British press would soon name him "The Butcher of the Bedouin", for his scorched earth policy. Any tribes not submitting to French rule (i.e. those aligned with 'Abd al-Qadir), "could expect to have their harvests torched, orchards chopped down, livestock seized, tents burned, men decapitated, women and children left destitute or imprisoned" (Kiser 2008: 142). One of Bugeaud's officers wrote that he would execute his orders punctually: "I shall burn everything, kill everyone" (Kiser 2008: 143).

It was during this period of French brutality that 'Abd al-Qadir's character truly became apparent. In contrast to the widespread French destruction of Arab lives and lands, he showed remarkable humanity, winning hearts and minds across the world, even as he lost ground in Algeria. He was ever ready to engage in prisoner exchanges, though Bugeaud largely denied 'Abd al-Qadir's requests. He freed French prisoners when he could no longer feed them, and severely punished his men for any maltreatment of prisoners. The only time that his forces massacred French prisoners occurred while he was away, and 'Abd al-Qadir always maintained that the killings were against his orders. Notably, the Amir sent all female prisoners to stay under the personal care of his mother, Lalla Zahra, as he did not fully trust his men to keep them safe. She fed the female captives well and nursed the sick with "maternal attention and sympathy" (Kiser 2008: 155). For 'Abd al-Qadir, kindly treatment of captives was simply fulfilling the *Sunnah* or way of the Prophet Muhammad, a way he lamented that all too few Muslims actually lived.

With much of his force destroyed after 1843, 'Abd al-Qadir evaded French capture for four years, despite Bugeaud's dedication of 18 French military columns to capture him. Finally, in 1847, he surrendered on the condition that he could live in peace in Egypt. The Amir maintained that if he thought resistance was feasible, he would have continued, but French domination was now so complete that he reasoned that continued fighting would only bring needless suffering on the Algerian people. Failing to honour their promise to the Amir that he be allowed to live in Muslim lands, the French government instead placed him under house arrest in France, with his family, servants, and close followers. During his exile in France between 1847 and 1852, a time when many members of his family and followers died of ill-health due to the limited resources they were given, 'Abd al-Qadir's celebrity only grew. From French generals and bishops, to those who guarded, met or corresponded with him, all were impressed by his stoic serenity, impeccable manners and graciousness, and dignity in a time of hardship. When his most implacable and brutal foe, General Bugeaud died, 'Abd al-Qadir wrote a letter of condolence to the General's family, sharing the many ways in which he respected the old French warrior.

During his time in France, the Amir developed a keen interest in Christianity, meeting with priests and bishops, and reading an Arabic translation of the Bible. Impressed by the shared emphases of Islam and Christianity, 'Abd al-Qadir wrote of having a vision of Abraham, which inspired him to "be a sign of the oneness of God, the merciful, patient, and loving God for all people" (Kiser 2008: 243). Although he was a deeply devout Muslim throughout his life, the Amir was always respectful of the piety and compassion he saw among Christians. He prayed together with the head priest of the Madeleine in Paris, and shared a profound mutual respect with the Dominican Sisters of Charity that were assigned to care for his family while in France. He wrote a letter to Sister Natalie, describing her as "a shining mirror of goodness made from the purest mother of pearl… In her, we have seen only a deep attachment to her religion, and a perfect intelligence" (Kiser 2008: 262). Sister Natalie wrote of 'Abd al-Qadir that, "Allowing for certain exceptions of a theological nature, there is no Christian virtue that [he] does not practice to the highest degree" (Kiser 2008: 262).

His allies in France grew, even as his promise of free passage to Muslim lands continued to be denied. The British press called him "The Caged Hawk" after William Thackeray (d. 1863) composed a poem with that title lamenting his fate. The French populace, initially hostile to him as a martial foe, grew to regard him with affection during his time in Bordeaux, so much so that locals gathered enough signatures to put 'Abd al-Qadir on the ballot for the French presidential election. Finally, with popular French demand, Napoleon III (d. 1873) freed him, granting him passage to Turkey, and offering him a generous annual stipend from the French government. 'Abd al-Qadir left with his family for Bursa, Turkey in December of 1852.

In 1860, the Amir moved with his family one last time, now to the ancient city of Damascus. His arrival was greeted with popular acclaim. Local Arabs celebrated him as a descendent of the Prophet, a religious scholar, a Sufi, and a famed warrior. These qualities gave him a status and renown that troubled the Ottoman rulers there, who watched him closely. They were becoming ever more uneasy as European powers pressed them to grant Christians in Lebanon and Syria more rights than they had traditionally had under Ottoman Islamic law. As protected minorities under the *dhimma* stipulates of the *shari'a*, Christians and Jews were allowed to practice their religion and enforce their own laws within their communities, but were not allowed to join the military or serve in the higher levels of government, and were required to pay a protection tax, the *jizya*. As the Ottomans engaged in reforms in the 1850s bringing religious minorities closer to Muslims in legal equality, Christians in Lebanon and Syria began to cease payment of the *jizya*.

Ottoman authorities in Damascus were now looking for ways to "correct" the Christians for their refusal to pay the minority tax, and hoped to employ local Druze, a Muslim sect, to carry out the ominous correction. 'Abd al-Qadir wrote Druze leaders letters counselling patience and condemning attacks on Christians, which were already beginning. The French agreed to arm a thousand of 'Abd al-Qadir's men, in the hopes that they might protect Christians facing an increasingly precarious fate. In July of 1860 anti-Christian riots broke out in Damascus. 'Abd al-Qadir organized his men and began escorting European diplomats, priests and nuns, and local Christians to his substantial compound, until over 1,000 refugees were sheltered there. When the local mob found out the Amir was sheltering Christians they approached his home and demanded that he hand them over. He warned them against violating God's law and shedding innocent blood. When they continued to demand the Christians, he warned, "As long as one of my soldiers is still standing, you will not touch them. They are my guests. Murderers of women and children, you sons of sin, try to take one of these Christians and you will learn how my soldiers fight" (Kiser 2008: 299). The crowd dispersed.

Figure 2.2: Painting of Amir 'Abd al-Qadir saving Christians in Damascus.[1]

As 'Abd al-Qadir and his men escorted throngs of Christians to Beirut, estimates of the number he saved rose to the multiple thousands. The French media universally lauded their former foe, praising his honourable protection of a people whose co-religionists he had so long fought. He always maintained his actions arose from obedience to the law of God, which in

1.   This is an image celebrating 'Abd al-Qadir al-Jaza'iri's famed protection of Christians in Damascus, Syria, during the anti-Christian riots that broke out there in 1860. The painting's style is characteristic of Orientalist artwork during the colonial period.

all religions counselled compassion for His creatures. Even President Abraham Lincoln was impressed enough to send the Amir two "finely engraved custom made colt pistols" (Kiser 2008: 303). His global celebrity now cemented, he received a steady stream of visitors from around the world during his final decades in Damascus, which were otherwise spent with his family and engaged in religious study. His death in 1883 was counted as a loss for the world by *The New York Times*, which described him as "among the foremost of the few great men of the century" (Kiser 2008: 323). Interestingly, his legacy continues to reverberate. A traditional Algerian song for the Amir, titled "Abdel Kader", became a top ten hit in France when a live version was recorded by artists Rachid, Khaled, and Faudel, staying on the charts between 1998 and 1999.

Throughout his life, 'Abd al-Qadir was renowned for his strict adherence to the law of the Qur'ān and *Sunnah*. And yet this adherence to the outward elements of Islam coincided with a profound devotion to one of Sufism's most famous mystical figures. Upon entering Damascus, for example, his first request to the Ottoman authorities was not for an audience with them, or to visit the grand Umayyad Mosque in the heart of the city, as one might expect, but rather to visit the tomb and mosque of the famous Sufi philosopher and saint Ibn al-'Arabi (d. 1240), whose life and thought will be discussed at greater length in Chapter 4. He would later move into the home where Ibn al-'Arabi died in Damascus. 'Abd al-Qadir often taught classes on Ibn al-'Arabi's thought in the Umayyad Mosque, writing hundreds of pages of commentary on the great *shaykh's* works. Finally, when 'Abd al-Qadir died, he was buried next to Ibn al-'Arabi in his mosque at the foot of Mount Qaissoun.

Sufi Leaders and Resistance to Colonization

As an esoteric or mystical tradition, Sufism is frequently associated with an inward, spiritual focus, unworldliness, and even passivity. During the late eighteenth and throughout the nineteenth centuries, however, Sufis formed some of the most organized and effective Muslim movements to resist European conquest, and were furthermore instrumental in promoting a revival of Islamic law and practice. As the life of 'Abd al-Qadir illustrates so well, Sufism in this era transcended stereotypes. He was however, only one of a number of Sufi leaders who led resistance movements.

Catherine the Great's (d. 1796) push to modernize Russia and establish it as a world power included a series of territorial expansions. The Russian invasion of the largely Muslim Caucasus region (today Chechnya and Dagestan) began in 1783, and was met with concerted resistance, organized by Naqshbandi Sufi leader Shaykh Mansur Ushurma (d. 1794), who achieved battlefield success until his capture in 1791. In a pattern that was repeated throughout Muslim lands during this era, Ushurma not only organized military resistance to European encroachment, but ushered in a revival of Islamic practice, emphasizing a renewed focus on following Islamic law among

Caucasian Muslims. In the nineteenth century, the Naqshbandi master Shamil Dagestani (d. 1871), known popularly as Imam Shamil, would perpetuate Ushurma's mission. Shamil effectively ruled much of Dagestan, Chechnya, and parts of Ingushetia between 1834 and 1859, while waging a defensive war against the Russians. Like Ushurma before him, he enforced a strict version of the *shari'a* in areas under his rule, flogging drinkers and banning tobacco, music, and dancing (Sirriyeh 1999: 41). Captured in 1859, Shamil was exiled in Russia, only being allowed to make his way to Mecca and Medina in 1870, where he would die the following year. Overall Naqshbandi and Qadiri Sufis contributed both to the further Islamization of the Caucasus region and resistance to Russian invaders, illustrating quite clearly that Sufism during this period was not something incompatible with an emphasis on Islamic law and fighting in defence of Muslim lands.

Meanwhile, in West Africa, the Tijani Sufi *shaykh* 'Umar Tall (d. 1864) proved an obstacle to French domination of the region in the nineteenth century. By the time he made the pilgrimage to Mecca in 1830, 'Umar Tall was already a renowned scholar, healer, and political leader. In Mecca, the head of the Tijani order appointed Tall to spread the Tijani path in West Africa (present day Guinea, Mali, and Senegal). The Tijanis were a new order, founded by Ahmad al-Tijani (d. 1815) in the 1780s in North Africa. The Tijanis were distinguished as an Islamic revivalist order, opposing what they saw as the deviant direction many of the other Sufi orders had taken, and considering themselves to be superior to the other orders in spiritual attainment and adherence to Islamic law and the Prophet Muhammad's *Sunnah*. After Tall returned to West Africa and gained a sufficient following, he began to organize a *jihad* against the surrounding pagan and later Muslim kingdoms. Just as he carved out a new Tijani kingdom, known as the Tukulor Empire, the French were establishing a presence on the coast of Senegal. Tall was initially uninterested in fighting the French and approached them for a treaty. However, the French were determined to expand their domination of West Africa and eventually fought Tall's forces in the Senegal River valley. Tall's role in resisting French domination was thus not one of choice but of necessity (Vikor 2015: 217). His primary interest was establishing (his understanding of) genuine Islamic rule in West Africa, not in fighting the French. The French quest to dominate the region, however, brought his Sufi kingdom into conflict with colonial expansion. Tall was killed in 1864 during fighting with another Muslim kingdom, and his own kingdom would be annexed by the French in 1897.

In East Africa, the British faced-off against a figure known as the Mahdi and his followers in the Sudan, engaging in large, bloody battles there. Muhammad Ahmad (d. 1885) was leader of the Samaniyya Sufi order, a branch of the *shari'a*-oriented Khalwatiyya order that spread in Sudan during the late eighteenth and early nineteenth centuries. In 1881, Ahmad declared himself to be the awaited Mahdi, someone described in *hadith* literature as a holy messiah-like figure who will come to earth to prepare the way for the return of Jesus before the world's end. The fact that unbelievers had come to dominate Muslim lands combined with the approaching year 1300 according to the Islamic calendar, fostered a sense among many Muslims during the late nineteenth century that the signs of the end times were manifesting (Sirriyeh 1999: 34). Offering a sweeping reform of the Islamic tradition, Ahmad built a revivalist movement premised on a return to the Prophet Muhammad's *Sunnah* and his early Islamic state in Medina. He first fought the Ottoman-appointed Egyptian rulers of the Sudan and then the British when they took over rule of the region, before his death in 1885. His Mahdist state would last until 1899, when it was destroyed by the British.

The Mahdi was not the only Sufi leader to establish an idealized state in East Africa. Late in the nineteenth century Muhammad 'Abdille Hasan (d. 1920), a leader of the Salihiyya order, organized resistance to British, Italian, and Ethiopian incursions into Somalia. While the British referred to Hasan as the "Mad Mullah", he successfully established a "Dervish State" in Somalia, which lasted between 1896 and 1920. Hasan's state mirrored the hierarchical structure of the Salihiyya order, with the *shaykh* at its head, and his functionaries carrying out administrative tasks under his direction. Like other movements during this period, the Salihiyya were *shari'a*-oriented, enforcing Islamic law within their domain and critiquing other Sufi orders in the region as straying from Islamic legal and theological orthodoxy. Hasan's centralized state proved unable to resist the modern weaponry of the British military and was destroyed in 1920, though he remained a symbol of Somali nationalism thereafter (Green 2012: 197).

Across the world in Indonesia, the Qadiri order was instrumental in spearheading an Islamic revival on the island of Java in the second half of the nineteenth century. Since the sixteenth and seventeenth centuries, Javanese Islam was largely Sufi-oriented. Javanese Sufism tended towards an emphasis on mystical knowledge rather than adherence to Islamic legal norms. Qadiri Sufis however promoted a renewed focus on the Qur'ān, Islamic law, and the practice of the Five Pillars in Javanese Muslim life, and further led and organized resistance against Dutch rule from 1880 to 1888. Although the Javanese rebellions were unsuccessful in shaking Dutch control, the revival of Islamic identity and *shari'a* adherence in the region would have a more sustained impact (Lapidus 2014: 732). As we will see in the next section however, the initial resistance offered by Sufi orders to European colonization would prove insufficient, and new forms of Islamic revivalism would challenge Sufism's place in Islam.

Sufis and Salafis in Colonial Algeria: Shaykh Ahmad al-'Alawi

After French forces defeated 'Abd al-Qadir and completed their conquest of the country, Sufis worked to maintain their position in Algerian society against new challenges. Their status as spiritual and political leaders however, was not what it was during 'Abd al-Qadir's heyday as leader of a vibrant Islamic state holding off the conquest of nonbelievers. As the great Sufi resistance leaders one by one were killed, captured, or chose to negotiate with Europeans, many Muslims began to look elsewhere for the standard bearers of Muslim independence and revival. Muslim trust in the renowned spirituality, even miraculous power of Sufi leaders as the "friends" of God was shaken as they failed to repel the French and in many cases worked with their new non-Muslim rulers to help govern Algerians (Sirriyeh 1999: 33).

Following the First World War, Algerian discontent with French rule grew. Almost 200,000 Algerians served in the French military during the war, with around 25,000 dying in combat (Abun-Nasr 1987: 328). Although the French government wanted to reward Algerians for their service to France with further equality under French rule, the French settlers in Algeria opposed any such changes to the colonial system, which they benefited from. Further, as French settlers began to colonize the Algerian countryside, occupying more and more of the available farmland, rural Algerians were forced to move to the cities for work. This urbanization of Algerian Muslim society combined with growing discontent set the stage for new, largely urban movements to emerge challenging colonial rule. One of the most important of these was the Salafiyya, a movement whose origins we will account for in greater detail later in this chapter. For our purposes here, it is important to note that Salafis believed that Islam was an inherently rational religion, one that could help Muslims revive their societies if they would only return to its original purity and dynamism, uncorrupted by later accretions, forgoing the mediation provided by the Sufis in particular. Making use of urban networks and print culture, the Salafi challenge to Sufism was a formidable one, as we continue to see in the twentieth and twenty-first centuries.

This new, more tenuous place for Sufism in Algeria is illustrated by the life and publishing of one of the region's most famous Sufi masters, Shaykh Ahmad al-'Alawi (d. 1934). Al-'Alawi was the founder of what would become a leading branch of the Darqawi order, the 'Alawiyya. The Darqawi order was itself a branch of the Shadhili order – the nature and founding of the Shadhili order will be discussed in Chapter 4. Emerging in the late eighteenth and early nineteenth centuries with the teachings of Shaykh Ahmad al-Darqawi (d. 1823), the Darqawiyya would become "the most widespread, numerous, and influential *tariqa* in North Africa" (Trimingham 1998: 111). Though having branches around the Muslim world, the Darqawi order was based outside of Fez, Morocco. Notably, the order authorized women to act as local deputies of the head *shaykh* of the order (*muqaddamat*), a position of authority not all orders in the region granted women. Al-'Alawi's branch of the Darqawi order would become particularly widespread. By the time of his death in 1934, al-'Alawi was thought to have around 200,000 disciples in Algeria, Tunis, Yemen, Ethiopia, Syria, and Palestine (Lings 1993: 10).

Al-'Alawi was born in Mostaganem, Algeria in 1869 to a relatively poor family. Working from a young age to help support his parents and two sisters, al-'Alawi intensively pursued studies of Islamic theology, law, and spirituality in the evenings, so much so that his first wife requested a divorce, which he admitted was warranted. He later joined the 'Isawi order known for performing various marvels like fire eating and snake charming, before finding such practices objectionable and seeking out a more qualified spiritual master. Al-'Alawi found what he was looking for in the Shadhili-Darqawi master Muhammad al-Buzidi (d. 1909). Al-Buzidi asked the young al-'Alawi if he would like to try to tame the most dangerous and venomous snake around, and when he said he would and asked where to find it, al-Buzidi responded, "I mean your soul which is between the two sides of your body. Its poison is more deadly than a snake's, and if you can take hold of it and do what you please with it, you are...a sage indeed" (Lings 1993: 52).

Figure 2.3: Portrait of Ahmad al-'Alawi, one featured in his tomb in Mostaganem, Algeria.

Al-'Alawi became a disciple of al-Buzidi's, and, following al-Buzidi's direction, abandoned both his snake charming and theological studies, focusing instead on the Sufi path of purifying the self through the invocation of God's Name (*Allah*) whilst visualizing the letters of the Name. Although al-'Alawi deeply loved pursuing theological studies, he obeyed his master's orders and gave them up. Al-Buzidi suggested that the study of theology would only confuse the mind, reflecting both a longstanding suspicion of dialectal theology within the Islamic tradition, and al-Buzidi's belief that the existential realization of God through Sufi practice was infinitely more significant and closer to the prophetic model. As we will see in the following section, al-'Alawi would return to his theological studies following the completion of the spiritual path, this time with a radically new perspective on their significance.

Eventually al-Buzidi would order al-'Alawi to begin teaching publicly, predicting that he would draw followers from far and wide. Following al-

Buzidi's death in 1909, his disciples had a series of visions and dreams confirming al-'Alawi as his successor. Besides his efforts in training disciples in the Sufi path, starting in 1910, al-'Alawi further began publishing works of Sufi philosophy and poetry. By this time the Salafiyya had taken root from Syria and Egypt to Algeria and Morocco. Much of their scorn for the superstition and degradation of Islam's old order was directed toward Sufism, a tradition more and more receiving the blame for the historically unprecedented low to which Muslim societies had sunk on the world's stage. The establishment of the printing press in Muslim societies meant that much of this debate over Sufism's place within Islam took place in the various periodicals and newspapers now circulating in countries like Algeria.

Although al-'Alawi did his best to remain above the fray of public polemics, in 1920 he published his first defence of Sufism in response to a widely circulated pamphlet by a religious scholar in Tunis entitled *A Mirror to Show Up Errors* (Lings 1993: 88). The circulation of print media among a growing, literate urban class, meant that public opinion could now be swayed in ways difficult to achieve a century ago. Al-'Alawi realized that the future of Sufism in Muslim societies required that it be defended in print. The Salafi author of the pamphlet argued that Islam was nothing more than the Qur'ān and the *Sunnah* of Muhammad, suggesting that Sufism was something else added onto this original essence. This idea that Sufism was a later interpolation as opposed to an organic outgrowth of the Islamic revelation is something we will see as a pattern across Muslim history.

Al-'Alawi responded by insisting that Sufis agreed fully with the statement that Islam's basis lies in the Qur'ān and *Sunnah*, but countered by suggesting that the Qur'ān had profound meanings far beyond the grasp of the most refined mind, let alone the average one. As we will see in Chapter 6, Sufis have since the earliest records of their teachings, based their path on the Qur'ān and the *Sunnah,* though their understanding of them at times contrasts sharply with that of more exoterically minded religious scholars. Al-'Alawi continued, in his response to the anti-Sufi polemic:

> It may well be that one who cleaves to externals can see nothing in the Book of God but what his own intelligence, such as it is, can apprehend and that he may belie what goes beyond this without realizing that in knowing the outside of the Book only he is as one who knows a fruit by nothing but its peel ... In saying: 'Islam is nothing other than the Book of God and the [Sunnah] of the Apostle', it is as if you said: 'Islam is what *I* understand of the Book and the [Sunnah], and no more'... which means that you set your own innermost perceptions on a level with the innermost perceptions of the Companions – nay, of the Prophets! (Lings 1993: 89–90).

Al-'Alawi continued to invoke authenticated sayings of the Prophet Muhammad (*hadith*) that describe an elect among the Muslim community, a special group of God's friends to whom He reveals the secrets of the Qur'ān and path of Muhammad. Who else, al-'Alawi asks, are this elect if not the Sufis who have devoted their lives to the remembrance of God and purifying their selves of evil?

The rest of his response to the Salafi attack on the Sufis, seeks to illustrate why the various practices of the Sufis – from the pursuit of ecstasy, dancing or swaying rhythmically, to the use of prayer beads – do not in fact fall under the condemnatory category of *bida'a* or reprehensible innovation/deviation in religion. This concept of *bida'a* is at the heart of the Salafi critique of Sufism. For Salafis, the practices of Sufism are not sufficiently traceable to the *Sunnah* of Muhammad and his Companions to warrant their acceptance as an authentic part of Islam. Instead, Salafis see the Sufis' collective practice of *dhikr* (which often involves rhythmic chanting and swaying, the use of music to induce ecstasy, and prayer beads to count repetitions of God's Names) and especially in their metaphysical doctrines (which tend to suggest that nothing really exists except for God) as later developments that deviate in significant ways from the Islam of the Prophet. As such, Salafis tend to condemn Sufism as a whole as an innovation and deviation from "authentic" or "pure" Islam.

In response to this critique, al-'Alawi notes a ruling by a medieval scholar who is one of the most revered and respected by the Salafi movement, Ibn al-Qayyim al-Jawziyya (d. 1350), himself a close disciple of Ibn Taymiyya (d. 1328), about whom more will be said in Chapters 4 and 6. Ibn al-Qayyim writes that the deliberate seeking of ecstasy, a practice known as *tawajud*, was in fact permissible. As such, al-'Alawi notes, it follows that the various practices of Sufism meant to engender ecstasy have received approval from one of the conservative medieval scholars most respected by contemporary Salafis (Lings 1961: 93). Al-'Alawi further emphasizes the presence of ecstasy and rapture among the *salaf* by highlighting Qur'ānic verses such as: *When they hear what has been revealed unto the Prophet, you see their eyes overflow with tears from their recognition of the truth* (5:83), and *Only those are believers whose hearts thrill with awe at the remembrance of God* (8:2). He concludes by arguing:

> If the grace of ecstasy is beyond you, it is not beyond you to believe that others may enjoy it ... None the less I do not say that dancing and manifestations of ecstasy are among the essentials of Sufism. But they are outward signs which come from submersion in remembrance. Let him who doubts try for himself, for hearsay is not the same as direct experience (Lings 1993: 95).

Continuing in this vein, he responds to the article's suggestion that anyone who thinks that dancing is permissible is a nonbeliever. Al-'Alawi asks, "Do you imagine that the Sufis hold dancing to be absolutely lawful, just as you hold it to be absolutely unlawful?" and suggests that "it behoves the learned not to pass any judgment about it until he knows what is the motive behind it, lest he forbid what God has allowed" (Lings 1993: 95). In general, al-'Alawi highlights the many Islamic traditions, both verses of the Qur'ān, and sayings of Muhammad's (*hadith*), that emphasize the centrality and pre-eminence of *dhikrullah* or the remembrance of God. It is upon this principle that al-'Alawi argues for a proper evaluation of the rituals of the Sufis: that which fosters the remembrance of God is to be praised and encouraged. On this he writes, "our performance of the rites of worship is considered strong or weak according to the degree of our remembrance of God while performing them", and notes that when the Prophet Muhammad was asked who was rewarded the most for their fasting, and prayer, and pilgrimage, he said, "The richest in the remembrance of God is the richest in reward" (Lings 1993: 97).

Al-'Alawi finally concludes by thanking his Salafi critics for pointing out the frauds and hypocrites among the Sufis, but suggests they go too far in condemning all Sufis and in failing to consider them as members of the Muslim community. In spite of al-'Alawi's attempt to preserve the unity of Muslims by arguing for their shared basis in the Qur'ān and *Sunnah*, the Salafi rejection of Sufism would only grow in intensity during the nineteenth and early twentieth centuries, such that, by the twenty-first, this rejection would manifest in the destruction of Sufi shrines the world over, a destruction that in many ways is the surface eruption of a much deeper fracture in the Muslim community. Interestingly, just as many Muslims were beginning to turn against Sufism during the nineteenth and twentieth centuries, Europeans were discovering in Sufism a philosophical and mystical approach they felt lacking in their own religious traditions. Al-'Alawi's teachings in particular would play a key role in the early transmission of Sufism to Europe and eventually North America.

Western Sufi Traditionalists

In the first decade of the twentieth century René Guénon (d. 1951), a young mathematics student in Paris, found himself increasingly drawn into the city's thriving occult underground. As he explored Paris's many secret societies (with teachings often traced to the Masons, the Knights Templar, or the Hermetic tradition), Guénon discovered a worldview that made sense of the various doctrines and religions he was exploring. Dating back to the Renaissance in Latin Europe, the perennial philosophy or *philosophia perennis* holds that there is a set of shared metaphysical principles that underlie humanity's diverse religions and philosophies; there is a fundamental unity to the world's wisdom traditions. It further proposes that this unity is rooted in an original, primordial wisdom, the *prisca theologica*, a tradition of wisdom that existed holistically in humanity's earliest years, but over time has fragmented and atrophied.

For Guénon, whereas pre-modern civilizations preserved this original wisdom in their esoteric, mystical traditions, modernity represented a break from tradition, falling into materialism and a rejection of the possibility of transcendent wisdom. Although the modern West appears to offer moral, scientific, and technological progress, Guénon believed that it is premised solely on material development, and as a result represents a profound deviation from the primordial tradition, leading to the decline of sacred knowledge, social fragmentation, conflict, and the eventual dissolution of human civilization. This rejection of modernity and valorization of traditional metaphysics, symbolism, and mysticism, is why Guénon's approach became known as Traditionalism. The capital "T" here indicating a discrete school of thought as opposed to a more general intellectual trend..

Guénon was first drawn to the non-dualistic metaphysics of the *Advaita Vedanta* tradition within Hinduism. Guénon was not simply seeking to learn the metaphysical principles however, but to be initiated into a spiritual path that allowed for the individual realization of these principles. This search for authentic initiation would eventually lead Guénon to Ivan Aguéli (d. 1917), a Swedish-born convert to Islam, Sufi, and artist. Aguéli, or Shaykh 'Abd al-Hadi Aqili as he was also known, managed a bookstore in Paris that formed an important node in the city's network of seekers. In 1912 Aguéli initiated Guénon into the Shadhili Sufi order, after which Guénon took the Muslim name 'Abd al-Wahid Yahya. Guénon would come to see Islam as a final revelation of the primordial tradition before the end of the world, one particularly accessible for Westerners, due to its shared emphases with Christianity, and the ease with which one could convert. Guénon did not believe that conversion to Hinduism was possible, as he thought that only one born in the Hindu caste system could be legitimately counted as a Hindu.

In 1930 Guénon travelled to Egypt, a country he would decide to make his home, seeing in Cairo at the time a society that, though changing, still offered the possibility of a lifestyle grounded in traditional principles. He adopted traditional Egyptian dress, joined a Sufi order in Cairo, and raised his family rather anonymously as a devout Muslim. And yet, despite adhering to Islam in practice, Guénon did not consider himself to have converted to Islam, nor did he think it was superior to any other traditional religious form. He held that an understanding of the fundamental unity of all religious traditions precluded the possibility of conversion. Guénon suggested that his practice of Islam was due to reasons of "spiritual convenience", meaning that the religion offered an accessible form through which to live the primordial tradition or perennial philosophy (Sedgwick 2004: 77).

Guénon would become a prolific author, writing 26 books. Despite remaining relatively unknown in academic literature, Guénon was critically important for the development of Sufism in the West in general and North America in particular. Though Guénon never recommended in print that his readers convert to Islam or practice Sufism, "most of those who were influenced by him did become Sufis" (Rawlinson 1997: 280). Hence many of Guénon's intellectual heirs followed Guénon's own example of Islamic practice, and were likely influenced by his understanding of Islam as the final manifestation of the perennial philosophy before the end of time.

Although Guénon is generally regarded as the founder of the Traditionalist school of thought, its most influential exponent was Frithjof Schuon (d. 1998). As a young man, Schuon became fascinated with religious traditions from around the world. His growing interest in Arabic and Islam was cemented through correspondence with Guénon who, in 1931, advised him that Westerners seeking an Eastern tradition should look to Islam (Aymard and Laude 2004: 15). In 1932 Schuon spent four months at al-'Alawi's Sufi centre in Mostaganem, Algeria. On his first meeting with al-Alawi, Schuon wrote, "One could compare the meeting with such a spiritual messenger with what, for example, it would have been like, in the middle of the twentieth century, to meet a medieval saint or Semitic patriarch" (Aymard and Laude 2004: 17). He described meeting with the renowned *shaykh* on numerous occasions during his four month stay. During this time, much of which he spent in a retreat cell, engaging with the Sufi practice of *khalwa* or spiritual retreat to focus on *dhikr*, he was initiated into the 'Alawi order. Schuon's stay at al-'Alawi's Sufi lodge however was cut short as French colonial authorities grew suspicious of a European living in an Arab religious centre (Fitzgerald 2010: 34).

In 1934, Schuon described mystically receiving the highest 'Alawi spiritual practice, the use of the Supreme Name in recitation (*Allah*), while reading the Hindu scripture known as the *Bhagavad Gita* in Paris (Sedgwick 2004: 88). He later found out that al-'Alawi had died that day. In 1935, Schuon returned to Mostaganem where al-'Alawi's successor, Shaykh Adda Bentounes (d. 1952), authorized Schuon as a representative (*muqaddam*) of the 'Alawi order. Upon returning to Europe, Schuon began initiating fellow Traditionalists who were themselves eagerly seeking a spiritual lineage within which to practice. Although he was never made a *shaykh* by al-'Alawi or his successor Bentounes, in 1936 Schuon experienced an inner conviction that he was in fact a *shaykh*, or spiritual master able to guide students and fully transmit the Sufi path. His inner sense that he was a *shaykh* was confirmed for him by a number of his followers who reported dreams revealing Schuon's new status.

Schuon would eventually establish a branch of the 'Alawi order known as the Maryamiyya, for Schuon's emphasis on the veneration of Mary as an embodiment of universal wisdom. Schuon's Maryamiyya order would prove appealing to academics in particular, many of whom, like Seyyed Hossein Nasr and Martin Lings (d. 2005), would become renowned scholars of Islam in North American and European universities, as we explored in Chapter 1. Like Guenon, Schuon was a prolific author, writing over 20 books on various aspects of traditional wisdom, metaphysics, and spirituality. In one of his most famous works, *The Transcendent Unity of Religions*, Schuon explained the Traditionalist understanding of how humanity's diverse religious doctrines can be understood as expressions of a single truth:

> If an example may be drawn from the sensory sphere to illustrate the difference between metaphysical and theological knowledge, it may be said that the former, which can be called "esoteric" when it is manifested through a religious symbolism, is conscious of the colourless essence of light and of its character of pure luminosity; a given religious belief, on the other hand, will assert that light is red and not green, whereas another belief will assert the opposite; both will be right insofar as they distinguish light from darkness but not insofar as they identify it with a particular colour (1984: xxx).

SUFI METAPHYSICS AND SPIRITUALITY IN THE COLONIAL CONTEXT: RELIGIOUS DIVERSITY AND SYMBOLISM

In reviewing the remarkable lives of 'Abd al-Qadir al-Jaza'iri and Ahmad al-'Alawi, what is not always apparent is the way in which an engagement with Sufi metaphysics and spiritual practice informed their ability to, with relative serenity, respond to the immense challenges posed by European invasion and domination, and the rise of anti-Sufi movements. Although 'Abd al-Qadir was famous the world over for his accomplishments on the battlefield, much less publicized was the intensive spirituality that was so foundational to his life. Léon Roches (d. 1901) was a French officer who pretended to convert to Islam and, as 'Umar ibn Rusha, was taken by 'Abd al-Qadir into his inner circle between 1837 and 1839. In his memoirs, Roches described the way in which 'Abd al-Qadir integrated spiritual practice into his everyday life. He noted that, when time permitted, 'Abd al-Qadir engaged in prayer outside of his tent, and that the Amir's religious exercises went beyond the daily prayers (*salat*) performed throughout the day:

> He gives himself up to meditation between each prayer, constantly touching the prayer beads. Every day, in his tent, or at the mosque when by chance he finds himself in a town, he gives a talk on the unity of God... He fasts at least one time a week, and what a fast! From two hours before dawn until sunset, he does not eat, drink, or even inhale perfume (Chodkiewicz 1995: 3).

Besides his daily devotion to prayer, meditation, and weekly fasting, Roches described witnessing the Amir in states of spiritual ecstasy (known as *wajd* in Sufi terminology). Returning from the battlefield in a state of what we would now call post-traumatic stress, but what Roches referred to as "a nervous excitement which I was unable to master", Roches relates in his memoirs being taken into 'Abd al-Qadir's tent, where the Amir personally saw to him, giving him new clothes and medicine. Falling asleep in his tent, Roches awakened to observe 'Abd al-Qadir:

> His lips, slightly open, seemed to be still reciting a prayer but never-theless were motionless. He had come to an ecstatic state. His aspirations toward heaven were such that he seemed no longer to touch the earth. I had on occasion been granted the honour of sleeping in ['Abd al-Qadir's] tent and I had seen him in prayer and been struck by his mystical transports, but on this night he represented for me the most striking image of faith. Thus the great saints of Christianity must have prayed (Chodkiewicz 1995: 4).

This impression of saintliness from a bygone era was one repeatedly noted by Europeans who met with 'Abd al-Qadir. Following his final move to Damascus in 1856, 'Abd al-Qadir was able to devote even more of his time to religious devotions, study, and teaching, no longer responsible for a fragile wartime state. His daily routine in Damascus was described by a British visitor, Charles-Henry Churchill (d. 1869), who spent the winter of 1859–60 there. Churchill related that 'Abd al-Qadir woke two hours before dawn, engaging in prayer and meditation until sunrise, before going to the mosque for public prayer, after which he returned home to read and write in his library until noon. 'Abd al-Qadir would then return to the mosque for the noon prayer, following which he held a three hour class in the mosque, reading from, commenting and answering questions on, a religious text (often one of the works of Ibn al-'Arabi). Then, following the afternoon prayer, the Amir returned home to spend time and dine with his family. He would return to the mosque for the sunset prayer, hold another class until the night prayer an hour and a half later, following which he was again reading and writing in his home library (Chodkiewicz 1995: 5–6).

'Abd al-Qadir's life of religious devotion was informed in particular by the works of Ibn al-'Arabi. Much of the writing described above involved work on his *Kitab al-Mawaqif* (*Book of Stopping Places*), a book that sought to revive the teachings of Ibn al-'Arabi in an age of science (Green 2012: 200). This engagement with Ibn al-'Arabi's thought was not simply textual, As we discussed in Chapter 1, Sufi practice is connected to a *silsila*, a chain of transmission of spirituality and blessing (*baraka*) passed on from master to disciple, and traced back to the Prophet Muhammad. Although all originating with Muhammad, some of these chains of transmission came to be associated with particular masters, usually within a particular Sufi order. Hence Sufis speak of the Naqshbandi or the Qadiri *silsila*. Ibn al-'Arabi's chain of transmission is known as the Akbarian *silsila* after Ibn al-'Arabi's title the *shaykh al-akbar* or "Greatest Master". Unlike the other chains of transmission however, the Akbarian chain is not affiliated with any particular order, and is usually transmitted discreetly. 'Abd al-Qadir received this transmission from his father, likely in his teens or early twenties (Chodkiewicz 1995: 7–8). Indeed, confirming the *shaykh al-akbar's* influence, 'Abd al-Qadir's affirms in a collection of his spiritual writings that Ibn al-'Arabi "is our treasure, from which we draw what we write, whether it be from his spiritual form (*min ruhaniyyatihi*) or from what he has himself written in his works" (Chodkiewicz 1995: 13). This reference to the "spiritual form" of Ibn al-'Arabi suggests that 'Abd al-Qadir encountered and learned from the spirit of Ibn al-'Arabi, a phenomenon known within Sufism as an *'Uwaysi* connection, usually between a Sufi aspirant and the spiritual form of a Sufi master or prophet – we will discuss this phenomenon further in Chapters 4 and 5. Ibn al-'Arabi himself is said to have had a number of *'Uwaysi* connections with the Prophet Muhammad, Jesus, and the mysterious immortal Khidr, about whom more will be said in Chapter 6.

'Abd al-Qadir's spiritual connection with Ibn al-'Arabi, and close study of his works, clearly informed the remarkably open and respectful way in which the Amir related to non-Muslims. His protection of Christian lives and holy places and his ability to recognize the piety and holiness he encountered in Christian nuns and priests are particularly noteworthy in this regard. Ibn al-'Arabi's writings offer one of the most explicit and thorough discussions of the necessity of religious pluralism within the Islamic tradition. Hence it is not surprising that, as a close student of Ibn al-'Arabi, 'Abd al-Qadir would prove to show a profound respect for other faiths.

Ibn al-'Arabi proposes that the diversity of religious perspectives we see among people is a necessary result of the nature of God Himself: religious plurality is not accidental, but rather grounded in ultimate reality. According to Islamic theology, although God is absolutely one in essence, He has an infinite diversity of qualities or Names (*asma'*). These Names or qualities are the origin of the spectacular diversity of the universe, which is their visible expression. Ibn al-'Arabi calls the manifestation of these Names in the cosmos *tajalliyyat* (singular, *tajalli*), an Arabic term meaning the self-disclosures of God, or theophanies. Commenting on Ibn al-'Arabi's thought in this regard, 'Abd al-Qadir writes:

> Our God, as well as the God of the Christians, the Jews, the Sabeans, and all the diverging sects, is One, just as He has taught us. But He has mani-fested Himself to us through a different theophany than that by which He manifested Himself in His revelation to the Christians, to the Jews, and to the other sects… Now all of that results only from the diversity of theophanies, which is a function of the multiplicity of those to whom they are destined and to the diversity of their essential predispositions (Laude 2011: 40).

As a result of God manifesting Himself in diverse ways to different people, based on their own nature and receptivity, the world is full of many religions, creeds, philosophies, and beliefs – none of which encompasses God in his totality. Hence, 'Abd al-Qadir continues, "None of His creatures worships Him in all His aspects; no one is unfaithful to Him in all His aspects", remarking that, if all know God in some respects and not others, then "error does not exist in this world except in a relative manner" (Chodkiewicz 1995: 19). The result of this Akbarian perspective is first an intellectual and religious humility, whereby one must acknowledge the inherent limitation of any religious view, including one's own: no one has a monopoly on the truth, and no one has a comprehensive or final word on God. The second result is a respect for all religions and beliefs: just as no one view encompasses the entire truth about God, no religion or belief is totally devoid of truth about God, and hence each belief offers a window onto one of God's Names or theophanies. Thus, Ibn al-'Arabi writes, "created beings have formed various beliefs about God and for me, I believe everything they have believed" (Chodkiewicz 1995: 19). And yet, none of these beliefs, though partially correct, can claim to be totally without limitation or error. Commenting on this, 'Abd al-Qadir proclaims:

> If you think and believe that [God] is what all the schools of Islam profess and believe – He is that, and He is other than that! If you think that He is what the diverse communities believe – Muslims, Christians, Jews, Mazdeans, polytheists and others – He is that and He is other than that! And if you think and believe what is professed by the Knowers *par excellence* – prophets, saints, and angels – He is that! He is other than that! (Chodkiewicz 1995: 127–28).

This perspective of Ibn al-'Arabi's on the divine roots of the cosmos and religious diversity came to shape much Sufi thought after him. In particular, his understanding of the world as the self-disclosure of God's Names (*tajalliyyat*) lent itself well to the various symbolic approaches to scripture and the universe that the Sufis specialized in. Ibn al-'Arabi's understanding of *tajaliyyat* was an articulation of one of Sufism's earliest concepts (as we will see in Chapter 6). If the cosmos itself is a site of God's self-disclosure, then the universe and everything in it ultimately acts as a symbol or sign of God, as the Qur'ān repeatedly affirms. This perspective was undoubtedly at the heart of 'Abd al-Qadir's notable serenity and dignity in the face of military struggle, evasion, defeat, and exile. All of the tumultuous events of his life were interpreted as *tajalliyyat*, signs and symbols of God's Names. Living a life of witnessing the *tajalliyyat,* recognizing God's qualities in every facet and event of one's life, is certainly one way of describing the Sufi path.

Sufis are, of course, not the only ones to perceive the world in a symbolic way. The idea that the visible world is a manifestation of higher realities is found in as varied philosophies as Platonism, Hermeticism, Jewish and Christian mysticism, as well as forms of Buddhism and Hinduism. Lings, who besides his work as a scholar was a leader of the Maryamiyya order, goes so far as to suggest that, "there is no traditional doctrine that does not teach that this world is the world of symbols (Lings 2005: vii). Within the Islamic tradition, a symbolic understanding of reality is traced to a variety of Qur'ānic verses and *hadith* texts. One of the most famous in this regard is a *hadith qudsi* or "sacred *hadith*" in which Muslims believe the Prophet Muhammad shared words of God that were not a part of the Qur'ān. One particularly loved by Sufis begins, "I was a hidden treasure and loved to be known, so I created the universe". The implication of this saying is that the universe as a whole is a means of knowing God, that everything in creation symbolically communicates something about God. The Qur'ān affirms that, "we will show them Our signs on the horizons and in themselves until they know it is the truth" (41:53), suggesting that both the outward and inward realms signify or symbolize God. As such, Sufis have approached all aspects of reality – whether the outward universe, inward self, or scripture – as fundamentally symbolic in nature, all signs of the one Reality underlying them all – the origins of Sufi understandings the Qur'ān's symbolic nature will be explored in Chapter 6.

Almost a century after 'Abd al-Qadir, al-'Alawi relates an interesting anecdote illustrating how Sufis experience the scripture of Islam, the Qur'ān. Once al-'Alawi's Sufi master, al-Buzidi, was convinced that he had practiced the invocation of God's name to a degree that he had achieved the spiritual fruits of the Sufi path, his master allowed him to return to his classes on Islamic theology. Al-'Alawi found however, that he experienced these classes, and the Qur'ān, in an entirely new way. "Another result of the invocation was that I understood more than the literal sense of the text. In a word, there was no comparison between the understanding which I now had and that which I had before, and its scope went on increasing" (Cadavid 2005: xv).

In essence, al-'Alawi began to experience the Qur'ān symbolically, with the rich variety of meanings encapsulated in each word rushing forth into his mind in an almost overwhelming fashion, compelling him to begin writing his insights down. He would further publish a commentary on a popular primer on the basics of Islam by the jurist Ibn 'Ashir (d. 1631), offering an explanation of the esoteric, or inward significance of the basic doctrines and practices of Islam. Al-'Alawi for instance, comments on Ibn 'Ashir's discussion of the basics of the daily prayer, *salat*. Al-'Alawi suggests that the prostration (placing one's forehead on the ground), which is an integral component of *salat*, is a symbol or expression of the extinction (*fana'*) of the self in God, while the *Ka'aba* in Mecca, which the individual faces while praying, represents the divine presence, such that facing Mecca is a symbol of dedicating oneself to the realization of God's presence (Cadavid 2005: 34). He even interprets Ibn 'Ashir's account of the requirements of women's dress as a symbol of God's relationship with the Sufi aspirant. Ibn 'Ashir relates the majority opinion within the Maliki school of Islamic law that "Save the face and hands of a free woman, all else must be covered, and is regarded as private parts". For al-'Alawi, the woman here described symbolizes God as the Beloved, "for to see the Beloved without veils is only given to those who show respect. Otherwise her beauty must be veiled, and her sun covered by a cloud" (Cadavid 2005: 42). Ibn 'Ashir's account reflects the traditional understanding of women's dress found in Islamic law, though it is important to point out that Muslims and Sufis have a range of approaches to this issue, as many female Sufi practitioners in the 'Alawi and other orders do not necessarily maintain these traditional clothing norms.

Al-'Alawi's discovery of not only the outward meaning of Islamic scripture and ritual, but also their hidden depths, reflects a longstanding Sufi understanding of reality as consisting of both the outward, visible, and apparent (*zahir*), and the inward, hidden, esoteric (*batin*). Regardless of the circumstances Sufis found themselves in – whether colonial conflict or medieval empires – outward realities were engaged from a perspective of inward transcendence that saw the divine perfection underlying the fortune or misfortune of their contexts. This understanding of reality as multi-layered, with the deeper layers of meaning only accessible to those whose souls have been sufficiently purified to perceive their more subtle nature, is characteristic of the Sufi tradition as a whole (Ohlander 2015: 58). Sufis have thus shared a world of scripture, doctrine, and practice with their other Muslim compatriots, but have understood all of these as having an inner dimension that only the realized Sufis can appreciate in their fullness. In other words, it is only with the unveiling (*kashf*) given by God to His friends that the full spectrum of meaning can be apprehended. As al-'Alawi puts it, the Sufis "participate in listening along with others but what they hear is different" (Cadavid 2005: 4). This "hearing" of a deeper meaning that others cannot hear, is the knowledge from God's presence, the *'ilm al-laduni* spoken of in the Qur'ān. Elaborating on this, al-'Alawi writes regarding the Sufis:

> Do not, therefore, think it strange, brother, if they understand from a word a meaning that is different from its apparent one. This is but evidence of the nobility of their station and the exaltation of their degree, for they understand matters in God. The Sufis declare that such understanding in God is proportionate to one's station before Him, and they are united in saying that a single word, which refers to a specific meaning, can have, for the worshipper, innumerable possible meanings and an inexhaustible number of subtle and rare nuances... A word may be outwardly plain, but the realized man can obtain something enlightening from it by means of symbolism and allusion (Cadavid 2005: 3–4).

As we will see throughout this book, Sufis have pursued this deeper understanding of scripture, self, and cosmos, and then sought to communicate this understanding, though always with an appreciation of the limits of human language in expressing such things. One of the ways that Sufis have sought to work with the possibilities and limitations of language is through the use of poetry, which revels in symbolism, imagery, and allusion, perhaps better equipped to communicate subtle spiritual states than prose. The colonial era in particular would see Westerners discovering forms of Sufi poetry that would have a profound effect on artistic movements in Europe and North America, from the nineteenth century into the twenty-first.

ROMANTICISM AND THE WESTERN
DISCOVERY OF PERSIAN SUFI POETRY

While European states were engaged in various forms of conquest of Muslim societies, irreversibly transforming them, Western intellectuals in the Romantic movement were themselves being transformed by one of Islam's richest sources of spirituality and culture: Persian Sufi poetry. Forming such a seminal part of the Islamic literary canon, Sufi poetry began to seep into European literature in the sixteenth century, when George Puttenham (d. 1590) translated a few of the famous Persian Sufi poet Sa'adi's (d. 1291) works into English. Sufi poems would gradually appear more frequently in European writings in the seventeenth century, although it was not until the late eighteenth century that Sufism became more broadly accessible to Western readers. This was accomplished in large part through the watershed efforts of Sir William Jones (d. 1794), a pioneering comparative philologist and Orientalist, and a judge and diplomat in the service of the East India Company in Bengal and Calcutta. Mehdi Aminrazavi remarks that it is "nearly impossible to overemphasize the importance of Sir William Jones in transmitting Oriental history and literature to the West" (2014: 3). Through various journals, and later through his collected works, Jones would introduce readers in Britain and North America to a variety of "Oriental" or Eastern philosophies and literatures. He notably translated some of Hafiz's (d. 1390) poetry in "A Persian Song", which was widely circulated in the late eighteenth century. As we will see later on in this chapter, Jones's philological work would help shape Western perceptions of Sufism more broadly, which would then have an effect on Muslim reformers and revivalists.

The poetry of Sufis like Hafiz and Sa'adi would prove an easy match with Romanticism. The Romantics were scholars, artists, and poets who rebelled against the staid rationalism of the Enlightenment, seeking to reconnect with the primal, mysterious, natural, and sublime. They shared a number of concerns with Sufis, including the underlying unity of religions, a passion for seizing the day, venerating beauty, and embracing the mystery of love (Lewisohn 2014: 22–40). Some of these shared concerns were rooted in Platonic philosophy and mysticism, which was a source of inspiration for both Romantics and Sufis. This encounter between Western intellectuals and the poetic culture of Islam in the early nineteenth century would set the stage for an enduring Western interest in Sufi poetry, as evidenced by the popularity of Rumi's poetry in the late twentieth century as we saw previously in Chapter 1. Although it was initially Persian poetry that Westerners were drawn to, later waves of translation would bring Arabic Sufi poetry to enchanted Western readers.

The story of this remarkable intellectual bridge between cultures has a varied history. The colonial era witnessed the widespread horrors of conquest and the destruction of non-Western cultures, but it was also a time of genuine translation, transmission, and transformation between East and West. Although European countries were in a position of power, the flow of influence was not simply West to East, but also East to West. Western engagements with Eastern thought and culture included both those that sought to establish and maintain a power-differential of West over East, by dehumanizing, reducing, and satirizing Eastern cultures, but we also find Western engagements that genuinely sought to translate and transmit Eastern cultural forms, and ultimately seek transformation through them.

Goethe, Romanticism, and the Arts of Translation, Transmission and Transformation

We find one of the best examples of this later sort of engagement with Eastern culture, with one of Germany's greatest literary figures and Romantic intellectuals, Johann Wolfgang von Goethe (d. 1832). For many historians and literati, Goethe represents the peak of modern German literature. His influence on German culture in general is paramount, as illustrated by the fact that the organization established by the German government to promote German language and culture is called the Goethe Institute. He was a poet, novelist, playwright, director, scientist, and statesman. Although he produced a wide-ranging and rich body of written work, Goethe is perhaps best known for his epic play *Faust*.

Among his many interests, Goethe had long been fascinated with Islam. He translated and edited Voltaire's (d. 1778) *La Fanatisme, ou Mahomet le Prophete* (*Fanaticism, or Muhammad the Prophet*) into the German play *Mahomet: Trauerspiel in funf Aufzugen* (*Muhammad: A Tragedy in Five Acts*), first staged in 1800. Prior to this, while in his twenties, Goethe had penned his own play entitled *Mahomet*, which, unlike Voltaire's work, was not a satire on religious imposture, but admired Muhammad's "natural power and sublime beauty" (Einboden 2014). Goethe would later turn this abandoned play of his into a poem entitled *Mahomets-Gesang* (*Song to Muhammad*), which celebrates both the sublimity of the natural world and Muhammad's call to prophetic mission, themes prevalent in the Qur'ān itself. Goethe was a profound admirer of the Islamic tradition as a whole. He understood the term "Islam" in its etymological meaning as a state of submission to God, and hence he famously wrote, *Wenn Islam Gott ergeben heisst, In islam leben und sterben wir Alle!* – "If Islam means submission to God, then we all live and die as Muslims" (Goethe 1819). Goethe was quite taken by the Qur'ān, and his interest in Islam's scripture only seemed to grow as he aged, as evidenced in his many references to it in his letters and poetry.

Goethe was not alone in his admiration of Islam and attraction to Arabic literature and culture. His friend Johann Gottfried Herder (d. 1803) was a fellow Romantic who saw in the Qur'ān a poetic sensibility and sublimity, a sensibility that he theorized had made its imprint on Asian and European poetic traditions. Friedrich Schlegel (d. 1829) similarly looked eastward for inspiration, first drawn to Arabic poetry, before developing a sustained interest in South Asian religion and philosophy, admiringly writing *On the Language and Wisdom of the Indians* in 1808 (Einboden 2014).

It was not until 1812, however, that Goethe would have access to Persian Sufi poetry. It was in that year that Joseph von Hammer-Purgstall (d. 1856), who had previously worked as a translator in the Ottoman court in Istanbul, published his landmark translation of Hafiz's famous work the *Divan*, from its original Persian into German. It is difficult to overestimate the significance of the *Divan* of Hafiz in Islamic cultures more broadly. Shahab Ahmed describes the *Divan* as "the most widely-copied, widely-circulated, widely-read, widely-memorized, widely-recited, widely-invoked, and widely-proverbialized book of poetry in Islamic history" (Ahmed 2016: 31). Hafiz's influence was so wide and deep between the fifteenth and late-nineteenth centuries in the Ottoman, Safavid, Timurid, and Mughal realms, where Muslim elites tended to read Persian, that Leonard Lewisohn describes these "Persianate civilizations of Islamdom" as "Hafizocentric" (Lewisohn 2010: 16). Testifying to the geographical reach of Hafiz's work, Ahmed notes that the two most influential commentaries on his *Divan* were composed in Sarajevo, Bosnia and in Lahore, Pakistan (Ahmed 2016: 32). The *Divan* consists of hundreds of Persian *ghazals* or rhyming couplets, which celebrate wine (real and divine), intoxication, eroticism, and humour, whilst offering a satirical take on the pious, the ascetic, and legalistic authorities in Islam. This charming marriage of spiritual profundity and satire would go on to have a profound influence on Goethe.

Interestingly, Hammer-Purgstall, in his preface to his translation of Hafiz's *Divan*, suggested that he sought less to translate Hafiz for Germans, than to translate Germans for Hafiz. His sentiment proved prescient, as the influence of his German *Divan* would succeed in re-shaping the German (and later American) literary imagination. For his part, Goethe was so taken with Hammer's *Divan* that he began studying Arabic and Persian, and started writing his own *Divan*. Of Arabic, he wrote to a friend, "in no other language, perhaps, is spirit, word and script so primordially bound together" (Einboden 2014: 55). His Arabic and Persian studies, along with his close reading of Hafiz, would lead to his famous *West-ostlicher Divan* (*West-Eastern Divan*), published in 1819. A landmark in the European cultural engagement with Islam, Goethe's work of narrative poetry was interwoven with references to Hafiz, the Qur'ān, and Islamic spirituality in general. Goethe engages in a dialogue with Hafiz in the text as follows, with himself named here as "Poet":

> Poet: Tell me why, Muhammad Shamseddin,
> you are 'Hafiz' to
> worthy folk.

Hafiz:
For asking, you
Merit thanks. I answer, then:
Legacy of the Qur'ān
I unaltered carry on
Hallowed in my memory
And, by acting piously,
Daily every injury
Ward away from me and those
Who the Prophet-word and see
Treasure and their duty heed.
So my name the people chose.

(Einboden 2014: 70)

This short excerpt from Goethe's *Divan* delves first into the meaning of Hafiz's name. *Hafiz* is an Arabic term used to describe one who has memorized the Qur'ān, and hence Goethe unpacks the poet's name by describing this meaning for his readers, further connecting Hafiz's often irreverent poetry to the scripture of Islam, a connection not all Western readers would make. Just as we saw in Chapter 1, where a variety of twentieth century artists found their work transformed by encounters with Rumi's poetry, so in the nineteenth century, we find the work of one of Europe's greatest literary figures transformed by his encounter with Hafiz.

Emerson, Transcendentalists, and Persian Sufi Poetry

Across the Atlantic, just as Goethe's *Divan* was planting Islamic reference and imagery into the soil of German literature, a young Ralph Waldo Emerson's (d. 1882) interests were being drawn eastward. Emerson would become one of America's most famous poets and essayists, and was the central figure of the Transcendentalist movement. With influences as varied as New England Unitarianism, English and German Romanticism, and Indian philosophy, Transcendentalists would popularize metaphysics and mysticism, and preach the virtues of nature, intuition, and individualism. The movement crystalized around Emerson's short work *Nature*, published in 1836, but included among its luminaries Henry David Thoreau (d. 1862) and Margaret Fuller (d. 1850). The interests of the Transcendentalist would coincide with those of the Theosophical movement later in the nineteenth century, both fostering a larger interest in the poetry and philosophy of the Middle East and Asia among North Americans.

Like the German Romantics, Emerson saw in the East an ancient heritage and wisdom, writing at age 17 that, "All tends to the mysterious East" (Ekhtiyar 2014: 55). It would take years however for these seeds of interest to mature, much of which was watered by his encounters with Indian scripture and philosophy, increasingly available in English translation. Starting in his teens Emerson came across Persian poetry, although it was not until he was in his thirties that he would have access to the six volumes of Sir William Jones's collected works, which he borrowed in 1840. Jones's volumes included extensive discussions and translations of Persian Sufi poetry, which clearly only increased Emerson's interest in the subject as the following year he acquired Hammer-Purgstall's German translation of Hafiz's *Divan*, along with an anthology of Persian poetry collected and translated by Hammer-Purgstall (Jahanpour 2014: 118). These German works would cement Emerson's interest in Persian Sufi poetry, particularly that of Hafiz and Sa'adi, an interest that would thenceforth shape his intellectual and literary concerns. Sa'adi in particular had been long known in the West, with his famous *Gulistan* translated into Latin in 1651 and in 1654 it was translated into German. From these early translations later French and English versions of Sa'adi's poetry would emerge. Sa'adi was respected as a poet of fine moral sentiment, and his poetry would prove popular for American audiences in the nineteenth century (Loloi 2014). In his poem *Saadi* (1842), Emerson eulogizes the famous Sufi poet, penning an ode to his uncompromising moral integrity, and highlighting some of the key themes of Sa'adi's poetry:

> O gentle Saadi, listen not,
> Tempted by thy praise of wit,
> Or by thirst and appetite
> For the talents not thine own,
> To sons of contradiction.
> Never, sun of eastern morning,
> Follow falsehood, follow scorning,
> Denounce who will, who will, deny,
> And pile the hills to scale the sky;
> Let theist, atheist, pantheist,
> Define and wrangle how they list, –
> Fierce conserver, fierce destroyer,
> But thou joy-giver and enjoyer,
> Unknowing war, unknowing crime,
> Gentle Saadi, mind thy rhyme.
> Heed not what the brawlers say,
> Heed thou only Saadi's lay.

(Emerson 1842)

From the 1840s onward, Emerson would include his English translations of Hafiz (from Hammer-Purgstall's German), among other Persian poets, in his writings. Altogether he translated around 700 lines of Persian poetry, half of which were by Hafiz (Jahanpour 2014: 128). His interest would culminate in the publication of his article "Persian Poetry" in *The Atlantic Monthly* in 1858. In the article he glowingly describes Hafiz as "the prince of Persian poets", and praises his self-reliance, "audacity", "fluent mind", and uncanny ability to craft "pregnant sentences" (Emerson 1904).

Emerson neatly captures Hafiz's oeuvre, observing that, "Hafiz praises wine, roses, maidens, boys, birds, mornings and music, to give vent to his immense hilarity and sympathy with every form of beauty and joy; and lays the emphasis on these to mark his scorn of sanctimony and base prudence" (Emerson 1904). He continues:

> The other merit of Hafiz is his intellectual liberty, which is a certificate of profound thought. We accept the religions and politics into which we fall, and it is only a few delicate spirits who are sufficient to see that the whole web of convention is the imbecility of those whom it entangles, – that the mind suffers no religion and no empire but its own. It indicates this respect to absolute truth by the use it makes of the symbols that are most stable and reverend, and therefore is always provoking the accusation of irreligion
>
> (Emerson 1904)

Hafiz's humour and love of beauty, his critique of sanctimony and convention, clearly resonated with the core values of the Romantics and Transcendentalists. Hafiz's boldness and self-confidence further resonated with the individualism of these movements, which encouraged people to think and feel for themselves, and trust their own ability to scale the heights of sentiment, intuition, and insight. The following translation of Hafiz by Emerson illustrates this well:

> Oft have I said, I say it once more,
> I, a wanderer, do not stray from myself.
> I am a kind of parrot; the mirror is holden to me;
> What the Eternal says, I stammering say again.
> Give me what you will; I eat thistles as roses,
> And according to my food I grow and I give.
> Scorn me not, but know I have the pearl,
> And am only seeking one to receive it.
>
> (Emerson 1904)

Emerson and the Transcendentalists would have a lasting legacy in North America, contributing to generations of interest in the sublimity of the natural world, self-reliance, free thought, and mysticism.

Jones and the Impact of Orientalism: The Separation of Sufism and Islam

Although Goethe clearly saw the connection between Persian Sufi poetry and Islamic scripture and practice, in general, European Orientalists largely saw Sufism as something separate from Islam, associating Islam more with rigid dogmatism and legalism rather than individualistic and satirical poetry. This separation drawn between Sufism and Islam developed alongside the remarkable discovery of linguistic families, and the racial theories that would later develop based on this discovery. These racial theories would then play a key role in crystalizing the distinction between Sufism and Islam among Orientalists.

Historically, in European and North American contexts, the idea of an "Orient" basically meant "the East" or more broadly the "non-West". "Orientalism" is a term that has been used in various ways, first to describe a form of academic inquiry that was devoted to understanding the languages, cultures, and peoples of the "non-West", and later as a *critical* label for this academic enterprise of studying non-Western peoples, based on the conviction that it was inherently biased, distorting, and harmful. There were a variety of scholars, artists, and government officials who either labelled themselves or were labelled "Orientalist".

Edward Said (d. 2003), a Palestinian-American Professor of Literary Studies and Literary Theory at Columbia University, wrote a watershed book titled *Orientalism* (1978) that would heavily influence a whole generation of scholars, altering the discourse on Orientalism as an academic enterprise. According to Said, Western scholars specializing in "oriental" languages and cultures, though claiming a sort of scientific objectivity, have historically acted – consciously or unconsciously – as handmaidens to empire, by producing knowledge claims based on sweeping generalizations and harmful stereotypes about the Eastern "natives". These generalizations and narratives perpetuated preconceived notions about "more" civilized and "less" civilized peoples.

These Orientalist patterns of representation have provided Western political leaders (that is, the architects and managers of empires and colonies) with habits of thought that make a master-servant relationship with non-Western societies appear justified and even morally desirable. Instead of remaining just academic discourse, Orientalism became a political process of homogenizing thought about Eastern "others", particularly but not exclusively in the Middle East and the Islamic world. One of the ways that Orientalist scholarship affected Western and later Muslim understandings of Sufism, was to effectively separate it from Islam, a separation in part fostered by the work of Sir William Jones.

In 1786 Jones famously gave the third presidential address to the Asiatic Society of Bengal. Jones's address was truly historical, irreversibly altering the way Europeans would see themselves and their relation to other peoples. Having learned to read Sanskrit and Persian (and by his death, almost 30 languages), Jones was struck by an uncanny correspondence between Sanskrit, Persian, and the classical languages of Europe: Greek and Latin. In his address, Jones described:

> The *Sanscrit* language, whatever be its antiquity, is of a wonderful structure; more perfect than the *Greek*, more copious than the *Latin*, and more exquisitely refined than either, yet beating to both of them a stronger affinity, both in the roots of verbs and in the forms of grammar,

than could possibly have been produced by accident; so strong indeed, that no philologer could examine them all three, without believing them to have sprung from some common source, which, perhaps, no longer exists (Masuzawa 2005: 150).

Jones's lecture would spark an interest in the literature of India, and the question of the nature of this "common source" that Jones described. This original source for all of these languages came to be referred to as the Indo-European language, an ancient language from which Indian, Persian, and European languages were thought to derive. What began as a linguistic category however, soon evolved into an anthropological one. In the mid-nineteenth century, European Orientalists began to refer to Sanskrit, Persian, and Greek as belonging to the Indo-European or, more concisely, "Aryan" family of languages. The word "Aryan" was derived from the ancient Persian and Sanskrit *arya*, meaning "noble", a term Persian and Sanskrit speakers used to refer to themselves. Though Jones's discovery could just as easily have led to a sense of humanity's shared history it would evolve into categories of differentiation based on race.

Notably, Wilhelm von Humboldt (d. 1835), a Prussian minister, education reformer, and linguist, hypothesized that a given language was intimately connected with the "race" or "nation" from which it originated. According to Humboldt, a race's mental power was determined by its language, which itself expressed the race's mental possibilities and limitations. Humboldt further suggested that the Indo-European languages presented the best climate for advanced mental formation, and apparently, historical destiny (Dickson 2015: 36–37). In contrast, he believed that the relatively stable grammatical structure of Semitic languages like Arabic and Hebrew reflected the rigidity and dogmatism of Semitic peoples, with the conclusion following that Semitic religions could not but be intolerant, philosophically barren, prone to fanaticism and legalism: none more so than Islam.

If Islam, a quintessentially Semitic religion, was by definition rigid, legalistic, devoid of philosophical sophistication and spiritual profundity, then the remarkable poetry of the Sufis, so beloved by Orientalists, Romantics, and Transcendentalists, could not be Islamic, and must instead be derived from an Aryan source, whether Indian, Greek, or Persian. This belief fostered the separation of Sufism from Islam in the minds of European scholars of the Orient. Jones hence described Sufism as a "metaphysical theology, which has been professed immemorially by a numerous sect of *Persians* and *Hindus*, was carried in part into *Greece*, and prevails even now among the learned *Muselmans*, who sometimes avow it without reserve" (Ernst 1997: 9). The underlying presumption in Jones's statement is that Sufism, like all genuinely creative mysticism and philosophy, is in essence Aryan and hence non-Islamic. This perspective carried the day for sometime among British Orientalists. E. H. Palmer, for instance, in his work *Oriental Mysticism* (1867), argued that Sufism is the "primeval religion of the Aryan race" (Schimmel 1975: 9). This discourse functioned to simultaneously a) distance Islam from the West, as each were thought of as, in essence, composed of fundamentally different peoples, natures, and ideas, and b) to carve out a space for Sufism to be included in the West as an Aryan phenomenon. This racial separation of Sufism from Islam would reinforce a growing sense among Salafi Muslims that Sufism was a foreign interpolation, corrupting the purity and dynamism of Islam as lived by the first generations of Muslims. In what follows we will see how the dynamics of the colonial era would inspire the rise of the Salafi movement and its growing suspicion of Sufism.

COLONIALISM AND THE RISE OF THE SALAFIYYA AND WAHHABIYYA

Although Western analyses of Muslim-majority societies too often frame them as monolithic in their identification with Islam, Muslim societies have traditionally consisted of layers of identity including familial or tribal affiliation, guild or profession, membership in a Sufi order, and ethnicity. As Muslim societies began to modernize however, these tribal, ethnic, religious order, and guild affiliations began to be replaced by the European Enlightenment model of citizenship, where people were more and more conceiving of themselves not as members of a tribe or ethnicity, but as individual citizens of a nation-state. This shift away from communal affiliation would affect how Muslims understood Islam. A new sort of Islam was needed for the modern individual and citizen, and for the nation-state, an Islam that stood in marked contrast to that found within Ottoman or Mughal societies for example, where Islam was embedded within and shaped by various communal networks and tribal or ethnic affiliations. The Islam of these pre-modern societies was dizzying in its diversity, with competing orthodoxies, heresies, and everything in between forming a vast array of religious expression. The new Islam however, would need to eliminate this messy diversity if it were to offer a vision consistent with the homogenizing tendencies of the modern nation-state.

As Muslim states began to adopt European-derived legal codes, national courts staffed by secular elites replaced the local *shari'a* courts run by Muslim jurists. Muslims were increasingly instituting and abiding by laws originating in Westminster and Paris, rather than Medina or Istanbul. Furthermore, as the traditional system of religious endowments that funded the institutions of traditional Islamic learning were nationalized and dismantled, Islamic scholars (known as the *'ulama* or "learned ones"), and jurists (known as the *fuqaha*), began to lose not only their public roles but their institutional basis as well. This marginalization of the Islamic scholars and jurists, although never total, opened up avenues for new forms of religious authority within Islam, forms of authority that were in many cases opposed to Islam's old order. Besides the *'ulama* and their institutions, Islam's old order was most visibly represented by the Sufi lodges and shrines (as will be discussed in Chapter 3), scattered across trade routes and towns, demarcating the sacred geography of Muslim societies. For a growing number of Muslims, this old order was associated with the passivity, decadence, and corruption that allowed for European powers to so handily take over Muslim lands.

If the eighteenth century saw the contraction of Muslim power, the nineteenth century witnessed its complete disintegration. By the early twentieth century, the majority of the Muslim world was under the direct or indirect political rule of European states, and the last remaining Muslim empire, the Ottoman state, collapsed completely following the First World War. This collapse precipitated the division of nearly the entire Middle East into British and French-ruled colonial states. During the height of the colonial era, the British would end up ruling over what are today India, Pakistan and Bangladesh, Malaysia, Nigeria, Sudan, Somalia, Kenya, South Africa, and Jordan. The French would include Algeria, Tunisia, Morocco, Senegal, Mauritania, Mali, Syria, and Lebanon, within their control, while the Dutch took over Indonesia, and Russia dominated the Central Asian republics of Kazakhstan, Turkmenistan, and Uzbekistan (Green 2012: 187). Never before in the history of Islam had Muslims experienced such a total loss of control over their own social and political destinies. The resulting encounter with foreign domination, economic exploitation, and imposed inferiority would inspire a range of responses as Muslims sought to gain independence from European rule, revive Islamic culture, and create modern societies that could compete on the global stage with the West.

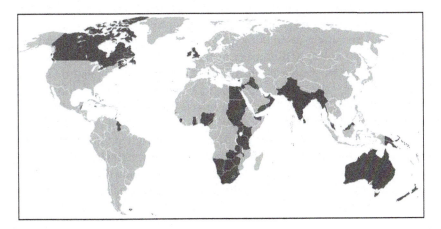

Figure 2.4: The British Empire at its territorial peak in 1921.

The Salafiyya and the Evolution of Opposition to Sufism

Such a state of affairs inspired intellectuals like Jamal al-Din al-Afghani (d. 1897) to call for the simultaneous embrace of European science and technology and the revival of a unified Islamic polity, based on a rational Islam purged of superstition. Al-Afghani's new, streamlined vision of Islam can largely be understood in relation to nineteenth century European discourse on religion, which tended to evaluate religions as either "primitive" or "advanced". Ernest Renan (d. 1892), for example, was an accomplished scholar of Middle Eastern languages and civilization. He was also a leading figure in what Edward Said (d. 2003) would call Orientalism, an approach to the languages and cultures of the East that was intertwined with colonialism and a sense of European superiority. Renan's worldview was shaped by the rationalist trend in European thought. He believed that the spread of the scientific method and rational, critical thinking among Muslims would lead to the demise of religious superstition and ill-founded belief, most notably Sufism.

It is important to point out here that, as previously discussed, European scholars of Islam during this period tended to be impressed by Persian Sufi poetry, but believed that Sufism as a practice had degenerated into a popular cult of saint-veneration, spectacle, and superstition. For Muslims familiar with European thought, Sufism on the ground appeared to be one of the elements of Islamic culture that would need to be purged for a rational, modern Islam to take shape. Hence European scholars played an important role in shaping Muslim perceptions of Sufism, and in some cases Muslim embarrassment of Sufism arose from seeing it through European eyes, as Muslims read European dismissals of superstitious, "wild" or "mad" dervishes (a term that will be discussed in the next chapter).

For European scholars of religion and culture, religions were believed to evolve from primitive superstition and polytheism to increasingly rational, monotheistic theologies in harmony with science (the most advanced religion not surprisingly resembling Protestant Christianity). Faced with the overwhelming power of European technology and influence of European notions of religion, people around the world began to reformulate their own traditions to (a) better reflect European ideas of cultural advancement and (b) to better unify their cultures in response to European domination. For example, Buddhist reformers like Shaku Kozen (d. 1924) proposed reviving the pure message of the historical Buddha, a message purged of superstitious and divisive doctrines and practices. This new, rational, unitary Buddhism would then foster a global Buddhist solidarity and help the Japanese counter European power. Similarly, The Brahmo Samaj was founded in 1828 as a Hindu reform movement, one that "promoted Hinduism as universal, monotheistic, rational, and grounded in the authority of scriptures rather than popular practices" (Knight 2015: 178).

Along the same lines, for al-Afghani, the original Islam of the *salaf* (the pious early generations of Islam) was an eminently rational religion that only needed a reformation to purify it of medieval superstition, and once purified, this original Islam could function as a means of unifying Muslims and countering European domination. Although valuing elements of Sufi spirituality, al-Afghani largely held Sufism responsible for Islam's fall into superstition and corruption. He criticized the Sufis of his day for betraying Islam's rationality, and succumbing to fatalism, passivity, and blind obedience (Sirriyeh 1999: 72). He blamed the success of the Crusades on Sufism's esoteric and mystical emphases, which for al-Afghani, distracted Muslims from social and political activism.

Al-Afghani's antipathy towards elements of Sufism was not simply a response to European perspectives however. Since the seventeenth century, Muslims were increasingly concerned about corruption and abuse within Sufi orders, many of which had become wealthy and powerful as a result of state patronage. During the eighteenth century, Sufis themselves founded movements to purify Sufism of corruption and decadence. As we saw previously in this chapter, many of the Sufi groups involved in the fight against European incursions were simultaneously religious reformers, seeking to ground Sufism more in the Qur'ān, *Sunnah*, and *shari'a*. Although the progenitors of the Salafi movement like al-Afghani saw some elements of Sufism as valuable for developing a reformed Islam (such as a layered understanding of Quranic interpretation and ascetic discipline), the Salafiyya would eventually align with the Wahhabi movement, which would seek not simply to reform Sufism, but to totally remove it from the Islamic tradition.

Al-Afghani's students, Muhammad 'Abduh (d. 1905) and later Rashid Rida (d. 1935), would take up Afghani's revivalist cause, disseminating his ideas in Egypt and throughout the Middle East. 'Abduh, who became the Grand Mufti of Egypt in 1899, favoured a return to the Islam of the *salaf* (the pious early generations of Islam) and criticized Sufi saint veneration and philosophy. Notably, in 1904, 'Abduh published a *fatwa* (ruling) declaring the practice of seeking the intercession (*tawassul*) of a prophet or saint with God to be a harmful innovation in Islam (*bida'a*), one that led to idolatry (*shirk*) (Sirriyeh 1999: 149). *Tawassul* involved prayers asking the Prophet Muhammad or deceased Sufi saints to intercede with God on one's behalf. Although the majority of Sunni scholars had affirmed its permissibility, 'Abduh suggested that this practice was not found among the *salaf* and should be opposed. As *tawassul* was particularly associated with Sufism, 'Abduh's *fatwa* against this practice had important implications for Muslim opinion regarding Sufis in Egypt and the larger Arabic-speaking world. 'Abduh also established the journal *Al-Manar* in 1897, which under the management of Rida, would become one of the premiere venues for the dissemination of Salafi thought.

'Abduh's *fatwa* further drew the Salafiyya closer to the Wahhabi movement in Arabia, a movement that Rida in particular was supportive of.
Founded by Muhammad Ibn 'Abd al-Wahhab's (d. 1792), the Wahhabi
movement, like the Salafiyya, drew inspiration from Ibn Taymiyya's
(d. 1328) thought. Ibn 'Abd al-Wahhab was particularly drawn to the
works of Ibn Taymiyya, which he believed offered a clear paradigm for
purifying Islam of innovation and idolatry. He shared with Ibn Taymiyya a
tendency towards literalism when it came to scripture. Ibn 'Abd al-Wahhab
saw the Qur'ān as a text with obvious meanings (*zahir*) to be understood
and applied, discounting and condemning expositions of the text's hidden,
layered meanings (*batin*) so loved by Sufi interpreters. He viewed Islamic
source texts as, collectively, "an instruction manual to a virtual utopia modelled after the Prophet's city-state in Medina" (Abou el Fadl 2005: 47). This
quest to recreate the purity of the first Muslim community was an absolute
one, requiring the utter condemnation of views, cultures, and persons that
stood as obstacles to the recreation of early Islam. Surveying the religious
practice of his Ottoman-ruled surroundings, he saw Islam's pure monotheism hopelessly compromised by saint-veneration, folk superstitions, and
philosophical Sufism.

Although inspired by Ibn Taymiyya, Ibn 'Abd al-Wahhab would take
his thought in unprecedented directions. Rather than critique and even condemn Muslims in general and Sufis in particular for deviating from the path
of the early Muslims, as Ibn Taymiyya had, Ibn 'Abd al-Wahhab suggested
instead that they had fallen into idolatry (*shirk*) and hence could no longer
be considered Muslims at all. Hence, unlike any previous Sunni thinker,
Ibn 'Abd al-Wahhab rejected Sufism totally, seeking to purge it entirely
from the Islamic tradition. He considered Sufi practices of saint veneration
and intercession to be clear cases of idolatry and unbelief. If the majority
of Muslims were in fact unbelievers, reasoned Ibn 'Abd al-Wahhab, their
blood and property was licit: they could legitimately be fought and killed
as apostates.

With the support of a local ruler, Muhammad Ibn Sa'ud (d. 1765), in
1746 Ibn 'Abd al-Wahhab formally declared a *jihad* against the surrounding Muslims of Arabia. By the early nineteenth century, his followers had
taken over the holy cities of Mecca and Medina, where they promptly
killed their Muslim opponents and continued to destroy Islamic holy sites
they deemed idolatrous. The Ottomans were shocked by the success of the
Wahhabi movement. Most of the Ottoman *'ulama* respected Sufism and in
many cases were Sufis themselves, well-versed in Ibn al-'Arabi's thought.
They condemned the Wahhabis as extremists and heretics. The Wahhabi
seizure of Islam's two holiest sites, the mosques of Mecca and Medina,
forced the Ottomans to act and restore their prestige and the guardians of
Islam. Under Ottoman leadership, an Egyptian army was sent to destroy

the Wahhabi state. Although the state was successfully crushed by 1818, Ibn 'Abd al-Wahhab's ideas had already spread. His simple call to purify Islam of idolatry, restore it to the pristine purity of prophetic monotheism and strict obedience to prophetic norms, resonated with Muslims from North Africa to India, many of whom were already critical of Sufi excesses and corruption.

In general, we find that anti-Sufi polemics were married to Islamic revivalism in various movements throughout the Muslim world in the eighteenth and nineteenth centuries, leading to a growing marginalization of Sufism, as Muslims sought to develop a new, modern Islam that drew upon the religion's ancient roots. Sufis certainly faced a number of challenges during the colonial period, and in some cases experienced the loss of their traditional structures of authority and influence under colonial rule, or were displaced by emerging anti-Sufi movements. However, a number of Sufis embraced the opportunities offered by the introduction of modern technologies into Muslim societies. Just as 'Abduh and Rida disseminated their increasingly anti-Sufi perspectives in print, with their journal *Al-Manar*, Sufis were better able to disseminate their teachings as well, whether by the printing press, which expanded into Muslim societies beginning in the 1820s, or via the new opportunities for transnational networking offered by steam-powered ships and trains, starting in the 1850s (Green 2012: 188). Sufis in many cases were actively involved in the spread of Islam during this period. One noteworthy example of the Sufi role in the revival and expansion of Islam is found in the Sokoto Caliphate of Nigeria, and one of its central leaders, Nana Asma'u.

Nana Asma'u (d. 1864) was a one of West Africa's most important religious teachers and community leaders. She was the daughter of Usman dan Fodio (d. 1817), an Islamic revivalist preacher, Sufi *shaykh* of the Qadiri order, and founder of the Sokoto Caliphate (in present day Nigeria). As we will see in Chapter 4, the Qadiri order has roots in the Islamic preaching of the order's founder, 'Abd al-Qadir al-Jilani (d. 1166). Like al-Jilani, Usman dan Fodio saw himself as tasked with reviving Islam in his age. He preached an integral Islam, one based on the Qur'ān, the *Sunnah* of Muhammad, Islamic law, and the practices and doctrines of the Sufi path. He was a close student of the works of the medieval synthesizers of the Sufi tradition, Abu Hamid al-Ghazali (d. 1111) and Muhyi al-Din Ibn al-'Arabi (d. 1240), both of whom will be considered at length in Chapter 4 (Mack 2015: 190).

His scholarly and saintly renown was such that he became known simply as the Shehu or *shaykh*. The dan Fodios were a family of religious scholars in the Fulani clan, in a region dominated by Hausa rulers. Although the local Hausa kings were Muslim, dan Fodio openly preached against their corruption, abuse of the poor, and deviance from *Sunnah*. As a result, dan Fodio and his family were exiled in 1804. The Shehu envisaged his task like that of the Prophet Muhammad's: to first escape the oppression of those resisting the establishment of Islam, and to then fight to secure a realm safe for the religion's practice. To this end dan Fodio launched what would become known as the Sokoto Jihad, a struggle against local pagan and Muslim rulers to eradicate corruption and idolatry, and to establish the teaching and practice of Islam in what is now north-western Nigeria.

Like her father, Asma'u was well-versed in the breadth of the Islamic tradition, including the Qur'ān, which she had memorized as a child, the sayings of the Prophet Muhammad (*hadith*), and in the doctrines and practices of the Sufi path. She was fluent in the local Hausa, Fulfulde, and Tamachek languages, as well as Arabic (Helminski 2003: 137). Although traditions of Islamic scholarship were frequently the preserve of men, the dan Fodio family made sure that male and female members alike were thoroughly educated. Her father set an important precedent for African Muslim women, in critiquing the cultural resistance to female education in the region (Mack 2015: 192).

Counting her father and grandmother among her teachers, Asma'u was tutored in the many hand-written books that the dan Fodio family carried with them in goat skin satchels. She would eventually become a well-known religious scholar, holding popular classes for both men and women. Increasingly Asma'u would draw students from all over the region, particularly women, who knew they had a welcoming but rigorous teacher they could approach. Although women did not customarily travel alone, Asma'u argued that they should be allowed to do so for the sake of religious study (Helminski 2003: 139).

Educating women would become one of her lifelong causes. For those women who could not travel due to the demands of marriage and young children, Asma'u pioneered a distance education model, whereby she personally trained older women and younger girls (those without family duties) in a series of religious lessons including Qadiri Sufi values and the basics of Islamic doctrine and practice. These women, known as the *'Yan Taru* ("The Associates") would then travel in small groups to remote rural areas, bringing education to women who would otherwise be totally isolated from such opportunities. Asma'u's reputation for learning grew, and she comfortably engaged with other, usually male, scholars of renown across Africa. Asma'u's *'Yan Taru* model of distance education outlived not only herself, but the Sokoto Caliphate itself. This model of travelling religious educators remains active in contemporary West Africa, still utilized by Qadiri women (Mack 2015: 194).

She was also famous for her poetry, written in Hausa, Fulfulde, and Arabic, which elegantly expressed religious teachings, the history of her family and the Sokoto movement, her grief over lost loved ones, and her longing for God. In the following excerpt of her poem *Tawassuli Ga Mata Masu Albarka*, she eulogizes famous Sufis, and particularly Sufi women, for the inspiration they provide in her own life:

> My aim in this poem is to tell you about Sufis
> To the great ones I bow in reverence.
> I am mindful of them while I am still alive
> So that they will remember me on the Day of Resurrection.
> The ascetic women are all sanctified
> For their piety they have been exalted...
> I remind you how they yearn for God.
> I swear by God that I love them all
> In the name of the Prophet, the Messenger of God.
> The scent of their yearning engulfs me.

(Helminski 2003: 140–41)

In the poem, Asma'u continues to describe the virtues of the Prophet's mother, wives, and daughters, as well as female Sufi figures from early and later periods of Islamic history. Asma'u herself would become an exemplar in her time of female piety, learning, mystical acumen, and communal leadership. She further illustrates how the spread and inculcation of Islam during this period was frequently indivisible from Sufi spirituality: Sufism and Islam were not seen here as two separate categories, but as a single, integral, phenomenon.

As we will see in Chapter 3, Sufism was intimately integrated into the Ottoman, Safavid, and Mughal empires, from their royal heights to the poor back alleys and streets wandered by mendicant bards. It was only with the decline of these empires that Sufism's place in Muslim societies was more easily challenged by the Salafi and Wahhabi movements, leading in many contexts to the emergence of a new sort of Islam with little memory of its Sufi roots. These Sufi roots, however forgotten they might be today, remain embedded across Muslim lands in the various shrines, poems, palaces, miniature paintings, folk songs and stories, that marked the multivalent culture of the Ottoman, Safavid, and Mughal empires.

Discussion Questions:

1. How did 'Abd al-Qadir al-Jazai'ri's life manifest his spiritual practice and philosophical perspective?
2. Briefly summarize the Salafi critiques of Sufism, and Sufi responses to these critiques, as discussed in this chapter.
3. What did Western Romantics find so appealing about Sufi poetry?
4. What is Orientalism and why did the Orientalists see Sufism as something separate from Islam?
5. How do the dynamics of the colonial era shape contemporary Sufism?

Further Reading:

Aminrazavi, M. (ed.). (2014). *Sufism and American Literary Masters*. Albany, NY: State University of New York Press.

Boyd, J., & Mack, B. (2013). *Educating Muslim Women: The West African Legacy of Nana Asma'u (1793–1864)*. Oxford: Interface.

Chodkiewicz, M. (1995). *The Spiritual Writings of Amir 'Abd al-Kader*. Albany, NY: State University of New York Press.

Kiser, J. W. (2008). *Commander of the Faithful: The Life and Times of Emir Abd el-Kader*. Rhinebeck, NY: Monkfish Book Publishing.

Lings, M. (1993). *A Sufi Saint of the Twentieth Century: Shaikh Ahmad al-'Alawi, His Spiritual Heritage and Legacy*. Cambridge: The Islamic Texts Society.

Said, Edward W. (1978). *Orientalism*. New York: Random House.

Sirriyeh, E. (2013 [1999]). *Sufis and Anti-Sufis: the Defence, Rethinking and Rejection of Sufism in the Modern World*. New York: Routledge.

3

COMMANDING SULTANS TO WANDERING
DERVISHES: SUFISM IN THE LATE MEDIEVAL ERA

The reign of Selim I (d. 1520) marked a watershed in the Ottoman Empire's remarkable history. Under Selim's capable and uncompromising leadership, the Ottomans would nearly triple their territorial holdings. With the defeat of the Mamluks the Ottomans came to rule the heartland of Islam: Egypt, Syria, and the Two Holy Cities of Mecca and Medina in Arabia. Selim strengthened the Ottoman claim to the caliphate, forcing the last 'Abbasid Caliph in Cairo, al-Mutawakkil III (d. 1543), to surrender the Prophet Muhammad's sword and mantle, important symbols of caliphal authority. Selim's remarkable conquests would set the stage for the Ottoman Empire's pinnacle under Sulayman the Magnificent (d. 1566).

Notably, after defeating a Mamluk army in Syria in 1516, Selim and his army rode into the ancient city of Damascus. Of the various sites he would visit in the city, one in particular would have seemed strange to local observers. In a small family cemetery near Mount Qaissoun on the city's outskirts, the fearsome conqueror humbly paid his respects to a little known tomb. It was the grave of Sufi saint and philosopher Muhyi al-Din Ibn al-'Arabi (d. 1240). After completing his conquest of the Mamluks, Selim would return to Damascus in 1517. This time he would commission the building of a mosque next to Ibn al-'Arabi's tomb. The new mosque was opened with great ceremony, indicating a renewed public recognition of Ibn al-'Arabi. Long a figure of controversy, even considered by some to be Islam's greatest heretic, Ibn al-'Arabi was venerated by Ottoman elites as one of Islam's greatest saints and scholars. In 1534, the Ottomans released a *fatwa* (religious decree) that "henceforth the works of Ibn 'Arabi should be officially studied throughout Ottoman lands" (Hirtenstein 1999: 242). Sufism's foremost metaphysician now had the official endorsement of Islam's most powerful, expansive, and long lasting dynasty. As a result, Ibn al-'Arabi's works – reviled in many conservative contexts – would now be widely studied and commented upon throughout the Ottoman realm, and his philosophy of the radical oneness of existence and the perfectibility of the human being would infuse the heart of the Muslim world.

Alongside the Ottomans, powerful Muslim empires like the Safavids in Persia and the Mughals in South Asia secured a realm in which various forms of Sufism could flourish and clash. In contrast to the previous chapter, where we saw Muslim empires collapsing and artistic and intellectual expressions of Sufism finding their way into the European consciousness, in this chapter we will explore how Sufism's manifold expressions permeated every corner of Muslim cultural life between the fifteenth and eighteenth centuries, a period later historians would refer to as the height of the "gunpower empires". Unlike the colonial period wherein Sufism's place in Islam came under concerted challenge, most Muslims during this era would not have thought of what we now call "Sufism" as being anything different from Islam itself.

Although Sufism was basically accepted as a natural part of Muslim life, the forms in which Sufism was expressed were highly contested. In the first section of this chapter, we will see that the Ottomans, Safavids, and Mughals all patronized forms of Sufi literature, sacred Sufi shrines, and Sufi orders themselves. Courtly life in these dynasties was imbued with the artistic aesthetics of Sufism. Commissioning, erecting, and preserving sacred buildings to honour the legacy of Sufi saints, rulers sought to show reverence and receive divine blessings (*baraka*). Specific holy sites venerating particular Sufi personalities would become places of homage. Many imperial leaders were known for visiting Sufi shrines and gleaning advice from Sufi Masters. Sufis as advisers would influence imperial culture and life. Particular Sufi orders would gain recognition and legitimacy due to their relations with the imperial courts, even the process of governing would be impacted.

Sufism, however, would take many forms in these empires – not all of which fit within the confines of the conventions, courtesies, intrigues, and hierarchies of courtly life. In contrast to the Sufism of imperial elites, in this chapter we will further delve into the far more marginal and mysterious world of the Sufi dervish, the wandering holy mystics that formed such a celebrated part of Muslim life in this era. In the third section of this chapter, we see how these various strands of Sufism come together in the shared sacred space offered by the Sufi shrines. Shrines were the homes of dervishes, sites of legitimation for sultans, pilgrimage destinations for Muslims seeking healing, blessing, intercession and the nearness to God offered by the saint's presence. We end the chapter describing how Sufism would influence the development of cities devoted to saints and a network of Sufi guilds would help these cities flourish in trade, commerce, the arts and sciences.

SULTANS, SHAHS AND SUFIS:
POLITICS IN THE LATE MEDIEVAL ERA

In stark contrast to the situation today – where commentators, both Muslim and non-Muslim, frequently dismiss Sufism as a marginal heresy that can be passed over when considering Islam – between the fifteenth and eighteenth centuries, Sufism *was* Islam, in its officially sanctioned forms, its popular cultural expressions, and in its philosophical articulations. Expressions of Islam that we now call Sufi were simply assumed to be normative aspects of a way of life shaped by the Qur'ān. In particular, the official Islam of the imperial courts, and the Islam invoked by imperial rulers to legitimize their rule, was generally Sufi in orientation.

Some of Islamic civilization's most powerful dynasties could only function as legitimately Islamic by paying homage to Sufi saints, whether living or dead, either through supporting Sufi orders or visiting and endowing Sufi shrines. The politics of ruling as a Muslim at this time simply assumed interacting with representatives of Islam, which included both authorities in Islamic law and the bearers of Islamic spirituality. Although a variety of dynastic formations crystalized and dissolved during this rich period of cultural creativity, three proved to have the most significant and long lasting influence on the Islamic world more generally. These three, the Ottomans, Safavids, and Mughals, are the subjects of our consideration here, in exploring the ways in which Sufis and sultans functioned most frequently in relationships of mutuality, though in some cases as we will see, in open conflict with each another. As the historian Marshall Hodgson observes:

> The age of the sixteenth and seventeenth centuries was one of the greatest in Islamdom's history. The artistic, philosophic, and social power and creativeness of the age can be symbolized in the spaciousness, purity – and overwhelming magnificence of the Taj Mahall at Agra (1974: 14).

The Taj Mahal remains a global symbol of Muslim architectural achievement and of love, as Shah Jahan (d. 1666) built the magnificent mausoleum as an architectural ode to his beloved, Mumtaz Mahal (d. 1631). It is a UNESCO World Heritage Centre and widely considered a "wonder of the world". In general, the cultural and artistic achievements of this era endure to the present, and are embodied in some of the most iconic structures produced by Islamic civilization.

The Ottoman Empire and Prominent Sufi Orders

There is no easy way to characterize the Sufis of the Ottoman Empire. This is largely because the various Sufi orders that flourished in the Ottoman realm occupied every conceivable strata of Ottoman society. In fact, particular orders came to be closely associated with different social groups, so much so that one could largely guess someone's Sufi affiliation based on their class or professional affiliation. To illustrate this fascinating dynamic of Ottoman society, we will explore three Sufi orders, in some cases quite different in orientation: the Mevleviyya, Bektashiyya, and Naqshbandiyya.

As we saw in Chapter 1, Rumi's poetry transcends time and place, having a popular appeal not only among medieval Muslims, but even for contemporary North Americans. Although less well-known in the West, Rumi's teachings also formed the foundation of a spiritual path. Following a pattern common throughout the medieval Muslim world, the disciples and descendants of Rumi formed a Sufi order maintaining the practices and spiritual discipline of their master. What would later become key practices of the Mevlevi order, including the whirling dance, sending new disciples to serve in the kitchen, and even the style of hat worn by Mevlevis, are traceable to statements and practices of Rumi and Shams, although they would crystallize in particular ways due to later influences.

As the Mevlevi order developed in the Ottoman Empire, it became increasingly associated with the cultural, intellectual, and political elite. Whereas some Sufi orders had an almost entirely rural basis, the Mevlevi order was found primarily in urban centres such as Istanbul, Damascus, and Konya, and was popular amongst rulers, musicians, writers, and scholars.

It was Rumi's son, Sultan Walad, who would codify Rumi's teachings into an order, establishing the Mevlevi authority structure by normalizing the positions of deputy (*nayeb*), and successor (*khalife*). Early records indicate that representatives of the Mevlevi order were required to be familiar with the order's terminology, wear the order's distinct clothing, as well as maintain piety and good manners (Lewis 2000: 425).

Sultan Walad further established a precedent in setting up the order's activities in Konya with state patronage. Later Mevlevi teachers would spread the order to other towns and cities in Seljuk and later Ottoman-ruled Anatolian peninsula, and in doing so, would seek patronage arrangements from the aristocracy and local governors. Official endowments from Ottoman sultans, including Bayezid II (d. 1512) and Murad III (d. 1595), funded a growing network of Mevlevi lodges. Eventually there were 14 large Mevlevi *tekkes* established in the cities of the Ottoman Empire, with 76 smaller lodges set up in provincial towns.

Mevlevi leaders became closely associated with Ottoman rulers, and eventually the head of the order would appoint leaders for each Mevlevi lodge with the approval of the highest religious authority in the Ottoman realm, the *shaykh al-islam*, as well as the Ottoman sultan (Lewis 2000: 426). It is interesting to note that due to its popularity Mevlevis were even given the privilege of anointing new Ottoman sultans with the ceremonial sword.

With the weight of official ceremony and elite culture, the Mevlevi order spread throughout the Ottoman realm. The Sufi order based on Rumi's teachings then, was important to the development of culture in the Ottoman Empire. Lewis writes, "the Mevlevi lodges came to function as a kind of art academy or cultural centre, as well as places for the practice of Mevlevi rituals" (2000: 426). When the study of Persian was forbidden in Turkish schools, Mevlevi lodges became study centres for Persian literature. It was during this period (the sixteenth and seventeenthcenturies), that the great Mevlevi commentaries on Rumi's *Mathnavi* were written, usually under the influence of Ibn al-'Arabi's school of thought. Rumi's mystical poetry was largely interpreted using Ibn al-'Arabi's mystical philosophy. By the nineteenth century, the Mevlevi order could be found in Anatolia, Syria, Egypt and Iraq.

While few questioned the Sunni orthodoxy of the Mevlevi order, the veneration of the Prophet's immediate family members by followers of the Bektashi order led many to consider them to be more Shi'a in orientation.[1] Traced to Haji Bektash Wali (d. 1337), the Bektashiyya began as a religious movement among frontier Turkish tribes. They integrated a number of Shi'a elements in their devotions. Bektashis celebrate the Shi'a holidays of Ashura and Nevruz, and recite poems and hymns in honour of the Prophet's family and the 12 Shi'a Imams of the *Ithna 'Ashari* or "Twelver" Shi'a sect. Frances Trix recorded an Albanian prayer from her Bektashi teacher Baba Rexheb (d. 1995) as follows:

> O Lord Most High!
> May your salvation and peace be upon the light of Muhammad, Ali, Fatima, Khadija, Hasan, and Husayn.
> And upon their holy descendants: Imam Zayn al-'Abidin, Imam Muhammad Baqir, Imam Ja'far al-Sadiq, upon Imam Musa Kazim, Imam Ali Riza, Imam Muhammad Taqi, Imam Ali Naqi, Imam Hasan 'Askari, and Imam Muhammad Mahdi.
> That all be remembered throughout life,
> And Your salvation be upon them all, Amin!
>
> (Trix 2009: 16)

1. The term Shi'a comes from the Arabic term *Shi'at 'Ali*, which means the "party" or "faction" of 'Ali, referring to the Muslims who believed that Prophet Muhammad had designated his cousin and son-in-law 'Ali as his successor. In Islam's early period, this movement of supporting 'Ali as the Muslim community's rightful leader developed into a sect that believed that religious and political authority were joined in the person of the *imam*. The *imam* is believed by Shi'a Muslims to be a divinely appointed guide for Muslims, beginning with 'Ali, and being passed on through his bloodline to his sons Hasan, then Husayn, and on through their descendants. The majority of Shi'a Muslims believe that the twelfth *imam* Muhammad al-Mahdi went into occultation in 941 CE and will return to earth prior to the return of Jesus. Ismaili Muslims believe that the *imams* continue to this day, with their leader the Aga Khan the current *imam*.

Alongside their Shi'a leaning, the Bektashis embraced the metaphysics of oneness expounded by Ibn al-'Arabi (described in further detail in the following chapter) and the sensibility of the *Qalandariyya* or mendicant dervishes (whom we will discuss later in this chapter). This varied mix of influences fostered an order rich with poetry, philosophy, and humour. The Bektashis were particularly influential in spreading Islam among the predominantly Christian populations of the Balkans, under Ottoman rule. Bektashi lodges hence took root in countries like Albania, Kosovo, and Macedonia. Christian influences are thus not entirely surprising, and may include the celibacy practiced by many Bektashi leaders or *babas* (a term meaning "father", commonly used as an honorific for a Sufi *shaykh* or saint), and the use of candles and religious icons in Bektashi tekkes or lodges, as well as the ritual use of wine. In general, Bektashis tended to understand Islamic norms as prohibiting drunkenness, not drink.

The order would, until the nineteenth century, be further well established in the centres of Ottoman power. Their affiliation with the special forces of the Ottoman military, the fearsome Janissaries, gave the Bektashis an official sanction in the increasingly Sunni-oriented Ottoman Empire they might not otherwise have had. This official sanction did not last, however; eventually the Janissaries were disbanded after multiple rebellions, some in response to pressures from Ottoman sultans to modernize the military. Finally in 1826 Sultan Mahmud II (d. 1839) used modern military technology to quash a Janissary rebellion, after which he outlawed the Bektashi order, executing some of its leaders and destroying Bektashi lodges or giving them to Sufi orders favoured by the sultan, such as the Naqshbandis, whose reputation for Sunni orthodoxy stood in marked contrast to that of the Bektashis (Trix 2009: 28). The Bektashi order would regroup however, and establish itself extensively throughout Albania in particular.

Unlike the Bektashi Sufis, whose often syncretistic practices were usually associated with a *bi-shar'*, "without religious law" position, the Naqshbandis were regarded as exemplars of a *ba-shar'*, "with the religious law", orientation (Frembgen 2008: 37). The Naqshbandis have long had a self-conception of being an order apart from the others. Within the Ottoman Empire, the Naqshbandis became highly regarded for their rigorous *shari'a* adherence, their claim to a superior spiritual method, and their transmission of Sufi literature. As noted in the introduction to this chapter, the Ottomans were particularly drawn to Ibn al-'Arabi. The Naqshbandis developed a reputation for expertise in the great *shaykh's* works, and this seems to have been one of the reasons why Ottoman sultans starting in the fifteenth century would extend invitations to Naqshbandi teachers to settle in Ottoman lands, build Naqshbandi centres, and commission Naqshbandi teachers to write commentaries on Ibn al-'Arabi's works (Le Gall 2005: 35).

More than many other Sufi orders, the Naqshbandi drew members from the *'ulama*, the class of jurists that shaped Islamic law and orthodoxy. This gave them an influence on key figures in the Ottoman religious hierarchy. Their strong orthodox credentials were highly consonant with official Ottoman claims to uphold Sunni orthodoxy, not only against internal subversion by heterodox groups but also in the larger confrontation with the Shi'a Safavid Empire to the east.

Notably, the Naqshbandi order maintains its lineage to the Prophet Muhammad (d. 632) through Abu Bakr (d. 634), in contrast to all other Sufi orders that trace their lineage through the Prophet's cousin and son-in-law 'Ali (d. 661). This *Bakri* lineage gives the Naqshbandis an emphatically Sunni orientation, as Abu Bakr's successorship to Muhammad is rejected by Shi'a Muslims and hence Abu Bakr is not venerated and even disparaged in non-Sunni traditions (Weismann 2007: 24). Given the Ottoman Empire's protracted conflict with the Safavids, the strong Sunni lineage of the Naqshbandis appealed to Ottoman elites, especially as they began to articulate their Sunni identity in opposition to their Shi'a rivals for Islamic leadership.

Safavids: Shi'as and Sufis

Religious and cultural solidarities made the Ottoman Empire a potent historical force, and yet these strengths also brought limitations. The centrality of Sunni orthodoxy in defining the Empire's identity and political legitimacy invited challenges from alternative currents of Islamic belief, from movements founded on different formulations of Shi'ism. The foundational role of Turkish peoples also imposed limits, and left imperial legitimacy open to contestation by those who were capable of harnessing non-Turkish identities to larger political projects.

Such was the case in lands once occupied by the pre-Islamic Persian Empire, where a charismatic religious and political movement succeeded in harnessing both Shi'a beliefs and latent Persian identity to create the Safavid Empire. From its inception, the new Safavid Empire was defined in opposition to the Ottoman status quo. Even though the movement itself arose from the predominantly Turkic region of Azerbaijan in what is today modern Iran, it found strength in the revival of Persian culture and in strongly articulated ideological opposition to the Sunni orthodoxy promulgated by the Ottoman court.

At the centre of this new movement was a man known as Shah Ismail (d. 1524), himself a member of a Sufi *tariqa* that had taken on esoteric Shi'a doctrines. In addition to his status as a political leader with expansive territorial ambitions, Ismail also grounded his authority in the charismatic traditions of the Safavi Sufi order, within which he was known as *Murshid-e kamil* (the perfect Sufi master). Upon attaining power, Ismail sought to universalize and institutionalize his order's beliefs, completely displacing Sunnism in the lands over which he gained control and harnessing Shi'a beliefs as a basis for political power. The result was an empire whose underpinnings were deeply opposed to the religious and political ideology of the Sunni Ottoman Empire, and the genesis of one of the most profound sectarian and political rivalries in Muslim history.

The Safavid transformation of Persia's religious landscape was sweeping. Ismail imposed strict adherence to the Shi'a creed and forced religious authorities to stress the Shi'a understanding of 'Ali as the rightful successor to Muhammad. This assertion of a Shi'a historical-political narrative was accompanied by a pointed critique (some would say demonization) of the Prophet's companions who were seen to have usurped 'Ali's rightful authority. Loyalty to the Imams, the divinely guided descendants of the Prophet, was also emphasized.

Despite the Safavid's Sufi origins, the new order was inhospitable to traditional Sunni forms of Sufi practice. Some of the new pilgrimage destinations associated with the Imams were themselves once shrines to deceased Sufi leaders, and the persistence of fully public and organized Sufi orders was seen as a threat to the new religious and political order. Ismail therefore sought to disempower the Sunni Sufi *tariqas* by exiling or executing their leaders, closing their places of worship (*khanaqahs*) and rescinding their endowments (Hodgson 1974: 23). Sufi beliefs and practices were either forced underground or adapted in ways consistent with the new Shi'a context. Sufi poetry, in particular, provided a medium for the persistence of Sufi culture, offering a framework within which individuals could negotiate between Sufi devotion and the new demands of Shi'a devotion. As Hodgson notes, the new religious landscape was marked by both transformation and continuity:

> On the level of folk religion, one can generalize the effects of the victory of the Shi'ah by saying that the (Shi'i) tragic drama of the world's history, with its coming finale where all would be righted, gradually replaced the Sufi mystical quest of the soul's love for God, with its exemplification in a hierarchy of saints. Of course, such a replacement took place at most only in the public framework of the religious imagination. The Sufi world image continued valid not only for those who would be personally mystics by temperament, but at least as a component in many persons' reading of the Shi'i world image (1974: 35).

The paradox of publicly mandated change and continuity at the level of folk religion can be seen quite clearly in practices of pilgrimage and saint veneration. In many cases, Sufi *khanaqahs* were replaced with *imamzadahs*, tombs of saintly descendants of an *imam*. At such locations, the Sufi saints were no longer the intercessors for prayer, but rather the *imams* and their descendants. Sufi rituals of celebrating the *mawlid* ceremonies of Sufi saints were replaced with mourning commemoration for *imams*. Such changes were by no means insubstantial, and yet the continued use of these pilgrimage sites as centres for popular spirituality enabled past traditions to persist. In some cases, the new *imamzadahs*, as in the Shah Cheragh shrine of Shiraz, the custodians of the site were associated not just with Shi'a religious learning but also with a Sufi *tariqa* that had adjusted to new Safavid reality.

Synthesis between Shi'a doctrines and Sufi metaphysics also occurred within the Safavid Empire's new religious institutions. Esoteric doctrine from classical Sufi synthesizers (a subject addressed in the next chapter) would be transformed in ways compatible with Shi'a exoteric orthodoxy, with the restructured Sufi teachings presented as acceptable forms of *irfan*, or gnosis. Whereas *ma'rifa* is a form of knowledge within Sufism that results from the engagement with Sufi practices under the guidance of a qualified *shaykh*, usually within the context of a lineage and order, *irfan* is a form of knowledge developed by an individual engaged in a philosophical as well as spiritual pursuit of truth.

Although the immediate impact of Ismail on Persian Sufism was disruptive, greater accommodation of the Sufi impulse occurred in subsequent generations. At the height of the Safavid Empire, under the imperial court of Shah Abbas, Sufism would experience a renaissance in cosmopolitan cities such as Isfahan and Shiraz. Like Suleyman in the Ottoman Empire (1520–1566), Shah Abbs I (1587–1629) presided over a time of great cultivation in the arts and sciences. Under his patronage and protection, esoterically oriented thinkers sought to harmonize systems of knowledge derived from Sufism with "illuminationist" philosophical traditions and Shi'a theological doctrines concerning the indispensable role of the *imams* in the quest for spiritual reality. Being protected by the court allowed scholars such as Mir Damad (d. 1631) and his student Mullah Sadra (d. 1640) to synthesize and preserve as well as develop and transform past elements of Persian and Islamic Sufi heritage, creating new traditions that henceforth took a central place in spiritual culture. Persian poetry from the pre-Safavid era experienced a rebirth of popularity, and works such as the Sufi-inflected compositions of Hafiz of Shiraz took on heightened prominence in courtly as well as popular culture. At the same time, related currents of philosophical, poetic, and artistic tradition were finding a welcome reception in Sunni imperial courts to the west and east, in Ottoman as well as Mughal lands.

The Mughal Empire and Sufism in South Asia

Sufism was also a defining element of the Islamic experience in South Asia, and was central to courtly life as well as popular devotion during the time of the Mughal Empire (1526–1858). Debates concerning the proper understanding of Sufism and its relation to Islamic orthodoxy as well as to the terms of interfaith coexistence had profound consequences. All of the early Mughal rulers, from Babur (d. 1530) to Aurangzeb (d. 1707), took Sufism for granted as a key element of Islamic spirituality and culture. Particular "readings" of Sufism often diverged, however, with consequences that persist and continue to shape South Asian realities in the present day.

When Babur founded the Mughal Empire in 1526, Sufism was already present in the northern Indian lands that he conquered – lands that had previously been ruled by Muslim as well as Hindu kings. Although his reign in these new lands was brief, Babur was known to visit the mausoleums of great Sufi personalities from the Chishtiyya Sufi order, especially Nizam al-Din Awliya (d. 1375) and Qutb al-Din Bakhtiyar Kaki (d. 1235) in the city of Delhi. Nasir al-Din Humayun (d. 1556), the son of Babur, manifested a similar respect for Sufi saints and institutions, as well as a passion for "mysticism, magic, and astrology" (Schimmel 2004: 28). When Humayun triumphantly returned from a period of exile in Persia to establish Delhi as the Mughal imperial capital, this city became for Indian Muslims a spiritual capital as well.

Arguably the most iconic of Mughal rulers, Humayun's son Jalal al-Din Akbar (d. 1605), cultivated not just the image of a great political leader but also that of a spiritual seeker. Following in the example of his father and grandfather, Akbar was known for making pilgrimage to Sufi holy sites, such as the tomb of Khwaja Mu'in al-Din Chishti (d. 1236), the founder of the Chishti Sufi order. One story states that Akbar, after the death of his twins, went to seek guidance from the Sufi holy man, Salim Chishti (d. 1572), who lived near Agra. During that visit Salim Chishti foreshadowed the coming of another child. Due to Akbar's gratitude and reverence, he named the child Salim after the Chishti master. This child would later be known as Jahangir, an honorific title which means "Seizer of the World". Fatepur Sikri, a small, elaborate city of monuments and shrines, was also built in honour of Salim Chishti and his shrine is still situated in the heart of the city today (see Figure 3.7). The city remains one of the best-preserved examples of Mughal architecture.

Sufism and Persian Miniatures

Figure 3.1: Miniature by the Hindu painter Bichitr of *Jahangir Preferring Sufi Shaykh to Kings.*

Despite the prohibition of figurative painting or sculpture in some of Islam's legal schools, Islam has its own venerable tradition of figurative art, generally referred to as "Persian miniatures", a tradition that began in the thirteenth century, and came to fruition in the fifteenth and sixteenth centuries, influencing Ottoman, Safavid, and Mughal art. Persian miniatures were paintings in illustrated books of poetry. Although figurative art was prohibited in copies of the Qur'ān, this prohibition did not extend to other books, including collections of tales, history, and poetry.

After the Mongol invasions devastated much of Islam's Eastern and Central lands, the Mongols converted to Islam. To establish themselves as legitimate Muslim rulers, they patronized Islamic art, culture, and spirituality, funding the building of mosques, schools, and commissioning the writing of religious and historical works. In Persian societies, the new Mongol rulers commissioned the writing of great historical epics, documenting the history of pre-Islamic Persian kings, the Islamic caliphate, and their own rule. Copies of these historical works, such as the *Jami' al-Tawarikh* or "Compendium of Chronicles", which date from the early fourteenth century, remain in museums and they are richly illustrated, early examples of what would later be known as Persian miniatures. Over time, later dynasties would support the development of miniature painting in further historical chronicles and books of poetry, raising the level of sophistication, detail, and beauty in these works.

The miniature, *Jahangir Preferring Sufi Shaykh to the Kings*, by the Hindu painter Bichitr (d. circa 1700), thought to have been painted in 1625, is a great example of Sufism and empire. In it, Jahangir is being visited by four individuals in order of significance to Jahangir: a holy man, an Ottoman Sultan, King James I of England, and Bichitr the artist himself. In this miniature, the Mughal emperor hands the Sufi Hasan Chishti a devotional text. It is with the dervish, not the rulers, that the emperor is interacting. By painting the Sufi *shaykh* at the level of the Emperor, Bichitr is commenting on Jahangir's spiritual inclinations and the influence Sufism had on the Mughal imperial court and life. Sultans often consulted Sufi teachers as spiritual and political advisers. At times, Sultans would use relationships with respected Sufi saints to legitimize their rule, the saint's *baraka* (or blessing) sought both as divine security and to religiously legitimize secular rule. The Emperor also has a large halo surrounding him, representing the sun of wisdom, or the divine, with the crescent moon upholding the halo representing the royal soul, in its capacity to reflect the sun's light. The minature also shows a European influence, with European-style angels, and some details of the figures depicted. This miniature painting then, is a product of a Hindu artist, commissioned by a Muslim ruler, reflecting Persian, Turkish, Indian, and European influences.

Said to be unlettered (*ummi*) like the Prophet Muhammad, Akbar took an immense interest in spiritual matters and often instructed his advisers to read to him from Sufi manuscripts in his library. He was often seen engaging in forms of contemplative worship, and was believed by some to have access to divinely revealed insight (*kashf*) and knowledge (*'ilm al-laduni*). Akbar's passion for religion and spiritual pursuits was a well-known part of his persona:

> Around 1575 Akbar was beginning to feel more secure in his power and had, at last, the opportunity to come into closer contact with religious ascetics, more specifically with the disciples of the late Mu'in ad-Din Chishti of Ajmer, and to spend more time discussing religion to them. He would spend whole nights in religious discussion and worship, 'and from a feeling of thankfulness for his past successes he would sit many a morning alone in prayer and meditation on a large flat stone of an old building which lay near the palace in a lonely spot, with his head over his chest, gathering the bliss of the early hours of dawn' (Wink 2009: 97).

Akbar's engagement with mysticism has given rise to much folklore, but it was his engagement with matters of interfaith relations and theology that has had the greatest – and most controversial – impact on his legacy. Both as the ruler of a multi-religious empire and as a seeker of spiritual truth, Akbar quite necessarily took interest in the diverse doctrines and teachings of his subjects. His approach to these matters, however, has been a subject of intense debate for centuries, with contemporary detractors upholding longstanding charges of syncretism and supporters regarding him as a bold pioneer of interfaith dialogue and understanding.

At Fathepur in 1576, Akbar took an unprecedented step, commissioning what he called an *'Ibadat khana* or "House of Worship" in which theological debates were established amongst "Sufis, philosophers, orators, jurists, Sunnis, Shi'is, brahmans, Jains, Christians of various denominations, Jews, Zoroastrians, and still others" (Wink 2009: 99). Although at first these discussions were limited to Muslims of divergent views, their inability to find common ground or even practice civility convinced Akbar to widen participation and include representatives of other belief systems as well. Not only allowing such debates but also presiding over them marked a significant departure from the normal practice of a ruler, implicitly suggesting that the sultan of the Mughal Empire somehow stood beyond the boundaries of conventional orthodoxy and sought for himself a more transcendent or encompassing account of the truth. After much intensive examination of different faith traditions and understandings within the House of Worship, and listening to the often fractious and undiplomatic theological assertions of diverse speakers, at times from distant lands such as Jesuits from Europe, Akbar eventually ended the debates at the *'Ibadat khana*. He continued, however, to take steps to make his position of spiritual universalism authoritative, for example, by pronouncing the principle of "peace with all" (*sulh-i kull*) as a basis for religious toleration. Within his court, Akbar also initiated a spiritually eclectic, esoteric fellowship within which he presided over various mystical forms of worship with his followers. Eventually associated with the term *din il-llahi*, or "religion of God", the precise character and intent of these practices has been a highly contested matter. It was criticized as a syncretistic amalgam of Akbar's. The *din il-llahi* was something of a "spiritual club" involving a small circle of elites who pledged unfailing allegiance to Akbar, and including a variety of rituals from different religious traditions, such as veneration of the sun (Schimmel 2004: 38).

Akbar's universalist preoccupation would evoke religious hostility from critics who suspected that he had abandoned Islam or overstepped his religious authority at the expense of the *'ulama*. The most formidable opposition to Akbar's court came from the Naqshbandi Sufi leader, Ahmad Sirhindi (d. 1624), who sought to be known among his followers as the *Mujaddid-e Alf-e Thani*, "the Reviver of second Muslim thousand years" (Hodgson

1974: 85). Recognized as the *qutb* or "pole" of his age by the Naqshbandis, Sirhindi wrote letters to members of the imperial court warning against religious syncretism and deviation. He also expounded on matters of Sufi metaphysics, seeking to undermine the basis for Akbar's form of universalism by refuting the idea of *wahdat al-wujud*, or "unity of being", which was one of the most influential medieval Sufi concepts within Mughal imperial courts. According to this teaching, derived from the works of Ibn al-'Arabi, the Creator and all creation are ultimately and essentially one (Ibn al-'Arabi's thought will be discussed at greater length in the following chapter). As an alternative, Sirhindi expounded a doctrine called *wahdat al-shuhud*, or "unity of witness". In Sirhindi's view, mystical experiences of unity with God are subjective in nature, and potentially dangerous insofar as they may be used as a basis for erasing distinctions between religions or disregarding religious laws and observances. Against the tendency of Akbar to assert metaphysical unity as the basis for his social and religious ethics, Sirhindi underscored the paramount and unchanging role of *shari'a* (Hodgson 1974: 85).

Although Akbar's son, Jahangir (d. 1627), would imprison Sirhindi for one year at a fort in Gwalior, and ultimately release him for repenting, his ideas would heavily influence debate over persistent questions that have divided South Asian Sufis and Muslims – questions that persist into the contemporary era. How flexible is Sufism's relationship with *shari'a*? How universal and inclusive can Sufism be without losing its Islamic character? How similar is Sufi thought and practice to the esoteric traditions of other religions, such as Hinduism and Buddhism? Can the pursuit of spiritual realization take priority over the external forms of theology and jurisprudence, or are these inner and outer aspects of religion fundamentally inseparable? Such questions had particular urgency in the pluralistic South Asian religious context, where the encounter between Hinduism and Islam was giving impetus to new religious movements such as Sikhism, but also resonated further afield in Ottoman lands, where questions concerning the boundaries of orthodox Sunni Islam vis-à-vis Shi'ism and the Christian West were also salient. As early as 1681, a deputy of Muhammad Ma'sum (d. 1686), Sirhindi's son, brought the Naqshbandiyya-Mujaddidiyya to Istanbul, where he was well received by the city's elite (Abu-Manneh 1982: 17). Later waves of the order would prove influential in the Ottoman Empire in the eighteenth and nineteenth centuries.

The question of how Islam and Sufism relate to specifically South Asian religious traditions produced divergent answers, dividing Mughal elites as well as subsequent generations of Muslim intellectuals. Outwardly, the theological assertions, forms of worship, and behavioural norms advanced by Islam and the various indigenous South Asian traditions differ profoundly.

Historically, many Sufis – including personalities who played a leading role in introducing Islam to South Asia – had prioritized spiritual essence over external form, preaching divine unity without punctilious attention to legal norms, and introducing new forms of devotion (for example, *qawwali* singing) that appealed in the South Asian context. Dissonance between Islam and Hinduism in particular was potentially a major source of conflict, and played a role in the emergence of Sikhism as a new religious force. Despite Akbar's efforts to bridge or transcend differences, disputation over persistent questions concerning Islam's relation to other faiths continued to build during the Mughal era, and would come to a tipping point during the time of Shah Jahan and his sons Dara Shikoh (d. 1659) and Aurangzeb Alamgir. A dual nature of Indian Islam became apparent in universalist and exclusivist forms of Sufism, respectively exemplified by the mysticism of Dara Shikoh and the legalism of his brother and rival Aurangzeb.

Jahanara: A Sufi Princess

Outside the bustling crowds of Nizam al-Din Awliya's shrine in Delhi, India, Jahanara (d. 1681), a Sufi princess, was buried in a small white marble tomb. Daughter of the Mughal Empire's Emperor Shah Jahan, and Empress Mumtaz Mahal (for whom the Taj Mahal was built), and sister to Dara Shikoh and Aurangzeb Alamgir, Lady Jahanara is known as a pious disciple of the Chishti Sufi order (Ernst 1999: 195). Her writings reflect her devotion as an imperial princess to the Sufi path and way of life. In contrast with the mendicant orders who took a vow of poverty to pursue their spiritual practice, Jahanara maintained her elite status while engaging in the dervish practice of *dhikr* through physical actions to connect with the divine.

In *The Confidant of Spirits*, Jahanara (also called Fatima) conveys her personal commitment to Sufi living. Utilizing the term *faqira*, Jahanara acknowledges her spiritual calling as a Sufi. This term was eventually invoked in the inscription at her tomb, which reads: "The annihilated *faqir* Lady Jahanara..." (Ernst 1999:194). In this work, she acknowledges that it was "with the aid of fortune and ascendant victory" (in Ernst 1999: 197) that she was able to make her pilgrimage "from the capital Agra in the company of my great father toward the pure region of incomparable Ajmer" (Ernst 1999) – where the tomb of Muʻin al-Din was located – during Ramadan in 1643. She evocatively describes her mystical experience of visiting the tomb as follows:

> Having entered the dome, I went around the light-filled tomb of my master seven times, sweeping it with my eyelashes, and making the sweet-smelling dust of that place the mascara of my eyes.

> At that moment, a marvellous spiritual state and mystical experience befell this annihilated one, which cannot rightly be written. From extreme longing I became astonished, and I do not know what I said or did...

If the sincerity, love and spiritual concentration of this annihilated one demanded that I should not go back home after having gone all the way to that blessed and gracious place, the corner of security – what can be done?

The Beloved has placed a noose on my neck,
And he pulls me wherever he wishes.

(Ernst 1999: 198)

In addition to *The Confidant of Spirits*, Jahanara compiled existing writings to produce well-regarded biographies of her living Sufi teacher, Mulla Shah of the Qadiriyya order, and the historical "famous Indian saint of the Chishti order, Mu'in al-Din (d. 1236)" (Ernst 1999: 194) and his followers (Adams Helminski 2003: 128). Jahanara also wrote *Risala-i sahibiyya* (Message of a Companion), in which she recounted her initiation into the Chishti order (Adams Helminski 2003: 128).

Figure 3.2: Dara Shikoh and his Sufi Qadiri teacher, Mian Mir.

According to historical accounts, Shah Jahan's favoured son, Dara Shikoh, was more passionately dedicated to mysticism and to mutual appreciation between Islam and Hinduism than to more mundane military and administrative affairs. In this respect, he appears to have been inspired by those of his ancestors who were absorbed in the quest for mystical truths and spiritual unity, without regard for potential risks, such as the charge of syncretism. Raised in a setting where Sufism was normative, Dara's intellectual and spiritual views were heavily influenced by the Qadiri Sufi order, while his sister the princess Jahanara was affiliated with the Chishti order. His Qadiri teacher, Mian Mir, was himself a crosser of religious boundaries, a former Jew named Sarmad Kasjani who had come to embrace Sufism and Ibn al-'Arabi's teachings concerning *wahdat al-wajud* (which will be discussed in the following chapter). These Sufi teachings, as well as encounters with Hindu holy men, led Dara to the conclusion that Sufi Islam and esoteric Hinduism offered different formulations of what are essentially the same truths. Inspired by this vision, Dara translated 50 of the Hindu Upanishads, texts known for their accessible mystical teachings, into Persian and even proposed that these texts might possibly be the *Kitab al-Maknun* ("hidden book") mentioned in the Qur'ān. He found further sanction for his belief in the divinely inspired nature of the Upanishads in Qur'ānic passages asserting that no race of people has been deprived of a messenger and revealed scripture (e.g. 57:25).

Dara's fascination with Hindu scripture was not an isolated phenomenon; there is a long history of Muslim (and Sufi) engagement with Hindu literature and practice. For example, one can see this relationship going as far back as Abu al-Rayhan al-Biruni's (d. 1048) Arabic translation of the *Yoga Sutras*. Muslim appreciation of Indian philosophy was fostered through the Neoplatonic Illuminationist (*Ishraqi*) school of thought and Islamic philosophy more widely, which made it easy for Muslims "to view yogic or Vendantic teachings as one more example of the adaptation of philosophy to local traditions" (Ernst 2013: 63). In terms of practice, particularly among South Asian Sufis like the Chishtis,

> it is obvious that Sufis paid close attention to sophisticated yogic teachings involving the subtle physiology of the chakras and the power of mantras, which were arguably quite similar to the subtle centres (*lata'if*) of Sufi meditation and the *zikr* [*dhikr*] formulas consisting of the Arabic names of God (Ernst 2013: 63–64).

Such views ran counter to prevailing religious views, and called into question not just conventional wisdom but also beliefs that provided a rationale for Muslim rule. Dara's brother, Aurangzeb Alamgir, considered such views heretical and, after moving to seize the throne from his father Shah Jahan, defeated his brother in battle. Executed alongside his sons by Aurangzeb, Dara became a martyr for his beliefs.

The rise of Aurangzeb marked a dramatic shift in the religiosity of the Mughal dynasty. Probably the most controversial figure in South Asian Muslim history, Aurangzeb campaigned to introduce traditional Islamic law and commissioned scholars of Islam to compile a codified body of Hanafi jurisprudence. He called this compendium *Fatwa-e-Alamgiri*. Taking exception to forms of aesthetic experience embraced by many South Asian Sufis, he prohibited the poetry of Hafiz and discouraged the performance of music (Schimmel 2004: 110). Seeking to assert the pre-eminence of Islam, he systematically removed temples, schools, and places of worship that facilitated the teachings of other religions, especially Hinduism. He nonetheless asked to be buried near the mausoleum of a Sufi in the Deccan region, presenting a very different face of the Sufi experience to that presented by Dara Shikoh. Austere in his personal religious practice, opposed to any form of syncretism, and asserting a legalistic vision of Muslim purity over and against the teachings of other religions, Aurangzeb did not wish to strengthen grounds for coexistence among faiths or to increase scope for forms of spiritual practice that diverged from the traditional consensus of legal scholars.

To this day, South Asian Muslims continue to debate the significance of these Mughal-era rivalries, with some embracing the legacy of Akbar and Dara Shikoh, and others affirming Sirhindi and Aurangzeb. Although actually practiced forms of Sufism cannot always be pigeonholed into one camp or the other, distinct tendencies are discernible: on the one hand, a more purist, communally minded, and *shari'a*-oriented form of Sufism that seeks to maintain a religious culture that corresponds more or less exactly with traditional Sunni orthodoxy in other regions, and on the other hand, a form of Sufism that downplays the significance of religious boundaries, fosters community between Muslims and Hindus at the shrines of saints, and embraces uniquely South Asian religious and cultural forms such as *qawwali* singing. Although these differences are not coextensive with the boundary between the modern states of India and Pakistan, the partition of these two countries in 1947 is to some extent reflective of differences that emerged centuries earlier, as Muslims sharing common reference points within Sufism diverged in their beliefs about the content of their own Muslim identities and on the extent to which their spiritual lives overlapped with those of their non-Muslim neighbours.

DERVISHES: THE WANDERING MENDICANTS OF ISLAM

As the preceding accounts demonstrate, Sufism was integral to the official high cultures of the three Muslim empires considered in this chapter – the Ottomans, the Safavids, and the Mughals. Sufism shaped the lives of political authorities, religious leaders, scholars, and artisans, and left a profound imprint on material arts as well as intellectual traditions. Yet the influence of Sufism was by no means confined to imperial courts and the institutions patronized by the likes of Akbar and Selim I. Sufism also found expression at a broader, popular level, manifesting in the lives of people without a formal education. Within this larger cultural milieu, Sufism was associated not just with the fine robes and distinguished clothing of palaces and seminaries, but also with the patched frocks of wandering dervishes.

The *dervish* or *faqir* was among the most intriguing characters found in the lands of Central and South Asia as well as the Middle East and parts of North Africa. Unfortunately, there is no consensus on the origin of the word dervish. In Persian, however, the term usually connotes "beggar" and literally means "the sill of the door" referring to one who actively begs from door to door. In the context of Sufism, the dervish would come to symbolize "the one who is at the door to enlightenment" (Friedlander 1992: 15). While the term can apply generically to any Sufi practitioner – for example, a Mevlevi "whirling dervish", as described in Chapter 1 – such usage of the word "dervish" for more mainstream Sufi adherents is derivative of a more specific usage connected to wandering or mendicant Sufis. Such Sufis achieved an iconic status, were not affiliated with specific Sufi orders, and idealized a path of poverty (*faqr* in Arabic) as prescribed by the Prophet Muhammad's tradition, "*faqri fakhri*" (poverty is my pride). In contrast to sultans and emirs who accumulated riches and aspired towards overwhelming material grandeur, dervishes and faqirs sought to embody contrasting principles of world renunciation and spiritual as well as material poverty.

Dervishes drew inspiration from the lives of the earliest Islamic mystics, who regarded renunciation of the material world and of egotistical inclinations as essential for spiritual growth. Believing that "[t]o possess anything means to be possessed by it" (Schimmel 1975: 121), the dervishes embraced poverty as a basis for spiritual practice and followed an ethic outlined by the early Sufi biographer Hujwiri:

> Dervishhood in all its meanings is a metaphorical poverty, and amidst all its subordinate aspects there is a transcendent principle. The Divine mysteries come and go over the dervish, so that his affairs are acquired by himself, his actions attributed to himself, and his ideas attached to himself. But when his affairs are freed from the bonds of acquisition, his actions are no more attributed to himself. Then he is the Way, not the wayfarer, i.e. the dervish is a place over which something is passing, not a wayfarer following his own will (Hujwiri, in Schimmel 1975: 123).

While not all Sufis became dervishes in a literal sense, as wandering mendicants utterly free of the world's fetters and pretensions, for many the term took on a powerful symbolic and metaphorical meaning, and dervishes were seen as exemplars who lived outside the bondage of egotism, greed, political ambition, and religious hypocrisy.

Because of their simplicity and non-attachment to the world, dervishes were often highly esteemed in Muslim culture. Farid al-Din Attar (d. 1221), an influential Sufi writer, described "love for the dervishes" as a key to spiritual attainment:

> If you are possessed of discernment joined with knowledge, seek the company of the dervishes and become one with them. Love for the dervishes is the key which opens the door into Paradise. The dervish's garment is nothing but a patched robe, and he is not led astray by earthly desires and passions (Farid al-Din Attar, in Friedlander 1992: xiv).

Though their practices took different forms and more "rustic" or countercultural dervishes at times drew reproach, a rich language developed to account for Muslim mystics who lived without regard for worldly rank or ordinary forms of security. Dervishes who were believed to be particularly inspired, through an all-consuming absorption in divine contemplation and loss of conventional awareness, frequently earned the title *majdhub* ("utterly attracted to God") or *majnun* (roughly, "possessed by divine madness"). Such terms were applied to a dervish who lived in union with God, experiencing the "ecstatic rapture by losing himself in God" (Friedlander 1992: 156). Sufi poets such as Nizami (d. 1209) used symbolic narratives in which losing one's own identity through intense preoccupation with a beloved figure led to the ultimate state of union with the divine Beloved. Others spoke of *hayra*, an experience of bewilderment or mystical perplexity, and similarly affirmed the loss of ordinary "sanity" as a basis for deeper spiritual realization.

Figure 3.3: *Dervish.*

Due to the fact that wandering dervishes "did not usually organize them-selves in centralized orders" (Knysh 2000: 272), they were largely discon-nected from institutionalized Sufism. Though often supported by popular piety, such dervishes could also engage in "blatant social deviance" (Kara-mustafa 2006: 13) from societal norms and authoritative power through reclusive lifestyles which exhibited extreme asceticism and antinomianism. Many dervishes, particularly those known as *qalandars*, expressed pious protest not only through the self-denial of renouncing property and material wealth but also through a rejection of employment, and marriage. Such non-conformism included seemingly "deviant" forms of behaviour and appear-ance, associated with a peripatetic homeless life of "voluntary poverty and mendicancy" (Karamustafa 2006: 14–16). The *Qalandariyya* movement in particular provoked criticism from more orthodox quarters for failing to stress devotion to traditional Islamic ritualistic practices and at times con-veying a complete indifference to communal values and norms. The *qalan-dars*, for example, became known for their deviation from conventionally accepted forms of dress and their adoption of "outrageous dress codes [that] clearly signified protest and rejection of social convention" (Karamustafa 2006: 18). Thus, the "anti-establishment" conduct of many dervishes earned both praise and blame, and in some cases dervishes were regarded as the "mouthpiece of social criticism" (Schimmel 1975: 111).

In addition to its significance as a form of protest against authority and conventionality, the lifestyle and dress of the wandering dervishes was also suffused with symbols of the Sufi path of piety. The defining worldly pos-sessions of these dervishes – for example, the *kashkul* (beggar's bowl), *tabar* (double axe), and *khirqa* (cloak) – are notable not just for distinguish-ing their carriers from other Muslims but also for their metaphysical and symbolic meanings as markers of a spiritual path.

Perhaps the most distinctive of the wandering dervish's possessions was the *kashkul* (beggar's bowl). Though on a surface level carrying a beggar's bowl could be seen as deviant or countercultural in a culture that valued self-reliance and communal responsibility, the significance of the *kashkul* for the dervishes was not merely practical and material. Rather, the *kashkul* was a constant reminder of one's ultimate poverty in rela-tion to God upon whom all surrender. Depending for one's basic, material sustenance from others, then, was a spiritual exercise that reinforced an existential posture. Usually formed in the shape of a boat, the bowl repre-sented not just the receptive nature required by the Sufi path, but also the journey of the spiritual traveller. Ironically, this symbol of the spiritual path was eventually appropriated in the artwork of high society and impe-rial courts, leading to the embellishment of a symbol of great destitution in lavish, gold- and silver-inlaid vessels presented as gifts (see Figure 3.4) (Renard 2005: 49).

If the *kashkul* is the symbol of spiritual passivity and receptivity, then the *tabar* reminds the dervish of the active duty to battle with the lower self. The *tabar* reminds the dervish to engage in what is known as the process of *jihad al-akbar* or "the greater struggle", the constant "inward combat... aimed at vanquishing one's ego/soul and its baser tendencies" (Renard 2005: 229). This struggle purifies the dervish and opens ways to experience higher stages of self. Dervishes were known to carry a *tabar* along with few other possessions, creating another clear marker of their vocation and status. The *tabar* was also adopted by some established Sufi orders as a spiritual symbol that could be placed on display at a meeting house along with a *kashkul*, often near a door or entrance.

Dervishes were also known to carry a *chantah* (rug bag) and, like other Sufis, *tasbih* (prayer beads). The rug bag provided a place for the dervish to store his or her sparse possessions. According to tradition, owning more than would fit in the *chantah* amounted to reaching a "state of forgetfulness" (Bakhtiar 1976: 38). *Tasbih*, known by some as "the Muslim rosary", are used by many Muslims for a variety of reasons. For Sufis, the *tasbih* is a symbolic tool for spiritual methods. For initiation on the spiritual path, *tasbih* may, for example, be given to a student from a teacher to encourage regular practice of remembrance throughout the student's daily life in order to receive the virtues of such remembrance. As reflected in the Prophetic tradition, "Repeat the Tasbih a hundred times, and a thousand virtues shall be recorded by God for you, 10 virtuous deeds for each repetition" (Henry and Marriott 2008: 90). The *tasbih* can also remind the adherent to actively invoke the Divine characteristics in order to witness and translate the symbols of the Divine in the nature of things. *Tasbih* then helps in the Sufi processes of meditation and contemplation which are both spiritual methods to master the art of concentration and the experience of being present.

Standards for clothing among wandering dervishes were also distinctively minimalist. Whereas the first Sufis were said to have worn simple clothing made of wool, dervishes became known for wearing a simple dervish *khirqa* (cloak) or *muraqqa'a* (patched frock). While cloaks were also used by established Sufi orders as a symbol of initiation or attainment on the spiritual path (Renard 2005: 63), dervish attire was most immediately recognizable for its exceedingly humble character. In contrast to the fine clothing of high society, wandering dervishes donned weathered garments held together inelegantly by patches, again symbolizing poverty and affecting an attitude of humility and self-abnegation.

Although dervishes became part and parcel of Sufi life, attitudes toward dervishes varied depending on the social and cultural context as well as perceived sincerity and spiritual depth. Just as the term Sufi itself became contested after Sufism entered the mainstream during the medieval era, the development of dervish subcultures also led to instances in which dervishes

Figure 3.4: *Kashkul*: Sufi begging bowl from Lahore, Pakistan.

were condemned for the "degeneration" of their practices (Schimmel 1975: 20). Despite problems with image and apparent inconsistency of dervish practices, there are many traditional and folkloric stories which suggest that rulers would sometimes seek wisdom or receive criticism directly from a dervish. One such tradition is connected to Baba Tahir, a well-known Persian dervish (referred to as a *qalandar* in Persian literary sources) of the eleventh century. In it, Baba Tahir critiqued the Saljuq Sultan Tughril Beg (who reigned from 1037–1063) by urging him to "establish a just society" (Renard 2005: 43). A poem by Baba Tahir reads:

> I am the mystic wanderer, known as Qalandar;
> I have neither a hearth nor a lodge.
> During the day I wander through the world and at night
> I sleep with a brick under my head.
>
> (Frembgen 2008: 2)

Another dervish tradition concerns the relationship between Otman Baba (d. 1478) and the Ottoman Sultan Mehmed II (d. 1481). According to this tradition, Otman Baba envisioned the coming of Mehmed II into power and yet he also foreshadowed Mehmet's failure to seize Belgrade (Karamustafa 2006: 48). Due to this dervish's uncanny abilities to predict the future, one biography states that Mehmed II "actually admitted that the 'real' sultan was Otman Baba" (Karamustafa 2006: 48). Yet another tradition found in the north-west province of today's Pakistan relates to Rahman Baba (d. 1711), one the greatest Sufi Pashtun poets. Known as "the Nightingale of Peshawar", Rahman Baba's poetry influenced religious leaders and politicians alike. In particular, his poems were used to inspire independence movements. As mentioned at the beginning of this book, within the context of Persian Sufism, one of the most well-known dervish and dervish traditions was found in Baba Kuhi of Shiraz, in southern Iran.

Figure 3.5: Mulla Nasruddin riding backwards on a donkey.[2]

2.   This Turkish miniature owned by Meena Sharify-Funk depicts a well-known story of Mulla Nasruddin riding his donkey backwards while leaving a village which he had visited. When asked the reason, he simply responded "I did not want to disrespect the people by having my back to them".

Mulla Nasruddin

'If you want truth', Nasruddin told a group of Seekers who had come to hear his teachings, 'you will have to pay for it'. 'But why should you have to pay for something like truth?' asked one of the company. 'Have you not noticed', said Nasruddin, 'that it is the scarcity of a thing which determines its value?' (Shah 1971: 90).

The title, "Mulla", refers to a male religious authority figure in Islam, and is used in areas such as Iran, Turkey, Afghanistan, and Central Asia. Mulla Nasruddin is a legendary thirteenth century satirical Sufi figure who is claimed by many – including Afghans, Turks, Kurds, Uzbeks, and Iranians – to be their own. In Arabic contexts, this figure is known as Joha. Nasruddin is particularly revered by dervish orders, who invoke his stories in their teachings as an illustration of "the antics characteristic of the human mind" (Shah 1983: ix). Even in spite of legally suppressing the dervish orders in the 1940s, Turkey continues to publish pamphlets about Nasruddin for tourism purposes. He remains the inspiration for folklore in places as varied as Georgia, Macedonia, Bulgaria, Azerbaijan, the United States, and Sicily (Özdemir 2011; Shah 1983: ix).

Depending on the reader's perspective, Nasruddin can be interpreted as holy (like the sober Sufi who abstains from worldly pleasures by adhering to doctrine) and/or a fool (like the ecstatic Sufi who is metaphorically intoxicated "in the love for God") – a distinction which is explored further in Chapter 5. This paradoxical "holy fool" character is featured in stories such as *Prayer is better than sleep*:

As soon as he had intoned the Call to Prayer from his minaret, the Mulla was seen rushing away from the mosque. Someone shouted: "Where are you going, Nasruddin?"

The Mulla yelled back: "That was the most penetrating call I have ever given. I'm going as far away as I can to see at what distance it can be heard" (Shah 1971: 98).

Nasruddin is characterized as devout yet irreverent, unpredictable yet consistently foolish, comical yet clever. Stories about Nasruddin use humour to represent and critique Middle Eastern cultural and religious norms, customs, beliefs, and institutions, and to destabilize widespread assumptions. By presenting lessons in a humorous way, Nasruddin holds up a lens to how people flatter political leaders and tell them what they wish to hear. He takes on the role of the fool, which allows him to be subversive without posing a real threat to venerated systems of authority.

While tales about Nasruddin defy classification (Halman 2003: 11), three key themes can be found in them, as showcased below:

1. **Bazaar haggling mentality** (i.e. outrageous reasoning that is nonsensical yet amusing and which challenges the status quo; ego-centric in that the individual seems driven by his wants; and idiotic yet transparent about his foolishness):

The Reason
The Mulla went to see a rich man.
"Give me some money".
"Why?"
"I want to buy…an elephant".
"If you have no money, you can't afford to keep an elephant".
"I came here", said Nasruddin, "to get money, not advice" (Shah 1971: 13).

Tit for tat
Nasruddin went into a shop to buy a pair of trousers.
Then he changed his mind and chose a cloak instead, at the same price.
Picking up the cloak he left the shop.
"You have not paid", shouted the merchant.
"I left you the trousers, which were of the same value as the cloak".
"But you did not pay for the trousers either".
"Of course not", said the Mulla – "why should I pay for something that I did not want to buy?" (Shah 1971: 24).

2. **Insha'Allah mentality** (i.e. the tendency to prioritize Islamic theology over philosophy, leave things to chance or fate, and assume a distinction between human and divine responsibility):

Assumptions
"What is the meaning of fate, Mulla?"
"Assumptions".
"In what way?"
"You assume things are going to go well, and they don't – that you call bad luck. You assume things are going to go badly and they don't – that you call good luck. You assume that certain things are going to happen or not happen – and you so lack intuition that you don't *know* what is going to happen. You assume that the future is unknown.
"When you are caught out – you call that Fate" (Shah 1971: 20).

If Allah wills it
Nasruddin had saved up to buy a new shirt. He went to a tailor's shop, full of excitement. The tailor measured him and said: "Come back in a week, and – if Allah wills – your shirt will be ready". The Mulla contained himself for a week and then went back to the shop. "There has been a delay. But – if Allah wills – your shirt will be ready tomorrow". The following day Nasruddin returned. "I am sorry", said the tailor, "but it is not quite finished. Try tomorrow, and – if Allah wills – it will be ready". "How long will it take", asked the exasperated Nasruddin, "if you leave Allah out of it?" (Shah 1971: 29).

3. **Challenges to rationalism** (by using inconsistent logic):

Inscrutable Fate
Nasruddin was walking along an alleyway when a man fell from a roof and landed on his neck. The man was unhurt; the Mulla was taken to hospital. Some disciples went to visit him. "What wisdom do you see in this happening, Mulla?" "Avoid any belief in the inevitability of cause and effect! *He* falls off the roof – but *my* neck is broken! Shun reliance upon theoretical questions such as: 'If a man falls off a roof, will his neck be broken?'" (Shah 1971: 26).

A word for it

Hearing that a man wanted to learn the Kurdish language, Nasruddin offered to teach him. Nasruddin's own knowledge of Kurdish was limited to a few words. "We shall start with the word for 'Hot Soup', said the Mulla. 'In Kurdish, this is Aash'. 'I don't quite understand, Mulla. How would you say 'Cold Soup'?'" "You never say 'Cold Soup'. The Kurds like their soup hot" (Shah 1971: 85).

Although their status in Muslim societies was always to some extent disputed and dervish practices have declined drastically in the modern era, the idea of the dervish became firmly established in Muslim cultures and took on a symbolic or iconic status. Within the larger contexts of Sufism and the literary as well as visual arts, dervishes came to represent wayfaring (*suluk*) along a spiritual path, and ways of life that highlighted the liminality of the human condition. Like a monk or wandering ascetic in the Christian, Buddhist, or Hindu traditions, the dervish symbolically represents the individual spiritual traveller (*salik*) in his or her complete dependence upon God. In their itinerant ways, dervishes embodied literally what was for most people a figurative journey through the world and back to God.

SANCTUARIES AND SHRINES:
ARCHITECTURAL ORDER AND SACRED SPACE IN SUFISM

In their wanderings, dervishes would often congregate at sacred sites, such as tombs of holy men and women. As they travelled from place to place to pay their respects to saints and to worship in holy places, dervishes actively contributed to the development of shrine culture in the Islamic world. They contributed to a broader cultural practice of *ziyara* (literally, "visitation") in which people would travel to specific holy sites in addition to the classical pilgrimage destinations in Mecca and Medina, to honour exemplars of Islamic spirituality, offer prayers in venerated settings, and seek divine blessings.

The *masjid* (mosque) is the ultimate sacred space in Islam, and offers the archetypal template for all holy places, including Sufi shrines. *Masjid* literally means the place of *sujud* or prostration, which is part of the daily Muslim ritual prayers. While the term is most often used to denote a house of worship constructed specifically for community gatherings and the offering of ritual prayers, *masjid* also has a broader meaning consistent with sayings of the Prophet Muhammad such as "Wherever you pray, that place is a mosque" (Akkach 2005: 193) and "the earth was placed for me as a mosque and purifier" (Nasr 1987: 37). In its most essential meaning, then, a *masjid* is a place where one humbly prostrates in submission to the Divine, existentially returning to a state of remembrance.

As Sufi groups expanded in medieval times (see Chapter 4), mosque culture developed in ways that reflected specifically Sufi forms of worship and remembrance. Not only did grand mosques in imperial cities come to accommodate Sufi gatherings and practices, but Sufi lodges, meeting houses, and saintly shrines evolved into major centres for pilgrimage and prayer. Thus, Sufi sanctuaries became important spiritual and cultural and artistic centres, embracing identifiably mystical forms of worship in addition to mainstream Islamic piety. During the period of the great empires described in this chapter, these sacred places were simultaneously honoured by imperial courts, destinations for wandering dervishes, and focal points of everyday spirituality and social interaction for the larger Muslim population: "From the thirteenth to the end of the eighteenth centuries, the veneration of shrines and holy places became the most widespread form of Islamic religious life. The Sufis and shrines provided ritual and spiritual counsel, medical cures, and mediation among different groups and strata of the population" (Lapidus 2002: 209). Hundreds and even thousands of shrines may be found in countries where Sufism particularly flourished, such as Morocco, where there is "roughly one shrine for every 6 square kilometres and 150 people" (Eickelman 2013). Pakistan, Syria, Iran and Turkey are some other countries replete with Sufi shrines and centres.

The Culture of Sufi Lodges and Mausoleums

The Islamic cultures of different geographical regions developed multiple terms to refer to centres for Sufi worship and social life, including *khanaqah*, *zawiya*, *ribat*, *tekke*, and *dargah*. While the terms differ in origins and original linguistic emphasis, they all convey the notion of a Sufi centre and place of residence and worship. In the Persian language the word *khanaqah* evokes the idea of "a place where one dwells", and thus emphasizes the sense that a Sufi setting is a place where one resides, either literally or else figuratively through a sense of spiritual belonging and association. *Zawiya* is Arabic and literally means "corner" (e.g. of a building or street), and suggests the integration of Sufi meeting houses within larger urban environments as convenient places of gathering. In contrast the Arabic term *ribat*, alternately "base" or "hostel", evolved from an original usage for a frontier outpost and often came to be associated with Sufi hostels. *Tekke* is Turkish and connotes "a place of rest or support", while in Indo-Persian contexts the term *dargah* denotes a "court" or a royal residential facility but is frequently applied to mausoleum-shrine-social centre complexes where saints are honoured and the hungry are offered food as well as shelter.

Across multiple regions, Sufi lodges had many features in common. They typically offered residential space for the head of a Sufi order and specific disciples, as well as a place for communal worship and rituals. The lodges were also centres for learning and for training in particular Sufi practices.

In some geographical locations the lodges of a particular Sufi order would become predominant, while in major metropolitan centres one could find lodges for many different orders – for example, Mevlevis, Naqshbandis, and Bektashis in Ottoman Istanbul. Some orders benefited from a patronage relationship with imperial powers, receiving resources that helped their centres to thrive as spaces for prayer, devotional gathering, and residential life as well as for schooling, medical care, and even burial. Many Sufi centres would be found in the heart of bustling cities surrounded by food and clothing markets.

Some, but not all, Sufi lodges have been built around shrines that host the mausoleum of a Sufi saint or dervish. (This can be seen in a story mentioned at the beginning of this chapter, of Selim I commissioning the building of Ibn al-'Arabi's shrine.) Similarly, many other Sufi shrines were also built around the burial place of a Sufi saint in order to honour the life and teachings of a particular friend of God. As the community of devotees grew over time, additional institutional structures – a formal mosque, lodgings, school rooms, etc. – would be developed to accommodate the needs of a particular Sufi group or emerging neighbourhood. The Sufi shrine component of a lodge, also known as *mazar* ("place of visitation") then would become not only a place for a specific Sufi group but also sacred space for pilgrims to visit and receive the *baraka* (blessing) of a particular Sufi master. The shrine itself would come to represent a comprehensive space for Sufi life, death, and reunion with God.

For many travellers to Sufi lodge-shrine complexes, taking time to pay homage to the centre's patron saint was a key purpose of their visit. Believing that saints had achieved a level of sanctity that could confer blessings on others, such visitors would seek communion at shrines with a great teacher and "friend of God". Although for Sufi practitioners this honouring of saints was deeply connected to the contemplative practices of their specific order, at a popular level shrines contributed to a culture in which the veneration of saints – as exemplary Muslims, and as potential intercessors for humanity – became increasingly central. For Muslim travellers and itinerant dervishes, the use of shrine spaces was deeply intertwined with the phenomenon of *ziyarat al-qubur* ("visitation of graves"), as a form of minor pilgrimage that complemented the major pilgrimages to Mecca and to the burial place of the Prophet in Medina. Some spiritual seekers even developed a practice of travelling from one city to another to glean from the different mystical schools of thought and Sufi teachers, becoming in effect disciples of many teachers. Some cities and regions became known for offering multiple shrines that pious visitors or travellers might feel blessed to visit, and some Sufi figures, such as 'Abd al-Qadir al-Jilani (d. 1166) would have multiple shrines scattered across different lands (for example, Iraq as well as Sri Lanka), each evoking the memory and spiritual sanctity of the saint even if his or her physical body were not present at the location.

Like any Muslim mosque, shrines to Sufi saints accommodated a variety of activities and rituals. In addition to regular mosque happenings like daily ritualistic prayer, Friday sermons and Qur'ānic readings, one could also find particular devotions to the Sufi saint, such as commemorations or celebrations conducted on regular calendar dates. The most typical of these ceremonies were the *mawlid* and the *'urs* celebrations. *Mawlid* connotes "day of one's birth"; in addition to its connection to the birthday of the Prophet Muhammad, the term can also be applied to the birth anniversary of a saint or holy figure. The *'urs*, literally "wedding", is an annual celebration that commemorates the death of the Sufi saint and his or her "mystical nuptial" or *'urs* with God (Frembgen 2008: 6). At most major shrines, services associated with the birth and death of a saint became major community celebrations.

In addition to being centres for a specific Sufi group, most Sufi shrines similarly functioned in a manner similar to a caravanserai, accommodating travelling Sufis of their own order as well as other visitors and spiritual seekers, and in some cases even political leaders or dignitaries from other religious communities. As was previously mentioned in this chapter, Mughal-era imperial rulers were known for visiting specific shrines for the *baraka* and also for building peaceful relations with fellow dignitaries of different religious affiliations. The Sufi shrine in South Asia was known for unifying people across differences in ways that traditional mosques did not (Schimmel 2004: 114). Centres for South Asian Sufism such as the *dargahs* of Mu'in al-Din Chishti and Nizam al-Din Awliya offered visiting non-Muslims, especially Hindus, solace and community solidarity in the form of shared meals and lodging.

In addition to their potential as places of meeting in which religious differences might be transcended, Sufi shrines also provided spaces in which women experienced a broader scope for their spiritual and social lives. In some cases, it could even be said that women more than men have dominated shrine culture. Some Sufi shaykhs and establishments were underwritten by affluent female patrons:

> Separate convents or refuges for Sufi women have been sponsored by female patrons at various epochs of Muslim history. For example, rabats [hospices or hostels] or shelters for women were constructed in premodern Cairo, Aleppo, and Baghdad. Their functions may have overlapped spiritual retreat with charitable shelter (Hermensen 2005: 768).

Certain aspects of shrine culture and Sufism are more accessible to women than men. For example, many ceremonies and commemorations

involve the preparation of special foods for devotional offering and/or char-
itable distribution:

> Sufi shrines are more accessible to females than many mosques
> because of the lack of formal regulations and the spontaneous nature
> of ritual expression. Visits to shrines may provide sanctioned outings
> for women that are undertaken for healing and other benefits beyond
> religious edification. Common disorders addressed by visiting shrines
> are infertility, mental disturbance, and marital problems. While women
> of all social classes may perform shrine visits, they provide in particu-
> lar an outlet for poorer women to picnic, visit, and relax (Hermensen
> 2005: 767).

The comparative freedom of women's participation and interactions at Pakistani shrines and lodges:

> These features [shops, schools, restaurants, entertainment facilities, etc.]
> of Pakistani society resemble those in other conservative Muslim soci-
> eties in the Middle East, and like in the Middle East, in Pakistan too
> the place of Sufi lodges and shrines has been recognised by scholars as
> one of the few contexts in which women can worship and mingle with
> women strangers, devotees or supplicants from different backgrounds,
> ethnic groups and classes (Werbner 2004: 376).

It is interesting to note that in contemporary times, there has been what
some call a "Talibanization of shrines": a process of banning women from
many shrines in India, or preventing women from entering the innermost
chambers of these shrines, where the saints' tombs are found (Merium
2012). Even though women continue to visit major shrines in India – such
as the shrine of Mu'in al-Din Chishti in Ajmer – women's access to the very
popular Delhi shrine of Nizam al-Din Awliya has been prohibited. In 2012,
seven of the 20 most prominent *dargahs* in Mumbai alone, including the
very popular Haji Ali mausoleum which receives up to 20,000 visitors per
day, banned women from entering their sancta sanctorum (Rahman 2012).
The authorities at such *dargahs* argue that they are correctly implementing
Islamic law, although little explanation is reported for why this particular interpretation of Islamic law has not been previously implemented at
shrines that have existed for centuries.

Throughout the Muslim world, there are numerous shrines. Each honours a different Sufi saint and the culture of that specific region as reflected
in the diverse architectural styles and designs. Below are just some examples of different Sufi sacred places.

Sufi Symbolism of the Shrine: Sacred Architecture and Geometry

With the need for sacred space devoted to Sufi activities came the development of sacred architecture in which the form of the building embodied

deep symbolic and cosmological meanings. Each aspect of the shrine (i.e. structure, design, patterns, and even colours) was intended to evoke and, ultimately, aid in the discovery of higher spiritual realities. Like the sacred architecture of other religious and spiritual traditions, the architectural symbolism and geometry found in Sufi sacred spaces is intended to represent the essential Divine order. The structure itself serves as a microcosm and reflects the maxim, "as above so below".

Figure 3.6: Jalal al-Din Rumi's *Tekke* (Museum) in Konya, Turkey.[3]

---

3.   This photo was taken by Dr. Eric Ross. For more about Ross' research see https://ericrossacademic.wordpress.com/

Figure 3.7: *Dargah* of Salim Chishti in Fathepur Sikri, India.

Figure 3.8: Farid al-Din Attar's mausoleum in Nishapur, Iran.

Figure 3.9: *Darou Khoudoss* in Touba, Senegal.[4]

In comparison to contemporary architecture that is largely utilitarian and devoid of mystical intentions, premodern architecture was an intersection of science and theology:

> Geometry, geography, and astronomy, an intertwined set of scientific enterprises, were often under the influence of theological, philosophical, and astrological speculations that were concerned with the origin, order, and purpose of the universe... If existence is meaningful only with God as its principle, then everything else in the world must likewise have a founding principle, including, one would think, the ordering of spaces and making of architecture (Akkach 2005: 158–59).

The vision behind the architectural work of Sufi shrines as well as great mosques was one in which engineering and metaphysics were integrated. Their outward form reflected not just technological abilities and advancements of the age, but also an understanding of cosmological truths and of the aesthetic features that might lend spiritual ambiance to a space of prayerful submission and contemplation.

Many Sufi personalities throughout Islamic history, such as Ibn al-'Arabi, articulated a vision in which the world is a reflection of higher realities – a formal manifestation of metaphysical symbols or images known as

4.   Darou Khoudoss, "the Abode of the Holy", is a mosque that was built in the place where Ahmadu Bamba, leader of the Muridiyya Sufi order, experienced spiritual retreats and received mystical visions. This photo was taken by Dr. Eric Ross. For more about Dr Ross' research see https://ericrossacademic.wordpress.com

"*'alam al-mithal*" (literally, "world of symbols"). The *'alam al-mithal* can be understood in the following terms:

> *'Alam al-mithal*, the 'world of similitudes' or the 'realm of images', is a product of medieval Muslim mysticism... *Mithal* equates 'symbol' in the sense of being a shadow of a higher reality revealed in a sensible form (Akkach 2005: 28).

For the Sufi, the more apparent aspects of existence in time and space point beyond themselves in an allegorical fashion. The created world points to its Creator and by extension the creations of humans should be constructed in a manner that honours the source of creativity and larger cosmic realities. The mosque, for example, can be seen as a symbol representing the order of the cosmos as a whole as well as the perfected human being within that larger order. This can be understood further in terms of nature, "through the Divine Command which placed nature as the Muslim's temple of worship, the sacred architecture of Islam becomes an extension of nature as created by God within the environment constructed by man" (Nasr 1987: 37). If the mosque or shrine is the focal point of human creativity driven by an intent to manifest "an extension of nature as created by God", other architectural creations are constructed in continuity to this larger aim to sacralise human life and activity (Nasr 1987: 37). Thus, the imperial palace and residential houses as well as the city itself become extensions of the ethos manifest in the mosque or shrine.

In structure, the dome of a mosque or shrine symbolizes the ultimate vault of heaven – the heavenly realms or skies which cover the world. It is the universal spirit which encompasses everything and unifies all differences. Thus, the dome represents the ideal of an encompassing circle in which all is One. In contrast to the circle which defies any otherness and endlessly speaks of eternity, the square base of the structure represents the more temporal reality of our earthy bodies and of the Earth itself as experienced in the four elements (water, air, fire, and earth) and the four cardinal directions. Muslim tilework and Arabesque patterns in mosques clearly display a diversity of individual forms united by an underlying, organic harmony. Such patterns directly manifest Sufi cosmology, which holds that all existent things are so many parts of one whole, participants in the One Being, or Reality: Allah.

In the overall structure and design, sacred mathematics and geometry are at the heart of sacred architecture. Sacred geometry is the science of interpreting geometric patterns in relation to cosmological understandings:

> The creation of shapes through the use of numbers and geometry, as mathematical expressions, recalls the Archetypes reflected through the World of Symbols. Mathematics, then, is a language of the Intellect, a means of spiritual hermeneutics whereby one can move from the sensible to the intelligible world (Bakhtiar 1976: 104).

In mosques and Sufi shrines, geometric shapes and a system of proportions created a means of expressing beauty, reminding the spiritual wayfarer to return to the Architect of this beauty. Through various artistic forms, including most prominently calligraphy and abstract ornamentation – the spiritual aesthetic behind sacred Islamic architecture sought to achieve consistency with the prophetic *hadith* that "God is beautiful and he loves beauty" – we will explore Sufism's relation with Qur'ānic calligraphy in Chapter 6. Such beauty could be manifested through careful attention to principles of harmony and symmetry:

> The art of pure ornament revolves around two poles: geometric pattern, the harmonic and symmetrical subdivision of the plane giving rise to intricately interwoven designs that speak of infinity and the omnipresent centre; and the idealized plant form or arabesque, spiralling tendrils, leaves, buds, and flowers embodying organic life and rhythm (Sutton 2007: 1).

Such geometrically patterned calligraphic and arabesque designs were used throughout the exterior and interior of Sufi sacred spaces, as well as with other spaces for Islamic worship.

CITIES OF SAINTS, GUILDS AND SHRINES

The period between the fifteenth and eighteenth centuries witnessed the culmination of Sufism's outward expression in Muslim societies. The majority of Muslims during this time experienced a worldview, social order, ritual life, and cultural landscape that were all unmistakably Sufi in orientation. When Muslims in the Balkans, Syria, Khorasan, and India participated in the utterly ubiquitous practice of making a pilgrimage to a local Sufi shrine to seek the blessing of the saint's presence, they did so operating within a holistic Islamic worldview that understood the cosmos as having an unseen realm within which the foremost spiritual practitioners had thoroughly immersed themselves. Sufi saints served as living testaments to scripturally revealed truths, which they actively conveyed through their teachings, poetry, writings, and deeds:

> It was Sufism that came to provide the... vocabulary in which the majority of Muslims experienced, by way of regular collective rituals carried out in institutionalized Sufi spaces – where 'higher Sufi thought tied sources of immediate relief and hope in every village and *qasbah* to Muhammad's revelation' – a most profound personal Real-Truth of their existence (Ahmed 2016: 20–21).

Sufism provided a vocabulary not only for the experiential encounter with God or Ultimate Reality, but for how this experience was expressed in various forms of architecture, music and poetry. In sum, virtually every conceivable aspect of Muslim life during this period would be related to what we now call Sufism.

From Fez, Morocco in the west to Shiraz, Iran and points further east, Sufism would help great cities become known across the Muslim world for their spiritual culture and saintly shrines. These spiritual centres would entice seekers, scholars, tradesmen, and people from all walks of life. In such cities, prospective visitors heard, they could find architectural, artistic, scientific, and literary genius. A combination of factors, including the exemplary dedication of leaders to spiritual institutions, the prevalence of dervish personalities, and the presence of a vibrant shrine culture, would all burnish the reputation of these great cities, which became known as "cities of saints" in the early and late medieval Muslim world.

Sufi shrines were at the heart of these cities, and having notable patron saints contributed considerably to a city's status. Capacity to claim such saints as Mulay Idris II, Ibn al-'Arabi, Shams al-Din Hafiz, Mu'in al-Din Chishti, and al-Hujwiri, for example, was a significant source of prestige for the cities of Fez, Damascus, Shiraz, Ajmer, and Lahore respectively. In many of such cities, shrines to key, defining saints could be found at the very core of the urban landscape, creating a symbolic centre for the larger environment. In addition, the newcomer could easily establish social connection with a variety of Sufi-oriented guilds (*asnaf*) or professional organizations which members consisted of craftsman and merchants which included "butchers, cooks, millers, bakers, weavers, tailors, dyers, tanners, silver- and goldsmiths, sword-makers, brick-layers, physicians, sailors, paper-makers, book-binders, carpenters, brokers, night-watchmen, porters, blacksmiths and saddle-makers" (Abdullah 2003). In such guilds, Sufi spirituality was interwoven with other aspects of professional practice:

> Most of the asnaf would start their meetings with a couple of hours of Sufi liturgy before settling down to deal with the practical issues confronting their trade. Sufi shaykhs were very often also the leaders of some of the asnaf, and the hierarchies of both groups tended to overlap (Abdullah 2003).

Where spiritual and professional leadership overlapped, the *shaykh* would be the spiritual model but also the administrator. In other cases, a particular Sufi order would be heavily populated with members from one or more different guilds, with many members also joining due to familial relations. The integration of urban crafts and Sufi spirituality, however, was a pervasive aspect of leadership within traditional Islamic guilds:

> Every traditional master craftsman was an initiate of a Sufi order – as some still are today. The master's success in continuing to invoke [divine remembrance] through his work determines the spiritual strength of the

> entire guild, as expressed in its work. The other members of the guild implement the designs, and while they may not be fully conscious of all the principles involved, their creative expressions attest to their Spirit, which will lie dormant within until their own [spiritual retreat] awakens it (Bakhtiar 1976: 94).

As Bakhtiar explains, traditional guilds fostered a convergence of artistic and spiritual ideals, with the master craftsman taking on a role in artistic training that was analogous to the role of the *shaykh* in Sufi spiritual culture.

The interrelations of Sufi orders, or *tariqas*, and traditional Islamic guilds served to advance both forms of social organization. In contrast to "purely religious organizations", most guilds were also established for "economic association, craftsmanship, or trade" (Trimingham 1998: 24). At the same time, a given guild would usually have distinctive connections to a specific *tariqa* or saint and drew upon the corresponding spiritual as well as social resources. Conversely, the professional and artistic pursuits of the guilds provided a means of spreading Sufi principles within a social context. Trimingham describes the interaction between *tariqa* and *asnaf* in the following terms:

> A particular guild and its members tended to be linked with a particular *tariqa* or saint. At initiations and other ceremonies, religious rites were a predominant feature, and it was behind the banner of that *tariqa* that the guild members proceeded to and from the *'id* prayer-ground. They were not secular associations, although centred on economic and social interests, but neither were they Sufi orders. The organization of the orders, however, owes much to that of the guilds (Trimingham 1998: 25).

These close associations between Sufi orders and guilds suggest that neither can be fully understood in isolation from the other.

In addition to providing a social and spiritual affiliation, Sufism also served to enrich the social and spiritual ethos of guilds, in ways that provided meaning as well as a broader sense of purpose and legitimacy. Each guild, for example, was under protection of a certain Sufi saint, and followed the morals and principles established by the saint and his order:

> In Fez 'Abd as-Salam ibn Mashish is the patron of the scribes (*habib at-tulba*); in Egypt the dancing girls (*'awalim* and *ghazawi*) were devoted to Ahmad al-Badawi. The Bayyumiya in Cairo was linked with the butcher's guild, and a champion of the rights of the poor, Ahmad Salim al-Jazzar, towards the end of the eighteenth century, seems to have been both guild-master and *khalifa* of a Bayyumi group at the same time (Trimingham 1998: 234–35).

The prevalence of such associations between guilds and saints suggests the pervasiveness of Sufi ideas and affiliations in society, as a mainstream element of the Islamic milieu.

The Sufi character of the guilds did not, however, require religious uniformity. Even while cultivating religious devotion towards a particular form of Islamic spirituality, guilds were also populated by many non-Muslim members. In such cases Sufi principles of universalism provided a means of accommodating non-Muslims (Hodgson 1974: 221). To a considerable degree, "Sufism supplemented the Shari'ah as a principle of unity and order, offering the Muslims a sense of spiritual unity" that was not dependent on the larger political system and which was not threatened by the presence of *dhimmi* non-Muslim peoples (Hodgson 1974: 221). Although the term is anachronistic, Islamic guilds performed functions comparable to those of many contemporary civil society organizations. Though not completely independent of family traditions and affiliations they were in nonetheless voluntary social organizations. While infused with religious practices and beliefs they could still remain open to non-Muslim membership. Like many Sufi orders, some Sufi guilds were even known to disassociate themselves from the imperial courts in order to "underline the alternative social outlook" (Hodgson 1974: 221).

Additionally, networks established by guilds transcended local political contexts. Together with Sufi networks spanning different cities, lands, and Islamic cultures, the guilds supported an early form of transnational social order by enabling travelling merchants to connect with fellow members of their association as they journeyed to different Muslim cities. This capacity of guilds to transcend boundaries and offer points of entry for travel and commerce greatly expedited the spread of Sufism throughout the Muslim world. Even while preserving local customs, guilds worked hand in hand with the Sufi orders to build bridges across regions and social systems. The mobility and spirit of exchange and fellowship fostered by guilds helped many guild-affiliated Sufi personalities to influence the development of the arts, trade, and science. While the influence of Sufi-affiliated guilds on the diffusion of artistic styles and crafts is easily grasped and appreciated, other impacts are more subtle, difficult to trace, or surprising. In the domain of trade, for example, the eventual worldwide use of coffee (*al-qahwa*) owes much to the Yemeni Sufis who discovered coffee's effects and then used it to encourage wakefulness during nighttime practices of *dhikr* (al-Hassani 2012: 36). Understanding the development of scientific knowledge in Islamic history would also be difficult without recognizing the impact of Sufism on their worldviews and the role of guilds in ordering the social context within which their discoveries and inventions were propagated.

Prominent Sufi Scientists Throughout Muslim History

Although the influence of Sufi ideas on many Muslim scientists was undoubtedly diffuse rather than direct, many well-known scientists were themselves also Sufis. They include:

Abd al-Rahman al-Sufi (d. 986), both a scientist and a Sufi, who wrote an influential treatise that would be used in the Muslim world and Europe on observational astronomy entitled, *Suwar al-Kawakib* (*Figures of the Stars*). In it he translated and transformed ancient Greek understandings (i.e. Ptolemy's *Almagest*) of the stars and provided outstanding illustrations of the constellations.

> With the rise of observatories and a greater interest in the night sky, Muslim astronomers from the ninth century onward were fascinated by the night sky and carried out substantial work on stars and constellations. These included 'Abd al-Rahman al-Sufi, a Persian astronomer who lived during the tenth century...in 964 described the Andromeda galaxy, our closest neighbour, calling it 'little cloud'. This was the first written record of a star system outside our own galaxy. He set out his results constellation by constellation, discussing the stars' positions, sizes and colours, and for each constellation he produced two drawings, one from the outside of a celestial globe and the other from the inside (al-Hassani 2012: 294).

He also is known for development of celestial globes and astrolabes. His legacy is immortalized in a crater of the moon named after him by the European spelling of his name, Azophi.

Umar Khayyam (d. 1131) was one of the most influential scientists in the medieval period. Although in the contemporary West he is mostly known for his book of poetry, *Rubaiyat of Umar Khayyam*, he was also a brilliant mathematician, astronomer and philosopher. His treatise on the principles of algebra further developed ideas from the founder of algebra, al-Khwarizmi (d. 850).

> Khayyam classified algebraic equations up to the third degree in rigorous and systematic manner and solved them through geometric means. In its thoroughness, clarity and manner of exposition as well as its mathematical content the *Algebra* of Khayyam must be counted as one of the masterpieces of Islamic mathematics and is still of value as a model for the way that algebra should be taught to young students (Nasr 1976: 85).

Qutb al-Din al-Shirazi (d. 1311) was among the foremost intellectuals of his age, a master of not only physics and astronomy but also of logic and medicine. Known for his work on planetary theory and even "credited for the discovery of the true cause of the rainbow" (al-Hassani 2012: 271), Qutb al-Din distinctly contributed to the great school and observatory of Maragha, Iran:

In Persia the criticism of Ptolemaic planetary theory was of much greater astronomical importance. In his astronomical masterpiece, the *Tadhkirah* (*Memorial of Astronomy*), Nasir al-Din al-Tusi criticized severely the shortcomings of the Ptolemaic planetary model. His associate Qutb al-Din al-Shirazi in his *Nihayat al-idrak* (*The Limit of Comprehension*) followed the suggestions of his teacher and applied the *Tusi-couple* to Mercury, while the Damascene Ibn al-Shatir applied the new theory to the motion of the moon and produced the lunar model identical with that of Copernicus... Without doubt this new planetary theory as applied by the entourage of Tusi at Maragha and later Islamic astronomers is the most important transformation brought about in this aspect of astronomy by Muslims. Through channels which are not completely clear – although it is known that Byzantine scholars translated some works of Islamic scientists into Greek during the Il-Khanid period – the fruit of the planetary theory of the school of Maragha reached Copernicus and later European astronomers, who used it in the new heliocentric world-picture which became dominant in the West after the 16th century (Nasr 1976: 109, 111).

Qutb al-Din also reportedly received through his father the *khirqa* of Shahab al-Din Suhrawardi (d. 1191). He then would write one of the most influential commentaries on Suhrawardi's *Hikmat al-Ishraq* and from it further developed the "physics of light" and thereby influenced a new generation of *ishraqi* philosophers (Nasr 1997: 429).

As these examples attest, the influence of Sufism on Islamic societies during the late-medieval and early premodern periods was pervasive, and manifest in social, commercial, artistic, and scientific as well as more purely religious domains of activity. The influence was so pervasive, indeed, that purporting to define a clear boundary between Sufism and Islam in these times would be a rather misleading exercise. Sufism was not generally perceived to be something separate from the deeper aspects of Islam rightly understood, and ideas about the authentic vision and ethos of Islam bore a substantial Sufi imprint.

Significantly, the Sufi aspiration to directly encounter revealed truth often trumped the authority of the law in the minds of Muslims during this period. If according to Sufi cosmology truth is a layered phenomenon that is only fully embodied by the perfected human or Sufi saint, then the realized Sufi has a stronger claim to the truth of Islam than the unrealized jurist, whose knowledge is not existential and embodied but intellectual and speculative only. As Rumi articulated by analogy, "The Law [*shari'a*] may be compared to learning the science of medicine, and the Path [*tariqa*] to regulating one's diet in accordance with the science of medicine, and the Real-Truth [*haqiqa*] to gaining health everlasting and becoming independent of them both" (Ahmed 2016: 22).

As a consequence of this widespread perspective, the authority of the Sufi outweighed that of the jurist in defining the meaning of Islam for a great many Muslims, common as well as elite, during this era. Of course the idea of the realized Sufi as the best representative of Islam did not always involve a sense of transcending the law. Sufi jurists were not uncommon and for many Sufis, as we have seen in this chapter and will see in following chapters, *haqiqa* is a level of realization that fulfils *shari'a* and is encapsulated by it. As we have discussed, these different conceptions of Sufism and the law were at the heart of tensions between different Sufi groups and personalities. As we will see in the following chapter, reconciling the metaphysical truths and mystical experiences of the Sufi path with Islamic law and orthodoxy more broadly was one of the key tasks of the great synthesizers of the medieval era.

Discussion Questions:

1. Describe the many different ways in which Sufism connects to Muslim empire.
2. How does the dervish culture compare to the imperial court life? (Explain how it intersects and how it does not.)
3. What were the main purposes for developing Sufi lodges and shrines?
4. What is the metaphorical significance of Islamic architecture as experienced in a Sufi shrine?
5. Help paint a picture of how Sufism influenced the late medieval period. Why do scholars argue that Sufism was the fabric of Muslim life?

Further Reading:

Akkach, S. (2005). *Cosmology and Architecture in Premodern Islam: An Architectural Reading of Mystical Ideas.* Albany, NY: State University of New York Press.

Bakhtiar, L. (1976). *Sufi: Expressions of the Mystic Quest.* New York: Thames and Hudson.

Hodgson, M. G. S. (1974). *The Venture of Islam: Conscience and History in a World Civilization, Volume 3: The Gunpowder Empires and Modern Times.* Chicago: University of Chicago Press.

Karamustafa, A. T. (2006). *God's Unruly Friends: Dervish Groups in the Islamic Middle Period 1200–1550.* Oxford: Oneworld.

Le Gall, D. (2005). *A Culture of Sufism: Naqshbandis in the Ottoman World, 1450–1700.* Albany, NY: State University of New York Press.

Schimmel, A. (2004). *The Empire of the Great Mughals: History, Art and Culture.* London: Reaktion Books.

SYNTHESIZERS AND SAINTS:
SUFISM IN THE MEDIEVAL ERA

A widely-quoted *hadith* of the Prophet Muhammad's that has proved pivotal to Islamic history and Muslim self-conception is narrated by Abu Hurayrah: "Allah will raise for this community at the end of every hundred years the one who will revive its religion for it" (Abu Dawud 37: 4278). Muslims have thus looked in each age for a figure whose life and work revived the spirit and practice of Islam. Although there is not always agreement among Muslims over who counts as a reviver or *mujaddid* in each age, both Abu Hamid al-Ghazali (d. 1111) and Muhyi al-Din Ibn al-'Arabi (d. 1240) have been considered as such, two figures we will explore in depth in this chapter.

As we saw in Chapter 3, it is difficult to overestimate the extent of Sufism's influence on the post-Mongol Islamic tradition between the fourteenth and seventeenth centuries. Alongside the integration of Sufi orders into the very structure of the Ottoman, Mughal, and Safavid empires, Sufi philosophy would shape the intellectual, artistic, and cultural traditions of the era. From the pens of royal scholars to the travelling bands of local singers, Sufi ideas found themselves seamlessly integrated into every corner of Muslim life, so much so that the later Orientalist suggestion that Sufism was something distinct from Islam would have struck the majority of Muslims during this period as rather odd, if not completely incomprehensible.

This profound synthesis of Sufism with Muslim life however would not have been conceivable without the intellectual efforts of Sufism's great medieval luminaries. The renowned saints (plural *awliya'*, singular *wali*) and synthesizers of the eleventh and twelfth centuries worked to integrate the foundational rules of Islamic law with the metaphysical scaffolding of Sufi philosophy, which together provided the framework for Sufism's holistic paradigm of moral guidance and spiritual realization. The paradigm developed by Sufism's great medieval architects would allow for the expansion of Sufi thought, social movements, and art throughout the era of empires. In particular, famous Sufi synthesizers like Abu Hamid al-Ghazali and Muhyi al-Din Ibn al-'Arabi articulated a symbiotic relationship between Sufism and Islamic law, while drawing out Sufism's metaphysical and cosmological implications. Like spiritual cartographers, they sought to map the inner universe (microcosm) and its integral relation to the outer universe (macrocosm). They were not founders of orders, but both al-Ghazali and Ibn al-

'Arabi were seen by later Muslims as the *mujaddids* or "revivers" of Islam in their age. Their wide-ranging scholarship and intellectual syntheses would chart a course for later Muslims in the centuries following them.

Socially, Sufism would develop one of the most important institutions of medieval Muslim societies: the Sufi order or *tariqa*. Sufi orders wove far-flung spiritual networks into the fabric of Islamic culture, shaping its primary expressions from Spain to India. The medieval period saw the consolidation of cosmopolitan urban centres across the Muslim world, connecting cities as far West as Seville to urban centres in Iraq, Persia, and India. These cities were nodes in a network of centres not only of shared commerce, but of ideas and spiritual practice. Sufi institutions such as shrines and lodges would be key institutions in these cities, hosting the development of spiritual practices such as the various forms of collective *dhikr* practice, which in some cases were integrated with the ritual use of music and dance. This sound mysticism will also be discussed in this chapter.

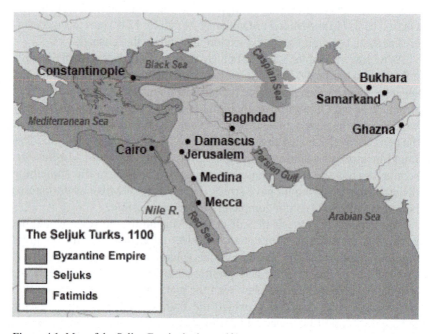

Figure 4.1: Map of the Saljuq Empire in the twelfth century.

SUFISM AND THE POLITICAL IN THE MEDIEVAL ERA

The sectarian tensions fostered by the imperial use of religious identity was a theme not only in the era of the "gunpowder empires", which saw the Ottomans and Safavids mobilizing Sunni and Shi'a identities to consolidate their rule. These tensions were further characteristic of imperial contests in the centuries prior. Political legitimacy proved to be an enduring dilemma for Muslims during the medieval period. For Shi'a Muslims, the preservation of Islam and protection of Muslims was the task of the *imam*, a divinely appointed descendent of the Prophet. For Sunnis however, the era of genuine, holistic leadership ended with the death of 'Ali ibn Abi Talib in 661, the last of the *rashidun*, or four Rightly Guided Caliphs. As we will see in Chapter 6, 'Ali is significant for both Sunnis as one of the *rashidun* and a transmitter of Sufi spirituality, and for Shi'a as the first *imam*. Following the rule of these four companions of Muhammad's, neither the Umayyad dynasty nor their successors the 'Abbasids were able to muster the religious legitimacy of Islam's first generation of leaders, and both dynasties were challenged with rival Shi'a claims to Islamic authority.

The late tenth and early eleventh centuries – dubbed by some as the "Shi'i century" – saw the rise of powerful Shi'a dynasties across the Islamic heartland. From Cairo, the Isma'ili Fatimids (969–1171) ruled over Egypt, North Africa, and the Hijaz (Mecca and Medina). The Fatimids claimed the caliphate for themselves, symbolically splitting the unity of Muslims and threatening the legitimacy of the 'Abbasid claim. Meanwhile, from Western Iran, the Shi'a Buyids (934–1062) consolidated their rule over Iran and Iraq. In 945 they took control of Baghdad, the seat of the 'Abbasid caliphate. The Buyids allowed the 'Abbasids to maintain symbolic authority in return for endorsement of their rule, though for many it was a clear blow to the Sunni caliphate. Sunnism itself appeared to be threatened by the growing hegemony of Shi'a powers.

Culturally, Islam's first dynasties saw the synthesis of Arab tribal notions of authority with Persian dynastic ones. Under the 'Abbasids, Arab tribal customs were increasingly codified in Islamic law in places like Medina and Kufa. Meanwhile, Persian kingship norms were enshrined in the court life of the 'Abbasid Caliphs in Baghdad, and Persian cultural forms were integrated into Islamic civilization with court sponsorship of the arts. By the tenth and eleventh centuries however, a third cultural influence began to shape central Islamic lands. Unable to expand eastward into China, Turkish nomadic tribes – many of which had converted to Islam – began a series of migrations into the Iranian plateau. Notably, the Oghuz peoples, led by the proudly Muslim Saljuqs, crossed the Oxus River in 1025 (Lapidus 2007: 117).

Tughril (d. 1063), the ambitious founder of the Saljuq dynasty, took the important Iranian city of Nishapur in 1037 and declared himself sultan. Under his rule, Saljuq warriors made their way to Baghdad in 1055, ostensibly to rescue the 'Abbasid Caliph al-Qa'im (d. 1075) from a Shi'a insurrection. In response to the widespread Sunni concern over the spread of Shi'a influence and social instability, the Saljuqs defined their rule as one of restoring Sunni orthodoxy and social order to Islam's heartlands. Like the Buyids before them, the Saljuqs situated their rule not as an usurpation of 'Abbasid authority, but rather as its guarantor. Within their complex and shifting relationship with the 'Abbasids, the Saljuqs essentially propped up the *symbolic* authority of the 'Abbasids, and in return the 'Abbasids conferred legitimacy on the Saljuqs' *actual* authority, as one executed on their behalf.

The Saljuq claim to Sunni orthodoxy was supported by their efforts to establish a network of Islamic universities with a systematized Sunni curriculum. The Nizamiyya were a series of universities established by Nizam al-Mulk (d. 1092), the Saljuq dynasty's most powerful administrator, and arguably one of Sunni Islam's most significant political figures. Nizam al-Mulk's academies, with their shared religious program, served a number of important functions in the Saljuq Empire. First, they trained a cadre of scholars who could disseminate an officially sanctioned version of Sunni orthodoxy that would unite the empire theologically. This was a particularly pressing matter in the eleventh century, as the lands of Islam were engulfed in sectarian feuds and religious, political confusion. Within Sunnism, various theological and legal schools engaged in bitter polemics and occasionally even violence. For the Saljuqs, not only did they want a coherent Sunnism for domestic stability, but they also needed a unified Sunni doctrine to counter the appeal of Shi'a dynasties and missionaries and the threat they posed to the legitimacy of Saljuq rule. The Fatimid's famed al-Azhar University gave Shi'a thought a sophisticated institutional basis, and made Cairo a centre of Islamic thought. Second, besides the project of Muslim unity fostered by the Nizamiyyas, they had the important function of training faithful administrators for the Saljuq regime (Safi 2006: 97). Scholars trained in these schools both staffed the Saljuq administration and anathematized the Shi'a opponents of the Turkish rulers with their writings and rulings.

The lynchpin of this Saljuq project of Sunni orthodoxy and legitimacy was Abu Hamid al-Ghazali (d. 1111). Notably it was the *sort* of Sunni orthodoxy that al-Ghazali would promote that makes him so relevant to the history of Sufism and Islam. Perhaps no name has been associated more with reconciling Sufism and *shari'a* than his. Further, it was al-Ghazali's close relationship with the Saljuq Turkish ruling elites that helped secure Sufism's place as a normative part of the larger Sunni curriculum of Islamic studies promoted by Saljuq authorities. This close relationship between Muslim ruling and Sufis, was a pattern that, as we saw last chapter, would continue to be replicated by later Muslim empires. Al-Ghazali did not accomplish this on his own of course: the Saljuqs were already building both *madrasas* and *khanaqahs* as the dual sites of Islamic study (and for them, legitimacy) (Safi 2006: xxv). Sufism was already making its way into the mainstream of Muslim life by the time al-Ghazali came on the scene. As we will see in the chapter that follows, authors such as Abu Talib al-Makki (d. 922) and Abu Nasr al-Sarraj (d. 988) in the tenth century, and 'Abd al-Rahman al-Sulami

(d. 1021) and Abu al-Qasim al-Qushayri (d. 1072) in the eleventh, developed influential works shaping Muslim perceptions of Sufism's orthodoxy. Al-Ghazali's works however would provide as unprecedented intellectual basis for Sufism's full integration into normative Islamic thought and practice (Keeler 2006: 6).

Al-Ghazali and the Politics of the Spiritual Quest

Al-Ghazali was born in Tus, a district in the Persian province of Khorasan, in 1058. In Nishapur, a city just south of Tus, he studied Islamic law and theology with Imam 'Abd al-Malik al-Juwayni (d. 1085), one of the era's most accomplished scholars, and a luminary of the Shafi'i school of law and Ash'ari schools of theology. Al-Juwayni also held the chair of Shafi'i law at the Nizamiyya academy in Nishapur. In 1091, Nizam al-Mulk appointed al-Ghazali professor of Shafi'i law at Baghdad's Nizamiyya academy, the foremost in the Nizamiyya network of universities, in the very centre of imperial power. At the age of 35, al-Ghazali became one of the most famous scholars of his time. Nizam al-Mulk bestowed upon him the titles of "Brilliance of Religion" and the "Eminence among the Religious Leaders" (Griffel 2009: 34). Al-Ghazali's fame spread far and wide, and even his theological opponents found him deeply impressive. He was not simply a famous theologian, but an important official in the Saljuq imperial apparatus, acting as something of a negotiator between the Saljuq rulers and the caliph's court in Baghdad. Al-Ghazali was, in a sense, the leading intellectual figure in the Saljuq project to establish an orderly, Sunni realm (Safi 2006). Although he was only a professor for four years in Baghdad, al-Ghazali was incredibly prolific during this period, writing upwards of 70 books while maintaining a busy teaching schedule. Many of these works sought to demonstrate the truth of Sunni Islam as against its doctrinal opponents, particularly Muslim philosophers and Isma'ilis.

Significant here is al-Ghazali's political theory. Omid Safi (2006: 110–11) observes that a close study of al-Ghazali's political writings reveal that his politics shifted significantly over time. Whereas his early writings evince a caliph-cantered notion of Islamic authority, his later writings centre more on the role of sultans who could effectively wield force and establish order. Al-Ghazali initially depicted the caliph as the key figure of power, describing the Saljuq sultans as his faithful military servants, defending his rule. In his later works however, al-Ghazali increasingly acknowledges the legitimacy of a power sharing agreement between the caliph and the sultan. Although "sultan" can refer to a leader in general, it was clear that al-Ghazali meant to affirm the authority of the Saljuq sultans. He argued that obeying a sultan, even if tyrannical or sinful, is preferable to rebellion as long as he effectively wields power and maintains law and order. With this ethos, al-Ghazali enshrined a sort of "might makes right" approach to political authority.

Like Thomas Hobbes (d. 1679) centuries later, al-Ghazali suggested that tyranny was preferable to anarchy, as long as the ruler could effectively use force to curtail the human tendency towards strife and sin. Al-Ghazali even suggested that the ability to assert raw force (*shawka*) is itself the condition for legitimate rule, and that the caliphate is only maintained with this force, which at the time only the Saljuqs could claim. Hence authority of the caliphate in a sense followed from Saljuq military power, and not the other way around.

Al-Ghazali's later writings further legitimated Saljuq rule in arguing that those who do gain leadership through the effective exercise of force are appointed by God – "'it is God Almighty who grants the rank of authority and sultanate'" (Safi 2006: 118). Muslims are hence obligated to obey the sultan, and his exercise of force is divinely mandated. For his part, the sultan is advised to keep company with and support the religious scholars, and to maintain social order and justice. As these were precisely the means by which the Saljuqs justified their rule, al-Ghazali's writings proved particularly efficacious to the Saljuq project.

The assassination in 1092 of al-Ghazali's Saljuq patron, Nizam al-Mulk, set off a period of political instability in Baghdad, with various Saljuq rulers jockeying for power. The political uncertainty in Baghdad mirrored in al-Ghazali's own growing uncertainty as to the authenticity of his faith. Seeking answers, al-Ghazali dove into the works of foundational early Sufis like al-Junayd (d. 910), and al-Qushayri (d. 1072). Although he had spent his intellectual career studying the law and engaging with philosophy, the Sufis suggested a different means of knowing, an alternative epistemology premised on *dhawq* or "taste". The Sufis held that the spiritual realities described in the Qur'ān could be "tasted" experientially, if the heart had been purified of lower desires and worldly distractions. Al-Ghazali's interest in Sufism was in part the result of the influence of his brother Ahmad al-Ghazali (d. 1123), who was already a renowned Sufi master and poet, one who never fully approved of his brother's more bookish approach to Islam.

The changing political winds, combined with his discovery of a deeper way of internalizing Islamic teachings, created a crisis of conscience for al-Ghazali. He began to question the nature of his path. How strong was his faith? How sincere was he in his practice? Did he love fame and renown more than God? How would he fare on the Day of Judgment? As these questions of authenticity came to haunt him, he considered leaving his prestigious academic post in pursuit of the deeper knowledge hinted at by the Sufis. Yet each time he considered this he was pulled back by his attachments to career, friends, family, and fame. Indeed, it is his deeply personal struggle with the contradictory pulls of family, career and the spiritual quest that make al-Ghazali's story so universal in appeal. Al-Ghazali recorded his struggle in his famous autobiography, *al-Munqidh min al-Dalal*, or "Deliverance from Error". He describes the tension reaching a fever pitch in which he succumbs to something of a breakdown. He loses the ability to speak. He physically can no longer teach; the crisis becomes acute:

> Thus I incessantly vacillated between the contending pull of worldly desires and the appeals of the afterlife for about six months, starting with July 1095. In this month the matter passed from choice to compulsion. For God put a lock upon my tongue so that I was impeded from public teaching... As a result that impediment of my speech caused a sadness in my heart accompanied by an inability to digest; food and drink became unpalatable to me... That led to such a weakening of my powers that the physicians lost hope of treating me (McCarthy 2006: 54).

Unable to speak, wasting away, and yet with no signs of physical malady, al-Ghazali's condition was a mystery to himself and his doctors. Finally he mustered the wherewithal to leave Baghdad in pursuit of spiritual knowledge, hoping that heeding the call of the spiritual quest would address his increasingly dire situation. With echoes of the story of the Buddha, al-Ghazali left a life of family, wealth, and fame, in pursuit of spiritual enlightenment.

It is important to emphasize here that al-Ghazali was also questioning his own politics at this time. He appears to have no longer felt comfortable earning his income from a state institution. Pious Muslim scholars and Sufis long stressed the importance of earning income in a way in accordance with the *shari'a*. Many scholars refused to work at state institutions such as the Nizamiyya, as they doubted the ethicality of the funding such institutions received. Famous Sufis such as 'Ayn al-Qudat al-Hamadhani (d. 1131) believed that the Saljuqs gained much of their wealth from unlawful seizure of lands and property. If this were the case, then taking income from a Saljuq institution meant earning an unlawful livelihood, one that would count against the scholar on the Day of Judgment. Joining the ranks of these pious rejecters of state employment, al-Ghazali abandoned his academic career.

To ensure that the Saljuq authorities did not get any suspicions about his leaving, al-Ghazali announced his intent to make the pilgrimage to Mecca. He then travelled to Damascus. Describing his life there, al-Ghazali wrote:

> My only occupation was seclusion and solitude and spiritual exercise and combat with a view to devoting myself to the purification of my soul and the cultivation of virtues and cleansing my heart for the remembrance of God Most High, in the way I had learned from the writings of the Sufis (McCarthy 2006: 55–56).

After staying in seclusion in Damascus for two years, often shutting himself in the minaret of the Umayyad Mosque, al-Ghazali continued his practice at the Dome of the Rock in Jerusalem and then at the sacred sites in Mecca and Medina. He made a pilgrimage to Abraham's grave in Hebron, where he vowed to never appear before a ruler – sealing his newfound commitment to distance himself from the halls of political power.

Al-Ghazali on the Nature of Love

Al-Ghazali applied his renowned ability to systemize and define to a variety of subjects, including to the topic of love, which soon became one of the most popular subjects in Islamic literature. He begins by discussing the causes of love. Al-Ghazali argues that love results from pleasure. Our nature inclines towards those things that give us pleasure, and we develop passionate love, in Arabic *'ishq*, when this inclination increases. Our five senses give us different kinds of pleasure. The pleasure of the eyes is beautiful objects, the pleasure of the ears beautiful sounds. However, Al-Ghazali contends that we have a sixth-sense, the heart (*qalb*). He says this is the most powerful sense, and the one that gives us the greatest pleasure. The heart perceives spiritual realities, which give spiritual pleasure. *Qurrat al-'ayn*, or spiritual pleasure is, according to al-Ghazali, the highest form of pleasure.

Al-Ghazali says that a person's first object of love is herself. We love our own existence, and hate the thought of non-existence, that is unless life gets so painful that it seems to be the better option. As a rule, we love anything that perpetuates and perfects our existence. Secondly, we love those who benefit us. In the case of a benefactor, the benefactor is loved not by virtue of himself but because of the benefit he provides us.

The third cause of love is the love of something by virtue of itself. For al-Ghazali this is the highest form of love. He uses beauty as an example. He argues that we love beauty in and of itself. Perceiving beauty is the essence of pleasure. Following Plato, al-Ghazali suggests that intangible objects, or qualities, can be beautiful. By intangible objects he means things such as virtue and good character. We perceive the beauty of virtue not with our five senses, but with the sixth sense, our heart, or our basic intelligence.

The fourth cause of love is a mysterious phenomenon al-Ghazali calls the hidden affinity between the lover and the beloved. Today, we might describe this as the notion of kindred spirits. Al-Ghazali quotes an Islamic scholar who says that if two spirits meet in heaven before coming down to earth, they will be natural friends in this life. This shares some analogy to the story in Plato's *Symposium* of the sexes pre-existing as one person, who are thenceforth split in half, with the one-half of the human being seeking their other half.

Al-Ghazali concludes that we love God because all four causes of love are joined in God, and really only exist in him. God is the originator of our existence, hence we love God by way of loving our existence. In other words, we love ourselves, and God created us, so we love God. Second, we love those who do good to us, and if we come to know God accurately, we know that God is our true benefactor, and the source of innumerable goods, or blessings that we enjoy. Hence we love God for the benefit he brings us. Third, we love God in and of himself. Al-Ghazali describes God as *al-jamil al-mutlaq*, or the "absolutely beautiful". Divine beauty is eternal, and goes beyond earthly, or even abstract, intangible beauty. Finally, we love God because of a hidden affinity with God. Al-Ghazali quotes the well-known verse from the Qur'ān that says that God breathed his spirit into Adam, and hence people share something of God's spirit. In some sense, our essence is the same as the essence of God, though God has this essence to a much greater degree (Abrahamov 2003: 42–62).

Al-Ghazali spent a total of twelve years travelling throughout the Middle East pursuing the spiritual practices outlined by the Sufis. After this period of intensive meditation, prayer, and seclusion, al-Ghazali confirmed through his own experience that the path of the Sufis bore the spiritual fruit they claimed it did:

> I knew with certainly that the Sufis are those who uniquely follow the way to God Most High, their mode of life is the best of all, their way the most direct of ways, and their ethic the purest (McCarthy 2006: 56).

The Sufi claim that another faculty of perception could be opened by purifying the heart, from which the perception of unseen worlds could occur, was confirmed for al-Ghazali during his years of practice. Al-Ghazali called this faculty the prophetic power – a faculty or "eye" to which all people had access, but only prophets such as Muhammad had fully opened. In his autobiography al-Ghazali outlines the various kinds of perception humans have, from the senses, to discernment, and intellect. He then describes a means of perception beyond all of these:

> Beyond the stage of the intellect there is another stage. In this another eye is opened, by which man sees the hidden, and what will take place in the future, and other things, from which the intellect is as far removed as the power of discernment is from the perception of intelligibles and the power of sensation is from things perceived by discernment... Just as the intellect is one of man's stages in which he receives an "eye" by which he "sees" various species of intelligibles from which the senses are far removed, the prophetic power is an expression signifying a stage in which man receives an "eye" possessed of light, and in its light the unknown and other phenomena not normally perceived by the intellect become visible (McCarthy 2006: 60–61).

Al-Ghazali continued to argue that, although one may not have had this prophetic faculty opened, this lack of experience does not warrant rejecting its possibility. He uses the analogy of someone born blind who, being told of colours and shapes only from hearsay, would neither understand them nor acknowledge their existence. Things we have never experienced may sound strange, outlandish, and improbable, until we encounter them for ourselves. Similarly, those Muslims who have never experienced this form of knowing described by the Sufis, should (according to al-Ghazali) not reject its possibility simply because they have no personal knowledge of it.

Al-Ghazali's reputation as a brilliant jurist, opponent of heretics, and protector of Islamic orthodoxy, likely gave his advocacy of Sufism a weight amongst Sunni Muslims that other, less established authors could have possibly mustered. Although the significance of al-Ghazali's influence is contested, historians have suggested that much of the later Sunni acceptance of Sufism as an integral aspect of Islam can be attributed to the success of al-Ghazali's advocacy of Sufism's legitimacy within Islam. In particular, he articulated the whole of the Islamic sciences as consisting of six disciplines: the first five being theology (*kalam*), jurisprudence (*fiqh*), the sources of the law (*'usul al-fiqh*), the study of *hadith*, and commentary on the Qur'ān *tafsir*. The sixth he reserved for the science of the inner world or *'ilm al-batin* (Karamustafa 2007: 107). This idea will be discussed in greater depth in Chapter 6, when connected to the Qur'ān's account of *'ilm al-laduni*, or knowledge directly from the presence of God. It was precisely this critical element of Islam that he suggested the Sufis had mastered.

It was after his pursuit of the Sufi path that al-Ghazali would write his most famous work, the "Revival of the Religious Sciences", or *Ihya 'Ulum al-Din*. The book was an instant classic and bestseller in medieval Muslim societies, from East to West, and remains so to this day. Addressing what he perceived to be an intellectual crisis in Islam, whereby its religious sciences had become nothing more than a worldly, dry, and hypocritical scholasticism, the *Ihya* offered a practical treatise for scholars and lay people alike, on how to live the Islamic faith with heart, sincerity, and spiritual felicity. In effect, he articulated an Islamic ritual and moral life infused with Sufism, or a Sufi life grounded in the practice of Islam. It was for this grand resuscitation of Islam's religious sciences that later generations would refer to him as the *Hujjat al-Islam* or "Proof of Islam".

Although al-Ghazali abandoned state institutions, he maintained a schedule of teaching and writing, only now he was teaching small circles of students in local devotionals not receiving government funds. These small corners of learning are where al-Ghazali would suggest the real lovers and knowers of God could be found, not amongst the proud scholars giving *fatwas* in the courts of rulers (Griffel 2009: 49). After returning to his home in Tus, he rejoined his family, building a small house and garden, teaching at a local school and Sufi lodge in his neighbourhood. Al-Ghazali had gone from being a famous scholar giving *fatwas* and keeping the company of rulers, to being one of the anonymous lovers of God, quietly teaching his neighbours and friends.

However, after years of anonymity, al-Ghazali returned to teaching at the Nizamiyya in Nishapur in 1106. The Nizam al-Mulk's son, Fakhr al-Mulk (d. 1106), had put significant pressure on al-Ghazali to return to public teaching. It was only after Fakhr al-Mulk guaranteed al-Ghazali's freedom to teach as he pleased however, that he consented to return to the Nizamiyya. Aware that he would receive criticism for this move, al-Ghazali legitimized his return to the Nizamiyya in his autobiography. He described consulting with people "of pure heart and religious insight" who affirmed that the religious failings and proliferation of false beliefs required al-Ghazali to leave seclusion and return to teaching publicly, despite the drawbacks of doing so.

As he suspected, al-Ghazali's teaching was controversial. More conservative scholars accused him of mixing Islam with philosophy, Zoroastrian doctrines, and unbelief. As al-Ghazali was ethnically Persian, some of this may have been Arab chauvinism, which has and continues to show up within Islamic thought from time to time. Eventually a group of al-Ghazali's scholarly opponents called for his execution, petitioning the Saljuq ruler, Sanjar, to call al-Ghazali to reckoning. In 1108, Sanjar met with al-Ghazali. Al-Ghazali's patron Fakhr al-Mulk had been killed by an Isma'ili assassin, and hence al-Ghazali was no longer under his protection, and had to make his case before the ruler. Al-Ghazali asked to be released from his teaching duties in Nishapur, but Sanjar was impressed by al-Ghazali and said that he should continue to teach publicly. Three years later, al-Ghazali would die where he was born, in Tus – his tumultuous and remarkable life coming full circle.

Al-Ghazali's life is illustrative of the ambiguous nature of Sufi relations with the political in medieval Islam. He began his career as a scholar closely aligned with a powerful Muslim dynasty, taking prestigious positions at state universities. However, with his embrace of Sufism, he distanced himself from power and politics, seeking a quiet, anonymous life of spiritual practice and teaching. However, the pressures of the world could not be put off forever, and al-Ghazali finally, reluctantly decided to return to teaching at a state institution, a move he felt compelled to justify in his autobiography, indicating the pious suspicion of such institutions prevalent during his time.

CONSTRUCTING A COSMOS:
CLASSICAL SUFI METAPHYSICS

Al-Ghazali's articulation of the *'ulum* or sciences of Islam (described earlier in this chapter) divides them into the *'ulum al-zahir*: the outward sciences, including theology, jurisprudence, *hadith* and Qur'ānic commentary, and the *'ilm al-batin*: the science of the inner world. For many Muslim intellectuals of this era, the ideal was to have a mastery of all of the *'ulum*, synthesizing outward and inward knowledge within a holistic paradigm and way of life. Al-Ghazali himself is widely reputed to be just such a synthesizer. However, many of the scholars of Islam, collectively known as the *'ulama*, remained what Sufis would call the *'ulama al-zahir*, or scholars of the outward sciences alone. Some of these scholars either totally rejected the possibility of an *'ilm al-batin* or were highly sceptical of any who claimed to have such knowledge. There was an inherent tension then between their exclusively textual claims to knowledge and the Sufi claim to a direct, experiential knowledge from the very source of the texts. This tension between different understandings of knowledge has been a perennial one throughout

Islamic history, from twenty-first century debates over what it means to be Muslim, to earlier debates over the legitimacy of an *'ilm al-batin*.

Following the intellectual foundation established by al-Ghazali, Sufism took shape as a respectable religious vocation, one essential to the institutions of power and authority in Muslim societies. However, it did not follow that Sufism was something entirely uncontroversial after the twelfth century, or that all of the *'ulama* were convinced by al-Ghazali's rhetoric. The Sufi claim to a higher, more direct form of knowledge would prove challenging and even unacceptable for some Muslim theologians and jurists who focused on the outward sciences. Although Sufis and these *'ulama al-zahir* often functioned in complementary ways, there was an inherent tension between their respective epistemologies.

For Sufis, and those *'ulama* who were themselves Sufis or at least sympathetic to Sufism, rational and textual forms of knowledge, though valid as far as they went, were in a sense secondary to an immediate, intuitive knowledge of spiritual reality. For the *'ulama al-zahir*, whose claim to authority was based on interpreting scriptures and applying legal methodology according to established traditions, the claims of others to have gained knowledge directly from God could be perceived as potentially destabilizing for the theological conclusions they came to based on more conventional kinds of scriptural interpretation. Indeed, medieval Sufis such as Ibn al-'Arabi frequently proclaimed that they, not the jurists and theologians, had authoritative knowledge of what the Qur'ān truly meant, based on *ma'rifa*: this more direct and profound sort of knowledge that trumped scholarly methods (Dickson 2015: 25). These claims had profound social implications. Where Sufis gained political patronage and popular support, even the concerted criticism of the *'ulama al-zahir* proved no match. There are numerous historical examples that show "the practitioners of Sufi epistemology are making 'normative' and 'authoritative' claims that contest, undermine, and put on the defensive legal epistemology and discourse" (Ahmed 2016: 93). Those *'ulama* who most feared the potential for claims of Sufi unveiling to contest and destabilize legalistic religious interpretations tended towards textualism, or scriptural literalism, and as a result emerged from Hanbalism's most conservative wing. Foremost among these was the Damascene jurist and scholar of *hadith*, Ahmad Ibn Taymiyya (d. 1328).

A controversial figure, Ibn Taymiyya was widely respected for his vast learning, but opposed by many for his literalistic theological views and vehement polemics, for which he was imprisoned on a number of occasions. Depending on whether one supported or opposed Ibn Taymiyya's project, he was either a pious preacher defending the authentic Islam of the first generations of Muslims, or an over-zealous, paranoid polemicist railing against Islam's natural diversity. His polemics arose out of a profound sense of crisis, greater than even the sectarian strife of al-Ghazali's age. Just as Muslims appeared to settle some of their most pressing sectarian issues, they faced the unprecedented devastation of the Mongol invasions. Led by Genghis Khan (d. 1227), the Mongols sacked and destroyed some of the most renowned centres of Muslim civilization and religious learning, including Bukhara (1220), Samarkand (1221), and later the centre of the 'Abbasid caliphate itself, the famous, cosmopolitan city of Baghdad (1258). Genghis Khan's grandson, Hulegu Khan (d. 1265), sent an emissary to the 'Abbasid caliph, al-Mustasim (d. 1258), giving the caliph the option of surrender. The caliph refused, and after a brief siege, the Mongols completely sacked Baghdad, emptying its famous libraries into the Tigris River, destroying its monuments, rounding up and decapitating its scholars, and massacring the caliph and his family. Baghdad would never fully recover from the destruction. The Mongol sacking of Baghdad marked the end of the 'Abbasid caliphate, and hence the end of a period of at least symbolic unity in Sunni Muslim societies.

Writing in this time of crisis, Ibn Taymiyya wanted to save Islam from what he believed to be its greatest enemies: the external threat posed by the Mongols and the internal threat posed by heretics of all kinds, most perniciously the Sufis. For Ibn Taymiyya, just as external invaders fragmented Muslim political power, Sufi excesses, innovations, and deviations threatened to fragment the coherence of Islam itself. Although Ibn Taymiyya did not oppose Sufism outright and was himself likely a nominal member of a well-known Sufi order, his works targeted central aspects of Sufism, laying the intellectual groundwork for later, more sustained anti-Sufi movements. He criticized the Sufi veneration of saintly masters and the prayers made at their shrines as compromising Islam's pure monotheism, which was supposed to limit veneration and prayer to God alone. He rejected the Sufi use of music and belief in saintly miracles as blameworthy innovations in Muslim doctrine. However, the majority of Ibn Taymiyya's anti-Sufi polemics were directed towards a single Sufi master and his intellectual heirs.

More than any other figure, Ibn Taymiyya was concerned about the growing influence of Muhyi al-Din Ibn al-'Arabi (d. 1240). In a sense, his focus on Ibn al-'Arabi was prescient, as Ibn al-'Arabi would indeed become the most influential metaphysician and cosmologist in the medieval period. Many Sufis consider Ibn al-'Arabi to be the *shaykh al-akbar* or "Greatest Master", offering Islamic mysticism's definitive articulation. His many works present a startlingly complex and comprehensive synthesis of the Islamic tradition that would prove popular in a variety of Muslim contexts, particularly in central Muslim lands recovering from the devastation of the Mongol invasions. If al-Ghazali laid the intellectual groundwork for Sufism's widespread acceptance within Sunni Islam, Ibn al-'Arabi built upon this foundation a remarkably intricate edifice of metaphysics and cosmology, one that continues to permeate Islamic thought, art, and culture.

It was this "philosophical Sufism" that most concerned Ibn Taymiyya, as it formed the basis for an increasingly popular understanding of Islam that made sainthood and a unitary understanding of the whole of reality its cornerstones. These emphases unequivocally affirmed the immanent (*tashbih*) presence of the sacred, in saintly people, and indeed throughout the cosmos. Ibn Taymiyya, in contrast, emphasized the uncompromisingly transcendental (*tanzih*) nature of God: God is to be understood as clearly distinct from His creation, residing in the highest heaven above. Because God is a being far above us, we relate to Him, according to Ibn Taymiyya, primarily through obeying His commands. For Ibn Taymiyya, Ibn al-'Arabi's full affirmation of God's transcendence *and* immanence, and his articulation of the cosmos' integral relationship to God's reality, violated the very core of Islam: *tawhid* or monotheism. We will see in what follows however, that Ibn al-'Arabi understood his writings as simply the most explicit metaphysical expression of Islamic monotheism as found in the Qur'ān and the traditions of Muhammad.

Whereas al-Ghazali hailed from some of the easternmost border regions of Islamic civilization, Ibn al-'Arabi came from its far west. He was born in Murcia, a town in south-eastern Spain, in 1165. Spain, under Arab Muslim rule, was known as *al-Andalus*. Although too little known in the contemporary West, al-Andalus's cosmopolitan culture is one that historians still marvel at today. Jews, Christians, and Muslims lived together in relative peace for centuries, a phenomenon rarely found elsewhere in Europe and the Middle East during the medieval era. Science, philosophy, literature, art and spirituality flourished under Muslim rule in Spain. Besides the cultural graces of Andalusian society, the natural beauty of Southern Spain contributed to the sense of enchantment al-Andalus gave to visitors, and to the almost otherworldly depiction of the region in medieval Arabic poetry. The poet Ibn Khafaja, in his *Diwan*, wrote:

> You who live in Al-Andalus, with its waters, its shade, its rivers, trees –
> how blessed are you! The Garden of Bliss is nowhere else than in your
> country, and if it was possible for me to choose between them it would
> be your country I would choose. Don't be afraid of going to Hell tomor-
> row; whoever has known Paradise will never enter Gehenna (Addas
> 1993: 11).

Ibn al-'Arabi came of age in Seville, which under the Almohads was a city of remarkable cultural florescence and learning. The near century of Almohad rule marked the final flowering of Arabic culture in Spain, and Seville was its epicentre. In her work, *Quest for the Red Sulpher: The Life of Ibn 'Arabi*, Claude Addas describes Seville as "a gigantic city, overpopulated, swarming with people, noisy, gaudy. Arabs mixed with Berbers and Andalusians, Muslims with Christians and Jews; the most depraved of libertines rubbed shoulders with the greatest of saints. It was a city of great – almost irresistible – temptation" (1993: 27).

Addas further notes that Seville hosted people of "the most diverse of talents: singers, poets and musicians mixed with *'ulama* and philosophers" (1993: 30). Ibn al-'Arabi was born into an aristocratic family. His father was a military officer in the personal service of the Almohad sultan, and the few available anecdotes of his life at this time indicate that Ibn al-'Arabi led a life typical of wealthy young Arabs, which included both the study of the religious sciences under the best *'ulama* in Seville, and considerable time for leisure and carousing with his aristocratic companions.

As a teenager, Ibn al-'Arabi partook of the all-night parties of music and dance that cosmopolitan Seville offered in plenty: "for the young Ibn al-'Arabi, twelfth-century Seville was no doubt the equivalent of today's London, Paris and New York all rolled into one" (1999: 36). His time as a young man of leisure was to be short lived. At the age of 16, Ibn al-'Arabi experienced a voice calling him to abandon his carefree lifestyle and devote himself to God. He recounts one of his first encounters on the Sufi path:

> This master came to Seville when I was just beginning to acquire knowledge of the Way. I was one of those who visited him. When I met him for the first time I found him to be one devoted to the practice of Invocation. He knew, immediately when he met me, the spiritual need that had brought me to see him.

> He asked me, 'Are you firmly resolved to follow God's Way?' I replied, 'The servant may resolve, but it is God Who decides the issue'. Then he said to me, 'If you will shut out the world from you, sever all ties and take the Bounteous alone as your companion, He will speak with you without the need for any intermediary'. I then pursued this course until I had succeeded (Ibn al-'Arabi 1971: 63).

Following this call he entered into *khalwa* (a retreat), the traditional Sufi practice of withdrawing from the world in seclusion for a set period of time, usually 40 days. Unlike most aspirants to the spiritual path, who spend years of disciplined practice seeking illumination, Ibn al-'Arabi appears to have been something of a spiritual prodigy. He reports entering retreat during the last hours of the night, and leaving retreat before sunrise, having received a powerful "opening" or illuminative experience. Shortly after Ibn al-'Arabi returned from retreat, his father arranged for him to meet the famous philosopher and judge, Ibn Rushd (d. 1198), or Averroes as he was known in medieval Europe. Ibn al-'Arabi describes their meeting as follows:

> One day I went to Cordoba to visit the *qadi* [judge] Abu Walid Ibn Rushd. He wanted to meet me personally because of what he had been told concerning what God had revealed to me in my retreat, for he showed great

astonishment at what he had heard. So my father, who was one of his friends, sent me to him on the pretext of doing some errand or other, but really in order for him to meet me. At the time I was still a boy, without any hair on my face. When I entered, he rose from his place, greeting me with great warmth and honour. He embraced me and said: 'Yes!', to which I replied: 'Yes!' He was even more pleased with me because I understood him. Then I became aware of what had given him pleasure and said to him, 'No!' At this consternation gripped him, the colour went out of his cheeks and he seemed to doubt his own thought. He asked me: 'What kind of solution have you found through divine unveiling and illumination? Is it identical with what we have reached through speculative thought?' I replied: 'Yes and No! Between the Yes and the No, spirits take flight from their matter, and heads go flying from their bodies'. Ibn Rushd turned pale, started to tremble and murmured the phrase: 'There is no power or strength save in God'. For he knew what I had alluded to (Hirtenstein 1999: 57–58).

Following his immediate, and powerfully transformative illumination in retreat, Ibn al-'Arabi left the company of his wealthy companions and began studying the religious texts with scholars in Seville. He further began a six-year spiritual apprenticeship with his first Sufi teacher. It was also during this time that Ibn al-'Arabi had his first encounter with the "master of the masterless", the immortal initiator into hidden knowledge, Khidr, about whom more will be said in Chapter 6.

One of the first stages of the Sufi path is renunciation, in which the aspirant abandons ties with the world in order to devote all their energy and focus on God alone. Beginning in his late teens, Ibn al-'Arabi started to frequent Sufi gatherings, which were generally attended by scruffy, impoverished ascetics and mendicants. His former companions were distraught at the poor company he had chosen, but Ibn al-'Arabi's priorities had drastically changed. At the age of 24, following the death of his first master, Ibn al-'Arabi began studying with numerous Sufi teachers in Seville, including an impoverished 90 year-old woman named Fatima bint Ibn al-Muthana. Ibn al-'Arabi and a friend built her a reed hut. She said of Ibn al-'Arabi:

> Of those who come to see me, I admire none more than Ibn 'Arabi. The rest of you come to me with part of yourselves, leaving the other part of you occupied with your other concerns, while Ibn 'Arabi is a consolation to me, for he comes to me with all of himself. When he rises up, it is with his whole self, and when he sits, it is with all of himself, leaving nothing of himself elsewhere. That is how it should be on the Way (Hirtenstein 1999: 79).

The year 1194 proved to be a year of trial and change for the young Ibn al-'Arabi. Both of his parents died that year – first his father, followed by his mother a few months later. Ibn al-'Arabi became the head of his household, and was responsible for his two sisters. At this time political pressures also made themselves known. King Alfonso VIII of Castile began an offensive against the Almohad kingdom, particularly the region of Seville. As he mobilized his forces to confront Alfonso's army, the Almohad Sultan Abu Yusuf Ya'qub al-Mansur offered Ibn al-'Arabi a position in his entourage and said he would ensure that Ibn al-'Arabi's sisters were married off to suitable husbands.

Refusing the Sultan's offer, Ibn al-'Arabi took his sisters to Fez in Morocco, where he found them husbands and where they settled. Ibn al-'Arabi was now free from worldly responsibilities. During the next few years Ibn al-'Arabi spent much of his time in Fez. He returned to Spain, the land of his birth for the last time in 1198. He attended the funeral of Ibn Rushd in Cordoba, and returned to the town of his birth, Murcia.

In January of 1199, Sultan al-Mansur died. For many Andalusians, this marked the end of an era, as al-Mansur was the last Almohad Sultan to effectively wield power in Muslim Spain. Perhaps Ibn al-'Arabi sensed that the sun of al-Andalus was beginning to set, as Christian armies continued to advance, and Muslim governments became increasingly unstable. Regardless, he left Spain that year for North Africa, and a year after that, in 1201, he set off from Marrakesh for the East, where he would spend the rest of his life.

Ibn al-'Arabi intended first to make the pilgrimage to Mecca. On his way to the holy city, Ibn al-'Arabi stopped in Tunis, Egypt, and Palestine. In Mecca, while praying at the Ka'aba, Ibn al-'Arabi met a young noblewoman who was to be a sort of muse for him, inspiring the composition of his greatest work of poetry, the *Tarjuman al-Ashwaq*, or "Interpreter of Desires". Ibn al-'Arabi describes his meeting with the girl, while praying at the Ka'aba, as follows:

> Suddenly a few lines came to my mind, and I recited them loudly enough to be heard not only by myself but by someone following me, if there had been anyone following me.

> Would that I were aware whether they knew what heart they possessed!
> And would that my heart knew what mountain-pass they threaded!
> Dost thou deem them safe or dost thou deem them dead?
> Lovers Lose their way in love and become entangled.

> No sooner had I recited these verses than I felt on my shoulder the touch of a hand softer than silk. I turned around and found myself in the presence of a young girl, a princess from among the daughters of the Greeks. Never had I seen a woman more beautiful of face, softer of speech, more tender of heart, more spiritual in her ideas, more subtle in her symbolic allusions... She surpassed all the people of her time in refinement of mind and cultivation, in beauty and in knowledge (Hirtenstein 1999: 148).

The young girl reprimands Ibn al-'Arabi for his lines of poetry, criticizing each one for failing to take full account of the nature of reality, and the knowledge "made known by non-existence". Ibn al-'Arabi would meet her again within days. She was the daughter of an eminent family of teachers in Mecca whom Ibn al-'Arabi came to know. Her name was Nizam. Like Dante's Beatrice, Nizam was, for Ibn al-'Arabi, a personification of wisdom and beauty. His love for her inspired a new stage in his life. Before setting eyes on Nizam, Ibn al-'Arabi had little interest in women. Though he did not seek to marry her, he did marry for the first time shortly after meeting her.

In 1204 he began a new chapter in his life, in which he was almost constantly travelling. Over the next 12 years Ibn al-'Arabi travelled widely throughout the Muslim East, including Palestine, Syria, Iraq, and Turkey. Ibn al-'Arabi settled in Damascus in 1223, where he remained until his death in 1240. In general, he appeared to have good relations with the rulers in Syria, and in Damascus Ibn al-'Arabi enjoyed the patronage of the Ayyubid princes who provided for him generously. He was able to write and teach in peace during his final years. He completed the first draft of his voluminous *Futuhat* in 1231, and a second draft in 1238. By the time of his death at 75 years of age, Ibn al-'Arabi was a renowned Sufi master, surrounded by disciples and students. He had lived and travelled through the various regions of the Muslim world, from the far West, through Africa, into Anatolia and the Middle East. He experienced the diverse range of Islamic expressions and intellectual traditions and encountered a variety of non-Muslim perspectives. This diversity of experience manifested in a broad-minded perspective that synthesized different systems of belief and thought. This encounter and embrace of religious and philosophical plurality would have a longstanding impact on later Muslims, such as 'Abd al-Qadir al-Jaza'iri, as we saw in Chapter 2.

The Nature of God and the Perfected Human Being

Along with his reputation as a *shaykh* or spiritual master, Ibn al-'Arabi is deemed by many scholars and Sufis to be Sufism's greatest metaphysician. His works provide an unparalleled explication of the different levels of reality, the relationship between God and the world, and the significance of the human being in the universe. Although his many works contain a dizzying variety of discourses, ranging from the meaning of Islamic ritual, to esoteric interpretations of Islamic apocalyptic imagery, from astrology and numerology to the varieties of spiritual experience, his metaphysics can be understood as revolving around two foci: the Absolute (*al-Haqq*) and the Perfected Human (*insan al-kamil*) (Izutsu 1983: 1).

In some sense Ibn al-'Arabi's thought is the metaphysical unpacking of the Islamic creed. God's oneness (*tawhid*) is explicated in terms of being or *wujud*. The Arabic word *wujud* derives from the trilateral root *wa-ja-da*,

Figure 4.2: Ibn al-'Arabi's shrine in Damascus, Syria.

which has the general meaning of finding, but can form the active "to find" and the passive "to be found". God as *wujud* is hence that which finds and that which is found. For Ibn al-'Arabi *wujud*, or Being, is one and only God truly has it: "*Tawhid* is expressed most succinctly in the formula, 'There is no god but God'. God is *wujud*, so 'There is no *wujud* but God'. Everything other than God is not *wujud* and can properly be called 'nonexistence' (*'adam*)" (Chittick 2005: 40). We can see here why Ibn al-'Arabi is often associated with the doctrine of *wahdat al-wujud*, or the "Oneness of Being". Although Ibn al-'Arabi never used the term *wahdat al-wujud,* with it only coming into vogue among some of his later followers (and detractors), most scholars agree that his works imply the term's ontology.

At the outset of our discussion of his understanding of reality, it is important to emphasize that Ibn al-'Arabi spoke of the Absolute as, in its most comprehensive sense, the "One/Many" or *al-wahid al-kathir* (Chittick 1994: 15). Although in its essence *wujud* is one (Allah), it appears as the many (the universe). Following the Qur'ān, which asserts that, "God is the light of heaven and earth" (24:35), Sufis have invoked analogies of light to describe God's relation to the world. If we think of God as pure light, then the world consists of the colours light reveals when shone through the prism of possibility. Without light the colours are nothing, and in a sense the colours we see through a prism are simply light. However light cannot be equated with them, and in itself remains colourless. Hence, for Ibn al-'Arabi, the subjects and objects that make up our world only exist through God. In themselves they are non-existent (not *wujud*), merely ideas (*al – a'yan* "entities") in the eternal knowledge of God, but they temporarily manifest a borrowed existence via God's existence (*wujud*). So the world and everything in it then is *huwa la huwa* or "Him/not Him", simultaneously God and not God, a dream-like realm "in between" Absolute existence (for which non-existence is impossible) and absolute non-existence (for which existence is impossible) (Chittick 1989: 82). It is for this reason that Ibn al-'Arabi labelled the world *khayal* or imagination. As in a dream, what is seen is an imagined version of reality, not reality itself. The imaginal forms (*amthal*) however symbolically express reality (*wujud*), as they are locations of God's self-disclosure (*tajalli*). Ibn al-'Arabi writes, "the Real discloses Himself within forms and undergoes transmutation within them" (Chittick 1989: 230).

Followers of Ibn al-'Arabi have mapped out the process of God's self-disclosure, beginning with Reality's most fundamental aspect, God's essence (*al-dhat*). The Qur'ān describes God as *al-Batin*, the inherently unknowable and un-manifest essence. However, the Qur'ān also describes God as *al-Zahir* – the apparent, known, and manifest. Although God's essence remains forever unknown, God can be known through his Names. Sufis long focused on God's Beautiful Names (*asma' al-husna*), which the Qur'ān is replete with, as a means to know God, and when invoked, as a means of manifesting God's qualities within oneself. Within Ibn al-'Arabi's school of thought the Names are understood as relations between the manifest God and the entities of the possible things. The Names represent God as divinity (*uluhiya*), expressed through God's actions as Lord (*rububiya*). God's acts bring the possible entities into existence within the intermediary realm between materiality and spirituality, the realm of forms or images (*amthal*), which themselves take shape in the sensible, material world, the realm of sensory witnessing (*mushahada*). So in one sense the visible world we experience is God as the Manifest (*al-Zahir*) through His Names. However, God in his essence is the un-manifest (*al-Batin*) and hence is transcendent to the world. Thus the world is simultaneously God in terms of the Names, and not God in terms of the Essence (*huwa la huwa*). Humans are tasked then with learning the language of symbols, of learning to read the world as a plethora of symbols of higher realities, as particularized expressions of the infinite forms inherent in the formless Absolute (*al-Haqq*).

Finally, it is important to highlight the dynamism inherent in the process of God's self-disclosure. According to Ibn al-'Arabi, God never manifests Himself in the same way twice, or to two people in the same way. Each person, at each moment, has a unique experience of Reality. Or, put alternatively, God manifests himself to each person, at each moment in a new and different way. Creation is forever new (*tajdid al-khalq*); God's self-manifestation is forever changing. This idea became a Sufi axiom: *La takrar fi'l-tajalli* – "There is no repetition in self-disclosure" (Chittick 1989: 103).

Besides articulating this metaphysics of "oneness", Ibn al-'Arabi was the first to fully explicate the Sufi doctrine of *walaya* or sainthood, which involved an intricate delineation of the hierarchy of saints, a specified number of which perpetually occupy the various levels of holiness and fulfil the divine functions allotted to them by God. God appoints his friends to watch over the world, and they form a hierarchy of power and blessing that secretly preserves the world throughout its term of existence. This concept, so central to Sufism, can be traced through Ibn al-'Arabi to the great scholar of *hadith* and mystic Hakim al-Tirmidhi (d. 869), and to a number of *hadith* attributed to the Prophet Muhammad, as we will consider in more depth in the following text box.

Levels of Perfected Humans: The Hierarchy of Saints

The Qur'ān describes both the *awliya' Allah* (10:62) and the *awliya' al-shaytan* (4:76), the "friends of God", and the "friends of the devil", suggesting an oppositional hierarchy of good and evil in the world. The general meaning of the term *wali* is closeness. So the friends of God are those brought near to Him in proximity. The Islamic tradition more broadly has unpacked this idea, articulating a hierarchy of friends or "saints" who occupy levels of increasing closeness to God, and are given corresponding responsibilities to carry out on His behalf. The first to write extensively on the subject of sainthood or *walaya* was al-Hakim al-Tirmidhi, who wrote the *Kitab Khatm al-awliya'* or *The Book of the Seal of the Saints*. His explication of this idea would prove controversial with some of the scholars of the *zahir* or outward understandings of Islam. Al-Tirmidhi wrote that the function of prophecy (*nubuwwa*) ends with the Day of Resurrection, when the divine law is redundant, however, he suggested that sainthood (*walaya*) is eternal, without end. Hence al-Tirmidhi argued that sainthood is superior to prophethood. Though this was frequently misinterpreted as placing the saints above the prophets, what al-Tirmidhi was actually saying was that the nature of *walaya* was superior, but that the prophets were saints first and foremost, and hence *walaya* was superior to *nubuwwa* in the persons or natures of the prophets, who themselves were superior to the saints (Chodkiewicz 1993: 30).

Early Sufi authors wrote sparingly on the subject, some describing a hierarchy of levels of sainthood, though not really explicating this in detail. Others like Abu Yazid al-Bistami (d. 874) simply said, "'the saint of Allah has no feature by which he is distinguished nor any name by which he can be named'" (Chodkiewicz 1993: 36). Later Sufis distinguished between limited and absolute sainthood: the one whose sainthood is absolute no longer experiencing the appetites of the self, emptied of personal will and desire, acting through

God and God acting through him. Descriptions of the nature of the different levels and roles of sainthood were generally incomplete and in many cases contradictory among early Sufi authors.

It was in the writings of Ibn al-'Arabi however that we see the Sufi conception of *walaya* presented in a systematic fashion. In his famous and lengthy work the *Futuhat al-Makkiyya*, he describes the different levels of sainthood in remarkable detail. He suggests that there are on the earth, at any one point in time, a total of 589 saints, occupying 35 different levels. The idea of this complex hierarchy of saints did not originate with Ibn al-'Arabi, but is found in a variety of *hadith*, whose authenticity has long been disputed, but whose influence on the Islamic tradition is notable. At the peak of this hierarchy is the *qutb* or "pole" around whom all else revolves. Ibn al-'Arabi describes the *qutb* as "'both the centre of the circle of the universe, and its circumference. He is the Mirror of God, and the pivot of the world'" (Chodkiewicz 1993: 95). The *qutb* is the leading figure of the four *awtad* or "pillars", each of whom protects one of the four directions. At any point in time there are four saints on earth fulfilling the role of the *awtad*, however, these saints are earthly representatives of the four prophetic *awtad* who exist in a spiritual form, perpetually. According to Ibn al-'Arabi, these four are Idris, Jesus, Elijah, and Khidr. Hence the earthly, saintly hierarchy represents a heavenly prophetic hierarchy of protectors.

After the four *awtad* are the seven *abdal* or "substitutes", each of whom watches over one of the seven geographical regions or climates of the world. Furthermore, each of them follows "in the footsteps" of a prophet, including Abraham, Moses, Aaron, Idris, Joseph, Jesus, and Adam. Regarding these seven, Abu Hurayra reports that the Prophet Muhammad said to him: "In a moment a man will come towards me through a door; he is one of the seven men by means of whom God protects the inhabitants of the earth". An Ethiopian man enters, described as bald with his nose cut off, carrying water on his head, a slave who washes and sweeps the mosque (Chodkiewicz 1993: 90). This innocuous, anonymous individual, who in worldly terms would be generally perceived as having a low status, is in fact one of the seven individuals tasked by God with the cosmic role of protecting all living things within their respective region. Later hagiographic tales only confirm this theme of a hidden council of saints tasked by God with preserving the world, generally consisting of people either obscure or not known for their religiosity. In one story, as one of the *abdal* is dying, the famous Sufi saint 'Abd al-Qadir al-Jilani attends a mystical council where he has a Christian from Constantinople make the profession of Muslim faith before investing him as the replacement for the *abdal* who had just passed (Chodkiewicz 1993: 91).

Ibn al-'Arabi further specified that this hierarchy of saints watching over the world consisted of both men and women, and that "each category that we speak of contains both men and women", such that any of the saints, from the highest *qutb* to the lowest of the 35 levels of sainthood, can be either male or female, as Ibn al-'Arabi affirmed again and again, "There is no spiritual quality belonging to men to which women do not have equal access" (Chodkiewicz 1993: 98).

For Ibn al-'Arabi, although God alone is *wujud,* human beings have the potential to manifest or reflect *wujud* comprehensively, unlike all other beings and things, which only manifest an aspect of *wujud*. This is the meaning of the Qur'ān's (and the Bible's) statement that humans are created in the image (*surah* or form) of God. This potential for human comprehensiveness means that humans can reflect all of God's qualities or Names. The fully realized human being or *insan al-kamil* (perfected human), manifests all of God's qualities, reflecting God's wisdom and compassion into the world. To do so however, the human has to be emptied of all created qualities, in a sense annihilated (*fana'*) to clear the ground for God's qualities to manifest and subsist (*baqa'*) in the perfected person. Hence Sufis have defended al-Hallaj's claim that "I am *al-Haqq*" ("the Truth" or "the Reality"), a figure who will be discussed at greater length in Chapter 5.

The process by which someone takes on God's qualities is known *al-takhalluq bi akhlaq Allah*, or "characterizing oneself with the characteristics of God". This is certainly one way to understand the entirety of the Sufi path: a gradual process of embodying more and more of God's qualities like generosity, justice, forgiveness, patience, wisdom, and love. As one invokes and more importantly lives these qualities, the aspirant fulfils more of the original human disposition (*fitra*) of innate goodness, which is created in the image or form of God. Once the individual manifests all of God's Names, they become marked by comprehensiveness and perfection. Thus they are able to act as a representative of God on earth, and carry out tasks of guardianship and protection of life, as envoys of God.

It was for this grand systematization of Sufi thought in terms of a metaphysics of unity and a cosmology of sainthood that Ibn al-'Arabi earned the title of the *shaykh al-akbar*, or the "Greatest Master". Some Sufi practitioners believe that Ibn al-'Arabi was the "Seal of the Saints". Just as Prophet Muhammad is believed by Muslims to have been the final prophet, hence sealing the line of prophets on earth (which according to Islamic theology is a line that begins with Adam), so Sufis believe that Ibn al-'Arabi was the final saint to inherit the comprehensive spiritual knowledge of the Prophet Muhammad, making him the Seal of the Saints, as Muhammad was the Seal of the Prophets. Ibn al-'Arabi has a providential role in preserving for posterity the comprehensive spiritual knowledge he inherited from the Prophet, a knowledge that none after him would be given.

Whether or not he is understood in this fashion, it is indisputable that Ibn al-'Arabi was a remarkably prolific and influential author, and, according to conservative estimates, wrote over 400 books. Some of these were quite short, while others, such as his famous *Futuhat al-Makkiyya* or "Meccan Revelations", are several thousand pages long. Besides the *Futuhat*, Ibn al-'Arabi's most notable and controversial work is his *Fusus al-Hikam*, or "Bezels of Wisdom". In the *Fusus*, a text that Ibn al-'Arabi says was given to him by the spiritual form of the Prophet Muhammad, Ibn al-'Arabi explores the metaphysical meaning of prophets mentioned in the Qur'ān, such as Abraham, Noah, Moses, Aaron, and Jesus. Most scholars agree that the *Fusus* expresses the quintessence of Ibn al-'Arabi's teachings, and that he composed the work to concisely summarize the entirety of his thought.

Although, as we have seen, both al-Ghazali and Ibn al-'Arabi distinguished the Sufi path from that of the theologians and jurists of the outward sciences, they shared with them an ethos of deep scholarship. In some sense, both of their lives represents the archetype of the pre-modern scholar or *'alim*, a polymath grounded in a range of intellectual traditions, who is further able to synthesize these traditions into a coherent vision of the whole.

SACRED SOUND:
MUSIC AND RITUAL IN CLASSICAL SUFISM

It is difficult to overstate the influence of Ibn al-'Arabi's complex metaphysics and cosmology on the late medieval Muslim worldview more broadly, from the Balkans to Bengal. Ibn al-'Arabi's ideas of universal oneness (*wahdat al-wujud*) and the perfectibility of the human being (*insan al-kamil*) would become central to the "Sufi-philosophical amalgam". This amalgam of philosophy and Sufism would find its way into popular poetry, narrative, and song across the Muslim world. Muslim literature and arts in the late medieval period were "marked by a developing and sophisticated discourse... that located the self in the cosmos and the cosmos in the self precisely in terms articulated by the Sufi-philosophical amalgam" (Ahmed 2016: 79).

It is important to note that the Qur'ān was at the heart both of this Sufi-philosophical amalgam and Muslim literature and arts. The word "Qur'ān" itself means "recitation". Hence Muslims have experienced the Qur'ān first and foremost as sacred sound. In a sense the Qur'ān sets a template of aural/oral culture for Muslims, one that has continued to flourish in a variety of forms, from the popularity of beautified recitation of the Qur'ān, to the call to prayer (*adhan*), and even storytelling and the public recitation of poetry. Sufis would develop this culture of sound into a spiritual science or mysticism of sound.

The Qur'ān commands above all else *dhikrullah* or the "remembrance of God", describing it as the greatest: "*Recite what has been sent to you of the Book by inspiration, and establish prayer, for prayer restrains from shameful and evil deeds, and truly the remembrance of God is the greatest. And God knows what you do*" (29:45). Sufis have thus made the remembrance of God their essential practice. The various Sufi orders eventually developed their own set of practices of *dhikr*. These have included, as just a few examples, the collective recitation of God's Names, the chanting of Allah or the first part of the shahadah: *la ilaha illa Allah*, reciting verses of the Qur'ān, invoking the names of prophets and saints, or sending greetings of peace and blessings upon Muhammad. The experience of the breath in all of these practices is essential. As such, Sufis have often coordinated the recitation of names or phrases with the breath, in most cases rhythmically, and with the body, in terms of precise postures thought to facilitate the effectiveness of the practice.

At least since the ninth and tenth centuries, Sufi poems were recited at Sufi gatherings, where they were vocally ornamented with melody, often accompanied by musical instruments, and in many cases, responded to with spontaneous dance. Known as the practice of *sema,* early Sufis such as al-Junayd (d. 910) connected the practice to the primordial covenant between humans and God spoken of in the Qur'ān, the famous day before creation when God calls upon the pre-created human beings, asking, "Am I not your Lord" (7:171), and they respond affirmatively that they witness God as their source. Junayd suggested that when people hear a beautiful, melodious voice singing, their deepest hearts are reminded of this primordial day, as the singing voice resembles God's beautiful voice asking people if they recognize Him that day (Ernst 1997: 184–85).

Alongside the Mevlevis, the Chishtis have been renowned musicians, and enthusiastically engaged in *sema* to engender an experience of closeness to God and ecstasy. Chishti musical traditions became more popularly known as *qawwali,* which to this day remains an immensely popular form of music in India and Pakistan. Abideen Pervez and the late Nusrat Fateh Ali Khan gained global recognition for their passionate performance of *qawwali* music. Sadly one of Pakistan's most famous *qawwali* singers, Amjad Sabri was killed in 2016 by the Taliban, who considered the centuries' old musical form to be blasphemous.

Similar to the Mevlevi *sema* the Chishti *qawwali* performance is a carefully programmed ritual. Although Chishtis were criticized by some of the *'ulama* for their emphasis on music, they tended to win the favour of sultans in South Asia, who were convinced in part by the power of the music itself. Indeed there are many traditions of "death by *qawwali*", in which Sufis particularly enraptured during a concert die, their souls so taken by ecstasy that they leave their body (Ernst 1997: 186–87). This confluence of life and death is further established by the timing of *qawwali* concerts: Chishtis tend to have some of their most elaborate musical performances on the anniversary of a saint's death, in an elaborate festival known as an *'urs* or "wedding". Reflecting the conventions of Persianate Sufi poetry, in which the saint's death was depicted as his or her wedding night with the Beloved, these festivals celebrate the day of the saint's death as they longed for a wedding with God.

Perhaps ironically, although ecstatic music and dance have become some of the most prominent symbols of Sufism, medieval Sufis like al-Ghazali and Ibn al-'Arabi tended to offer at best a qualified approval of music, and frequently opposed many forms of Sufi music as running contrary to the spirit and letter of Islamic law. Ibn al-'Arabi sharply dismissed Sufi musical gatherings: "There is no religion in drum, flute, and games; religion is in the Qur'ān and good morals. When I heard the book of God, it moved me; that is [true] *sama*"" (Ernst 1997: 183). Music itself has had an ambiguous and even contradictory place in the Islamic tradition. Muslims had, since the origins of Islam, appreciated the power of the human voice to inspire desired emotions (Ernst 1997: 180). The call to prayer (*adhan*) and recitation of the Qur'ān, though not technically considered music, are both ornamented melodically when recited, clearly making use of the human voice to inspire a sense of awe, repentance, devotion, and transcendence. The Sufi use of melodically recited poetry then, can be understood in this larger context of the Muslim use of vocal ornamentation for religious purposes. However, alongside the longstanding Muslim appreciation of the religious function of vocal melody, the various legal schools of Islam shared a suspicion of music as something sinful, associated with drunkenness and sexuality. Some legal scholars prohibited music outright, with the exception of religious hymns performed by men, accompanied only by a small drum. This negative attitude towards music can be accounted for in part by the fact that the culture of Arabia during the time of the Prophet Muhammad had not developed instrumental music as an art form, and it tended to be associated in that culture with the immorality and worldliness of courtly life (Ernst 1999: 95). This ambiguity towards music in the Islamic tradition is clearly reflected in Sufi discourse, which tends to carefully delineate the permissible, even recommended spiritual approach to music, and its discouraged or prohibited worldly alternative.

As previously mentioned, the term Sufis used for the spiritual experience of music was *sema* – originally an Arabic term that literally means "listening". The term "listening" centres the practice on the listener. Indeed Sufi scholars argued that *sema* was something virtuous or licit based largely on the condition of the one listening. If one's intent and desire was for God, then music could offer one of the best ways to facilitate an experience of divine intimacy. However, if one was simply amplifying one's lusts and desires through the same music, it became something disliked or prohibited (Ernst 1997: 181–82). But Islam is not limited to legal debates. Islamic civilization came to include elements running directly counter to legal discourse, with notable phenomena like wine drinking, musical concerts, and figurative painting, for example, all becoming key components of high Islamic culture, especially in the Persian cultural sphere of influence. Ruzbihan Baqli (d. 1209), hailing from Shiraz, Iran, wrote a number of influential Sufi works in Arabic and Persian, including a commentary on the Qur'ān and a visionary diary. He also wrote a manual for Sufi novices, *The Treatise on Holiness*, in which he addresses the question of music and spirituality. With his characteristically rich, hyperbolic imagery, Baqli writes that:

> Those whose physical natures are living, but whose hearts are dead, should not listen to music, because it bears harmful fruit for them. One whose heart is cheerful, regardless of whether he has reached the Beloved or not, should be listening to music. In music there are a hundred thousand pleasures, one can travel the path of mystical knowledge for a thousand years; this feat would not be easy, even for a knower of God, on the basis of religious devotion alone (Ernst 1999: 97).

Baqli suggests that music can open doorways to mystical pleasure and knowledge that are otherwise difficult to access, and hence is of great benefit to the genuine seeker. He traces the spiritual use of music to the early Sufi figures of Baghdad like Sari al-Saqati (d. 867) and Abu Bakr al-Wasiti (d. 932).

The early Sufis of Baghdad certainly used and discussed music, though its practice became more popularly associated with Sufism in the eastern Persian province of Khorasan. Abu Sa'id ibn Abi'l Khayr (d. 1049), himself a member of the Persian elite, played a seminal role in institutionalizing the Sufi use of music. Abi'l Khayr embodied the larger Sufi practice of appropriating secular cultural practices for spiritual ends. Traditionally, Persian aristocrats enjoyed concerts centred on the musical recitation of poetry accompanied by instruments and wine drinking. This poetry famously (or infamously) celebrated wine, intoxication, passion, and love. Abi'l Khayr utilized this poetry in his Sufi lodges as a means to engender *wajd* (spiritual ecstasy). Although this practice remained controversial for some Sufis, it spread widely throughout the Muslim world, with some Sufi orders developing their most important collective practices around the *sema*. Notably, as described in the previous chapter, the order based around the teachings of the famous Sufi poet Jalal al-Din Rumi, the Mevlevi order, utilized a highly structured form of *sema* as a keystone of its collective ritual life, giving us the famous "whirling dervishes", now so iconic of Sufism in general. The particular musical form used was based off of Ottoman classical music, and took shape in the eighteenth century.

THE INSTITUTIONALIZATION OF SUFISM: THE RISE OF SUFI ORDERS

After al-Ghazali secured Sufism's place within the orthodox sciences of Islam, and Ibn al-'Arabi offered a comprehensive synthesis of Sufism's worldview, Sufism shifted from being an intellectual system and spiritual path pursued by the few, to being a widespread social movement followed by the many. Although Sufism's influence was *indirectly* or *implicitly* spread via popular literature, poetry, and music, it was most directly disseminated through the formation and spread of the great Sufi orders of the medieval period. A Sufi order is called a *tariqa* (plural *turuq*). The word *tariqa* means "path" or "way"

Figure 4.3: *Sema.*[1]

and refers both to the social organization (the order or brotherhood), and to the devotional practices that form the basis of the order's structure and ritual.

As Sufism grew as a socio-spiritual movement within Islam, sites of Sufi activity shifted from the master's home or workplace, to lodges built specifically as centres of Sufi training and outreach. Along with shrines,

1.   A watercolour painting in the Shirazi style (c. 1582) depicting a sema. This picture is notable in that four women and a child are part of the Sufi circle, suggesting their initiation into the practices of the order. Permission to share this painting was given by the Aga Khan Museum.

these public centres of Sufism would compete with mosque culture as the definitive Islamic sites in this era. In southern Iran for example, Abu Ishaq al-Kazaruni (d. 1035) established a network of around 70 Sufi lodges. Celibate and vegetarian, al-Kasuruni preached an Islam of "charity and generosity to all living beings" (Karamustafa 2007: 115). To this end, al-Kazaruni's centres were built along trade routes, offering shelter to travellers, merchants, and the poor. Run by his disciples, these lodges were not primarily Sufi training centres but important sites of social service (Green 2012: 58). For his disciples however, he taught a way of life involving observance of Islamic law, avoiding the company of the rich and powerful, an hour of *dhikr* daily, and service to all. Meanwhile in Northern Iran, Abu Sa'id ibn Abi'l Khayr established a lodge exclusively devoted to Sufi training, offering a semi-monastic approach to the spiritual path. He established ten rules for his disciples, including remaining in a state of ritual purity at all times, avoiding gossip in mosques and shrines, performing the daily prayer in congregation, to recite the Qur'ān in the early morning hours and perform *dhikr* in the evening, and to welcome the poor and needy (Schimmel 1975: 243).

Within a century we see Sufi lodges emerging as important religious and social centres in the Muslim West. Under the rule of Saladin (d. 1193), the famed opponent of the Crusaders and founder of the Ayyubid dynasty, Sufi lodges flourished in Egypt and Syria, often receiving generous patronage from the Sultan himself. The association of Sufism with the official favour of respected Muslim leaders like the great Saladin certainly gave Sufism a new-found respectability among Muslims. This close relationship between imperial elites and Sufis would be a template for later empires, which hosted a saturation of Muslim culture with Sufism, as we saw in Chapter 3. Muslim traveller writers from the period marvelled at the serene beauty of the lodges, with their courtyards and fountains, and admired the spirituality of Islam's elect (Schimmel 1975: 232). Lodges for women were reported in cities like Aleppo, Baghdad, and Mecca (Karamustafa 2007: 126). Sufism now had an institutional presence across the entire Muslim world, one that was supported by the Islamic state and venerated by the Muslim populace. Following the Ayyubids and the Saljuqs, medieval Muslim rulers tended to build Sufi lodges as much as they did universities of Islamic law and theology: Sufism had come into its own.

With Sufism's doctrinal basis firmly established by al-Ghazali and Ibn al-'Arabi, and its institutional presence secured in the growing network of lodges, Sufism was institutionalized in a series of religious orders. These allowed Sufis to reproduce their path across time and space. The head of a Sufi order would appoint deputies to carry the teachings to other centres which were either regional or distant. This established a network of centres all connected by a shared master, lineage, and practice. Masters would often appoint successors before their death, and hence the particular branch of Sufi teaching represented by the master could be passed on for generations. Orders soon began to develop unique initiation rituals, rules for members, forms of *dhikr* and *khalwa*, signs of membership including distinct clothing, hairstyles, and even handshakes. Each order further developed its own orientation towards things like money, music, dance, art, and politics, with some shunning and others embracing these things to various degrees. However, it is important to point out that some orders functioned more as loose affiliations rather than established networks.

Just as the foundations of many of these orders were being laid in the thirteenth century, one of Islamic civilization's most devastating periods began with the widespread destruction of the Mongol invasions. Within a century however, the Mongols converted to Islam, and like the Saljuqs and Ayyubids before them, they legitimized their power through religious patronage, including building lodges for and allying with Sufis. As the medieval period progressed, the orders would continue to grow, encompassing thousands of members over wide-ranging areas of the Muslim world. Even the chaos and confusion engendered by the Mongol invasions did not slow this process. By the fourteenth century, Sufi orders were integral to the structure of Muslim societies. In many contexts the orders were Muslims' primary source of Islamic teaching. They offered Muslims a network of support and accountability for maintaining the laws and rituals of Islamic life, and connected them to the Prophet Muhammad's blessing and power through *silsila* (the master's lineage). The orders were central to the elite and popular practice of Islam, and they were as much sources of popular festival as they were sources of education, music, spirituality and literature. In certain regions of the Muslim world, almost every adult male had some affiliation with a Sufi order. Sufi teachers played key roles in the conversion of non-Arab peoples to Islam, and entire ethnicities came to be associated with a specific order. For example in Indonesia, the sixteenth century saw the spread of Sufism among Muslims, particularly in Aceh. Hamza Fansuri (d. 1590) for example, transmitted Ibn al-Arabi's philosophy through his Malay poetry (Knysh 2000: 286).

The outward manifestations of Sufi orders, ranging from colourful parades, cloaks, musical performances, or extensive lodges, are understood by Sufis themselves to be distinctly secondary to the order's inward aspect. The outward trappings of a Sufi order are merely the vehicle through which the master transmits the grace and blessing of the lineage, traced back to Allah through the Prophet Muhammad. For Sufis, it is this initiatic grace that charges the practices of the order with spiritual efficacy, and exposes the aspirant to a stream of spiritual power that opens doors to the unseen (*al-ghayb*) that would otherwise remain inaccessible. From the outside perspective of the observer or scholar, Sufi orders appear to be a network of sacred sites, with shared texts, traditions, and ritual practices. From the inside however, they are first and foremost a lineage of masters, who, as heirs to the Prophet Muhammad, transmit on a stream of *baraka*, grace, directly connecting the aspirant to the founder of their religion and ultimately to God.

In his classic work on the formation of Sufi orders, J. Spencer Trimingham divides the development of Sufism into three phases: (1) mystical schools, (2) *tariqa* lines, or lineages of spiritual practice, and (3) Sufi orders. In the first phase, "mystical schools", a master, in Baghdad or Khurasan, for example, begins to teach a circle of disciples the spiritual path, though at this time unaffiliated with any institutional form. Later the teachings of a particular master became more systematized, which Trimingham describes as the second phase, the formation of *tariqa* lines, in which a set of teachings and spiritual practices, the particular way or *tariqa* of a teacher, is codified and reproduced over time. Third, this coherent spiritual method then crystallizes into a concrete order, with a set hierarchy, initiation system, and sometimes, geographical affiliation (Trimingham 1998: 2–30). To illustrate this process, we will explore the formation of four important Sufi orders – the Shadhili, Qadiri, Naqshbandi, and the Chishti. Although there are numerous orders that could be chosen, including the Kubrawi, Nimatullahi, the Rifa'i, and the Suhrawardi, these four are some of the most widespread and historically influential orders, to this day, and as a result, they collectively cover a wide swath of Islamic civilization's geographical regions.

Abu Madyan and the Shadhili Order

Originating in North Africa, where the eponymous founder, Abu 'l-Hasan 'Ali al-Shadhili (d. 1258), established his first *zawiya*, the Shadhili order came to fruition in Egypt under the Mamluks. This pattern of transmission from West to East would continue throughout much of the order's history. As we saw in Chapter 2 however, the Shadhili order, via Ahmad al-'Alawi, would also play an important role in transmitting Sufism to Europe and North America, with the development of the Traditionalist school of thought. The order became formalized through the writings of important Shadhilis such as Ibn 'Ata Allah (d. 1309) as it spread throughout Egypt and North Africa. Traditionally, the Shadhilis proudly represented a strictly orthodox, sober form of Sufism. Unlike some early Sufis who advocated the abandonment of the world, the Shadhilis emphasized the importance of maintaining an ascetic lifestyle in the midst of work and family, with most learning a trade to support themselves.

Although each Sufi order traces its lineage back to the Prophet Muhammad, there is frequently a particular personage in the lineage who played a formative role in developing the order's approach to the spiritual life. For the Shadhili order, this person is Abu Madyan (d. 1198) – the great pillar of the *Maghrebi*, or Western Sufi tradition (the Maghreb being the Arabic term for North Africa), sometimes called the "Junayd of the West" (Nasr 2007: 187). As his spiritual influence spread throughout North Africa, he became increasingly eulogized as the "Shaykh of Shaykhs, Imam of the Ascetics and the Pious, Lord of the Gnostics, and Exemplar of the Seekers" (Cornell 1996: 2). Ibn al-'Arabi deeply respected Abu Madyan and longed to meet him. Though their meeting could not take place physically, biographical material suggests that the two Western Sufis shared a profound bond. Claude Addas contends that, "It was with Abu Madyan that the Sufi trend which is unique to the Maghreb really asserted itself" (1993: 60). By starting the story of the Shadhili order with Abu Madyan, we can see how his teachings were gradually transmitted as a particular spiritual method or way, which then provided the foundation upon which the Shadhili order was built.

Figure 4.4: *Zawiya* of Abu Madyan in Ubbad, Algeria.

Abu Madyan was born in the Cantillana fortress just outside of Seville. Orphaned as a child, he suffered as a labourer under his cruel brothers before fleeing in search of a better life. After time spent as a soldier in Marrakesh, he went to Fez where he studied religion at its famous University of *al-Qarawiyyin* (also written Al Quaraouiyine or Al-Karaouine), before attaching himself to a Sufi master. Notably Abu Madyan discovered al-Ghazali's *Ihya 'Ulum al-Din*, which would become one of his favourite texts, one he would later require his students to study. Al-Ghazali's powerful synthesis of Sufism and *shari'a* would become a hallmark of Abu Madyan's way. An early biographer shares an anecdote of Abu Madyan's, in which he recounts his practice of memorizing verses of the Qur'ān and *hadith* in ruins outside Fez. There he befriends a deer, who would approach and sniff him thoroughly before laying down in front of him (Cornell 1996: 4–5). The anecdote illustrates Abu Madyan's scriptural devotion, asceticism, and emerging saintly qualities, with accounts of wild animals approaching and being comfortable around a saint a recurring theme in Islamic hagiography.

After studying with a Berber Sufi *shaykh* famous for his healing abilities, Abu Madyan settled in the busy port city of Bijaya, and later died in Tlemcen, in present-day Algeria. Later accounts suggest that he made the pilgrimage to Mecca, where he studied under 'Abd al-Qadir al-Jilani (d. 1166), after whom one of the first Sufi orders would be founded (see below). However, close scholarship on these stories reveal them to be likely "pious fictions" developed by followers to account for the affinity between al-Jilani's and Abu Madyan's spiritual methods (Cornell 1996: 10–11). Most North African Sufi orders trace their lineage back to Abu Madyan, though Abu Madyan himself never founded an order. Abu Madyan taught many disciples and gave popular public talks in Bijaya. Like other *shari'a* oriented Sufis, Abu Madyan's approach was neither world denying, nor antinomian. He advocated adherence to the spirit and letter of Islam, and held that Sufis should neither shy away from social responsibilities nor abandon moral reform.

Abu Madyan's path involved rigorous ascetic practices including fasting three months of the year, while further emphasizing personal integrity and social justice. He sought to clearly distinguish false or wayward Sufi teachers from those who were authentic, and proposed that a knowledge of Islamic scripture and law, combined with self-denial and impeccable moral integrity, were sure signs of a genuine teacher. The following are a few examples of his recorded aphorisms, famous for the concise way in which they express spiritual truths and which give a sense of the flavour of his approach:

> The duration of your life is but one breath. Take care that you master it
> and that it does not master you.

> The heart has no more than one face at a time, such that when it is occupied with one thing it is veiled from another. To take care that you are not drawn to anything but God, lest He deprive you of the delights of intimate converse with Him.

> The most harmful of things is companionship with a heedless scholar, an ignorant Sufi, or an insincere preacher.

> Spiritual work is of no benefit when accompanied by arrogance, and idleness is not harmful when accompanied by humility.

> Poverty is an illumination as long as you hide it; reveal it and its light disappears (Abu Madyan, in Cornell 1996: 118–24).

Abu Madyan's particular emphasis on social justice caught the ear of the Almohad caliph Yaqub al-Mansur (d. 1199), who was concerned about the political implications of Abu Madyan's message. Fearing he might be a source of sedition and rebellion, al-Mansur had Abu Madyan summoned to Marrakesh to address his concerns. Abu Madyan never made it to the Almohad capital, dying on his way there in 1198, just outside of Tlemcen. We may conceive of Abu Madyan's teaching during his life as falling within Trimingham's first phase of Sufism's development: an informal mystical school.

In face-to-face interactions, Abu Madyan trained a close circle of disciples in a particular approach to the spiritual path, here marked by adherence to the *shari'a*, frequent fasting, social responsibility and personal integrity. Much of his focus was on the intensive training of a few close disciples, fulfilling the role of a *shaykh al-tarbiyya* or "master of spiritual training", as opposed to a Sufi theoretician. Following his death, Abu Madyan's nucleus of closely trained disciples moved throughout North Africa, spreading his teachings as far as Egypt, Syria, and Yemen. The transmission of Abu Madyan's way can be thought of in terms of Trimingham's second phase: a *tariqa* line, or mystical way.

At this point, Abu Madyan's approach transcends the group of disciples he trained, as these disciples now transmit his way to a new generation of disciples: a wide-ranging body of Sufi practitioners now share an approach to the path originating with Abu Madyan. This is not the final phase however. Abu Madyan's "way", or particular approach to spirituality, was transmitted by his student 'Abd as-Salam ibn Mashish (d. 1228), to his eminent disciple Abu 'l-Hasan 'Ali al-Shadhili, whose teachings become organized into an order.

Al-Shadhili had previously spent time studying Sufism in Iraq with a disciple of the famous Sufi Ahmed al-Rifa'i (d. 1182), before meeting Ibn Mashish in Morocco, who he would take as his primary spiritual master. He spent years with his beloved master before leaving for Tunisia, after Ibn

Mashish was murdered on the orders of a local ruler. In Tunisia al-Shadhili gained a reputation for healing and miracles, and his resulting popularity with the locals garnered the fear and loathing of the powerful scholars of the University of *al-Qarawiyyin*. He then settled in Alexandria, where he was popular among scholars and lay followers. He died on his way to Mecca in upper Egypt (Knysh 2000: 208–209).

Although he did not leave behind a large body of writings, al-Shadhili's disciples gathered together anecdotes about his life, his sayings and his prayers, to form the basis of the Shadhili order (Knysh 2000: 209), representing Trimingham's third phase of Sufi development, in which a mystical way is crystallized into an order. Al-Shadhili maintained Abu Madyan's emphasis on devout observance of the *shari'a*, scriptural study, self-denial, moral integrity, and social justice, and these have been the hallmarks of the Shadhili order since. Trimingham understood this movement from informality and intimacy to codification and popularity as an unfortunate reification and decline of Sufism, from a pure mysticism, to a popular social institution. Today, scholars are likely to acknowledge that mysticism need not be divorced from overtly social functions, or popular appeal.

'Abd al-Qadir al-Jilani and the Qadiri Order

Although not as famous in the West as Ibn al-'Arabi or Rumi, 'Abd al-Qadir al-Jilani occupies a preeminent place in Islamic spirituality as well as in popular Muslim imagination. If Abu Madyan can be thought of as the "Pole" of the West, so Abd al-Qadir can be considered the "Pole" of the East. Some even consider him the "Pole", or highest master, of the entire Sufi tradition. Although he never founded an order, the order bearing his name became one of the earliest and most widespread in the Muslim world, changing the face of Islamic spirituality while imbuing popular cultures from Africa, through Central and South Asia, into East Asia as well.

During the three centuries following 'Abd al-Qadir's death, branches of the Qadiri order emerged as far afield as what is today known as Algeria, Nigeria, the Sudan, Bosnia, Turkey, Iraq, into Afghanistan, Sri Lanka, and Thailand, Indonesia, and Malaysia. Each order developed its own symbols, rituals, and litanies, with only some of these being ascribed to 'Abd al-Qadir – the remainder being evidentially later additions to the order's practice. In many of these cases, 'Abd al-Qadir functions as a symbol and inspiration, rather than as a teacher whose teachings are practiced through a direct line of transmission.

In popular literature, poetry, and song throughout the Muslim world, 'Abd al-Qadir is colourfully depicted as the archetypical saint, one given miraculous powers and knowledge of the unseen world; a spiritual hero who conquers the forces of evil and establishes the good in people's hearts.

Millions, especially in South and Southeast Asia where he remains popular, see him as an intercessor with God on behalf of Muslims in peril.

Despite his legendary status and renown for the miraculous, 'Abd al-Qadir was a sober Sufi, and a strict follower of the conservative Hanbali school of law. As is apparent from his recorded speeches at universities and Sufi lodges in Baghdad, 'Abd al-Qadir was a revivalist preacher, who spoke in prophetic voice, with a clear sense of his own divinely ordained mission to renew the spirit and letter of Islamic practice, and return the people to the path of God. Like Abu Madyan, 'Abd al-Qadir was both a powerful public orator and a master to a close circle of disciples. Also, like Abu Madyan, 'Abd al-Qadir married a profound spirituality with an emphasis on the sacred law, morality, and social justice.

His life began in poverty and obscurity, but ended in fame and renown. Born in Jilan, a district in North Iran, 'Abd al-Qadir left for Baghdad when he was just 18 years-old. He avoided studying at the famous Nizamiyya Academy, which was likely due to his Hanbalism, as the Nizamiyya Academies were predominantly Shafi'i and Ash'ari in orientation. After studying Hanbali law and *hadith* for a number of years in Baghdad, 'Abd al-Qadir studied Sufism with Abu'l Khayr al-Dabbas (d. 1131), who subjected him to intensive practices of self-denial (Knysh 2000: 180). He continued to practice his master's severe way, spending at least 10 years in seclusion in the desert surrounding Baghdad, fasting frequently, spending nights in prayer. 'Abd al-Qadir's, in a purportedly autobiographical account, describes how he began preaching:

> One morning I saw the Messenger of Allah. He asked me, 'Why do you not speak?' I said, 'I am but a Persian, how can I speak with the beautiful Arabic of Baghdad?' 'Open your mouth', He said. I did. He blew his breath seven times in my mouth and said, 'God, address mankind and invite them to the path of your Lord with wise and beautiful words'.

> I performed my noon prayer, and turned to see many people waiting for me to speak. When I saw them I became excited and tongue-tied. Then I saw the blessed Imam 'Ali. He came to me and asked me to open my mouth, then blew his own breath into it six times. I asked, 'Why did you not blow seven times like the Messenger of Allah?' He said 'Because of my respect for him', and disappeared.

> From my open mouth came the words, 'The mind is a diver, diving deep into the sea of the hearts to find the pearls of wisdom. When he brings them to the shore of his being, they spill out as words from his lips, and with these he buys priceless devotions in Allah's markets of worship...'. Then I said, 'In a night such as one of mine, if one of you should kill his low desires, that death would taste so sweet that he would not be able to taste anything else in this world!'

> From then on, whether I was awake or asleep I kept my duty in teaching. There was such an immense amount of knowledge about faith and religion in me. If I did not talk and pour it out, I felt that it would drown me. When I started teaching I had only two or three students. When they heard me, their numbers increased to seventy thousand (Bayrak 1992: xix–xx).

His preaching only began after his return to Baghdad following this lengthy period of seclusion. 'Abd al-Qadir did not appear as a Sufi, but maintained the dress of the jurists. He was a fiery orator, calling for repentance and purification, and the scrupulous practice of Islam. He drew increasingly large crowds in Baghdad, and soon led schools, lodges and mosques.

Because his recorded speeches do not contain much in the way of explicit mystical teachings, many scholars remain baffled as to how this revivalist preacher and jurist in Baghdad came to have a reputation as one of the highest spiritual masters and saints in the Islamic tradition, with some depicting him as the pinnacle of sainthood, the "Pole" of the universe itself. There is no simple explanation for 'Abd al-Qadir's fame. He clearly had a profound influence on many Muslims during his life. Significantly, his sons, disciples and later biographers would spread accounts of his spiritual power, miracles, and sincerity, shaping later Muslim perceptions of 'Abd al-Qadir. Like al-Ghazali and Ibn al-'Arabi, 'Abd al-Qadir is thought by some to be a reviver or *mujaddid* of his age.

Although 'Abd al-Qadir was both a teacher of the law, as well as a spiritual master, his sons each took over one of these functions. His son 'Abd al-Wahhab (d. 1196) inherited his father's college, while his son 'Abd al-Razzaq (d. 1206) inherited 'Abd al-Qadir's Sufi lodge. Both institutions were lost with the sack of Baghdad by the Mongols in 1258. Following the Mongol destruction of Baghdad, 'Abd al-Qadir's descendants and students were scattered, transmitting his teachings to Yemen, Egypt, and Syria. During his life 'Abd al-Qadir tended to tailor spiritual exercises to the needs of each of his disciples, like a physician carefully prescribing the remedy needed for the variety of illnesses. This approach of his perhaps translated into the relatively structure-free form of the Qadiri order, which fostered a wide range of spiritual techniques in its various branches (Knysh 2000: 185).

The Naqshbandi Order

The Naqshbandis are also a prominent Sufi order with a long history of association with Sunni political elites, as we saw in the previous chapter. In contrast with the later visibility and public prominence of the Naqshbandiyya however, the order began rather secretly as a Central Asian Sufi methodology known as the "Way of the *Khwajagan*" or "masters". Their secrecy was connected with their political context: non-Muslim, Mongol rule of Central Asia meant that early Naqshbandis were unable to establish public institutions and political relationships until later in the order's history when they functioned under Muslim rule. The first of the *Khawajagan* or masters was Abu Ya'qub Yusuf Hamadhani (d. 1140), although it was his successor Khwaja 'Abd al-Khaliq Ghujduwani (d. 1179) who would establish the unique approach of the Naqshbandi order, including the silent *dhikr* (remembrance of God) and the eight original precepts of the Naqshbandi path. These remain a key part of Naqshbandi practice, and are (1) the constant remembrance of God throughout the day; (2) making the return to God one's sole purpose; (3) vigilantly maintaining watchfulness over one's thoughts; (4) concentrating on God's presence; (5) mindful breathing; (6) journeying home to God; (7) watching one's steps; and (8) solitude in the crowd, being outwardly with people but inwardly with God (Lizzio 2014). The Naqshbandis traced their practice of the silent *dhikr* to Abu Bakr (d. 634), who, as the first Caliph recognized by Sunnis, placed Naqshbandis firmly within the Sunni fold.

Baha'-al-Din Naqshband (d. 1389), after whom the order is named, was said to have been initiated into the path directly by Ghujduwani, who died two centuries before Naqshband. This would set a trend among Naqshbandis that continues to this day, namely the initiation and training of a living Sufi aspirant by the spiritual form or *ruhaniyya* of a master who has long since passed from physical existence. Naqshband would contribute an additional three of the order's 11 precepts: (1) temporal awareness, or awareness of how one is spending one's time, (2) numerical awareness, keeping count of the repetitions of one's *dhikr*, and (3) heart awareness, or mentally imprinting the name of God on one's heart (Lizzio 2014). According to Naqshband, *"The exterior is for the world, the interior for God* or in Arabic, *al-zahir li 'l-khalq al-batin li 'l-Haqq"* (in Trimingham 1998: 63).

The Naqshbandi order grew from the spiritual tendencies that took shape in Central Asia, in particular from a movement known as the *Malamatiyya* – the "People of Blame". The *Malamatiyya* attempted to closely emulate the Prophet Muhammad's model, which included an integration of spiritual depth with the social roles of everyday life, and the practice of constant self-critique or "blame". Hence the *Malamatiyya* sought to blend in with the crowd, to avoid any spiritual ostentation or egoic temptations that arise from being perceived as a "special" or "spiritual" person. They would even go so far as to purposely do something considered odd or disreputable, to ensure that they avoided the egoic satisfaction of social approval. The ideal of being a spiritually realized, self-critical person who is hidden in the crowd was one the *Malamatiyya* sought to realize. Emerging from this early spiritual tendency, the Naqshbandi order developed an approach to the spiritual life characterized by sobriety, shunning the devotional musical concerts known as *sema*, downplaying feats of charisma and miracle, and favouring development through spiritual companionship (*suhbat*) rather than *khalwa* (periodic retreat) (Knysh 2000: 221). They were further known for their emphasis on adherence to the *shari'a,* and their critique of other orders the Naqshbandis deemed to be wayward or lax in their belief and practice.

Contrary to Ghujduwani's advice to avoid rulers or service to them, Naqshband developed close ties to the Timurid (1370–1507) dynasty, setting a precedent for Naqshbandi involvement with a variety of political dynasties thereafter. These political alliances were fruitful for the order, as by the sixteenth century the Naqshbandis had established themselves as the predominant form of Sufism in Central Asia. Naqshbandi *shaykh* Ubayd Allah Ahrar (d. 1490) is exemplary here, both for his role in spreading the Naqshbandi order in Central Asia, and also for his remarkable economic ventures and political influence. Ahrar is recorded as having accumulated hundreds of villages and farms, making him the largest landowner in the region. He is said to have staved off conquest, shielded peasants from oppressive taxation, and advised Timurid Sultans on how to better rule by Islamic ethical norms (Le Gall 2005: 138). Ahrar's sons and successors would thenceforth assume roles as political advisers and spiritual mentors to sultans in Central and South Asia, frequently intermarrying with Timurid and Mughal royal families. This close relationship with Timurid and later Mughal elites would be mutually beneficial: the sultans gained religious legitimacy and access to spiritual *baraka* through Naqshbandi endorsement and affiliation, and in return the Naqshbandis received patronage and an elevated social status (Buehler 1998: 63).

The establishment of the Naqshbandis in Central Asia would soon lead to their spread into the Ottoman Empire, where they were generally well received by Ottoman elites, as a particularly Sunni, orthodox form of Sufism in line with official Ottoman doctrine. Then, in the sixteenth and seventeenth centuries, the Naqshbandi Sufi leader, Ahmad Sirhindi (d. 1624), would lead to a revival of the order in South Asia and later throughout the Middle East and Central Asia. This was discussed at greater length in Chapter 3.

The Chishti Order

Arab Muslim armies, within a century of the Prophet's death, conquered the western provinces of the Indian Subcontinent in 711. Starting in the year 1000, a second wave of Muslim conquests in India began, this time from Central Asia. Although Sufis found their way into the region during this period, Sufism would only act as a decisive influence on South Asian Islam in the late twelfth and early thirteenth centuries (Schimmel 1975: 345). Much of this impact was a result of the immense popularity of the Chishtiyya, and the saintly renown of the order's founders.

It is interesting to note that, "the Chishti order of Sufis is essentially an Indian one. Other branches emanating from the town of Chisht in modern Afghanistan did not survive for long in the Perso-Islamic world" (Hodgson 1974: 114). This is largely due to the founders' conscious adaptation of Sufi practice to an Indian, Hindu context. Unlike the majority of Sufis, and perhaps reflecting Hindu norms, many Chishti dervishes were celibate. Chishti himself was for many years, but after settling in Ajmer, he took two wives, seeking to imitate all of the Prophet's practices, including marriage. In contrast with the Naqshbandis, who that sought to maintain clear borders between Muslims and Hindus, the Chishtis comfortably adopted Hindu practices, including prostrating before the spiritual master and shaving the head of new disciples. This approach resonated with efforts of Mughal leaders like Akbar (d.1605), who sought to draw out the shared values between Muslims and Hindus. Also, unlike other orders, the Chishtis did not require conversion to Islam to enter the order. This set an important precedent in disconnecting the Sufi spiritual path from Muslim identity. In some localities Hindus made up the majority of a Chishti *shaykh's* followers. At its core, the Chishti path was a vibrant branch of Islamic spirituality, however, it was a branch premised on adapting this spirituality along the cultural contours of a predominantly Hindu society.

The founder and arguably most influential representative of South Asian Sufism remains Mu'in al-Din Chishti (d. 1236), born in Sijistan, an eastern province of Persia. He was forced out of his home by invasions, and wandered for many years before reaching Delhi in 1193 and then settling in Ajmer: "his dwelling place there soon became a nucleus for the Islamization of the central and southern parts of India" (1975: 345). Chishti missionaries were very active in the region and responsible for much of Islam's spread. Their simple message of love of God and service to humanity, and their emphasis on accepting all, regardless of caste or creed, gained them widespread respect and popularity in India.

Chishti, following al-Bistami, held that the Sufi should possess "a generosity like that of the ocean, a mildness like that of the sun, and a modesty like that of the earth" (Schimmel 1975: 346). This spiritual humanism had tremendous appeal in the polyvocal religious climate of medieval India, and to this day Hindus and Muslims alike congregate at the shrines of Chishti saints for stirring music, such as *qawwali*, blessing, and shared devotion. Although universal in orientation, Chishti held that dervishes must be scrupulous in their religious and moral practice. Besides following the moral and ritual guidelines of the *shari'a*, a Chishti dervish was expected to abide by nine stringent conditions, which effectively guaranteed their poverty, humility, generosity, and devotion:

1. One should not earn money.
2. One should not borrow money from anyone.
3. One should not seek help from anyone even if one has not eaten for a week.
4. If one gains food, money, clothing, such wealth should be distributed to others before the following day.
5. On should never curse anyone, or respond to attack, but pray for one's enemies.
6. All of one's good deeds should be understood as the *shaykh's* grace, or the intercession of the Prophet Muhammad with God on one's behalf.
7. One should take personal responsibility for all evil deeds and seek to avoid them.
8. One should regularly fast during the day, and spend one's nights in prayer.
9. One should speak only when it is necessary to do so, otherwise remaining silent.

Besides their association with music, the Chishtis were famous for their service to those on the margins of society. Mu'in al-Din was reported to have held that the highest form of worship was to assist the helpless and to feed the hungry. This ethos of helping the poor took shape in Chishti Sufi centres in South Asia, which tended to include a *khanaqah* for Sufi activity, a fully-equipped kitchen (*langar khana*) to feed the poor on a daily basis, and a main gathering hall (*jama'at khana*) (al-Huda JRS 17 [2003]: 63).

Following his death in 1236, Mu'in al-Din Chishti's shrine in Ajmer became an important centre of Sufi practice, as well as a popular pilgrimage site. There are huge cauldrons on the premises which for centuries have been used to cook food for the poor and for travellers. Notably, Chishti's daughter, Bibi Hafiz Jamal, is buried next to him and is considered to be his spiritual partner. The importance of Chishti's status in South Asian Islam was reflected in the range of political rulers who have felt compelled to sponsor and support his shrine. This aspect of shrine culture was discussed in greater detail in Chapter 3: "the structural development of the shrine (*dargah*) was largely due to political patronage from the Delhi Sultans, Mughal rulers, Rajputs, Nizâms of Hyderbad, the British empire and the modern Indian government" (al-Huda JRS 17 [2003]: 63). In the sixteenth and seventeenth centuries, Mughal rulers – including the famed Akbar – expanded Chishti's shrine complex (*dargah*), constructing larger, more ornate prayer halls and facades, as well as a college on the site, known as the famous *Fatehpur Sikri*, discussed in Chapter 3. Chishti's shrine was particularly loved by those rulers who sought a spiritual and theological reconciliation of Hinduism and Islam, as his teachings seemed to lend themselves so well to this project. Even the British Queen Mary endowed repairs to Chishti's shrine in 1911. Today, the shrine hosts large crowds who gather for *qawwali* performances of devotional songs to the saint, who is said to manifest most powerfully at sunset.

Like a Sufi practitioner emerging into the world after 40 days of isolation in retreat (*khalwa*), Sufism itself emerged from the hidden margins of Islamic history, and took its place in the very centre of Islamic civilization during the medieval period. In the eleventh and twelfth centuries, the seeds that had germinated underground in Islam's early years sprang forth into the daylight of Muslim public life, bringing to fruition Sufism's cultural, philosophical, and political implications. Synthesizers and revivers like al-Ghazali and Ibn al-'Arabi forged intellectual paradigms that integrated Sufi forms of knowledge with the outward sciences of Islam, paradigms that would shape the classical Islamic tradition for centuries to follow. As a result, post-Mongol Islam would be deeply Sufi in orientation, from Spain through to the Middle East and into South Asia. In the next chapter however, we follow Sufism's trail underground, back into the formative period of Islam, examining the seeds, both doctrinal and practical, planted by Islam's earliest spiritual luminaries.

Discussion Questions:

1. Briefly describe al-Ghazali's politics and how they changed throughout his life.
2. Is *wahdat al-wujud* or "the oneness of being" an adequate description of Ibn al-'Arabi's thought? (Why or why not?)
3. How have Sufis understood the role of music in the spiritual life of Islam?
4. Briefly describe the development of orders within Sufism.
5. Why was this era known as an age of synthesis? What were the different currents of thought that were brought together during this period?

Further Reading:

Ahmed, S. (2016). *What is Islam? The Importance of Being Islamic*. Princeton, NJ: Princeton University Press.

Chittick, W. C. (1989). *The Sufi Path of Knowledge: Ibn al-'Arabi's Metaphysics of Imagination*. Albany, NY: State University of New York Press.

Chodkiewicz, M. (1993). *Seal of the Saints: Prophethood and Sainthood in the Doctrine of Ibn 'Arabi*, trans. Liadain Sherrard. Cambridge: The Islamic Texts Society.

Ernst, C. W. (1999). *Teachings of Sufism*. Boston, MA: Shambhala.

Moosa, E. (2005). *Ghazali and the Poetics of Imagination*. Chapel Hill, NC: The University of North Carolina Press.

Rosenthal, F. (2007). *Knowledge Triumphant: The Concept of Knowledge in Medieval Islam*. Boston, MA: Brill.

Safi, O. (2006). *The Politics of Knowledge in Premodern Islam: Negotiating Ideology and Religious Inquiry*. Chapel Hill, NC: The University of North Carolina Press.

Trimingham, J. S. (1998). *The Sufi Orders in Islam*. Oxford: Oxford University Press.

A REALITY WITHOUT A NAME:
EARLY SUFIS AND THE FORMATION OF
TRADITION

As we have seen throughout this book, the external manifestations of Sufism are all vehicles for the transmission of *baraka*, the spiritual force and blessing that the master transmits to disciples through companionship and teaching. For Sufis, the essence of the matter then, is not the outward trappings of Sufism, its lodges, orders, shrines, festivals, and rituals, but this inner, unseen spirit that transforms those who encounter it and infuses these various aspects of the tradition. As we saw in the beginning of this text, in Manhattan, Lex Hixon was invested with the *baraka* of the Jerrahi order, symbolized by the turban his master placed on his head. It was the reception of this *baraka* that authorized Hixon as a *shaykh* in his own right. In Chapter 2, we witnessed the efforts of Sufis like 'Abd al-Qadir al-Jaza'iri and Ahmad al-'Alawi to preserve and exemplify the *baraka* of their path in the midst of colonial invasions and the rise of anti-Sufi movements. Then, in Chapter 3, we learned that even the great sultans and caliphs of Islam's empires sought out the *baraka* of Sufi saints in visiting their resting places. In Chapter 4, we found one of Sufism's most influential figures, Ibn al-'Arabi, in one of his first encounters with a Sufi teacher, affirming that it is ultimately the *baraka* of God that determines one's success on the path – not one's own efforts, despite the necessity of the discipline of the path.

As the great synthesizers of the medieval Islamic tradition Al-Ghazali and Ibn al-'Arabi would seek to articulate in their many treatises, the wholeness of Islam consists of the outward forms of the religion, animated by this inward spirit or *baraka*. They were, in a sense, the lead architects of a new synthetic orthodoxy that integrated the spiritual idealism of Sufism with the doctrinal realism of Islamic law and theology. To understand their projects, and the need for such a reconciliatory synthesis, we explore in this chapter the first four centuries after the Prophet Muhammad's death in 632. This time is known as the formative period of Sufism, when the religion of Islam shifted from being a new, marginal Arabian religious movement to becoming the basis for poly-cultural and wide-ranging empires: the Umayyads of Damascus and the 'Abbasids of Baghdad. Under the umbrella of empire, competing schools of thought formed and debated what it meant to be Muslim – to live in accordance with Qur'ānic precepts as exemplified by the model of the Prophet Muhammad.

This decisive age would see the birth of institutions and forms of religious thought that would shape the communal and devotional life of Muslims for centuries to come. While the institutions and modes of reasoning that eventually took root may now seem to have been inevitable, early generations of Muslim scholars actually engaged in vigorous debates about how best to know God's will for humanity, and how to understand and practice Islamic precepts. To cite just one example of these multivalent intra-Islamic debates, today many Muslims equate Muhammad's *Sunnah* (his "way" or lifestyle) with *hadith* (authenticated reports about what he said or did). However, during this formative period, Muslims engaged in a sustained dialogue on the value of *hadith* for accessing the *Sunnah*, with key figures arguing for alternative means of accessing the *Sunnah* as being superior.

Sufism emerged from within this religious landscape in which strong disagreements flourished, particularly between jurists and philosophers – that is, between those Muslims who regarded juristic reasoning as the definitive method for establishing and maintaining religious community, political order, and authoritative norms for social and spiritual life, and those Muslims who granted a greater role for philosophical reason in deriving the norms to guide individual and communal pursuits. Out of these debates, which were highly connected to the development of the first Muslim states (i.e. the formation of the imperial caliphate), one witnesses the early Sufi ascetics and mystics navigating through the politics of piety.

We begin with the great political debates in Baghdad during the ninth and tenth centuries, where we will trace socio-political reasons for the significant influence of a Baghdadi master, Abu al-Qasim al-Junayd (d. 910), whose followers would play a profound role in the formation of classical Sufism. In particular, we examine the conflicted relationship between the jurist Ahmad Ibn Hanbal (d. 855) and a leading Sufi figure known as Harith al-Muhasibi (d. 857), as well as the impact of the Inquisition of 877–878 on early "ecstatic" and "sober" Sufis as they navigated controversies over certain metaphysical claims and reacted to the notable death of Sufism's famous "martyr of love" Mansur al-Hallaj (d. 922). The reader will also learn an important political genealogy of the early Sufis that ties al-Junayd to "the patriarch of Sufism", Hasan al-Basri (d. 728) whose life would influence many future Sufis, particularly those who emphasized renunciation of worldly gain and an austere life dedicated to spiritual practice.

Before matters of mysticism and religious orthodoxy could be debated in the halls and seminaries of Baghdad, Sufism was first, as Abu'l Hasan Fushanji (d. circa tenth century) famously said, a "reality without a name", cultivated in the ascetic practices and mystical principles of Sufism's spiritual pioneers. Sufism however was not alone in this respect. The early Islamic sciences – legal, theological, and mystical – took centuries to crystalize into their medieval forms. Like Islamic law, Sufism formed around the teaching circles established by the Prophet Muhammad's prominent Companions (*sahaba*). As the Companions settled in cities like Kufa, Basra, and Fustat, their knowledge of the Qur'ān and *Sunnah* was shared with their closest followers, who in turn passed these teachings on to the next generation. As these teachings were transmitted across time, they began to take shape as separate disciplines of law, theology, and spiritual practice. In particular, Sufism's early pioneers, who have sometimes been referred to as "proto-Sufis", emerged as exponents of the Qur'ān's hidden or esoteric meanings, as rejectors of the new-found wealth and worldly status attainable within early Islamic empires, and as proponents of relating to God not simply as a law-giver and lord, but also as an intimate friend and lover. Hasan al-Basri, for example, was said to have been raised in the home of one of the Prophet's wives, and studied under 'Ali, the famed repository of Muhammad's spiritual teachings. Al-Basri then settled in Basra in Southern Iraq, where he gained renown as a pious ascetic, preacher, and mystical teacher. Another seminal figure of this era whom we will consider is Rabi'a al-'Adawiyya (d. 801), the great female Sufi and representative of the path of divine love.

In exploring the early Sufis, this chapter also offers a glimpse into their well-known contributions found in the voluminous works of Sufi biographers, especially Abu al-Qasim al-Qushayri (d. 1072). Their legacies were recorded in aphorisms, pious narratives, and poetry of spiritual longing and discovery. Many of these early Sufis were able to convey their messages and life's practices artistically, through poetry, which would influence a plethora of generations to come.

THE POLITICS OF PIETY:
EARLY SUFISM AND THE DEBATES OVER BEING MUSLIM

If Sufism had emerged as a unified and homogeneous system, there would have been little need for the great Sufi synthesizers of the medieval age, except perhaps to bridge the divide between esoteric and exoteric expressions of Islamic faith. In its beginnings, however, Sufism was far from a unified system. Rather, early Sufism was more akin to a diverse collection of fabric patches, each woven from the spiritual practices and teachings of a different mystic and his or her associates or successors, but not integrated with other patches, in the manner of a patchwork frock. In fact, just such a frock would become one of the most recognizable signs of Sufism, worn by mendicant dervishes as a symbol of poverty and transmission of *baraka*, as discussed in Chapter 3. The Sufi tradition of bestowing a frock or robe (*khirqa*) upon an aspirant represented the master's passing on to the disciple the *baraka* of the path that originates with God through the Prophet Muhammad. The diversity of these patches, or different ascetic and spiritual examples, together with the practices and patterns created by early theologians, prophetic tradition collectors, jurists, and philosophers, gave rise to vigorous debates about what it means to be a good Muslim. The Arabian Peninsula, Iraq, Syria, and Egypt became the crucibles of diverse authoritative personalities, schools of thought and political parties, each arguing their own particular understanding of how to define the norms guiding human behaviour and relationships.

In the beginning, amongst the first generations of "successors" to the Prophet (i.e. early Muslims who came after the Prophet Muhammad's immediate Companions), was the famous ascetic Hasan al-Basri. He and his followers in the area of Basra, Iraq, established the precedence of *zuhd* (ascetic practices) which would eventually become central to Sufism more universally. Like other early Sufi ascetics, al-Basri modelled an austerely devotional approach to the religious life that provided a marked counterpoint to the lifestyles followed by those who had embraced the immense wealth and power available in the metropoles of an emerging Islamic empire. Al-Basri taught Muslims to be God-fearing, rejecting any illicit gain, and to struggle against hypocritical rulers and caliphal tyrants. He warned the devout against being lured into the corruption of wealth and land appropriation. His message of scrupulous adherence to Islam's ethical norms, sincerity, repentance, and renunciation, would inspire subsequent generations of Muslim devotees: hermits, wandering mendicants, lovers of God, and ascetic soldiers. Members of each of these groups would develop Sufism in different ways.

For example, it is interesting to note that Al-Basri inspired the development of *futuwwa*, "a code of spiritual chivalry" (Knysh 2000: 214) for a variety of ascetic soldiers such as 'Abd al-Wahid (d. 793), who established "the first Sufi 'cloister' (*duwayra*) on the island of 'Abbadan" (Knysh 2000: 17). The adherents of this *duwayra* were mostly *ghazis*, military guards who were known for combining "military service with acts of worship and supererogatory piety" (Knysh 2000: 17). They also were known for their vigilance in constantly reciting the name of the one God, which later would be developed into the main Sufi ritual of *dhikr* (Knysh 2000: 18).

In particular, Al-Basri's thoughts on self-awareness would influence Harith al-Muhasibi, a leading theologian and psychologist with strong Sufi influences who came to be known as al-Muhasibi (literally, "the one who takes account") for the emphasis he placed on monitoring one's own innermost thoughts and feelings. Al-Muhasibi "examines or calls into account – with equal precision and subtlety – the stations and moments of egoism and the various forms it can take" (Sells 1996: 171). It was in 846 when al-Muhasibi used dialectical reasoning to debate the Mutazilites, a school of rationalist theologians with which he had once been affiliated. His rising prominence in Baghdad caught the attention of Ahmad Ibn Hanbal, a conservative and literalistic jurist, who regarded al-Muhasibi's science of psychology as a *bid'a* or "reprehensible innovation" (Knysh 2000: 44). Ultimately, Ibn Hanbal forced al-Muhasibi into exile and refused to pardon him. Al-Muhasibi would then be isolated from his Sufi community but his work on the "science of the soul" or psychology, would influence Abu Talib al-Makki (d. 996), whose understandings would in turn inspire al-Ghazali's most popular works of Sufism – texts which remain influential in Muslim spirituality to this day.

The Influence of Ibn Hanbal and the Mutazilites on Early Sufism

As discussed in Chapter 2, Ibn Hanbal's ideas – and the Hanbali school of law and theology which arose as his legacy – have influenced a variety of anti-Sufi personalities and movements throughout Muslim history. So, who was Ahmad Ibn Hanbal and what was his relation to Sufism during the ninth century? Ibn Hanbal promoted a strict literalist interpretation of the Qur'ān and *hadith*, and opposed any rationalist argumentation or Sufi interpretation. Living in Baghdad, the capital of the 'Abbasid Muslim empire, he became one of the most popular religious leaders in the *Ahl al-Hadith* (a group of scholars who were the main opposition to the Mutazilites, the Muslim rationalist school of thought). The *Ahl al-Hadith* would categorically and uncompromisingly challenge all ideas championed by Muslim rationalists, and did much to establish an intensified aversion toward theological "innovation" in Islamic thought.

In particular, Ibn Hanbal is best known for his staunch and unwavering opposition to the caliph al-Mamun's (d. 833) decree in 833 that all religious scholars were to adhere to the Mutazilite doctrine of the created Qur'ān. This doctrine stressed the idea that the Qur'ān was created by God and hence not eternal, whereas Ibn Hanbal emphasized that the Qur'ān was co-eternal with God, thus uncreated. Characteristic of his approach, Ibn Hanbal anathematized any Muslim who believed otherwise:

> The Qur'ān is God's Speech, which He expressed; it is uncreated. He who claims the opposite is a [heretic], a non-believer. And he who says, 'The Qur'ān is God's Speech', and stops there without adding 'uncreated', speaks even more abominably than the former. He who maintains that our sounds (which render the Qur'ān) and our recitation of the Qur'ān are created, is also a [heretic], and he who does not declare all those people infidels is like them! (Halverson 2010: 41).

As a result of Ibn Hanbal's refusal to declare his allegiance, he was persecuted, imprisoned and exiled from his community. Due to his steadfast refutation of al-Mamun and courage during persecution he acquired a larger-than-life reputation and was reinstated by the caliph al-Mutawakkil (d. 861), who declared the doctrine of the uncreated Qur'ān as the official position of the 'Abbasid Empire.

The ultimate triumph of Ibn Hanbal in this clash with al-Mamun had many implications for religious and intellectual as well as political life. Ibn Hanbal's successful challenge to the caliph's attempt to impose his own theological orthodoxy from the top down set a lasting precedent. In addition to putting a check on the caliph's power to define religious norms and beliefs, the outcome of the dispute promoted a decline in the standing of Muslim rationalism and insured the long-term supremacy of jurists and *hadith* scholars in establishing orthodoxy for the Islamic community. Ibn Hanbal's approach to Islamic law became one of four acknowledged schools of Islamic law, known for placing the greatest emphasis on literalism and taking the most conservative approach to questions of interpretation. Significantly, these developments did not stop the spread of Sufism, but they did profoundly shape the context within which Sufi ideas were articulated and practiced. Henceforth, Sufis would need to relate their understandings of Islamic spirituality to a more concrete set of orthodox beliefs and structures, and to be discrete with respect to politics and intellectual debates. For some Muslims, Sufism and Hanbalism were perfectly compatible, as we see in the examples of 'Abd al-Qadir al-Jilani and 'Abdullah Ansari (d. 1088).

Perhaps no Sufi premise attracted more opposition than the idea that the relationship between an individual and God might be likened to the relationship between a lover and his or her beloved. This idea, closely associated with the use of romantic metaphors and narratives in poetic verse, prompted the rise of what has been called an erotic mysticism, of which al-Muhasibi was a leading proponent. In his question and answer style, al-Muhasibi wrote:

> I said: God grant you compassion, what is the characteristic of sincerity? He said: The disentanglement of the self from a relationship of transaction with the lord Most High, and the observance of the reward of God Most High, without any desire for praise or any aversion to blame (Sells 1996: 174).

When individuals influenced by al-Muhasibi sought to develop these themes further, speaking particularly about the pursuit of union with the divine Beloved, they encountered intense opposition from conservative theologians and jurists who were scandalized by the introduction of seemingly profane themes into spiritual discourse. Convinced that faithfulness and righteous behaviour depended on firm notions of divine transcendence and a concomitant fear of God's displeasure on the part of the believer, they argued that professions of love for a divine Beloved would inevitably lead to a collapse of this belief in God's transcendence, as well as licentious behaviour and disregard for divine law.

The emergent Sufi emphasis on love as the principal impetus to faith – and indeed on the analogous nature of human and divine love – did give rise to transgressive behaviours, albeit not precisely in the manner anticipated by those with puritanical sentiments. One keynote of the emergent love mysticism was the use of *shatahat*, ecstatic outbursts or utterances expressing a divine intoxication: a verbal response to communion with the divine Beloved, whose presence was vibrantly accessible within this world and not merely in the afterlife. One of the most famous exponents of this message, a follower of al-Muhasibi was Abu al-Husayn al-Nuri (d. 907) who became known for his dramatic displays that conveyed not just a spiritual message, but also a critique of clerical and political power structures. For example, one narrative describes al-Nuri as smashing the Caliph's wine jars (Melchert 2015: 18); other accounts describe the impact of his "profane" erotic love poetry (Knysh 2000: 61) on his scandalized critics.

Ecstatic outbursts such as al-Nuri's ultimately proved intolerable to powerful orthodox figures, giving rise to another inquisition (877–878) when a prominent preacher from Basra, Ghulam Khalil (d. 888), brought charges of blasphemy on more than 70 Sufi personalities. To prevent a calamity, al-Nuri is said to have selflessly proposed that if authorities were to execute anyone, they should take his life first. This magnanimous gesture won the hearts of the court, resulting in a retrial and ultimately acquittal (Schimmel 1975: 60).

Given the central role of Islam in the functioning of the 'Abbasid state, controversies over religious and spiritual matters had clear political implications and consequences. The inquisition against transgressive Sufi figures was not the first instance of repressive religious policies by the 'Abbasids, which had previously backed theological rationalists against textual literalists at the behest of the caliph al-Mamun. While Ibn Hanbal was temporarily on the losing side in this clash, the tide soon turned in a manner that returned Ibn Hanbal to prominence and assured the prevalence of his more austere theological and legal positions during the reign of subsequent caliphs. It was this pendulum swing towards puritanism that brought many Sufis into perilous circumstances, sometimes pitting those who adhered more carefully to official orthodoxy against those who less cautiously celebrated an ecstatic communion with a loving God who transcended the world and was nonetheless present within created beings and forms.

While this rift among Sufis could be overstated, political pressures and religious critiques prompted the emergence of more visible distinctions between followers of different paths – namely, paths of "sobriety" and of ecstasy. This distinction became explicit during the time of the Inquisition of 877–878, when al-Junayd of Baghdad, himself a disciple of al-Muhasibi and an admirer of al-Nuri (referring to him as the "Commander of the Hearts"), distanced himself from the practices and professions of many ecstatic Sufis and reasserted the orthodox character of proper Sufi practice. While sources differ with respect to the extent to which he actively condemned those tendencies which had come to be regarded as heterodox, what is clear is that the "Sufi" label had become a liability and that al-Junayd, a recognized authority on mysticism, sought to disassociate himself from individuals whose utterances, practices, and political stances attracted the attention of authorities. The external pressures to take such a stance were extremely powerful; Melchert reports that "al-Junayd himself escaped arrest by asserting that he was not a Sufi at all but a student of jurisprudence" (2015: 16). While al-Junayd did not actively partake in the inquisition against fellow mystics, and indeed moved across the Tigris River to a location more distant from the centres of political decision-making and controversy, he adopted a position of "overt political conformism" (Knysh 2000: 55) and sought to remain on good terms with the religious and secular authorities of Baghdad.

There are strong indications, however, that al-Junayd's position was more one of tactical retreat than of surrender or recanting. In his writings, al-Junayd actually defended al-Nuri by developing concepts to make controversial accounts of Sufi unitive experience acceptable to the scholarly establishment (Knysh 2000: 54). At the same time, his name and example became synonymous with a more cautious mysticism, less inclined to provoke opposition and eager to assert its theological orthodoxy, using nuanced language to contextualize mystical experiences within an accepted theological framework. Rather than broadcast the esoteric vision of union with a divine Beloved to the masses, al-Junayd believed in reserving more esoteric teachings for advanced practitioners who were spiritually ready and prepared to understand. Ultimately, al-Junayd's emphasis on sobriety over mystical intoxication would heavily influence future generations of Sufi personalities and institutions. To this day, many Sufi orders (e.g. Qadiri, Suhrawardi, and Kubrawi), trace their *silsilas* (spiritual chains of transmission) through al-Junayd and are known as "Junaydi." As reflected in the statement below, for al-Junayd, being a Sufi was a way of constant purification and persistent inner striving to return to one's origin (as represented in the primoridal covenant, Mithaq, which will be covered in Chapter 6).

> Know that you are veiled from yourself by yourself. You will not attain Him through yourself. You will attain Him only through Him… He protects you from yourself, and brings you to Himself through the passing away of your passing away in your attainment of your aim (Sells 1996: 255).

The object of this spiritual struggle was to realize perfect *tawhid* (unity), through which man can bear witness that God is one from eternity to eternity. To provide guidance and structure for spiritual aspirants and to explain different varieties of mystical experience on the path to realization, al-Junayd helped conceptualize different stations and stages on the Sufi path. A major aspect of al-Junayd's teaching about stages is his emphasis on *sahw* (the state of poverty and sobriety) as contrasted to *sukr* (intoxication), together with an insistence on the need for a would-be spiritual aspirant to have a binding and disciplined relationship with a *shaykh* (spiritual teacher). The following quotation by a student of al-Junayd reveals al-Junayd's distinct position:

> Intoxication is a mystic term denoting ecstatic love for God; Sobriety proposes the attainment of some end. Bayazid and his disciples, who think Intoxication the higher way, maintain that Sobriety stabilizes human attributes which are the greatest of all Veils between God and man. But my own Shaykh, following al-Junayd, used to say that Intoxication is a playground for children, and Sobriety a mortal battleground for men (Glasse 1989: 212).

Sufism, to al-Junayd, was a path to profound experiences of unity with God, but it was also a systematic and sober doctrine. Moreover, Sufis were not to be wandering mendicants who advocated personal "union with God"; rather, Sufis were encouraged to renounce spiritual individualism and integrate mysticism into everyday life. Thus, al-Junayd's "sober mysticism" was not only a reaction to the orthodox theologians and jurists and the Inquisition of 877–878 but also a response to the influence of popular "drunken Sufis"; especially Bayazid al-Bistami (d. 874) who is known as the founder of the 'drunken', ecstatic school of Sufism, and Husayn Ibn Mansur al-Hallaj, perhaps the most famous of all intoxicated Sufi personalities.

For centuries, al-Junayd's critical position towards his contemporaries' ecstatic utterances and his lack of support for political and social activism have been critically counterpoised to al-Hallaj's disruptive spirituality and politics. Remembered not just for his provocative spiritual statements but also for sermons that aroused mass support and sometimes protest against injustice, al-Hallaj was as much a political figure as a mystic.

Divergent understandings of God's relationship with the world and with each individual believer were at the core of many theological debates in the early 'Abbasid era. For more austere and "sober" interpreters of scripture, this relationship was above all one of *tanzih* (divine transcendence), according to which God's being stands apart from the world to such a degree that no worldly object can be meaningfully compared with Him. Indeed, any suggestion of likeness between creature and creator – any blurring of distinctions or softening of the proclamation that "nothing is like him" (Qur'ān 42:11) – threatens to undermine an uncompromising conviction in God's transcendent unity, as well as the authoritative corpus of religious norms that provide the pattern for human service and divine sovereignty. Among Sufis, however, this affirmation of divine transcendence is balanced by a complementary principle of *tashbih* (immanence) according to which God is not only distant but also near – in the language of the Qur'ān, "closer than the jugular vein" (Qur'ān 50:16). From this perspective, the created world partakes of and reflects God's qualities, which are described in scriptural terms that connect to relationships in daily human life. For example, God may be described as the Compassionate, the Merciful, and the Forgiving as well as the Exalted or Sovereign, and all of these qualities can be recognized and experienced – albeit in finite ways – in the world. As a way of relating to God, *tashbih* emphasizes possibilities for spiritual intimacy and loving connection, and not just a more austere relationship of master and servant.

Whereas many Islamic mystics – including spiritual pioneers such as Hasan al-Basri – have promoted ascetic and ritually intensive systems within which *tanzih* is the overriding principle, developments such as the love mysticism of al-Muhasibi, al-Nuri and al-Bistami pushed in the direction of a new synthesis, in which nearness to a divine Beloved is a real and accessible goal, and in which intimate human relationships provide valid metaphors for the encounter with God. A disciple of al-Nuri as well as of various other Sufi teachers, al-Hallaj would become known for pushing the principle of *tashbih* to its fullest possibility, insisting that nothing – including the condemnation of worldly authorities – should stand in the way of loving union between the human and God. Where al-Junayd, an elder and acquaintance of al-Hallaj, emphasized prudence and discretion in publicly discussing spiritual aspirations toward union with God, al-Hallaj called openly upon the people of Baghdad to seek God within their own hearts, realize the inner meanings of external rites, and challenge injustices which many religious and political elites were all too willing to tolerate. Abandoning caution, al-Hallaj took to preaching spontaneously, jubilantly in the markets and mosque entrances of Baghdad. The following speech given by him in a Baghdad market illustrates the nature of his public rhetoric:

> I have embraced, with my whole being, all Your love, O my Holiness! You have manifested yourself so much that it seems to me that there is only You in me! I examine my heart amidst all that is not You, I do not see any estrangement between them and me, only familiarity between You and me! (Massignon 1982: 143).

He took positions that simultaneously inspired the public and invited opposition, and became known for provocative ecstatic utterances – most notably, "*Ana al-Haqq*" ("I am the Truth"). Such erasures of distance between the human and God – according to which separate human consciousness becomes totally effaced, and God may speak through the mystic – scandalized much of Baghdad's religious establishment as much as his political stances alarmed those with vested interests in the status quo. Al-Hallaj preached openly against the inequality and injustice inherent in the 'Abbasid economic order, where merchants and aristocrats reaped growing profits from the labour of plantation slaves and shop workers. Although not without powerful allies in the 'Abbasid court as well as among Sufis and the broader public, al-Hallaj's insistence on confronting what he saw as idolatrous beliefs that separated humanity from God ultimately led to a martyrdom that he willingly embraced. Refusing to recant and embracing suffering as a path to absolute unity with God, al-Hallaj faced persecution, imprisonment, and eventually execution in 922.

> There can be no distance for me
>   distancing you from me
> When I have achieved certainty
>   nearness and distance are one.
> Even if I am abandoned,
>   abandonment will be my companion.
> How can it be abandonment
>   while love is one?
> To you, praise in success,
>   in the pure absolute
> For a servant of true heart
>   who will bow to no other than you.
>
>   (Sells 1996: 274–75)

In many respects, the life of al-Hallaj represents a culminating point in early Sufism. His affirmation of the possibility of complete human union with the divine would remain controversial for centuries (and to this day), even as his acceptance of a punishing martyrdom served to enhance his stature as a Sufi who embraced *fana'* (loving annihilation in God) in the most existentially powerful way possible. Far from discrediting al-Hallaj, martyrdom transformed him into an archetype – an example toward which few could remain neutral. Though defeated in Baghdad, his school persisted, with many of his followers (i.e. Ibn Khafif, d. 982) migrating to Persia.

Subsequent generations would often juxtapose the example of al-Hallaj with that of al-Junayd, with the former embodying a Sufi path of love and intoxication (*sukr*) and the latter representing a path of gnostic sobriety (*sahw*). Where al-Hallaj became the preeminent Sufi martyr, al-Junayd became the exemplar for those who sought the enduring institutional development of Sufism, by carving out a viable theological niche and conscientiously relating to Islamic political and religious authority. While the precise character of the historical relationship between these two towering figures is difficult to discern – they were contemporaries, yet al-Junayd died 12 years before al-Hallaj's martyrdom – stories have been passed down to convey their contrasting positions on the proper expression and ultimate meaning of Sufi positions. According to one story, al-Hallaj once declared his realization that "I am the Truth" in the presence of al-Junayd, who responded, "Not so, for it is through al-Haqq that you exist". For al-Hallaj, union with God was the preeminent goal of the spiritual quest, and this goal of dissolving one's separate existence in the reality of God – spiritual annihilation or *fana'* – can and must be declared openly and sought without reservation. For al-Junayd, humans cannot attain union with God without God's permission, and experiences of union should not be understood to be stable or lasting. After the ecstasy of union, the mystic returns to the world, developing *baqa'* (subsistence) in God and retaining a separate identity.

THE QUEST FOR TRUTH:
EARLY SUFI PRINCIPLES AND PRACTICES

Islamic spirituality, like empire, law and theology, formed during the eighth and ninth centuries, and was subject to debates over the nature of the Qur'ān, Muhammad, and the ideal Muslim self and society – debates that affected all aspects of the emergent Islamic civilization. In their quest for truth, early Sufis developed and shared with fellow seekers a variety of principles and practices to explain esoteric experience. By the tenth century, Sufi science, *'ilm al-tasawwuf*, was established as a widely recognized category of knowledge.

The beginnings of Sufi systems of knowledge were intertwined with the development of *shari'a* (Islamic law) which, in its embryonic stage, meant a path to lead a righteous life by, ultimately, submitting to the will of the one God (Sells 1996: 12). Influenced by the work ethic demonstrated by Islamic scholars (*'ulama*) of *hadith* and *shari'a*, many of whom travelled great distances seeking knowledge of the sayings and traditions which formed foundations for the legal schools of thought and Islamic jurisprudence (*fiqh*), the great Sufi biographers engaged in similar processes of travelling, gathering, compiling, and recording to make available the exemplary lives and thought of the early Sufi masters.

These manuals, often in the form of encyclopaedic guidebooks, preserved records of the early Sufi way of life as well as accounts of essential practices, and became catalysts for moulding the future of classical Sufi traditions. The following quotation by Abu 'Abd al-Rahman al-Sulami (d. 1021), one of the most influential early Sufi biographers, reveals the significant role a biographer played in this formative period:

> [I]t occurred to me to collect something of the *adab* of those mystics and friends of God (*awliya' Allah*) well advanced in the spiritual path who are called Sufis (*al-sufiyya*): they are those who disciplined themselves by following the example of the 'People of Purity' (*ahl al-safa*) and shaped their character (*takhallaqu*) according to their morals (*akhlaq*). In this way, those who criticise them altogether without really knowing the truth can learn about them, their way of life and their customs, so that they may think about them as they deserve (al-Sulami in Biagi 2010: 1–2).

Due to significant contestation among Muslims who differed in their convictions about how to define and live Muslim piety – a source of divisive conflicts in the eighth and ninth centuries – the importance of offering knowledge about the lives and wisdom of the early Sufi personalities was paramount. Additionally, the work of early Sufi biographers served to reconcile Sufi teachings and practices with the orthodox Sunni creed (Knysh 2011: 222) while establishing the practice of Sufi hermeneutics as based in the Qur'ān and *hadith* (which will be discussed further in Chapter 6).

The voluminous works produced by biographers covered a variety of themes, such as Sufi rules of conduct and norms of pious behaviour, Sufi rituals and terminology, and the nature of exemplary Sufi personalities. Biographers recorded the lives and teachings of a great diversity of early Sufi figures, particularly from Egypt, Arabian peninsula, Mesopotamia, and Persia, and conveyed their understandings of principles and practices leading to knowledge of God and an exemplary spiritual life.

As they recorded teachings from diverse sources, biographers came to distinguish between two key modalities of knowledge: *'ilm*, or discursive learning, and *ma'rifa*, experiential and/or intuitive knowledge of God. Referring especially to the knowledge produced by Muslim jurists and theologians but also to outward knowledge of topics related to mysticism, *'ilm* denoted external knowledge, or knowledge *about* a topic or object that was still in some sense separate from the state or condition of the knowing subject. In contrast, *ma'rifa* connoted a transformative and deeply internalized variety of knowledge within which this separation between knower and known no longer prevailed. While the biographers conveyed respect for *'ilm* as beneficial in preparing for transformative knowledge, their new emphasis on *ma'rifa* underscored the importance of knowledge that leads to spiritual elevation, nearness to God, and refinement of character.

Their detailed accounts of Sufi saints and teachings illustrated the content of this transformative knowledge, and communicated a message that these exemplary Muslims had overcome the gross as well as subtle forms of hypocrisy that are always present when development of rational intellect – which can potentially encompass vast knowledge about religion and religious sciences – exceeds unitive knowledge rooted in the heart of the knowing subject, or gnosis. However important the former variety of knowledge might be, the biographers' accounts suggested *'ilm* must lead to *ma'rifa* if it is to lead to the ultimate aims of religion. To reach these aims, personalized guidance and divine grace – and not mere book learning – were necessary, as al-Ghazali would so effectively emphasize in his *Ihya 'Ulum al-Din*. The seeker of truth, the biographers attested, must seek direct guidance from teachers or *shaykhs* such as those described in the biographical accounts.

While this emphasis on unitive knowledge or gnosis did not begin with the biographers, the completion of new, encyclopaedic works gave new weight to the subject in religious thought and elevated the teachings of early Sufi personalities. Among the many Sufi lives recorded in their works, biographers gave particular credit for the distinction between *'ilm* and *ma'rifa* to Dhu'l Nun al-Misri (d. 860). Dhu'l Nun is reported to have said in this regard, "All that the eyes behold is related to earthly knowledge, but that which the hearts know is true certainty" (Arberry 1979: 94). For Dhu'l Nun, the essential goal of the mystical life was to internalize the qualities of God within the self, and thereby transform it – that is, to realize or know God by becoming one with God's qualities. Such knowledge was necessarily transformative with respect to character and behaviour. "The conduct of a Gnostic towards others", Dhu'l Nun attested, "is like the conduct of God Most High – he endures you and is forbearing with you because he imitates the characteristics of God" (Al-Qushayri in Von Schlegell 1990: 20). Like many other early Islamic mystics, Dhu'l Nun taught that it was possible for a seeker of truth to consciously and assiduously imitate the character traits of God, and thereby receive divine grace in ways described in a sacred saying of the Prophet, or *hadith al-qudsi*: "My servant ceases not to draw nigh unto Me by works of devotion, until I love him, and when I love him I am the eye by which he sees and the ear by which he hears. And he approaches a span I approach a cubit, and when he comes walking I come running" (Schimmel 1975: 133). As discussed in Chapter 4, later Sufis, such as Ibn al-'Arabi, would describe this process as *takhalluq bi akhlaq Allah* or, "assuming the character traits of Allah". Focusing on the invocation and contemplation of divine names, particularly the *asma' Allah al-husna*, or "ninety-nine most beautiful names", Sufis taught that moral traits and virtues could be acquired in this manner. If a seeker required patience, a teacher might prescribe repetition of the divine name "*Ya Sabur*" (the Patient). A need for realization of divine mercy might similarly be inculcated through the divine name "*Ya Rahim*". At the heart of this teaching method was a principle that Dhu'l Nun articulated in the following manner:

> Dhu'l-Nun was asked, 'By what means do you know your Lord?' He replied, 'I know my Lord by my Lord. If it were not for my Lord, I would not know my Lord'. It is said, 'The scholar is a source of imitation, and the Gnostic is a source of guidance' (Al-Qushayri in Von Schlegell 1990: 21).

Ultimately, the sole source of divine knowledge and spiritual transformation was God alone, who could be known through concentration on his divine names and through related practices prescribed for the seeker by a qualified teacher of *ma'rifa* – a gnostic who had "known God by God".

Some Principles and Practices of Early Sufis

In his highly influential work, *Al-Risala al-Qushayriyya* ("Al-Qushayri's Epistle"), the biographer al-Qushayri states that the first significant stage for many early Sufis was *tawba*, the act of turning to God and away from all that was not God. Like other early Sufi writers, he defined this turning and returning to God as the act of repentance and the seeking of divine forgiveness. According to al-Qushayri and his account of early Sufis, *tawba* is a way of "emptying or polishing the heart" through the act of repentance. He attributed this daily, constant practice to the Prophet Muhammad, who in a tradition is reported to have said, "My heart is clouded, so I ask forgiveness of God seventy times a day" (Al-Qushayri in Von Schlegell 1990: 11). Seeking forgiveness, then, is a response to the experience of forgetfulness and offers a means of "remembering" oneself back to conscious presence with God. Asking forgiveness polishes one's heart of any experience other than God – worldly impressions that distract from divine remembrance.

As is evident in the works of al-Qushayri as well as al-Sulami and Abu Nu'aym Ahmad ibn 'Abdullah al-Isfahani (d. 1038), the early Sufis were very aware of human conditions (i.e. sorrow, fear, envy, pride, hunger) that created the illusion of separation from God. At the same time, they also recognized that some of these conditions or emotional states corresponded with principles that could encourage repentance and progress as a traveller on "the path of God". Sorrow (*huzn*), for example, was viewed as a virtue that enabled humans to experience forgiveness. "Sorrow is a condition that rescues the heart from being scattered in the valleys of forgetfulness. And sorrow is one of the qualities of the people of the Path" (al-Qushayri, in Von Schlegell 1990: 76). The key of course, was to be sorrowful for the right reason – that is, for one's existential separation from God.

Fear, another complex human condition also mentioned by the biographers, was usually divided into two concepts: *khawf* and *taqwa*. *Khawf* suggests a more externally oriented movement of the mind and emotions, premised on the insecurity of one's own self in relation to the outside world: to be frightened of something outside of oneself. *Taqwa*, in contrast, is an internalized atonement of the mind and emotions through accountability to God and to a higher aspect of one's self. *Taqwa* suggests a mindfulness or alertness of spiritual awareness in which one refrains from disobedient acts and seeks to engage in virtuous conduct – in deeds based on qualities such as honesty, sincerity, and generosity. Thus, *taqwa* has often been translated as "fear or awareness of God" and described as the basis of morality. Dhu'l Nun was known for saying, "There is no life except with men whose hearts long for *taqwa* and whose joy is in remembrance. Content are they with the spirit of certainty and its goodness like the nursing child in his mother's lap" (Al-Qushayri, in Von Schlegell 1990: 27).

In contrast to fear of God and emotional states that pointed to one's need for divine assistance, al-Qushayri noted how other, more outwardly focused conditions such as *hasad* (envy) and *ghiba* (backbiting) led away from the path of realization. Rather than being rooted in fear of wavering from the path of God, these conditions were based on the fears for the lower self. Al-Qushayri spoke of these conditions in general terms as well as through references to specific stories of early Sufis:

> There is a root of all sin. Guard yourselves against them and beware (form of *taqwa*) of them. Beware of pride, for pride caused Iblis to refuse to prostrate before Adam. Beware of greed, for greed caused Adam to eat of the tree. And beware of envy, for it was from envy that one of the two sons of Adam killed his brother.

> Among the signs of the envier are that he flatters others when he is with them, slanders them when he is apart from them, and savours their misfortune when it befalls them.

> Let the Muslims' benefit from you be these three qualities: If you cannot be helpful to him, then do not harm him. If you cannot bring him delight, then do not cause him sorrow. If you cannot praise him, then do not find fault with him.

> 'So-and-so has slandered you'. Hasan a-Basri replied by sending a tray of sweets to the man, noting, 'I hear that you have bestowed upon me your good deeds. I would like to repay you'.

> Ibrahim Adham was invited to a feast which he attended. When they mentioned a man who had not come, it was said, 'He is so tedious'. Ibrahim remarked, 'This is what this soul of mine has done to me: I find myself in a gathering where backbiting takes place'. He left, even though he had not eaten for three days (Al-Qushayri, in Von Schlegell 1990: 101–108).

In offering such teachings and principles, al-Qushayri sought to convey the way of the Sufi, and provide spiritual seekers with a means to engage in a psychological battle for the soul. *Tawba* constantly enabled one to choose a way of living that was directed toward God.

Another principle in most of the early biographers' compilations was *zuhd*, the renunciation of all things connected to this world. *Zuhd* empowered one to abandon bad habits that would lead to the condition of forgetfulness. From renouncing inner attachments (e.g. past memory, judgments, ways of being) to resisting outwardly temptations (e.g. material wealth, property, and for some Sufis even family), there were a variety of opinions about the actual content of practising *zuhd*. Of course, renunciation of the material world would lead some early Sufi mystics to embrace austere practices, such as using only a brick for a pillow, preferring to sleep in a seated position, or refraining from sleep altogether. Other Sufis were known to care neither for their outward appearance nor for their attire, with some barely wearing anything and others refraining from any regular daily consumption of food (e.g. eating a date per day or waiting for food to be given). An extreme example can be found in a statement attributed to Abu 'Uthman al-Maghribi (d. 983): "The devoted to the Lord eats only every forty days, and the one devoted to the Eternal eats only every eighty days" (Al-Qushayri, in Von Schlegell 1990: 81).

Divine hunger (*ju'wa*) and humility (*tawadu*) were practices associated with *zuhd*. Ultimately, embracing divine hunger accompanied the pursuit of freedom from longing for the material world:

> 'Abu Nasr at-Tammar reported, 'Bishr came to me one night, …he explained, "I have craved eggplant for years, but it has not been destined for me to eat it". So I assured him, "But there is eggplant that is lawful in this dish". He replied, "[I cannot eat it] until I am free from the longing for eggplant"' (Abu 'Ali al-Daqqaq d. 1015, in Von Schlegell 1990: 83).

Ultimately, in renouncing this world, the early Sufi sought to focus his or her efforts on the other world. Hasan al-Basri was known for many sayings about asceticism, one being, "Be with this world as if you had never been there, and with the Otherworld as if you would never leave it". Ibrahim ibn Adham (d. 777), a student of al-Basri's life and thought, is credited with making the first classification of the stages of "Sufi asceticism". Among many later Sufis ibn Adham was regarded as "the key of mystical sciences" who provided "a proverbial example of true poverty, abstinence, and trust in God" (Schimmel 1975: 37). For ibn Adham, *zuhd* was to be experienced in three distinct forms: "(a) renunciation of the world; (b) renunciation of the happy feeling of having achieved renunciation; and (c) the stage in which the ascetic regards the world as so unimportant that he no longer looks at it" (Schimmel 1975: 37).

The biographies contain many other quotes about renunciation from early Sufis. Al-Qusahyri offered the following words of wisdom in his collection, each drawn from a different Sufi figure:

> Renunciation is trust in God Most High (*tawakkul 'ala Allah*) combined with the love of poverty (Abdallah ibn al-Mubarak).[1]

> One will not attain true renunciation until he possesses these qualities: action without attachment, speaking without ambition, and glory without having power over men (Yahya ibn Mu'adh).[2]

---

1. Abdallah ibn al-Mubarak (d. 797) is famous for his *Kitab al-Zuhd, Book of Renunciation,* a collection of *hadith* that highlighted the ascetical, world-renouncing behaviour of the early Muslim community.
2. Yahya ibn Mu'adh, is known as "the Preacher" (d. 872), of the Karramiyya movement of the Khorasan.

> Renunciation is this: the heart is empty of that which the hand is empty of. He also said, 'erasing [the world's] traces from the heart' (al-Junayd).

> Renunciation is a king who does not dwell anywhere but in a polished Heart (Bishr al-Hafi).[3]

Closely linked to this renunciation of the material world (*zuhd*) was the related principle of abstaining from material comfort (*wara'*). Although not regarded as ends in themselves, most early Sufis regarded these principles as crucial for renouncing the lower self and abstaining from baser tendencies of the ego. Thus, renunciation and abstinence were keys to the process of spiritual transformation. Al-Qushayri, for example, reports that Dhu'l Nun was once asked the question, "When may I renounce the world?" His answer was both laconic and exacting, "When you renounce yourself" (Al-Qushayri, in Von Schlegell 1990: 44).

In order to renounce the world and self, many early Sufis retreated from the world to practise *khalwa*, or spiritual retreat. Creating a physical distance from the world enabled the Sufi to establish a sense of constant vigilance of self (*muraqaba*), and supported efforts to abstain (*wara'*) from worldly appetites (*shahawat*) and affirm a life of poverty (*faqir*). Keeping with a much older Near Eastern practice, Sufis would sometimes retreat for 40 days of concerted spiritual practice. Later, different Sufi orders would develop the practice of retreat in various ways, diverging in terms of length of time, practices undertaken during retreat, supervision by *shaykh*, and type of location.

Taken together, these principles and practices of the early Sufis offered the biographers and those who drew upon their works a framework for a Sufi psychological system oriented towards spiritual realization. Practices like *taqwa* and *muraqaba* were central to this Sufi psychology, together with a critical process known as *muhasibat al-nafs* – the constant analysis and critique of the soul. This process then "taught the relentless fight over man's lower nature, not just the outward struggle of the ascetic against the 'flesh', but a subtle psychological analysis of every thought as well as uninterrupted spiritual training" (Schimmel 1975: 54).

The continual practise of specific principles were mandatory for *muhasibat al-nafs* and *dhikr*, the act of remembering God was the essential principle and practice that enables the lower self to be annihilated (*fana'*) for the Divine attributes to subsist (*baqa'*). As we have seen in previous chapters, *dhikr* can be experienced in a variety of ways through invoking the Names of God, chanting Qur'ānic verses, whirling in a commu-

---

3.   Bishr al-Hafi, "the Barefoot" (d. 842) was a student of al-Junayd (al-Qushayri in Von Schlegell 1990: 40–46).

nal gathering, playing particular contemplative music, etc. The method of *dhikr* has always been used to develop concentration (*mushahada*) focusing one's attention on the Divine alone.

As reflected in the biographies, the lasting impact of *dhikr* empowers the human to experience a diversity of mystical states. *Fikr* has been defined as "reflection or the power of thought and cogitation. It is the ability to put together the details accumulated by the senses and acquired through the imagination" (Armstrong 1995: 50). More broadly *fikr* can mean contemplation or meditation, being in a state of serene awareness and observation. Although not something that can be engendered by practice alone, Sufis believe that extended periods of retreat, purification, meditation, and *dhikr*, open the aspirant to divine grace, which can manifest as *kashf*. As we have touched upon throughout this book, *kashf* is an experience of God "unveiling" or self-disclosing, generously removing the veil of ignorance so that the practitioner has a sudden, direct knowledge of Divine Reality. This encounter with God can produce awe and fear if it reveals one of God's names of Majesty (*Jalal*), or sweetness and bliss if it discloses one of God's qualities of Beauty (*Jamal*) (Armstrong 1995: 109).

The Islamic tradition in general values dreams as a means of knowledge, with *hadith* traditions indicating that authentic or true dreams are an aspect of prophecy available to all. Among Sufis, a *ru'ya* or dream-vision occurs when a particularly lucid, vivid dream involves the transmission of higher knowledge, either from God, the Prophet Muhammad, another prophet, or a saint. As Ibn al-'Arabi describes in his *Fusus*, dream-visions clothe sacred "meanings" (*ma'ana*) in symbolic "forms" or images (*suwar*). The symbolic language of dreams is one that an advanced practitioner intuitively knows, reading the dream-vision's symbolic message. For a beginning practitioner however, dream-visions are usually brought to the *shaykh(a)* to have the meaning of the images drawn out (Armstrong 1995: 200–201). Finally, those Sufis who are believed to be God's friends (the *awliya'*) are thought to be given the ability to transcend the limitations of the material world and perform miraculous actions or (*karamat*). Sufi manuals generally advise against and even forbid the displaying of miracles, which are thought to be largely secondary to the purpose of the path, which is knowledge of God, rather than supernatural fireworks.

Rabi'a al-'Adawiyya: "The Crown of Men"

'Oh Lord, if I worship you out of fear of hell, burn me in hell. If I worship you in the hope of paradise, forbid it to me. And if I worship you for your own sake, do not deprive me of your eternal beauty' (Rabi'a in Sells 1996: 169).

One of the most famous early Sufis who was mentioned by many Sufi biographers was Rabi'a al-'Adawiyya. Interestingly, it was Rabi'a who was "the first figure from the history of Sufism to be introduced into European literature" (Schimmel 1975: 8). Rabi'a's legend was brought to Europe by Jean de Joinville (d. 1317), the chancellor of Louis IX (d. 1270), in the late thirteenth century.

Rabi'a was born and lived in Basra, Iraq. She died in 801. Due to the advanced nature of her spiritual states many Sufis held that there were none equal to Rabi'a. She would become an icon of the lover of God, with biographers like Attar considering her to be far above her contemporaries and later Sufis. She was hence given the title the "Crown of Men" (*Taj al-Rajal*).

As we find in Attar's famous work *Conference of the Birds*, the author writes ecstatic praise of Rabi'a's status:

> No, she wasn't a single woman
> But a hundred men over...
> From foot to face, immersed in the Truth,
> Effaced in the radiance of God,
> And liberated from all superfluous excess.
>
> (Attar in Nurbakhsh 1990: 15)

Attar also praises her in his *Memoirs of the Saints*: "That noble recluse who dwelled behind the cloisters of God's elect, a matron of sanctity beneath sincerity's veil, on fire with love, totally consumed with yearning, arduously enraptured by God's proximity, that apostle of Mary's purity, acknowledged by all men was Rabi'a al-'Adawiyyah, God's mercy rest upon her" (Attar, in Smith 2001: 21). He also wrote, "Both in terms of her spiritual transactions and gnosis of God, Rabi'a was unexcelled in her time and was accredited by all great men of her age" (Attar in Nurbakhsh 1990: 16).

These statements along with the title, "Crown of Men" are very telling. In the Islamic and Sufi traditions, one tends to find two opposite honorific titles: "Crown of Men" and "My Soul as a Woman". "The Crown of Men" is connected to the honorific tradition that states: "'When a woman walks in the way of God, she cannot be called a 'woman'" (Arberry 1957: 40). Such a woman is a man, or in the Arabic word, *rajul*, and the Persian *mard*, which represents an additional difficulty in understanding the role of women in the theory and practise of mysticism. The noun, "man", can be used to designate any individual who earnestly strives toward God, without making any direct reference to the gender identity of the person in question.

In contrast, you also find another honorific tradition which equates the soul with the woman. The Arabic word for soul is *nafs*, which is a feminine noun that appears in the Qur'ān "in three particular forms regarding the levels off the soul: *nafs al-lahwama, nafs lahwama, nafs al-mutmainna*. The last case is the highest attainment of the feminine gender. This is why so many Sufi personalities (especially poetical personalities like Rumi and Ibn al-'Arabi) used the images such as the "bridal soul" or "the saints are the brides of God". To these figures, the soul in its purest form/level was symbolically represented as and personified by a woman. As 'Abd al-Rahman Jami (d. 1492), the famous Persian Sufi poet and commentator on Ibn al-'Arabi, also said about Rabi'a: "If all women were like the one we have mentioned, then women would be preferred to men" (Schimmel 1997: 78).

Rabi'a was known for many mystical qualities – namely, spiritual piety (*taqwa*), mystical knowledge (*ma'rifa*) and ascetic restraint (*zuhd*)); however, she is best known for extolling the way of *mahabba* (Divine love and closeness with God). *Mahabba* to Rabi'a was an uncompromising way for Muslims to perceive and encounter the Divine. This encounter took the form of the classical Sufi "love triangle" of Love, Lover, and Beloved. In this triangle, one's thoughts are about Love, one's words are directed towards the Lover, and one's deeds are for the Beloved. This type of love is captured in her poetry:

I have two ways of loving You:
A selfish one
And another way that is worthy of You.
In my selfish love, I remember You and You alone.
In that other love, You lift the veil
And let me feast my eyes on Your Living Face.
That I remember You always, or that I see You face-to-face-
No credit to me in either:
The credit is to You in both.

(Rabi'a in Upton 1988: 23)

According to Rabi'a, love is immanent in every moment that the soul spends in communion with God, and can only be experienced when concern for the self – even desire for Heaven and fear of Hell is set aside. As reflected in the following famous story attributed to her God's Wrath and God's Mercy are transcended through His Love:

> Once, in the streets of Basra, she was asked why she was carrying a torch in one hand and a pail in the other, and she answered: 'I want to throw fire into Paradise and pour water into Hell so that these two veils disappear, and it becomes clear who worships God out of love, not out of fear of Hell or hope for Paradise' (Rabi'a, in Smith 2001: 123).

In classical and contemporary times, her sayings regarding selfless love and devotion to God have become well-known proverbs throughout the Muslim world and many contemporary famous female Arab singers like Feyrooz (b. 1934) and Umm Kulthum (d. 1975) have made her sayings into popular songs. Due to such popularity and having been a woman, Rabi'a has also become an archetype for many historical and contemporary Sufi women, such as the women in Rkia E. Cornell's translation of *Early Sufi Women* (see the textbox in the last section of this chapter).

Rabi'a was not the only early Sufi in the formative period to extoll the way of love. Other Sufis such as al-Bistami and al-Hallaj were known for experiencing and explaining love's diverse manifestations including *shawq* (longing for the Beloved), *irada* (desire to be in love), *'ubudiya* (servitude towards the Beloved), and *sidq* (intimacy with the Beloved). Particular emphasis on the human's love of God and God alone was the ultimate act of being human. As stated by al-Junayd in the work of al-Hujwiri, "Love is the annihilation of the lover in His attributes and the confirmation of the Beloved in His essence" (Von Schlegell 1990: 40).

Muhabba, then, is unconditional love that transforms the one who desires God to the one whom God desires. To desire not to desire:

> Desire to bring man nearer to God… God's love for the servant is His desire to bestow blessings specifically on a given servant, just as His mercy for him is His more general desire to bestow blessings… God's desire to extend rewards and blessings to the servant is called 'mercy', and His desire to confer nearness and exalted states on him is called 'love'… as for the servant's love of God, it is a state experienced in his heart, too subtle for words. This state brings him to glorify God and to try to gain His pleasure. He has little patience in separation from Him, feels an urgent longing for him, finds no comfort in anything other than him, and experiences intimacy in his heart by making continual remembrance of Him… There is no clearer or more understandable description of love than love [itself] (al-Qushayri, in Von Schlegell 1990: 326–27).

Out of *muhabba* develops *'ishq* as the highest stage before the complete annihilation in God. *'Ishq*, to al-Hallaj, was divine love which was the "essence of the essence of God and the mystery of creation" (Schimmel 1975: 72). Other early Sufis like al-Nuri however, saw *muhabba* as a higher stage of love than *'ishq* (Lewisohn 2015: 159). Although Hasan al-Basri tended towards a rhetoric of fear of God, he is also one of the first Sufis to speak of God's passionate love (*'ishq*), in a *hadith qudsi* transmitted from him by 'Abd al-Wahid ibn Zayd:

> As soon as My dear servant's first care becomes remembrance of Me, I make him find happiness and joy in remembering Me. And when I have made him find happiness and joy in remembering Me, he desires Me and I desire him (*'ashiquni wa 'ashiqtuhu*). And when he desires Me and I desire him, I raise the veils between him and Me, and I become a cluster of knowable things (*ma'alima*) before his eyes (Lewisohn 2015: 152).

The mystery of love has long been thought to transcend the rational mind. The ordered, sober prose of logic seemed distinctly incapable of expressing the depth, power, and profundity of love. Building upon the poetic sensibility of the pre-Islamic Arabs, the Qur'ān, and the literature of early Muslims, Sufis began to utilize poetry as a literary form more suitable to point to that which transcended language altogether, the divine mystery of love.

EARLY ARABIC SUFI POETRY: THE ART OF MYSTICAL ALLEGORY

Throughout all ages and cultures, poetry has been and continues to be an eloquent means for expressing the vicissitudes of human life. Many of the early Sufis were able to convey their messages and life's practices through eloquent Arabic poetry that would influence a plethora of generations who followed. Arabic poetry (whether pre-Islamic or Islamic) and all its metrical forms originates in the desert. It was cultivated and maintained by nomadic, pastoral people – the Arab Bedouin – who were constantly on the move in search of fresh, seasonal pastures. Many scholars of Islamic literature claim that it was through the rhythms of the caravan's paces and the rhythms of the songs (*al-huda*) which were produced in accordance with these paces that meters of Arabic poetry emerged (Ullah 1963: xii). Accustomed to the rhythm of the camel's walk or the horse's gallop, Arab Bedouins developed lyrics in harmony with their desert surroundings. In turn, they produced a melodious means for conveying the range of human emotion and feeling as well as their appreciation for the beauty and splendour of the desert environment.

For the pre-Islamic nomadic Arabs as well as for modern-day city-dwellers, Arabic poetry was and remains the peak of Arabic eloquence and culture. By evoking perennial realities such as death, time, and change, poetry brings us into contact with our own existential limitations. As portrayed in the poems found in this section, the desert is a mirror that reflects some of the most basic and essential of human experiences, needs and longings. It is a place of expansion, openness, emptiness, and simplicity; yet it is also a place of wandering and struggling – with oneself and with others.

Ironically, it was in the vacant sparseness of the desert that the Arab voice developed its superluxuriant vocabulary and complex syntactical system which would culminate into an astonishing explosion of poetic brilliance. From the Hijaz and Najd in Arabia through Mesopotamia, the rich diversity of the Arabic language (as seen in the variety of ways to express one manifested form [e.g. the word "wind" has over ten forms and meanings, from gentle zephyrs to torrent storms]) empowered the poet with a plethora of words to describe the desert's multi-faceted dimensions – physically, symbolically, and metaphysically.

Ultimately, to be a nomadic traveller of the desert was to live in constant transformation (*taqallub*), and thereby live beyond the compass of the settled verities of urban life. This symbolic openness of nomadic life to transformation was evoked by many early Sufis.

> Whenever a poet emerged in an Arab tribe, the other tribes would come and congratulate it. Feasts would be prepared, and women would gather together playing on lutes, as people do at weddings; men and boys would exchange the good news. For the poet was a defence to their honour, a protection for their good repute; he immortalized their deeds of glory, and published their eternal fame (Ibn Rashiq of Kairouan, in Arberry 1957: 14).

From the early Sufi perspective, poetry was not simply a vehicle for defending one's honour and tribe; it was the highest expression for the decipherment of God's signs. In other words, the poet was not only the mediator of the tribes but also a mediator of image and substance. He/she was endowed with the ability to penetrate into the veil of appearances in order to depict the essential character of the image being portrayed. In early Arabic Sufi poetry, the distinction between the subject and object vanishes, emphasizing the unity of spiritual and material realms. Many early Sufi principles, practices, and experiences that were discussed in the second section of this chapter were conveyed and distributed in the poetry of early Sufi personalities.

The Arabian Ode as a Vehicle for Early Sufi Expressions of Faith

From pre-Islamic times to the contemporary era, the foremost form of Arabic poetry has been the *qasida*. It was the quintessential way to capture and immortalize love, honour, humility, brevity, glory, and all of the time-less qualities moulding human behaviour and relations amongst the multitude of Arabs. The *qasida* was a "microcosm" of Arabian life:

> [The *qasida*] draws a precise horizon, reducing a comprehensive aesthetic vision to a microcosm. From this microcosm, as a pattern of the mind, a habit of thought, or a mode of vision, it then seems to fulfil a need for a comprehensive synthesis of an entire culture's view on world, life, and historical experience (Stetkevych 1993: 1).

The *qasida* was a glimpse into both the individual and communal life of the poet. Through the voice of the poet we get a snapshot into the life of his tribe as a whole living entity (full of complex relations and moral codes) as well as into his own subjective interpretive reality. In particular, a synthesis emerges through the poet's mastery over the constant tension of contrasting the kenosis and plerosis. Kenosis, like the Sufi principle *fana'*, is the process of "emptying", of abandonment, where the poet severs all ties with the Beloved, and plerosis is a process of "filling", of reconnection, relation, and ultimately union, akin to the Sufi principle *baqa'* (Sperl 1989: 10).

The most celebrated pre-Islamic collection of *qasida* poetry is known as the *Mu'allaqat*, "the hanging ones" which were honoured through the ritual of being "embroidered in gold on rare Egyptian cloth and [then] suspended from the ancient shrine in Mecca known as the Kaaba" (Sells 1989: 3). To Arabic literary scholars, the *qasida* (as seen in the *Mu'allaqat*) has been conceptualized as consisting of three distinct episodes/stages: *nasib*, *rihla*, and *madih*. As will be described in further detail, the *qasida* starts with the mood of loss, then the quest for lost love, and finally, the climatic arrival home.

In pre-Islamic times, the *qasida* was conceptually known as erotic (focusing on the amatory relationship of humans) or secular (expressing tribal pride and defiance). However, with the emergence of Islam, the *qasida* in particular and Arabic poetry in general would undergo dramatic changes. The birth of Islam and the literary content and style of the Qur'ān changed Arabic literature in all its manifestations.

Although, at times, the totalizing nature of legal discourse within Islam created something of an antipathy toward sensuality that marginalized many a poet, the poetic spirit of the pre-Islamic heritage was not abandoned; rather it was transformed. With the exception of poetry commissioned for the benefit of the state and ruler, Arabic *qasidas* began to experience a metamorphosis of variant degrees from the erotic to the spiritual. Masters of transmutation, the Sufi poets of the formative era, utilized the schemata of the *qasida* to synthesize the sensuous nature of pre-Islamic poetry with that of Islamic spirituality. In turn, new types of metaphorical poetry emerged, the most predominant being the "love-poem", also known as the *ghazal*. A notable influence here was the longstanding Persian courtly tradition of love poetry celebrating wine and romance – subjects that Sufis would utilize as metaphors for the intoxicating, ecstatic relationship with God (as we have briefly discussed in Chapters 1 and 2).

Such innovative yet unorthodox, "rebellious" poetry would not originate and blossom in the central core of the Muslim world, Arabia; rather, it would plant roots in the periphery, as in Iraq and Muslim Spain. It manifested in different degrees of non-religious poetry so popular among Muslim royalty and aristocratic elites, as well as in early Sufi poetry. Such gnostic thinking was developed in the poetic works of Rabi'a, Dhu'l Nun, al-Bistami, al-Nuri, al-Junayd, and al-Hallaj, all of whom interpreted human love as a spiritual Divine union of attraction. This stream of thinking would later develop in 'Abbasid times with the apophatic efforts of such individuals as Ibn al-Farid (d. 1235) and Ibn al-'Arabi.

Nasib Stage: Longing for What was Lost

The *nasib*, or *dhikr al-diyar* (relic rememberance), is the nostalgic prelude for the average *qasida*. It is the image of a lover (usually the poet) lamenting the absence of his/her beloved. This image is often depicted in the setting of a deserted campsite or a dwelling of ruins (*al-atlal*), metaphorically symbolizing a past ideal time and space for love. As invoked by the poet, the *nasib* establishes a mood saturated in haunted emptiness, in remorseful alienation, and in fleeting passion. The following are examples of the *nasib*, as found in the first verses of pre-Islamic as well as early Islamic poets:

> The tent marks in Minan are worn away,
> Where she encamped and where she alighted,
> Ghawl and Rijam left to the wild,
> And torrent beds of Rayyan
> naked tracings, worn thin, like inscriptions
> carved in flattened stones.
> Dung-stained ground that tells the years passed
> since human presence, months of peace gone by…
>
> (Labid, in Sells 1989: 35)

In the shadow of archaic desolation – as represented by his lover's abandoned abode – the poet reminiscences about a lost peace: a paradise for-
saken with only an archetypal memory to replace it. Although the desert
seems so bleak and so vacant in appearance, the poet (a master of diction,
syntax, and detailed reflection) interprets its every form as a reminder of
their love. As a consequence, ultimately, the poet is existentially as well
as physically "lost", for they no longer possess that which made them so
whole and at peace.

Yearning for a time before the time present and recapitulating that time
as absolute is nostalgia. This past time represents an ideal model for present time and reinforces an inevitably crystallized view of human life. It
is memory, the act of remembrance, which creates the feeling of remote-
ness, of distance. This reality of desolation is connected to the sense of
loss, a sense of not being whole – in unity with the self. An ideal, although
phantom in nature, emerges from the reconstruction of a past image. This
brooding reality is ironic due to the fact that the idealized past continues to
exist only as an imitation or reconstruction in the present. The poet seeks
to escape from the present, suspending the immediate reality in favour of a
presumably ideal and final "past originality".

For the pre-Islamic poets, the *nasib* was only a beginning that was necessarily followed by the journey and then the *madih*. However, in early
Islamic poets, such as Hasan ibn Thabit (d. 674), the *nasib* became the
whole poetic experience.

> At Taybah there remain the Prophet's
> Relics and a luminous
> Encounter place, while other relics fade
> And waste away.
> Indelible are the signs of that inviolate abode,
> Where the Guide's pulpit stands on which he used to mount.
> It stands so clear, the contours firm – and there
> His precinct with a prayer-place and mosque.
> There his chambers are, there
> The Lord's light found its repose,
> To give him light and warmth –
> Signs which will not be effaced as time goes by,
> Finding renewal in each decay.
> There I recognized the Prophet's traces
> And where I saw him last,
> A grave in whose dust he, hidden, lies.
>
> (Hasan ibn Thabit, in Stetkevych 1993: 61)

For Hasan ibn Thabit's love lyrics transformed into poetic elegies signify
the yearning for a time that was perfect, the time of the Prophet Muhammad.
In the *nasib*, emphasis is placed on a virtue of longing for a past originality negating any possibility for transformation. The poet is caught between

praising for what was and sorrowing for what is. The ruins are no longer desert encampments; rather they are lost prophetic sanctuaries:

> The holy places lie in empty patches
> For want of the live prophecy
> Which once they knew,
> A desolation but for the life which is the tomb
> Which hosts the one lamented...
> His mosque, and all that's lonely in his loss –
> Ravaged the place he stood, the place he sat.
>
> (Hasan ibn Thabit, in Stetkevych 1993: 61)

Remembrance is subjugated to the consciousness of separation; however, paradoxically, from the early Sufi perspective, it is through the process of longing (*shawq*) – with memory as its beginning stage – that the seeker once again becomes whole, at peace in love. For early Sufis, like al-Hallaj, the *nasib* is a vehicle to attain the state of longing in order to invoke a yearning for nearness to the Beloved. This longing connotes both separation and unification. The process of longing is embedded in the nature of separation; however, the ultimate aim of longing is to be reunited, as eloquently depicted by the following poetic lines:

> One with Thee make me, O my One, through Oneness
> Faithed in sincerity no path can reach.
> I am the Truth, and Truth, for Truth, is Truth,
> Robed in Its Essence, thus beyond separation...
>
> (al-Hallaj, in Lings 2004: 28)

According to al-Hallaj, the stage of *nasib* is the beginning of divine nostalgia, which lifts the lover out of the present back to a timeless origin which is Presence itself. Therefore, the *nasib*, for early Sufis, is a powerful prelude directing the poet-lover to an origin.

As depicted by so many poets, the nostalgic experience of reality is a state of suffering. The memory, not reality, of love leads to the experience of enduring distress. Longing has diminished the poet to abandon his passion, his Beloved, languishing in lament and wishing for annihilation. He is in exile from love and from the source of love. He is caught in the paradox of absence and presence where time and space are demarcated as realities of isolation. Such ambiguous language is reflected in the works of al-Nuri:

> Some have desired through hope to come to Thee,
> So, I have severed every thought from me,
> And died to selfhood, that I might be Thine.
> How long, my heart's Beloved? I am spent:
> I can no more endure this banishment.
>
> (al-Nuri, in Arberry 1957: 78)

However, for the early Sufi such paradox of annihilation (*fana'*) and sub-sistence (*baqa'*) is the goal, for it is through the experience of exile that yearning is created as a catalyst for inspiration to experience different states of being, such as love, union and self-transcendence. Such ambiguity is also conveyed in the works of al-Hallaj, as blatantly stated in the following verses:

> Until I pass all bounds in deserts
> Of the proximity in which I wander
> I look then in a watery surface
> But do not cross my imagined limits
> I come yielding to him at the end
> Of a tether in my submission's hand
> His love brands my heart with
> Passion's brand, O what a brand!
> My being's witness departs from me
> In nearness until I forget my name.
>
> (al-Hallaj, in Wormhoudt 1975: 92)

Rihla Stage: Journey for Love and Union

As the *qasida* continues, the lamenting lover leaves the ruins of his Beloved and sets out on a journey, *rihla*, by camel or by horse. At this stage, the pre-Islamic poet decides to either engage in a passionate pursuit of love by following the traces of his lover's caravan or to escape from love by surren-dering to endless war:

> By my soul, I made it a story of
> Riders, I was at peace and I got a war...
>
> (Zuheir ibn Abi Sulma, in Wormholdt 1975: 108)

Either way, he or she has now become a traveller, a *salik*, of the desert way, revealing in every step the secret of his longing, that being love. To be a traveller is to acknowledge the impermanence of life – that in life change is inevitable – and turn to the present reality. *Salik*, in early Sufi thought, meant the wanderer on the Sufi path (*tariqa*) who undergoes different states (*ahwal*, singular *hal*) and stations (*maqamat*, singular *maqam*) (Schimmel 1975: 98).

To early Sufi poets, the journey represents the notion that a Sufi is always in the making and never fully made, reflecting the Sufi sentiment, "We are God in the making". The *rihla*, or journey of individuation, is the formation of an archetype. The *rihla* that establishes the poet in motion is the isthmus mediating the temporal and the archetypal:

> I die, but my passion for Thee dieth not.
> Unfulfilled are my longings to drink deep Thy love.
> My desires are the essence of all desire; Thou art they...

Thou art the goal of my quest,...
Art Thou not guide to lost travellers in bewilderment,
And saviour from the brink of the crumbling precipice?

(Dhu'l Nun, in Lings 2004: 8)

For early Sufis, like Dhu'l Nun, this isthmus between the temporal and archetypal is living in the reality of "neither this nor that" and yet "both this and that". The poetic themes involved in this stage are drunkenness, love-madness, and perpetual wandering as well as the bewildered search to "belong". In this state, the self starts to dissolve and the process of annihilation (*fana'*) commences.

The nature of love is to make the lover unconditionally submissive in obedience and service to his or her Beloved. Echoing the outlawed, pre-Islamic poet, Antara ibn Shaddad's (d. 608) sentiment, "'Twas then her beauties first enslaved my heart", Rabi'a too develops her own notion of "love is slavery" (*al-hawa riqqun*). For Rabi'a, the slave of God, is in total bondage completely dependent upon his/her masterful Beloved:

No-one can claim to be sincere in love
Who doesn't forget the sting of the Master's whip
In the presence of the Master.

(Rabi'a, in Upton 1988: 35)

For the early Sufi, poetry elevates the Beloved to the highest station of his or her desire. Sufi poets, like Rabi'a, would use this combination of admiration and annihilation to transform the sensuous, amatory love into spiritual, esoteric love.

Uniting with the one who was lost is the object of a lover's journey, and if the lover cannot obtain such subsistent unity they may forever be annihilated. Although the nature of language is implicitly dualistic (e.g. subject and object; passive and active; feminine and masculine), suggesting an inevitable reality of separation, the poet's use of syntax and metaphor fuses together the lover and Beloved, creating an ambiguous blurring of worlds. The early Sufi poet, ultimately, annihilates all notions of "other". In other words, the tool of the poet (that being language) is limited to the function of its parts (that being words); yet, paradoxically, language's overall objective is to unite all its parts into one comprehensive whole.

I would, so overflowing is my love for Him,
Remember Him perpetually, yet my rememberance –
Wondrous to tell – is vanished into ecstasy,
And wonder upon wonder, even ecstasy,
With memory's self, in nearness-farness vanished is.

(al-Nuri, in Lings 2004: 18)

For the early Sufi and others who were influenced by their lives and thought, language is a tool to express the inexpressible: it is a method to portray a paradox of Oneness. For to the Sufi, the Beloved is God. Therefore, the longing for the Beloved is a yearning to reunite with the Oneness, as beautifully depicted by al-Hallaj:

> I saw my Lord with the eye of the heart.
> I said: 'Who art thou?' He answered: 'Thou'.
> Thus where no where hath, as from Thee,
> Nor is there, as to Thee, a where.

> (al-Hallaj, in Lings 2004: 28)

Through themes such as divine manifestation in creation and mystical union with the divine, poetry becomes a source of incantations for meditation and contemplation on the paradox of mutuality.

> I am he whom I desire, whom I desire is I;
> We are two spirits dwelling in a single body.
> If you see me, you have seen him,
> And if you see him, you have seen me.

> (al-Hallaj, in Ernst 1997: 153)

Such paradoxes of mutuality provide a transformed setting for human love, realized through a state of unconditional surrender, a state of freedom, of peace. To a Sufi, poetry is the highest form of synthesizing subject and object into one entity wherein the reader no longer can distinguish between the two. Such synthesis is the affirmation, the realization, the integration, and the proclamation of the sacred saying (*hadith qudsi*) from the Prophet Muhammad, "When I love my servant... I become the hearing with which he hears, the seeing with which he sees, the feet with which he walks, the hands with which he touches, the tongue with which he speaks" (Sells 1996: 22). In poetry the poet does not negate human life and all its multiple manifestations as but illusions; rather the poet embraces human reality and interprets it as Divine manifestation.

Madih Stage: Praise in Glorification and Honour

In the final stage of pre-Islamic *qasida*, the poet has arrived at the abode of praise, either of his individual self or communal self, his tribe. After the journey of individuation, there comes a time of boasting which signifies deliverance from an archetypal past. For early Islamic poets (such as Hasan ibn Thabit), the *madih* usually connoted the praising of the Prophet Muhammad. Instead of lamenting for the parting of a lover, the *madih* invokes the unification of one's self with a "home". The *qasida* has come to a full circle: that which was once lost is finally regained in a new form; the pride in the familial tribe fills the void of desire. In other words, beyond loss and at the height of love, praise dominates.

> From a clan whose fathers have shown the way.
> For every warrior band, there is a guide and a way.
> Their honour untarnished, their action never fallow,
> Their judgment does not lean with the winds of desire.
> When trust was portioned out among the tribe,
> The divider bestowed on us the greater share.
> Be content with what the sire has given.
> He who portioned merit out among us is most knowing.
>
> (Labid, in Sells 1989: 43–44)

Praise can manifest in self-glory or tribe glorification (*fakhr*). Whether personal or tribal, *fakhr* is a reflection of past victories and an upholding of the code of honour and valour. A spirit of gallantry is depicted in this stage in order to symbolize the prominent virtues of courage, fearlessness, devotion, and discipline – all of which helped the protagonist of the poem to undertake the journey.

Like a river running to the sea, for the early Sufi, the *madih* stage is the completion of the mystic's journey. It is the dissolution of self into the emanation of the Divine. *Fakhr* would transform from self and tribe glorification to the Divine glorification as reflected in the following lyric of al-Junayd:

> They enjoy God's nearness under the shadow of His Glory
> Where their spirits move and stir
> They go there to find honour and sagacity,
> And return with all perfections.
> They march with the unique glory of His attributes
> Trailing the robes of Unity.
> What happens next is beyond description.
> Let it remain a secret.
>
> (al-Junayd, in Nadeem 1993: 48)

The concept of chivalrous behaviour was inherently embedded in the moral and social livelihood of desert Arabs. As seen in more of the "heroic poetry", the poet portrays himself or his tribe as those facing "perilous encounters, adventures, chases…" (Stetkevych 1993: 37), creating the concept of an all-embracing power, an untouchable archetype. It was common for a poet to project an image of himself as a moralist warrior whose honour is rooted in peace and not war or vengeance, one who values kindness over pride.

Such poetry can be found in the work of Zuhair ibn Abi Sulma (d. 609), who was known to have prophesized that the Arabs were to receive a messenger from Allah (Beeston 1983: 31). The following verses are from his *Mu'allaqat*:

> You said: If we gain a treaty by wide
> Wealth and kind words we'll have peace
> So by it you came to the best land
> You were far from stubbornness and sin
>
> (Abi Sulma, in Wormholdt 1975: 19)

For the early Sufi, it is the highest honour to become the servant of one's Beloved. This chivalrous honour is known as *futuwwah*. This code of honourable conduct is irrevocable certitude to behave fearlessly for love and in love. As commented on by al-Sulami:

> *Futuwwah* is a state of mind. It means placing other people above oneself. It is being generous and altruistic. It is self-denial, immunity to disappointment, indulgence toward other people's shortcomings. It is fearless struggle against tyranny, and above all, it is love. Love is the essence of *Futuwwah*; love of God, love of His creation, love of Love (al-Sulami, in al-Jerrahi 1991: 13).

The stage of praise expresses the conditions of joy and fulfilment as associated with reunion. This profound happiness of homecoming gives way to deep satisfaction: feelings of peace. If the *rihla* involves the trials and tribulations of love, it is the *madih* that establishes peace, order and restoration of unity. As so eloquently stated by al-Junayd, "They march with the unique glory of His attributes. Trailing the robes of Unity" (Farrin 2011: 238).

The conclusion of the *qasida* is love and peace: the stage of complete surrender in the Divine. A trend that reoccurs throughout early Sufi poetry is the conceptual representation of love as peace between lover and Beloved, between sensual and spiritual worlds.

For early Sufi poets and many classical and contemporary Sufi poets who would be influenced by them, poetry was a mirror of life's multifaceted realities, depicting in the most eloquent ways the layers of mystical significance as experienced through human perception. They were masters of the word for they treated the word as the highest artistic expression to celebrate life's encounters with the Divine. The poetic intensity of the early Sufis is indicative of their sensitivity to human well-being in all its manifestations, inner and outer. Additionally, it is through poetry that we come to understand the growth of early Sufism through symbol and method.

EARLY SUFIS AND THE FORGING OF A SPIRITUAL PATH

Sufism's formative period – between the seventh and tenth centuries – was a dynamic time that witnessed the emergence of diverse renunciants, ascetics and mystics. The end of this period saw the first systematization of Sufi knowledge by the early Sufi biographers, who sought to establish Sufism as a discipline grounded in the recorded lives of the pious, and in their principles and practices. Before Sufism became a household term among Muslims however, it existed in an undefined way, embodied in the lives of early Muslims remarkable for their devotion and self-denial. As discussed at the beginning of the book, al-Hujwiri notes that there are a number of possible etymological origins for the term Sufism (*tasawwuf*): it has been connected with the Arabic word for purity (*safa*), and the Greek work for wisdom (*sophia*). Historically, the term seems to have originated as a reference to Muslim ascetics who wore wool (Arabic: *suf*), a material that Christian hermits had long worn as a symbol of renouncing worldly comforts. Historical sources show that asceticism (i.e. voluntary poverty, frequent fasting, abandoning sleep for nocturnal prayer vigils) was a widely held ideal among early Muslims. The first recorded application of the label, "Sufi", to an ascetic was in the eighth century (Melchert 2015: 13). The term did not appear more regularly until later in the ninth century, when Sufi circles in Iraq came to prominence. As Islam became the religion of a rapidly expanding Arab empire in the Near East, devout Muslims began to feel that the Qur'ānic imperatives of frequent worship and non-attachment to worldly wealth and achievement were being forgotten. Known as *zuhhad* (ascetics) and *'ubbad* (worshippers), some Muslims gained renown and notoriety for their poverty, fasting, fear of divine punishment, and frequent worship.

Mystics, Hermits and Ascetic Warriors

Perhaps no name is associated more with Islam's early ascetic tradition than Hasan al-Basri. Should one follow the various trails of Sufi lineage (*silsila*) back far enough, one will find they often converge upon al-Basri, indicating quite clearly the ways in which Sufism is thought to have emerged from Islamic asceticism. In 642, al-Basri was born to Persian parents in Medina, Arabia, which was the political capital of the Muslims at that time. It is interesting to note that al-Basri's father was enslaved during a military campaign of the second Caliph 'Umar (d. 644) and taken back to Medina. In the course of dividing spoils of war, his father, along with his wife-to-be from his own village, was given to Umm Salama (d. 680), a wife of the Prophet Muhammad. Umm Salama gifted both to one of her close relatives, where they were ultimately wed and freed by the couple who received them.

According to some traditions, al-Basri would then become a student of 'Ali ibn Abi Talib at the age of 14. After the death of 'Ali in 661, al-Basri would leave for Iraq where he would establish his own *madrasa* or theological school in Basra (hence his name al-Basri or "the Basran"). As previously mentioned at the beginning of this chapter, his thought and school would influence a variety of individuals significant in Sufism's early development, some of the most notable include: Wasil Ibn Ata, the founder of the Mutazilite school of thought, (Islam's first rationalist form of theology), Abd al-Wahid ibn Zayd (founder of the first Sufi cloister), Rabi'a al-'Adawiyya (the famous female Sufi saint), and Harith al-Muhasibi (Baghdad's leading Sufi psychologist).

As previously mentioned, another well-known early Sufi and a wandering hermit was Dhu'l Nun al-Misri or Dhu'l Nun the Egyptian. He was born of Nubian parents, and lived most of his life in Egypt. His shrine is in the City of the Dead, Cairo. Depicted in Farid al-Din Attar's *Tadhkirat al-Awliya'* (*Memorial to the Saints*) and Jalal al-Din Rumi's *Mathnawi*, the following is a story of how Dhu'l Nun came to be named:

> Once a saintly dervish took passage in a ship in which some gold was lost. One by one the passengers were searched, and although the gold was not found, everyone decided to blame the dervish. They abused him mercilessly and yet he remained silent until he finally exclaimed, "Oh, God, Thou knowest!" Immediately thousands and thousands of fish emerged, each with a perfect pearl in its mouth. The dervish collected a quantity of pearls and dropped them on board the ship, and then he sprang aloft, sitting high in the air like a king. The people on the ship were amazed and exclaimed that the pearls were from God, and belonged to no one else. High above them before the ship's mast the dervish said, "Begone! The ship for you, God for me, so that a beggarly thief may not be in your company! I am happy, being united with Him and separated from His creatures". And that is how this dervish came to be called Dhu'l-Nun (the Fish) (Attar, in Arberry 1966: 90–91).

Besides developing the concepts of *'ilm* and *ma'rifa* as previously discussed, Dhu'l Nun is also reputed to have reconciled ideas from ancient Egyptian mystery schools and alchemical traditions (although some of these links are apocryphal) with that of Islam.

Dhu'l Nun influenced many students including al-Muhasibi and Abu Yazid al-Bistami. As discussed previously in this chapter, al-Bistami would become an icon of the "intoxicated" Sufi, and is generally considered a founder of the "drunken" or ecstatic school of Sufism. He especially influenced Persian Sufi thought and practice; however, such seminal figures as Ibn al-'Arabi would consider al-Bistami to be a *qutb*, or a supreme Sufi master of his era (Abrahamov 2014: 37). He was born a grandson of a Zoroastrian in Bestam in north-eastern Persia. He died in Bestam in 874 and his mausoleum still stands there.

Being the founder of the ecstatic school of Sufism, he is famous for the boldness of his expression of the mystic's complete absorption into the Absolute. This absorption is best seen in one of his most well-known sayings: "Lover and Beloved are One. Glory be to Me! How great is my majesty!"

> The vestiges of knowledge are effaced; its essence is noughted by the Essence of Another, its track lost in the Track of Another. Thirty years God was my mirror. But now I am my own mirror; that which used to be I, I am no more. To say I and God denies the Unity of God. I say I am my

own mirror, but it is God that speaks with my tongue – I have vanished.
I glided out of my Bayazidhood as a snake glides from a cast skin. And
then I looked. And what I saw was this: Lover and Beloved and Love are
One. Glory to Me! (Glasse 1989: 76).

Figure 5.1: Shrine of al-Bistami in Bestam, Iran.

Figure 5.2: Tomb of al-Bistami.

To al-Bistami, the Sufi is a pure mirror who reflects the tendencies/char-
acteristics of God. Besides being known for his desire for union with the
Divine, he was also the first to describe the mystical experience in terms of

the image of the *mi'raj*, the heavenly journey of the Prophet. This would greatly influence the imagination of Sufis who would follow him (i.e. Ibn al-'Arabi).

Additionally, being one of the earlier Sufis, he is also known for having formulated the Sufi understanding of *fana'*, annihilation in God, and *baqa'*, "permanent life in God". Both concepts would contribute to the development of mystical psychology. It was al-Bistami's emphasis on an authentic mystical experience of total annihilation of the human self in God which would represent a shift away from the Basrian ascetic renunciant tradition (Knysh 2000: 71).

A Selection of Early Sufi Women

Like the other traditional disciplines that make up the *'ulum* or 'sciences' of Islam, Sufism has been largely the preserve of men. However, Sufism has long had notable female luminaries that indicate a significant cohort of female practitioners, a cohort that has not always been as prominently featured historically. Contemporary scholars of Islam are increasingly uncovering and recovering the rich history of female spirituality in Islam. For example, recent scholarship has discovered a much greater number of *muhaddithat* or female scholars of *hadith* than previously thought to be a part of the tradition. The popular *tabaqat* genre of Sufi literature, which catalogues or cateogorizes Sufi biographies, includes mention of a number of Sufi women famous for their sanctity, miracles, and wisdom. For example, 'Abd al-Rahman al-Sulami wrote an appendix, *Dhikr an-niswa al –muta'abbidat as-sufiyyat* (*The Book of Sufi Women*), to his famous *Tabaqat as-Sufiyya* (Categories of the Sufis) in which he states in his introduction that these women were spiritual exemplars:

> Masters of the realities of the divine oneness, recipients of divine discourses, possessors of true visions and exemplary conduct, and followers of the ways of the prophets (Cornell 1999, 48).

Cornell, translator of al-Sulami's book (1999), points out that this book was separated from the original work soon after al-Sulami's death and thought lost until it was rediscovered in 1991 making it one of the earliest manuscripts on Sufi women. The book contains 82 notices on Sufi women representing the regions of Iraq, Iran, and Syria. The following are brief biographies of some early Sufi female personalities mentioned by as-Sulami.

Mu'adha al-'Adawiyya (seventh century) founded the first school of female asceticism in Basra and was responsible for initiating the way of disciplined servitude to God (Cornell 1999: 61). Her spiritual method stressed this principle through "prayer, fasting, and the performance of night-vigils" (Cornell 1999: 61). *Tawakkul* (trust in/reliance on God) "was also a central part of her doctrine" (Cornell 1999: 61). She "used to pray six hundred prostrations (*rak'at*) every day and night. She would read her nightly portion of the Qur'ān in the standing position" (Cornell 1999: 264). Desirous of meeting death while in prayer, she refrained from sleeping during the night and wore "only thin garments" (Cornell 1999: 264) to enable the cold to keep her awake (Cornell 1999: 264). "When overcome by the need for sleep, she would get up and wander around the house, saying, 'Oh Self! Eternal sleep is ahead of you. If I were to die, your repose in the grave would be a long one, whether it be sorrowful or happy!'" (Cornell 1999: 264). She once said to a woman whom she had nursed as a child: "'Oh daughter, be cautious and hopeful of your encounter with God, the Glorious and Mighty, for I have seen that when the hopeful person meets God, he is made worthy by his devoted servitude, and I have seen the God-fearing person hoping for safety on the day when humanity stands before the Lord of the Worlds!'" (Cornell 1999: 266). The utterance left her "overcome by weeping" (Cornell 1999: 266). "Mu'adha lived during the time of A'isha [wife of the Prophet Muhammad] and transmitted hadith from her" (Cornell 1999: 268). Hasan al-Basri is among those who would transmit reports on her authority (Cornell 1999: 268).

Hafsah bint Sirin (eighth century) had memorized the Qur'ān by the age of 12 (Cornell 1999: 270) and was known for "her unique ability to interpret" its teachings (Cornell 1999: 62). She would say to her young students: "'Give of yourselves while you are still youths. For I see true spiritual practice only among the youths!'" (Cornell 1999: 270). Her spiritual practice included an emphasis on prayer, fasting and Qur'ānic recitation, and she would spend most of the hours of her day in her private place of worship leaving only upon the "full light of day" (Cornell 1999: 270) (in the morning) and returning in time for the noon prayer. "'She would recite half of the Qur'ān every night and would fast every day'", except for certain holidays (e.g. the *'Eid*) (Cornell 1999: 274). It is related that although the oil of her lamp would sometimes go out while she was praying in the night, it "would continue to illuminate her house until daylight" (Cornell 1999: 274).

Hukayma or Halima of Damascus (ninth century) was a descendent of the Prophet Muhammad and an important figure in Syrian women's Sufism. Some biographers confer the masculine title for a teacher, *'ustadh,'* upon her (rather than *ustadha*), as she was considered as having transcended the social limitations of her femininity with her renowned expertise in the formal Islamic sciences and matters of doctrine (Cornell 1999: 59). Attesting to the wisdom implied in her name, which means 'Dear Sage' or 'Dear Philosopher', Rabi'a bint Isma'il related the following story about a visit with her: When "'I entered Hukayma's room while she was reading the Qur'ān and she said to me, 'Oh, Rabi'a! I have heard that your husband is taking another wife.' 'Yes,' I said. 'How could he?' she replied. 'Given what I have been told about his good judgment, how could his heart be distracted from God by two women? Have you not learned the interpretation of this verse: 'Except one who comes to God with a sound heart' [Qur'ān 26, 89] 'No,' I said. Hukayma said, 'It means that when one encounters God, there should be nothing in his heart other than Him'" (Cornell 1999: 126). "'As I left Halima, I was so deeply moved by her words that I rocked back and forth as I walked in a kind of trance, but felt embarrassed at my condition – that a passerby might think me drunk'" (Adams Hemlinski 2003: 35).

Fatima of Nishapur (ninth century) of Khurasan, is known as one of the greatest female Sufi personalities similar to Rabia al-Adawiyyah, and was highly praised by her contemporaries. Her student, Abu Yazid al-Bistami once said of her: "'In all of my life, I have only seen one true man and one true woman. The woman was Fatima of Nishapur. There was no station (on the way) about which I spoke with her, but that she had already experienced it herself'" (Adams Hemlinski 2003: 47). Like few other exceptional women, she had been elevated to the ranks of honourary men by being called *'ustadh'* by the prominent Sufi scholar Dhu'l Nun (Cornell 1999: 45). In a famous story, she reminds Dhu'l Nun that the essence of Sufism is not to be found in paranormal states but in spiritual practice. Here, she describes and comments on true Sufis:

> A people who have staked their aspirations on God,
> And whose ambitions aspire to nothing else.
>
> The goal of this folk is their Lord and their Master,
> Oh what a noble goal is theirs, for the One beyond compare!
>
> They do not compete for this world and its honors,
> Whether it be for food, luxury, or children,
>
> Nor for fine and costly clothes,
> Nor for the ease and comfort that is found in towns.
>
> Instead, they hasten toward the promise of an exalted station,
> Knowing that each step brings them closer to the farthest horizon.
>
> They are the hostages of washes and gullies,
> And you will find them gathered on mountain-tops (Cornell 1999: 15–16).

Lubaba al-Muta 'Abida, otherwise known as 'Lubaba the Devotee' of Syria and Jerusalem, "was a specialist in the ways of gnosis (*ma'rifa*) and self-denial (*mujahadat*)" (Cornell 1999: 82), "scrupulousness (*wara'*) and reclusiveness (*nusuk*)" (Cornell 1999: 124). She once stated: "'Knowledge of God bequeaths love for Him; love for Him bequeaths longing for Him; longing for Him bequeaths intimacy with Him; and intimacy with Him bequeaths constancy in serving Him and conforming to His laws'" (Cornell 1999: 124). About self-denial, she said: "'The more I observe self-denial, the more comfortable I become with this practice. Thus, when I get tired from human encounter, I find intimacy in the remembrance of God. And when human discourse tires me, I take my rest in dedication to the worship of God and fulfilling His service'" (Cornell 1999: 82).

'Aisha bint Abu 'Uthman Sa'id (tenth century) of Nishapur, formerly one of the most important cities of the Islamic world, is known for having a high spiritual state and being able to conform "to the requirements of the moment" (i.e. "firmly maintaining what [was] required [of her] at the present moment") (Adams Hemlinski 2003: 46). She once said: "'When one feels lonely in his solitude, this is because of his lack of intimacy with his Lord'" (Adams Hemlinski 2003: 47). And that: "'He who shows contempt for God's slaves shows his lack of knowledge of the Master. For he who loves the Craftsman glorifies the Craftsman's handiwork'" (Adams Hemlinski 2003: 47).

Umm Ahmad bint 'Aisha, daughter of 'Aisha bint Abu 'Uthman Sa'id, "remained inside her home for fifty years" (Cornell 1999: 218) without leaving once. She was "known for her spiritual motivation (*himma*), her spiritual state (*hal*), and her moral conduct (*khuluq*)" (Cornell 1999: 218). She once said: "'Knowledge (*'ilm*) is the life of humanity, spiritual practice (*'amal*) is its conveyance, intellect (*'aql*) is its ornament, and gnosis (*ma'rifa*) is its illumination and insight'" (Cornell 1999: 218).

RISE OF THE BAGHDAD SCHOOL
AND SUFISM'S FOUNDATION

In the middle of the ninth century, having been influenced by the ascetic personalities and movements of Basra and Kufa, Baghdad not only became a political and cultural centre but also a home to prominent Sufi figures such as Sari al-Saqati (d. 867) and Abu Bakr al-Kharraz (d. 899), and of course al-Nuri, al-Junayd, al-Hallaj.

Sari al-Saqati abandoned the life of a merchant in the 'Abbasid capital and sought spiritual refuge in Basra and Abbadan with other Iraqi world-renouncers. In 833, he eventually returned to Baghdad and would gain many students from Iraq, Iran, and Syria, including his most famous students, al-Kharraz, al-Nuri, and al-Junayd. In al-Kharraz's works, such as *Kitab as-Sidq* (*Book of Truthfulness*) and *Kitab al-Kashf wa al-Bayan* (*Book of Unveiling and Elucidation*), he would develop certain Sufi concepts that would have an enduring influence throughout Sufi history and would earn him the title of "the Tongue of Sufism" (Knysh 2000: 57). These included the development of stations on the Sufi path for different classes of seekers, the articulation of *fana'* and *baqa'*, the differences between sainthood and prophethood, and the overall formation of mystical vocabulary. This led to Sufi interpretations of grammar and composition and the art of *isharat* or communication through symbolic allusions (hints).

The famous founder of the "sober" Sufi school of thought, al-Junayd, would credit al-Kharraz for his ideas on *fana'* and *baqa'*. Al-Junayd came from Iran; born in Nihawand and settled in Baghdad where he studied law according to the Shafi'i school of thought. Influenced by his uncle, al-Saqati, al-Junayd would follow and eventually succeed his uncle as a spiritual leader and master in Baghdad. "As reported by one of his fellow Sufis, al-Haddad, 'If intellect (*'aql*) were a man, it would have the form of Junayd', a saying that alludes to the seriousness, sobriety, and penetrating mind of the master" (Schimmel 1975: 58). Al-Junayd has since become the foremost representative of sober or orthodox Sufism, a path deeply mystical in orientation, but unlike al-Bistami's approach, circumspect in its discourse, with an emphasis on maintaining the norms of Islamic theology and law. Despite the emerging difference between the sober and ecstatic approaches to Sufism, represented by al-Bistami and al-Junayd, both were premised on the shared idea of *walaya/wilaya*.

Al-Junayd was not a prolific author, and yet the extant works attributed to him (letters and short treatises) reveal his absolute concern with the nature of the *awliya'* the "friends" of God, and the quality of "friendship" and "guardianship" (*walaya/wilaya*) that distinguishes them from others:

> God has select ones among His worshippers and pure ones among His creatures.

> He has chosen them for friendship, selected them [for] His graciousness and [thus] set them aside for Himself. He has made their bodies to be of this world, their spirits of light, their ideas of spirit, their understanding of the throne of God, and their intellects of the veil.
>
> (Karamustafa 2005: 65)

According to al-Junayd, the *awliya'* "are the instruments of God through whom God guides humanity to Himself and the springs with which He showers His mercy on His creatures" (Karamustafa 2005: 69). Later Sufis would insist that their entire path was premised on the existence of this select group of guides brought close to God, who in turn share their knowledge, light, and blessing with their close disciples, Muslims, and all people and creation in general. Interestingly, early Sufi conceptions of the *awliya'* overlap significantly with early Shi'a understandings of the divinely appointed guides who succeed Muhammad and lead Muslims, the *imams*.

Walaya in Sufism and Shi'ism

It is important to point out that although Sufism is quite often defined as *the* esotericism of Islam, it is better thought of as *one* of *two* major forms of Islamic esotericism, the other being Shi'ism. For both Sufis and Shi'a Muslims, Islam has an outer, exoteric form (*zahir*) and in inner, esoteric meaning (*batin*). The fact that two of Islam's earliest developments (both traditions took shape during the eighth and ninth centuries) are premised on this idea of a hidden or secret meaning to the religion, certainly adds weight to the historical claim that the Prophet Muhammad's message included an esoteric element.

Where Sunni and Shi'a Muslims differ however, is over the question of *who* inherits knowledge of the outer and inner aspects of Islam from the Prophet. Who among Muslims has exoteric and esoteric knowledge? Generally speaking, Sunnis believe that exoteric knowledge is inherited by the jurists (the *'ulama* or *fuqaha*), while esoteric knowledge is inherited by the *awliya'*, the "friends" of God, or Sufi saints. In contrast, Shi'a Muslims believe that both exoteric and esoteric knowledge were inherited by a single figure: the *imam*.

Shi'a Islam is based on the idea that God's mercy includes His provision of guidance to humanity. Hence He sends not only prophets like Muhammad, but also appoints a guide for each generation to ensure that the prophetic message is preserved over time. This guide is called an *imam* in Shi'ism, literally "one who stands before" others, leading the way. The *imams* are appointed by God to preserve the true meaning of the Qur'ān for Muslims after the Prophet. The *imam* is both an *'alim* (scholar-jurist) and a *wali* (saint) for Shi'a Muslims. Based on the Abrahamic model of transmission of prophetic authority through familial descent, Shi'a believe that the Imamate is something found exclusively among Muhammad's descendants, specifically within the lineage initiated by 'Ali and Muhammad's daughter Fatima (d. 632) and their two sons Hasan (d. 670) and Hussein (d. 680).

Various traditions from the early Muslim community indicate that 'Ali was not only the Prophet's cousin, son-in-law, and faithful follower, but that he was also the inheritor of comprehensive knowledge from the Prophet. Both Sunni and Shi'a traditions famously describe 'Ali as the "gate" to prophetic knowledge. Although Sunnis did not believe that prophetic knowledge and authority were transmitted exclusively through descent, they did respect and revere Muhammad's family and their descendants. Sufis in particular shared with Shi'a Muslims a belief that the line of descent through Hasan and Hussein included men of esoteric knowledge. Although not imbuing the *imams* of Shi'a Islam with the absolute authority given to them by Shi'a Muslims, Sufis revered them as sources of sacred knowledge, both outward and inward.

Like the early Sufi masters, the *imams* were renowned for their piety, devotion, and asceticism, and as with Sufism, this lifestyle was associated with holiness and esoteric knowledge. In the *Nahj al-Balagha*, a collection of 'Ali's sayings and sermons, 'Ali is recorded as suggesting that those devoted to a life of piety "see what others cannot see and they hear what others do not hear. They have access to divine secrets" (Takim 2006: 57). Hence we find the *imams* of Shi'ism figuring prominently in Sufi *silsilas*. All but the Naqshbandi Sufi order trace their lineage through 'Ali, while most Sufi orders consider Ja'far al-Sadiq (d. 765) and 'Ali al-Ridha (d. 818) to be key transmitters of their tradition. Notably, al-Ridha is recorded as being the teacher of Ma'ruf al-Karkhi (d. 815), who would bring Sufism to Baghdad, where it would become more widely known through such famous early Sufis as al-Junayd and al-Hallaj, as discussed earlier in this chapter.

The key difference in Sufi and Shi'a esotericism lies in their respective conceptions of *wilaya/walaya*. Both traditions are premised on the notion that, for each generation of people, God selects a number of individuals to dispose of His affairs on earth as sacred guardians and protectors of the world, and as transmitters of blessing and esoteric knowledge (the *awliya'*). For Sufis, however, this quality of *wilaya* is something that can be bestowed by God upon anyone. Anyone who undertakes moral purification and spiritual discipline of the Sufi path can experience an unveiling of esoteric knowledge, including access to the hidden meanings of the Qur'ān, can transmit *baraka*, and can even perform miracles. At least in principle then, anyone can be a *wali*.

According to Shi'a doctrine however, a distinction is made between *wilaya* and *walaya*. Although any believer can manifest a certain degree of *walaya* (friendship and closeness to God), Shi'a doctrine holds that *wilaya* (guardianship and authority) is given by God *exclusively* to the *imams*. For Shi'a Muslims then, there can be *awliya'* who are not *imams*, although they are usually found in the company of the *imams* as their disciples, and their authority and knowledge is always of a lower order. The *imams'* unique stature is such that they are thought to exist as lights revolving around God's throne before their earthly existence takes place. It follows that the *imams* do not *acquire* esoteric knowledge, blessing, and miraculous power through spiritual practice (although spiritual discipline is thought to play a necessary role in the manifestation of *wilaya*), but rather the *imams* are born with their *wilaya* fully intact. Similarly, comprehensive esoteric knowledge, including the hidden meaning of the Qur'ān, is found only with the *imams*, and can only be learned through them. Hence the Shi'a have described the *imams'* prophetic inheritance as a *wilaya al-mutlaqa*, or "absolute" *wilaya*, including a complete inner and outer knowledge, a sinless nature, and infallibility. These qualities of the *imams* are usually conceived of in such a way as to distinguish Shi'a conceptions of the *imams* from the Sufi conception of the *wali*, although they do overlap to a significant degree.

Schools of thought, traditions, and practices all seen in retrospect by later Muslims as the inevitable results of predetermined developments, in fact were the results of negotiations taking place among Muslims, with a variety of possible outcomes. In this respect, Sufism is no different. As we have seen in this chapter, early Sufism was akin to a variety of patches yet to be sown together in a patchwork frock. The esoteric and ascetic elements of the early Islamic tradition had not yet crystalized as either Sufism or Shi'ism. The Sufi attempt to express the inexpressible nature of mystical experience would find a home in the Arabic language, with its sophisticated tradition of poetry and rich depth of linguistic meaning. Although they would take shape in divergent forms, these disparate elements had shared roots in the Qur'ān and the life and practice of Muhammad. Foundational to all Islamic esotericism, the idea of an elect group chosen by God for closeness to Him, given esoteric knowledge, and tasked with guardianship of believers and creation in general, has its roots in the sacred sources of Islam, as we will see in the next chapter.

Discussion Questions:

1. How did the debates found in the formative period of Sufism from 700–1000 help to shape the age of synthesizers (discussed in Chapter 4)?
2. What were some of the main theological differences between al-Muhasibi and Ibn Hanbal, as well as between al-Hallaj and al-Junayd?
3. What were some of the principles and practices that early Sufis are known for developing?
4. Why would Sufi biographers be so important to the formation of Sufism?
5. How did pre-Islamic poetry influence early Sufi Arabic poetry? Provide a few examples.

Further Reading:

Cornell, R. E. (trans.). (1999). *Early Sufi Women: Dhikr an-Niswa al-Muta 'Abbidat as-Suffiyyat by Abu 'Abd ar-Rahman as-Sulami*. Louisville, KY: Fons Vitae Publishers.

Karamustafa, A. T. (2007). *Sufism: The Formative Period*. Berkeley, CA: University of California Press.

Melchert, C. (2015). "Origins and Early Sufism". In *The Cambridge Companion to Sufism*, ed. Lloyd Ridgeon, 3–23. New York: Cambridge University Press.

Sells, M. (1996). *Early Islamic Mysticism: Sufi, Qur'ān, Miraj, Poetic and Theological Writings*. New York: Paulist Press.

Von Schlegell, B. R. (1990). *Principles of Sufism by al-Qushayri*. Berkeley, CA: Mizan Press.

6

SOURCES OF SUFISM:
TRANSMISSION OF THE PROPHETIC WORD

As Rumi noted long ago, although the roads to Mecca are many, their goal
is one. In attempting to conceptualize Sufism, it is useful to think of it as a
tradition of roads or *tariqas* (recall the word *tariqa* literally means a "road"
or "path"), all of which lead back to Mecca, to the place of origin. Of course,
this is the nature of the Islamic tradition as a whole. As an object of history
and analytical category, Islam can be defined as "the historical phenomenon
that has proceeded from the human engagement with the idea and reality
of Divine Communication to Muhammad, the Messenger of God" (Ahmed
2016: 7). In other words, all things Islamic have their roots in Mecca, where
Muhammad first heard the prophetic call. This fact is symbolically enacted
daily with the *qibla* or direction toward which Muslims perform their daily
prayer.

Although the varied forms of Sufi thought and practice that we have
explored throughout this book have multiple sources, their roots can all be
traced back to the Qur'ānic revelation and the Prophet Muhammad's experience of it. The formulations of Islam that came to define the tradition arose
from the different ways in which Muslims have engaged with the Qur'ān.
In this chapter we consider in particular those verses of the Qur'ān and
sayings of the Prophet Muhammad that Sufis have engaged with, and as a
result that have come to shape Sufi thought and practice. We also consider
the way in which Sufis have engaged with the Qur'ān, for their encounter of
the text differs in notable ways from a strictly theological or legal approach.
We further explore Muhammad's life in regards to his spiritual practice,
moral example, and metaphysical significance. It is important to emphasize
at the outset of this chapter that for Sufis, neither the Qur'ān nor the Prophet
Muhammad are of the past, but rather both have a living presence that is
encountered in the present moment. To return to origins, then, is not simply
to go back to the past, but to fully encounter the present.

For Muslims, the Qur'ān represents the divine word or *logos* made first
into a recitation and then into a book. Muslims have thus developed a reverence for both recitation and the written word, and traditions of beautifying
them. As we find in this chapter's third section, some of Islam's most widespread and profound art forms directly result from this reverence, notably
the art of Qur'ānic calligraphy. Esoterically, Sufis took the letters of the

Arabic alphabet as symbols not only in a linguistic sense, but in a cosmic sense as well: some of Sufism's most elaborate metaphysical systems have been expressed utilizing letters as cosmic symbols.

Finally, although Sufis trace their path to Muhammad, many believe that Sufism can be more broadly understood as the esoteric aspect of all genuine revelations, and as such, Sufism can be thought to have existed since the origin of humanity. Therefore, even if Sufism may not have originated outside of the historical Islamic tradition, it has undoubtedly integrated various mystical and philosophical systems prevalent in the Near East. As such, we will consider the influence of some of these, including Neoplatonism, Hermeticism, Zoroastrianism, and Christian Mysticism. These influences include metaphysical, moral, practical, and aesthetic strands, all of which will be illustrated using concrete examples from these various traditions.

THE POLITICS OF EARLY QUR'ĀNIC HERMENEUTICS

To all Muslims, the word beyond comparison – the language that exists beyond all rules and standards and yet simultaneously creates all rules and standards – is the Qur'ān, the Holy Book, the revealed message of Islam. It is the miracle, *al-Mu'ajizah*, the source of all Muslim ways of knowing (whether orthodox, rational, or mystical), and it is the basis for all spiritual experience as well as the source of legitimacy for all social and moral values. Linguistically, it is the foundation of classical Arabic and the standard for eloquent literary expression.

The significance of the Qur'ān as the origin and central source for the development of Sufism cannot be overstated. As manifested in Qur'ānic concepts, principles, and practices (some of which were outlined in the previous chapter), the Sufi way of life was and has been embedded in experiencing the Qur'ānic revelation exemplified in the model of the Prophet Muhammad. Within 300 years after the death of the Prophet in 632, Sufi Qur'ānic hermeneutics – the art of Sufi interpretation of the Qur'ān – would emerge and develop into a complex, diverse web of understandings. Sufi interpretations of the Qur'ān, however, were by no means uncontested, and were a key thread in great debates about how to be Muslim as well as the nature of the Qur'ān and the varieties of Qur'ānic knowledge. These debates over appropriate methods for studying the Qur'ān, and comprehending its symbolic themes and stories, came to have great significance in defining the content of Islamic practice and spirituality, and have persisted from formative times to the present.

Sufi writers played a key role in early debates over Qur'ānic interpretation, in disagreements about what constituted "legitimate" or authoritative commentary and experience. These debates revolved around the very nature of claims that could be made about the Qur'ān as a source of spiritual and moral guidance, and gave rise to schools of thoughts that have since been characterized as esoteric or exoteric. Where a more esoteric approach was upheld, the Qur'ān was understood as a source of spiritual inspiration that was profoundly personal in nature, and which could not be limited by purely formal and literal expositions. In contrast, scholars who emphasized exoteric knowledge of the Qur'ān, frequently sought to delegitimize subjective experiences of the text and establish objective criteria for valid interpretations of the Qur'ān's theological and behavioural meaning.

Esoteric Qur'ānic Commentary of Ja'far al-Sadiq

Although many early Sufis engaged in commentary on the spiritual message of the Qur'ān, the most important early Sufi commentary on the Qur'ān is attributed to Ja'far al-Sadiq (d. 765). Recognized by Sunni Muslims as a renowned scholar of religious sciences and descendent of the Prophet, al-Sadiq is also regarded as the sixth *imam* in Shi'a thought. His wide-ranging legacy has influenced a variety of intellectual movements (Sells 1996: 21), including alchemy, theology, mysticism, jurisprudence, and Qur'ānic hermeneutics.

For Sufi thinkers, al-Sadiq articulated the basis of a method for understanding the Qur'ān through spiritual hermeneutics, by means of which a spiritual aspirant could inwardly receive knowledge and inspiration directly from God's presence (*'ilm al-laduni*). Conceiving of the Qur'ān as a multifaceted scripture suffused with outward as well as hidden, inward meanings, al-Sadiq and other Sufi commentators emphasized the presence of different layers of meaning – the clear expression (*'ibara*), the allusion (*ishara*), subtleties (*lata'if*), and realities (*haqa'iq*) (al-Sadiq in Mayer 2011: xxxi; Ja'far 2011: xxxi). Whereas the most unambiguous and outwardly clear levels of exoteric meaning established a common level of understanding for communal religious and social practice, these outward meanings did not by any means exhaust the riches that could be obtained from study and contemplation of the scripture. For the most dedicated practitioners, the Qur'ān was also a source of symbolic reference points for divine knowledge and spiritual realization, accessed through a dialogue "between personal, mystic experience and the text" (Sands 2006: 2).

Where exoteric commentators understood the Qur'ān as a singular and, for the most part, unambiguous source of revealed guidance for humanity, al-Sadiq and the Sufis who drew inspiration from his example (e.g. al-Makki, al-Ghazali), believed that the Qur'ān was also a vehicle for God's ongoing, spiritual self-disclosure directly to those who are able to perceive it. "I swear by God", al-Sadiq stated, "that God has disclosed himself (*tajalla*) to His Creation in His speech but they do not see" (Sands 2006: 31). From this standpoint, a proper attitude toward the Qur'ān made possible a direct and living encounter with God's continual manifestation, by means of which attributes such as divine majesty might speak – always anew, and in unendingly unique ways – to the heart of seekers.

Although the subtle spiritual meanings that could be accessed through God's spiritual disclosure were without limit, al-Sadiq and his Sufi commentators provided specific methods for experiencing *tajalli* or divine manifestation. Another oft-cited statement by al-Sadiq offered instruction: "I kept repeating the verse in my heart until I heard it from its Speaker and my body was unable to stand firm when I saw His power". Followers of al-Sadiq understood this to mean that reciting Qur'ānic passages with the proper intention, focus, and preparation could open a door not just to spiritual feelings and intuitions, but to an encounter with a living divine presence, as if one were hearing the verses spoken directly by God. Carrying this idea forward, Sufis (e.g. al-Kharraz and al-Makki) went on to articulate different types of listening to and hearing of the Qur'ān – first hearing it as if the Prophet were directly reciting it, then hearing it from the angel Gabriel, and finally hearing it straight from the presence of God Himself, without intermediary (Sands 2006: 30–31).

Al-Sadiq's teachings supported the later Sufi conviction that direct spiritual experience of God constituted the ultimate end of Islamic practice. Sufis trace many core concepts, including witnessing (*mushahida*), self-annihilation and subsistence in the Divine (*fana'* and *baqa'*), remembrance of God (*dhikr*), and love or knowledge of God (*ma'rifa*) directly to al-Sadiq (Mayer 2011, xvi). One additional and equally central concept attributed to al-Sadiq is *kashf*, or spiritual unveiling. For al-Sadiq, God's self-disclosure to humanity could be likened to the sudden removal of a veil. For the one seeking direct knowledge of God, this could occur in many ways and at different levels, but always with the implied occurrence of a flash of insight or realization. As with *tajalli*, or God's self-disclosure, there could be no end to the ways in which God might unveil aspects of His reality and nature, and the object of spiritual life was to prepare oneself for recurrent glimpses of divine insight, without an intermediary.

The influence of al-Sadiq's interpretation of *tajalli* and *kashf* is reflected in a variety of Sufi thought throughout the history of Islam and Sufism. Here are just some examples:

> As for the love which You deserve, it is that You remove the veils so that I can see You (a saying by a saintly woman whom Dhul'l Nun encountered as retold by Ibn al-'Arabi in Twinch 2010: 114).

> Poor people! They get their knowledge from the dead, but we get our knowledge from the Living One who never dies (al-Bistami in Sands 2006: 51).

> The one who claims that the Qur'ān has no other meaning than what exoteric exegesis has provided should know that he has acknowledged

his own limitations and therefore is right with regards to himself, but is wrong in an opinion that brings everyone else down to his level (al-Ghazali in Sands 2006: 50–51).

God discloses Himself (*tajalli*) to the lover in the names of engendered existence and in His Most Beautiful Names... When the lover assumes the traits of His Most Beautiful Names, he is overcome by the same assumption of traits that takes place in the path of the Folk of Allah (Ibn al-'Arabi in Chittick 1989: 43).

Exoteric Critiques of Sufi Qur'ānic Commentary

Despite their profound influence on Sufism and the emergence of such influential exponents as al-Ghazali, Sufi ideas of *tajalli* and *kashf* as a means of direct spiritual encounter with God produced enduring controversy and exoteric critiques. Many religious authorities either rejected the possibility of such direct spiritual experience, or argued strongly in favour of external criteria for evaluating "subjective" claims to divine knowledge. Consistently, these critics invoked Islamic traditions that admonished against reliance on "personal opinion" when interpreting the Qur'ān. According to one prophetic tradition, "The Prophet said, 'Whoever speaks of the Qur'ān from his personal opinion (*ra'y*), let him take his seat in the Fire'" (Sands 2006: 47). In another tradition on the same subject, the Prophet's companion Abu Bakr stated, "'What earth would carry me, what heaven shelter me, if I were to speak of the Qur'ān from my personal opinion (*ra'y*) or of what I do not know?'" (Sands 2006: 47). By invoking these traditions, critics relegated the spiritual testimonies of many if not most Sufis to the realm of the subjective – and therefore unreliable – personal conjecture, and argued that knowledge of the authentic traditions of the Prophet Muhammad was the key criterion for evaluating all interpretations of the Qur'ān and establishing their soundness. Thus, their contention was that knowledge of the Qur'ān can "never be received directly without the intermediary of the *hadith* and Traditions" (Sands 2006: 52). Claims to divine intimacy or unveiling were viewed with great skepticism, and the notion of *'ilm al-laduni* (knowledge given to a soul directly from God's Presence) was often equated with dangerously heretical or misleading forms of esotericism, or *'ilm al-batini*.

As described in Chapter 4, Ibn Taymiyya was among the most persistent and formidable critics of Sufi ways of knowing, and grouped the testimony of many Sufis with the heretical ideas of the *batiniyya* – that is, of those who propound hidden, esoteric knowledge but actually lead Muslims away from the sound knowledge of exoteric faith and practice (Sands 2006: 52).

Particularly opposed to the idea of *kashf* (understood as unmediated spiritual knowledge received directly from God), Ibn Taymiyya stated that spiritual disciplines and practices such as purification of the heart only yield genuine knowledge when they are bound by strict allegiance to the Prophet and his example:

> It is not possible for anyone after the Prophet to know by himself without the intermediary of the Prophet… The speech of the Messenger is clear in and of itself. There is no unveiling to anyone nor is any analogy of it equal to it. An 'unveiling' or 'analogy' of someone is sanctioned only when it is consistent with [the speech of the Messenger]; otherwise it contradicts it. However, what is called an 'unveiling' (*kashf*) or an analogy (*qiyas*) does contradict the Messenger and is therefore a false analogy and false imagination. This is what was meant when it was said, 'I seek refuge in God from philosophical analogy and Sufi imagination' (Sands 2006: 52–53).

For Ibn Taymiyya, this idea of the prophetic example as the indispensable criterion for evaluating claims of spiritual experience meant that all claims of spiritual knowledge should be rejected if they appear incompatible with known sayings of the Prophet Muhammad, and of his example as communicated by the first generations of pious Muslims (*al-salaf al-salih*) who witnessed his conduct. He articulated a strong opposition between the prophetic *hadith* (sayings) and *Sunnah* (normative practice), on the one hand, and more ecstatic and nonconformist ways of knowing and experiencing God, on the other. Thus, he carried forward and embellished on past arguments against ecstatic Sufism (see Chapter 5), and set in motion a critical discourse that would become even more restrictive in future generations, for example in the Arabian peninsula during the lifetime of Ibn 'Abd al-Wahhab (see Chapter 2). Though at times showing sympathy to some forms of spiritual practice, his arguments would eventually provide the basis for forms of religious puritanism that categorically rejected Sufism altogether.

Despite the stringency of such critiques, Sufism and Sufi epistemology of the Qur'ān continued to flourish for centuries, drawing in no small part on the arguments al-Ghazali and other synthesizers (i.e. Ibn al-'Arabi). For al-Ghazali, spiritual insights attained through contemplation of scripture and personal purification were in no way reducible to personal opinion (*ra'y*), and could be reconciled with exoteric knowledge when understood correctly in the context of personal spiritual development and the metaphysical insights of those who were prepared to understand.

LIVING SOURCES OF SUFISM: THE QUR'ĀN AND THE PROPHET

It can be argued that the Qur'ān is not so much analogous to the Bible in Christianity, but to Jesus, as the living Word or *logos* of God. Indeed, for Muslims and Sufi-oriented Muslims in particular, the Qur'ān is not a dead text but a living Word. Each word of the text then, encapsulates a reality, a being. One might say that the name of one's friend brings to mind one's friend, but the richness of the being of one's friend as a living person goes far beyond the letters of their name. For Sufis, each word of the Qur'ān can be understood to, like a friend's name, point to a richness of being and world of meaning. This is why Sufis have long loved analogies of oceans and seas for the Qur'ān, as a near infinite depth of meaning to be explored.

There are numerous stories in the Sufi tradition that illustrate how Sufis have developed a profound relationship with particular chapters of the Qur'ān. One of Ibn al-'Arabi's teachers, Fatima Bint Ibn al-Muthana, for example, was said to have had a particular relationship with the opening chapter of the Qur'ān, the *Fatiha*, whereby she related to the chapter as a being that could be literally sent to follow and guide those away from wandering astray (Ibn al-'Arabi in Austin 1971: 143–46).

For most Muslims, the recitation of specific chapters in the Qur'ān, Qur'ānic verses and/or words has always been the essential way for devoting one's life to God. However, for Sufis, the practice of memorization, recitation, and contemplation becomes an "internalization of the sacred text", which allows for an intimate understanding of the Qur'ān's many different levels of meaning (Ernst 1997: 36). Again, using the analogy of a being or person, verses of the Qur'ān were approached as beings that could be known from a variety of perspectives with different aspects of their nature, underlying which however, is an essential core of mystery that remains on some level unfathomable. The general Sufi understanding of reality as having a visible and accessible aspect (*zahir*) and an invisible and mysterious aspect (*batin*) included the Qur'ān, which was thought to have both a visible nature (the possible meanings of the Arabic words), and an invisible nature (the interior or being of the text) that was unveiled through mystical experience. Sufi commentators on the Qur'ān then tended to emphasize a series of binaries inherent in the nature of the text, binaries that acted as revolving poles of possibility, including the literal and allegorical, the majestic and the beautiful, the transcendent and the intimate. These multi-faceted understandings of the revelation would open the doors to the development of Sufi hermeneutics and different methods of study and practice.

Prominent Qur'anic Themes Found in Sufism

An early, traditional Sufi saying states that a devout Sufi can find up to 7,000 meanings in a single verse (Schimmel 1994: 161). This idea that the meaning of the Qur'ān is in no way reducible to a singular, surface-level reading constitutes a keynote theme of Islamic mysticism, and is central to the way Sufis have engaged the holy text to contemplate additional themes of spiritual life. The Qur'ān, Sufis suggest, is suffused with a plethora of meanings, and offers not only the outward forms of religious life but also keys to inwardly realizable mysteries.

Most of the Qur'ānic themes explored by Sufis pertain to terms that are already present within exoteric theological and legal discourse, but which take on additional layers of significance and depth within a mystical context. One of the most influential of these themes, for example, pertains to Qur'ānic passages describing a primordial covenant (*al-'Ahd*, or *al-Mithaq*) between God and humanity, as recorded in chapter 7:172:

> When your Lord drew forth from the children of Adam, from their loins, and made them bear witness to themselves: 'Am I not your Lord?' [*Alastu bi-rabbikum?*] They replied, 'Yes! We have borne witness'.

Sufis and other interpreters have understood this passage to mean that, prior to birth in this world, every human soul has already acknowledged God as the eternal Lord, and as the only reality worthy of worship and devoted service. From this primordial acknowledgement of divine sovereignty flows an obligation among all children of Adam to uphold an awareness of God's status as the one and only Lord, and to constantly bear witness to divine unity (Schimmel 1994: 179).

This idea of a primordial covenant between God and humanity has both exoteric and esoteric implications, with Sufi interpreters framing their teachings as a basis for spiritually exploring the latter. Exoterically, teachings concerning this covenant provide a basis for understanding Islam as the natural human religion, whose principles each human soul has already accepted before birth. In light of this, a person who was raised in a different religion and then embraces Islam is "reverting" to truths known since pre-eternity rather than "converting". At an esoteric level, the idea of a pre-existing covenant is taken to a deeper, spiritual plane, in which the seeker of God is invited to return to the pure, primordial state in which his or her soul testified to God's reality not on the basis of hearsay or received belief, but rather on the basis of standing directly before the divine presence. In practice, this means receiving an intimate relation of closeness between God and humanity, His creation. The Sufi returns metaphysically to the pre-eternal experience of the "Day of Alastu", when all children of Adam testified to God's Lordship in and through a state of spiritual purity – a state that is still accessible as the essential foundation for knowing God.

But how does one recover the state that he or she had on the "Day of Alastu", the face before you were born? For the Sufis, an answer is to be found in contemplative practices that are similarly grounded in divine revelation, and which enable the seeker to encounter God's presence through His signs. This possibility is suggested in various Qur'ānic verses, with many Sufis pointing particularly to 41:53 which states, "And We shall show them Our Signs in the horizons and in themselves". The Qur'ānic text contains numerous passages highlighting ever-present signs of God's reality in the created order, and this particular selection also hints that signs of God can be found within the human person. Sufis understand these signs not just as "proofs" of God's sovereignty, reality, or status as Creator, but also aspects of a more existential process through which God's presence can be traced and experienced. A clue to this possibility of a more profound and living realization of God can be found in chapter 2:115: "To Allah belong the East and the West: whithersoever Ye turn, there is Allah's Face. For Allah is All-Embracing, All-Knowing". God's signs – and indeed presence – are everywhere present, and everything that exists can be taken as a sign from and of God. Witnessing these signs, however, requires spiritual capacity and awareness. The mirror of one's being, so to speak, needs to be polished until it is able to clearly reflect the divine reality.

Many Muslim spiritual thinkers have articulated this correspondence between the created world and spiritual signs through the metaphor of a book. As Schimmel articulates, "the world is, as it were, an immense book in which those who have eyes to see and ears to hear can recognize God's signs and thus be guided by their contemplation to the Creator Himself" (1994: xii). If all that exists is a sign from God, then all of creation from nature (e.g. the stars, the weather, the plants, the animals, etc.) to the human soul is an expression of God's Truth (as we discussed in Chapter 2). By interpreting His signs one comes to understand God and indeed his or her own deepest nature. "It was We", states the Qur'ān 50:16, "Who Created man, and We know what his soul whispers to him: for We are nearer to him than his jugular vein". As the jugular is a primary conduit for blood and hence life, God is even closer to the human essence, as the very source of life itself, and, as Ibn al-'Arabi would later articulate, as *wujud* or being/ existence itself.

Contemplation of God's creation, then, provides clues and glimpses that lead toward intimacy (*uns*) and mystical connection with the Creator, particularly when this contemplation of the book of nature takes into account what is taught about the Divine nature in the book of revelation. The very diversity of phenomena in the created world, the Qur'ān suggests, testifies to the many different qualities of God. Traditional Islamic teachings concerning "the ninety-nine beautiful names of God" (*asma' Allah al-husna*) arise from Qur'ānic teachings that correlate observation of relationships within creation to what can be known and experienced among God's attributes and qualities. The Qur'ān for example, states that God is both the Manifest (*al-Zahir*) and the Hidden (*al-Batin*), the possessor of majesty and glory and also the subtle. He is both the seen and the unseen. Contemplating creation with awareness of divine attributes, then, is key to a larger process of purifying the heart and effacing those aspects of the lower self or ego that interfere with the approach to God. Contemporary Sufi teachers, such as Bawa Muhaiyaddeen (d. 1986), who we introduced in Chapter 1, taught his followers that the direct way to know and experience God was to live the qualities or names of God in one's everyday life. He was invoking here the Sufi tradition of *takhallaq bi-akhlaq Allah*, whereby the qualities of God are invoked within one's own soul, as discussed in various places in this work.

Teachings concerning God's signs in nature and within the human person should not be taken as a reduction of God to what is visible in creation, or as a contradiction of God's transcendence. While God is revealed by the created order, the entirety of God's being transcends the capacity of human sight. As verse 6:103 states, God is ultimately beyond the grasp of human sense perception: "No vision can grasp Him, But His grasp is over all vision; He is Subtle: well-aware". Similarly, while created forms may be witnessed in ways that give testimony to their Creator, the Creator Himself is beyond comparison: "There is No Thing Like Him" (42:11).

Muslim scholars have traditionally classified the Names of God as either names of majesty (*Jalal*) or beauty (*Jamal*). The Names of Majesty, include *al-Qawi*, "the Powerful"; *al-Qadir* "the Determiner"; and *al-Malik* "the Sovereign". These particular names are associated with qualities like majesty, rigour, transcendence, power, awe, and are sometimes described as God's masculine qualities. In contrast, other names like *al-Wadud*, "the Loving"; *al-Latif*, "the Subtle"; and *al-Wali* "the Close Friend", are associated with God's feminine qualities, such as mercy, love, and intimacy. The Names of God, each with its own quality, have long been invoked by Sufis as a means of healing, enlightenment, strength, and assistance, forming an integral part of the Sufi practice of *dhikr* or the remembrance of God.

According to the Qur'ān, the divine nature ultimately transcends any ordinary human experience or language, and approaching God requires scrupulous dedication to following the example and teachings of the prophets, whom God has offered as models for remembrance:

> And [remember] when God made the covenant of the prophets: 'By that which I have given you of a Book and Wisdom, should a messenger then come to you confirming that which is with you, you shall surely believe in him and you shall help him'. He said, 'Do you agree and take on My burden on these conditions?' They said, 'We agree'. He said, 'Bear witness, for I am with you among those who bear witness' (3:81).

The prophets, then, are the ultimate witnesses to God's reality and unity, offering the revealed guidance as well as applied examples of the conduct that leads to realization of the deepest meaning of the divine-human relationship. For Sufis, if the human task is to return to the primordial state on the Day of *Alastu*, then the prophets and the *awliya'* are the models of how one makes the journey of return.

Figure 6.1: The Prophet Muhammad and companions advancing on Mecca accompanied by angels Gabriel, Michael, Raphael, and Israel.

"The Perfected Human": the Prophet Muhammad

If the Qur'ān is the Word of God and His signs are everywhere to Sufis then the Prophet Muhammad who experienced the totality of the Qur'ānic revelation was the perfect human model to live up to. As stated in the Qur'ān 33:21: "Ye have indeed in the Messenger of Allah an excellent exemplar for him who hopes in Allah and the Final Day, and who remembers Allah much". Thus to Sufis, Muhammad is venerated as the ideal, Perfected Human (*insan al-kamil*) making him the ultimate last Prophet. One important illustration of this principle is found in the following *hadith*:

> The Prophet of God, peace and blessings upon him, said: 'Truly, God provided me with the best rules of conduct and perfected my *adab*. Then He ordered me to uphold noble traits of character, by His words: "Hold to forgiveness; command what is right; but turn away from the ignorant"' (al-Sulami 2010: 3).

The concept of *adab* would become paramount for Sufi practice, with the saying, "All of Sufism is *adab*" an oft-quoted tradition (al-Sulami in Sands 2006: 30). This term would be defined in a range of ways, including referring to holding one's tongue, and maintaining remembrance of God within one's inner heart. This understanding of Muhammad as the exemplar of *adab* par excellence, fuelled the collective task of gathering reports narrated through the early Muslim generations regarding every conceivable detail of Muhammad's life, from his appearance, clothing choices, preferences, eating habits, behaviour with his family, friends, and followers. For many Sufis, following this example in a detailed manner – including how long to grow one's beard, the colour of one's clothing, and how one brushes one's teeth or enters a room – forms an integral part of the spiritual path.

Besides his appearance, behaviour, preferences, and etiquette, Muslims gathered descriptions of Muhammad's spiritual practice. These begin with reports in the early biographies of Muhammad that suggest he practised a form of spiritual retreat (*khalwa*) one month each year. This practice is associated with the onset of prophecy. Indeed Muhammad experienced the first revelation of the Qur'ān while he was in the midst of one of these retreats. For Sufis such as the Khalwatiyya, this practice of Muhammad's forms an important precedent for the Sufi practice of retreat, wherein almost constant meditation and prayer take place for a period of a month or 40 days.

After the revelation of the Qur'ān began, Muhammad was commanded to awake and pray through some of the night and to fast. Muhammad's close companions similarly engaged in these practices of night devotion and denial of the lower self's demands for food and drink. As we discussed in the previous chapter, the *zuhd* movement of the eighth and ninth centuries is a continuation of this practice, one that Sufis would take up as an effective means to simultaneously train the lower self, and to polish and open the heart. Much of this movement involved pursuing extra devotions above and beyond the requirements of the *shari'a*. The efficacy of this approach for Muslims is illustrated in the following *hadith*:

> My servant draws near to me through nothing I love more than the religious duty I require of him. And my servant continues to draw near to me by supererogatory worship until I love him. When I love him, I become the ear by which he hears, the eye by which he sees, the hand by which

he grasps, and the foot by which he walks. If he asks me for something, I give it to him; if he seeks protection, I provide it to him (Ernst 1997: 51).

This famous *hadith* has been viewed as a divine charter for mystical experience. The individual worshipper can become increasingly close to God through continued devotion until they are united by love. For Sufis, Islam is the complete and exclusive surrender of the faithful to God's will and the perfect acceptance of the injunctions as preached in the Qur'ān. But the principle and practice of Islam is interconnected with two other principles found in the Qur'ān: *iman* and *ihsan*. *Iman* is usually translated as "faith/spirituality/self-confidence", and it constitutes the interior aspect of Islam which can lead to *ihsan*.

Ihsan is the Muslim responsibility to obtain perfection, or excellence, in worship, such that Muslims try to worship God, Allah, as if they see Him. There is a *hadith qudsi*, recorded in both *Bukhari* and *Muslim*, that is used by Sufis to develop an understanding of *ihsan*: "[Ihsan is] to worship God as though you see Him, and if you cannot see Him, then indeed He sees you". This idea of *ihsan* and God always seeing man is found in the Qur'ān. For example, verse 7:54 states, "Mercy is with those who practice *ihsan* [al-Muhsinun, 'those who do well']". For some Sufis, the path of Sufism is the human quest to reach a state of salvation and oneness, the state of *ihsan*.

Ihsan, then, is a means for created beings to return to the divine source, but how have Sufis understood the divine's impetus to create the world and beings in the first place? Simply put, based on another famous *hadith qudsi*, Sufi interpreters have suggested that the impetus for creation was love, or the "*ishq-i-haqiqi*", the true love that desired to make the hidden treasure manifest: "I was a hidden treasure, and I longed (desired or loved) to be known; so I created the world, in order to be known". Creation is ultimately due to God's willingness and desire to see Himself instantiated in the world, conceived in the widest possible sense as including everything that exists in one way or the other, that is everything falls under the scope of God's creative command to be. Ibn al-'Arabi would state about this *hadith* that God longs both to be instantiated and to see Himself instantiated in the world. In other words, as the mirror metaphor towards the end of the passage clearly indicates, God creates the world or becomes instantiated in the world in order to see Himself as the other or in the other, this instantiation is rooted in a divine desire for love: to experience oneself in the other, and to have the other experience oneself.

God's desire to create manifests in His creation of the first light of existence, a light through which the cosmos is made, and a light by which the created travels back to God. In the Islamic tradition, this first light is called the *Nur Muhammad* (*al-Nur al-Muhammadiyya*) or the Light of Muhammad. It is one of the central themes (if not *the* central theme) of the Prophet

Muhammad's spiritual legacy (Schimmel 1987: 123). This concept is known as the "essence of the Prophet", also called *al-Haqiqa al-Muhammadiyya* (the Reality of Muhammad). This association of Muhammad and light is found in the Qur'ān, wherein Muhammad is referred to as "a shining lamp" and as "a light". According to Islamic esoteric thought, this essence of the Prophet was created before the creation of the world, when "Allah took a handful of light and commanded it to be Muhammad". From it the world itself was created. This term is a shared esoteric tradition in Sunni, Shi'a, and Sufi histories. Each, of course, would have their own developments of this term.

One tradition states that the origin of the term *Nur Muhammad* is attributed to Ja'far al-Sadiq. As in many other early Sufi thinkers such as Muqatil and al-Hallaj, al-Sadiq derived his inspiration for this term from the Qur'ān and the *hadith*. From the Qur'ān, one particular verse, 24:35, inspired him which is also known as "the Light verse". It states:

> Allah is the Light of the heavens and the earth; the likeness of His Light is as a niche wherein is a lamp – the lamp in a glass, the glass as if it were a glittering star – kindled from a Blessed Tree, an olive tree that is neither of the East nor of the West, whose oil well nigh would shine, even if no fire touched it: Light upon Light; Allah guides to His Light whom He will. And Allah strikes similitudes for man, and Allah has knowledge of everything.

Early Muslim scholars such as al-Sadiq, suggest that the lamp (*misbah* in Arabic) in this verse is actually a symbol for Muhammad (connecting this to the Qur'ān's description of Muhammad as a lamp in the verse mentioned earlier):

> Through him the Divine Light could shine in the world, and through him humankind was guided to the origin of this Light. The formula 'neither of the East nor of the West' was then taken as a reference to Muhammad's comprehensive nature, which is not restricted to one specific people or race and which surpasses the boundaries of time and space (Schimmel 1987: 124–25).

It is with this more universal meaning of Muhammad that we find al-Sadiq explains why other prophets like Mary, Moses, Joseph, and Abraham are also *muhammad*. In this case, they are described as such based on the *meaning* of the name, as "one who is praised". So the *Nur Muhammad* can be conceived as a light from which emerge other lights, being the other prophets, who, like Muhammad, are praised (*muhammad*) for their state of total submission to God, and transmission of the divine word (Mayer 2011: liii).

This connection between *Nur Muhammad* and the concept of the divine word draws a comparison to the *logos* doctrines of Greek, Jewish, and Christian thought. *Logos* is an ancient Greek term that refers to the creative power of the Divine Word (*logos* meaning "living word") as it manifests through a messenger. It is because the word is associated with both light and a living, divine presence, that we see in the following section, the ways in which the divine word of the Qur'ān has been engaged and beautified in Islam.

'Ali ibn Abi Talib

Born in what is known as the "City of Peace", Mecca, at its holiest destination, the *Ka'aba*, and buried in the Valley of Peace, *Wadi al-Salaam*, in Iraq, 'Ali ibn Abi Talib came to be known as one of the most influential personalities in Islam and Sufism. Reports suggest that he was named by and raised with the wisdom of the Prophet Muhammad. Like the Prophet, 'Ali too became an exemplary model of morality, chivalry, honour, and humility. A plethora of poems praise 'Ali and encourage the emulation of his spirit:

> Abu Hasan you are always near us
> When we have no fear or dread
> Allah bless the fast days though they
> Pass without taste of food or drink
> Since they enhance our assemblies and
> The union of heart bent to heart
> I turn my eye to the spring morn of
> Wisdom and culture fine and books
> Meeting you is joy and peace to souls
> Not everyone after you has a heart
> You turned men's hearts from friends
> To you since you had true humility.
>
> (Ibn Rumi [d. 896], in Wormholdt 1977: 18)

Muslim biographers noted that his distinguished characteristics as an incomparable leader earned him many epithets, such as "*Amir al-Mu'mineen*" ("The Prince of the Faithful"), "*Asad Allah*" ("The Lion of God"), and "*Dhu'l-Fiqar*" ("The Possessor of Two-Edged Sword"). As reflected in the numerous legendary stories about 'Ali in battle, he was a man of heroic courage, irresistible charisma and holiness, and power and awareness. 'Ali's courage coincided with his humility and sincerity; for although he was an excellent warrior, he was also reputed to be a man of his word and a seeker of reconciliation and peace in internal and external human affairs. Even though 'Ali was celebrated for his wisdom in early Islamic jurisprudence, he was also well-steeped in literary criticism, the study of linguistics, art and poetry.

'Ali was not only known as an accomplished military commander and peacemaker, he was also held to be an influential intellectual, so much so that there is a famous *hadith*, "I am the City of Knowledge and 'Ali is its Gate". Inheriting the spiritual as well as political transmission of knowledge from the Prophet Muhammad, 'Ali was inextricably linked to both esoteric and exoteric understandings of reality. Muslim historians suggested that it was hard to find a discipline that 'Ali was not master of, for he seemed to have delved into the whole range of disciplines, such as jurisprudence, rhetoric, philosophy, mathematics, logic, astronomy, medicine, and history.

When comparing 'Ali's words to later Sufi works, such as those of al-Hallaj or Ibn al-'Arabi, the spirit and form of 'Ali's words can be found. In particular, the *Khutbah al-Bayan*, the *Last Speech of 'Ali* is seen by many Sufi orders as the culmination of his life's work, where 'Ali claims:

> I am the Sign of the All-Powerful. I am the gnosis of the mysteries. I am the Threshold of Thresholds. I am the companion of the radiance of divine Majesty. I am the First and the Last, the Manifest and the Hidden. I am the Face of God. I am the mirror of God, the supreme Pen, the *Tabula secreta*. I am he who in the Gospel is called Elijah. I am he who is in possession of the secret of God's Messenger (Corbin 1993: 49).

It is no wonder that most of the diverse Sufi orders (i.e. Rifa'i, Qadri, Mevlevi, etc.) link their chain of transmission to 'Ali, thereby acclaiming 'Ali as "the Father of Sufism".

THE ORIGINS OF SUFI COSMOLOGY AND METAPHYSICS: THE WORD

From the very beginning of Islam, listening to and reciting the Qur'ān has been a core practice of Islamic spirituality. In listening to the sacred word and then reciting it, practitioners of Islam emulate the spiritual experience of the Prophet Muhammad receiving the Qur'ān from the Angel Gabriel, and then articulating it as transformative speech. The spoken word thus lies at the very heart of Islamic spirituality and culture. As mentioned in Chapter 4, the Sufi tradition reflects this Islamic emphasis on auditory and oral experience, and the methods of spiritual practice developed by Sufis have centred around attaining realization by means of contemplation focused on divine words. In Chapter 3, we saw how the word was celebrated visually, in calligraphic representations of the Qur'ān found in shrines and mosques, as one of the key components of sacred architecture in Islam.

Qur'ānic Calligraphy and Sufism

Both in Islamic religious culture more generally and in the Sufi tradition, the centrality of the divine word led not just to perfunctory written preservation of oral revelation, but also to a flowering of artistic efforts to write the divine word in beautiful ways. For many Sufis this practice of writing the sacred word took on added levels of significance, encouraging them to play an active role in the development of Qur'ānic calligraphy. They experienced calligraphy as an attempt to communicate spiritual truths and realities:

> Islamic calligraphy is the visual embodiment of the crystallization of the spiritual realities (*al-haqa'iq*) contained in the Islamic revelation. This

calligraphy provides the external dress for the Word of God in the visible world but this art remains wedded to the world of the spirit. For according to the traditional Islamic saying, 'Calligraphy is the geometry of the Spirit' (Nasr 1987: 18).

Islamic religion, culture and civilization would not be the same without the presence of calligraphy as manifested in a variety of forms from religious texts and poetry to architecture and objects of everyday life. Calligraphy is "the progenitor of traditional Islamic visual arts" (Nasr 1987: 19).

In their pursuit of calligraphy, Sufis emulated the broader norm within Islamic culture to give deep respect to the capacity of the written word to convey revealed truths. They regarded Qur'ānic calligraphy as a holy art that offers *baraka* to the recipient of its beauty and wisdom. They contemplated not just the divine words and chapters in themselves, but also the Arabic letters as constituent elements of divine speech. The practice of calligraphy thereby became integrated with other methods of Sufi practice, and included reflection on sacred and symbolic qualities of Qur'ānic words.

'Ali ibn Abi Talib, who was previously noted as the progenitor of many Sufi orders, is credited not only as the founder for the study of rhetoric (*al-balagha*) and Arabic syntax (*'ilm al-nahw*), but also as the developer of Kufic, the oldest style of Qur'ānic calligraphy. Sufi legend claims that following in the tradition of Prophet Idris, who is believed to have invented a writing system with no curved lines known as *ma'qili*, 'Ali developed the Arabic script of "Kufic" (Schimmel 1984: 3). Known as the "liturgic script par excellence" for early Qur'āns, Kufic consisted of a division of 1/6 curved and 5/6 straight lines. Although many different calligraphy styles would follow 'Ali's Kufic, most calligraphers place much significance on their link to 'Ali, "the first master of calligraphy" (Schimmel 1984: 3). Some Sufis (e.g. Mir 'Ali of Tabriz) even claim 'Ali as the principal source of inspiration for their own inventions in calligraphy (Schimmel 1984: 47).

'Ali's dual status as the progenitor of many Sufi orders and of the art of calligraphy has reinforced natural connections between Sufi practices and the practice of writing in Arabic as a spiritual as well as artistic discipline. Just as various Sufi orders are careful to trace their spiritual lineages to Muhammad by means of 'Ali, Sufi calligraphers of different styles and techniques similarly honour 'Ali as the source of their artistic as well as spiritual pedigrees. In ways that mirror the Sufi master-disciple relationship, serious students of calligraphy are expected to study with a certified calligraphic master who ultimately has the right to bequeath an *ijaza* – a certificate of permission to be a *khattat*, or recognized calligrapher and member of a certain calligraphic school. Historically, Sufi orders provided highly conducive contexts for the study and development of calligraphy, with a variety of different orders becoming known for their own distinctive contributions to the art and its diverse formal expression. These orders included the Mevlevi, Naqshbandi, Qadiri, Khalwati, and Dhahabi, as well as many others.

Figure 6.2: *Surah al-Qalam* (The Pen), 68:1.[1]

To practise calligraphy as an integral component of their spiritual practice, many Sufis found great inspiration in Qur'ānic passages affirming the sacred nature of writing. Of particular significance were verses attributing cosmological significance to the pen (*al-Qalam*) and the "preserved tablet" (*Lawh al-Mahfuz*). References to the pen can be found in what are understood to be the first two revealed chapters of the Qur'ān: 96:1–5: "He [God] taught humans by the Pen!" and 68 which begins with, "Nun [an Arabic letter], and by the Pen! And by the record which humans write…". The idea of the "preserved tablet" as a spiritual reality or metaphor appears in a later Qur'ānic chapter, 85:21–22: "Verily, this is a glorious Qur'ān, inscribed on the Preserved Tablet".

The scriptural prevalence of ideas linked to writing provided great inspiration to Sufis and Sufi calligraphers. Qur'ānic passages conveying the

---

1.   Qur'ān 68:1: Nun, wa'l qalam wa ma yasturun, (By the Pen and by that which (men) write), Celi sülüs calligraphic piece by Nuria Garcia Masip, 2008. For more of Nuria's artwork, see http://www.nuriaart.com

idea of a heavenly pen (*al-Qalam*), for example, suggest a correspondence between human practices of writing and God's acts of teaching humanity through the creation of holy books. The idea of a divine book or tablet (*al-Lawh*) upon which all is recorded similarly infuses macrocosmic significance into the microcosmic practice of human writing, while evoking an ancient Middle Eastern belief that all holy and sacred books have been written on a heavenly book or tablet which also contains the mysteries of the universe as well as the secrets of human lives.

The presence of such content within the Qur'ān was a source of great inspiration for Sufi cosmology as well as for the calligraphic arts. Ibn al-'Arabi considered the Qur'ānic pen to be a symbol of the "First Intellect" and an embodiment of the creative principle present within *al-Badi'* ("The Originator"), one of God's names. By its very nature, calligraphy provided a living reminder of divine creativity and its manner of manifesting the unseen. The pen of calligraphy evoked the Primordial Pen by which all was created. The pursuit of excellence in the arts of calligraphy invited further reflection on how one's human state of being might be brought to a state of perfection, within which a created human being might become a mirror of the Divine.

Sufi reflections on these themes were extensive. One influential school of thought, based particularly on Ibn al-'Arabi's synthesis of Sufi ideas, reasoned that if the "pen" mentioned in the Qur'ān is Originator of everything and the *Lawh al-Mahfuz* ("preserved tablet") preserves all that has been written by the Pen, then the first visual point inscribed by the cosmic pen would represent the "primordial dot". This "primordial dot" was itself a symbol of Divine Ipseity (self-identity) and the basis of creation.

Such formulations proved immensely significant for calligraphers, as they infused the craft with layers of mystical and exoteric meaning. For technical and spiritual reasons, "the science of the dot" became a central preoccupation of calligraphy. Ibn Muqla (d. 940), a native of Shiraz, Iran, developed his influential science of dot-based proportions during al-Hallaj's lifetime (1984: 94). Significantly, one of Al-Hallaj's many mystical treatises dealt with the idea of the dot as a metaphysical reality and spiritual symbol. As mentioned in Chapter 5, Iran (and Shiraz in particular) became one of the more significant places where al-Hallaj's ideas were embraced and carried forward in the years after his execution. Shiraz's status as a centre for calligraphy, book-making, and other arts – including the production of "pens of the highest quality" – may well help to explain the warm reception that al-Hallaj's ideas received in the city during the classical period of Sufism.

Both Sufis and Sufi calligraphers regarded the dot not just as the beginning of all letters, but also as a sign of God's creative power. The dot provided a multivalent symbol that simultaneously evoked the origination of letters, the origins of the universe, and even 'Ali as the originator of calligraphy and as a critical source for Sufi lineages. When referring to the dot underneath the second letter of the Arabic alphabet, *ba*, Sufis explained that it represented not only the beginning of words, but also the "First Intellect" manifesting from the unknown Divine Essence and even 'Ali himself in his extensive wisdom. Like a dot in writing starts a pen's journey, so too does the First Intellect stir life into motion and energy. Evoking this primordial creativity, 'Ali helped to give form and inspiration to traditions of gnosis and calligraphy.

Figure 6.3: "I believe in the religion of love".[2]

2. This calligraphic piece by Hassan Massoudy is a saying by Ibn al-'Arabi from his book of poetry, *Interpreter of Desires*: "I believe in the religion of love, wherever its stages may go, love is my religion and faith". Hassan Massoudy, a native of Najef, Iraq, is a world-renowned master of contemporary Arabic calligraphy whose works bring light to a variety of classical Sufi personalities and their well-known sayings. To see more of Massoudy's artwork visit http://www.massoudy.net

The Sufi Art of Letter Mysticism

> We were lofty letters not yet pronounced
> latent in the highest peaks of the hills.
> I was you in Him, and we were you and you were He
> and the whole is He in Him – ask those who have attained.
>
> (Ibn al-'Arabi, in Schimmel 1984: 89)

For Sufis, language is an intertwined combination of revelation and logic. Language is understood to have a divine origin, and yet historical investigations concerning the developmental origins of signs, words, and grammars are not denied. These processes of linguistic development are believed to be like the continuous processes of creation, evolving organically yet guided by divine purpose. Moreover, the process of tracing the meaning of a word back to its root is, in many respects, comparable to the search for essence, and for spiritual sources of human experience. Language, then, is a divine code, associated with the abstract principles through which the universe was created. The letters of alphabets have metaphysical significance as well as practical utility; they are sometimes even understood to be "beings", or the equivalent of "cosmic DNA". The entire text of the Qur'ān can be experienced as a window upon Reality through the medium of language. While meanings can be disputed or forever rediscovered in new ways, the idea that language is impregnated with inherent meaning and significance is deeply rooted. Because the Qur'ān was revealed in Arabic, Sufis have sought access to spiritual experience through the medium of the Arabic language. However, other Muslim languages such as Persian, Turkish, and Urdu were also regarded as suitable vehicles for communicating mystical ideas, particularly in the form of poetry.

For the Sufi, language provides a systematic (but not necessarily "linear") means of attaining to and expressing spiritual states of being, and is therefore concerned not only with the management of social relationships but also with divine-human communication. Deep penetration into the forms of language can reveal an underlying grammar and a generative sound code that correspond with higher, more abstract levels of reality emanating from the divine source. Such profound contemplation of language – particularly but not exclusively the language of a holy book or saints – intensifies and enriches a spiritual path, providing a point of contact with God as the source of this language, and helping to clear the way for revelatory experience of the transcendent.

The goal of Sufi contemplation is to attain oneness with the One, beyond all ordinary ideas of "relationship". Although all of creation attests to its origin in God, and can by analogy be understood as a collection of letters or signs created by God's pen, this "alphabet of existence" is itself ultimately an expression of God that is (in the metaphysics of Ibn al-'Arabi) "not other" than He. Thus, language simultaneously evokes diversity and unity:

> Letters written with ink do not really exist as letters, for the letters are but various forms to which meanings have been assigned through convention. What really and concretely exists is nothing but the ink. The existence of the letters is in truth no other than the existence of the ink, which is the sole, unique reality that unfolds itself in many forms of self-modification. One has to cultivate, first of all, the eye to see the self-same reality of ink in all letters and then to see the letters as so many intrinsic modifications of the ink (Persian mystic Haydar-i Amuli, in Izutzu 1971: 66).

Language to a Sufi is perceived in a paradigm of revelatory experience wherein "the word" is the most refined and eloquent means of exchange, whether cosmological or social. Paradoxically, language can itself suggest a means of annihilating language in pursuit of that which lies behind it, thus transcending "the word" in order to experience "the word" in all of existence. To arrive at this non-dualistic realization is "to have no relation" – and therefore to be at One, to be all and whole. Contemplation of a spiritual language such as Arabic in light of such a non-dual aspiration facilitates revelatory experience and contributes to the realization of *wahdat al-wujud*, the "unity of being".

As previously mentioned, Sufis regard the words, verses and chapters of the Qur'ān not just as written language but also as beings which guide humans back to divine unity. Even the constituent elements of language, the letters, have divine power, and the disciplines of writing have spiritual significance. From a Sufi perspective, the science of letters (*'ilm al-huruf*) or letter mysticism (*al-huruf al-mana'*) is the art of expressing meaning from the letters and their multiple combinations and interpreting that meaning as it connects to a higher, cosmological order. Letters, therefore, are phonetic as well as phenomenological signs that are valued not only for semantic value but also for existential/spiritual value and arithmetic value. Following in the tradition of the Prophet Muhammad, "to worship with total presence as if one is actually seeing one's Lord in all things", the Sufi extends this aspiration towards spiritual presence and vision into language, as reflected in the Sufi saying that "there is no letter which does not worship God in a language" (Schimmel 1984: 81).

One of the most significant figures in the development of this Sufi view of language was al-Sadiq. His writings emphasize the esoteric significance of the letters and their role in the larger scheme of creation and existence:

> In the first place a thought surged in God, an intention, a will. The object of this thought, this intention, and this will were the letters from which God made the principal of all things, the indices of everything perceptible, the criteria of everything difficult. It is from these letters that everything is known (Schimmel 1994: 151).

According to a Qur'ānic commentary attributed to al-Sadiq (Mayer 2011: 4), al-Sadiq inherited a book of esoteric teachings from 'Ali, inscribed on lamb's skin (*jafr*). His teachings on the Arabic letters are attributed to this source, hence the science of interpreting the multiple meanings of the letters and numerical values assigned to them would be called *jafr*. The study of *jafr* is thought to reveal a mathematical structure that underlies the Qur'ān. For example, certain phrases are repeated in a mathematical pattern. This kind of numerological analysis of Arabic formulas has strong resemblance to the Kabbalistic practices of Jewish mysticism.

Figure 6.4: *Alif.*[3]

Many Sufis find support for such mystical understandings of language from Qur'ānic teachings about how God taught Adam the names of all things (i.e. taught him about their true inner nature), and in the mysterious invocation of combinations of isolated or abbreviated letters that preface 29 of the 114 Qur'ānic chapters. Some examples of these "mysterious letters" (*muqatta'at*) are found in chapter 68, "The Pen", – the second chapter revealed to the Prophet Muhammad which starts with the letter "*nun*" – and chapter 2 in the written Qur'ān, which begins with "*Alif, Lam, Mim*". In Sufi understandings, the sacred character of each letter is symbolized in both its form and in its meaning: "Each letter has a 'personality' of its own and symbolizes in its

3. This calligraphic piece is by Nuria Garcia Masip. For more about the artist see http://www.nuriaart.com

visual form a Divine Quality since the letters of the sacred alphabet correspond to features and qualities of God as the Divine Scribe" (Nasr 1987: 30).

Alif, being the first letter of the Arabic alphabet, is "the letter par excellence" from which all letters are derived. Its vertical, linear form is a perfect symbol of the unifying Principle of "as above, so below", wherein the heavens and the earth are ultimately one. Sahl al-Tustari states, "*Alif* points to God who is the *alif*, the one who has connected all things and yet is isolated from all things". For many Sufis, *alif* provided a powerful metaphor for the purified state towards which the spiritual seeker aspires to return. A desire to become the *alif* of Allah is often found in mystical poetry, as in Hafiz's statement, "There is no trace upon the tablet of my heart save the alif of stature of the Friend. What can I do, my master taught me no other letter" (Nasr 1987: 31).

The Story of the *Alif* by Bullah Shah

The following is an excerpt from the contemporary Sufi Hazrat Inayat Khan's *"The Inner Life"* (1979: 40–41), which is the first volume of his collected writings:

In the life of Bullah Shah [d. 1757], the great Sufi saint of Punjab, one reads a most instructive account of his early training when he was sent to school with boys of his own age. The other boys in his class finished the whole alphabet while he was mastering the same letter. When weeks had passed, and the teacher saw the child did not advance any further than the first letter Alif, he thought that he must be deficient and sent him home to his parents, saying, "Your boy is deficient, I cannot teach him".

The parents did all in their power for him, placing him under the tuition of various teachers, but he made no progress. They were disappointed, and the boy in the end escaped from home, so that he should no longer be a burden to his own people. He then lived in the forest and saw the manifestation of Alif which has taken form in the forest as the grass, the leaf, the tree, branch, fruit, and flower; and the same Alif was manifested in the mountain and hill, the stones and rocks; and he witnessed the same as a germ, insect, bird and beast, and the same Alif in himself and others. He thought of one, saw one, felt one, realized one, and none else besides.

After mastering this lesson thoroughly he returned to pay his respects to his old teacher who had expelled him from school. The teacher, absorbed in the vision of variety, had long ago forgotten him; but Bullah Shah could not forget his old teacher who had taught him his first and most inspiring lesson which had occupied almost all of his life. He bowed most humbly before the teacher and said, "I have prepared the lesson you so kindly taught me; will you teach me anything more that may be to learn?" The teacher laughed at him and thought to himself, "After all this time this simpleton has remembered me". Bullah Shah asked permission to write the lesson, and the teacher replied in jest, "Write on this wall". He then made the sign of Alif on the wall, and it divided into two parts. The teacher was astounded at this wonderful miracle and said, "Thou art my teacher! That which thou hast learnt in the one letter Alif, I have not been able to master with all my learning", and Bullah Shah sang this song:

Oh! Friend now quit thy learning,
 One Alif is all thou dost need.
 By learning thou hast loaded my mind,
With books thou hast filled up thy room.
But the true knowledge was lost by pursuing the false,
So quit now, oh friend, the pursuit of thy learning.

This story speaks both to the spiritual significance that Sufis have ascribed to letters, and to the special status of *alif* as the character which begins the Arabic alphabet and the word, "*Allah*". Sufis have regarded *alif* as the foremost and most elemental of the letters, even depicting it as the letter from which others have been derived. Similar to the Biblical and Qur'ānic story of Adam made in the likeness of God, so too are the letters made in the image of the *alif*. Al-Muhasibi communicates this understanding with a story: "When God created the letters he ordered them to obey. All letters were in the shape of alif, but only the alif kept its form according to the image in which it was created" (Schimmel 1984: 94).

If all letters come from the *alif*, as this story depicts, why learn the others? Although *alif* possesses a special status, Sufis have attributed spiritual meaning and significance to each of the other letters of the Arabic alphabet. Each letter is understood to have inherent qualities that are themselves manifestations of divine attributes and names. Taken together, the alphabet has provided Sufis with a way of thinking about an underlying "software" of creation through which God continually creates and recreates the universe. This understanding can be related to the "two dimensions" of calligraphy:

> The richness of the Arabic script comes from the fact that it has fully developed its two 'dimensions': the vertical, which confers on the letters their hieratic dignity, and the horizontal, which links them together in a continuous flow. As in the symbolism of weaving, the vertical lines, analogous to the 'warp' of the fabric, correspond to the permanent essences of things – it is by the vertical that the unalterable character of each letter is affirmed – whereas the horizontal, analogous to the 'weft', expresses becoming or the matter that links one thing to another (Burckhardt 1967: 159).

Far from regarding the letters as arbitrary building blocks of human language, Sufis have perceived cosmic significance in an alphabet that provides a medium for weaving the very tapestry of existence, and that manifests itself in divine as well as human speech.

Figure 6.5: Ibn al-'Arabi's Cosmology of the Letters.[4]

SUFISM AND ANCIENT NEAR EASTERN TRADITIONS

According to many Sufis, tracing the historical origin of timeless truth is an impossible task. Indeed, the history of esoteric traditions is by nature difficult to pin down with any certainty. Their secretive and symbolic nature alongside the prevalence of shared themes across a variety of religions and cultures, make questions of origin both fascinating and elusive. Traditionally, Western scholars of religion operated on the assumption that ideas were transmitted over time, moving in a relatively linear fashion from one group to another, explaining the resemblance between the thought of say Plotinus (d. 270) and Ibn al-'Arabi, for example. For adherents of the Perennial philosophy (from the Latin *philosophia perennis*) however, the shared themes we find in different esoteric traditions arise not simply because ideas spread over time, but because sages from different times and places encountered

4. A cosmological chart initially created by Titus Burckhardt (1977: 32–33) and recreated by Laleh Bakhtiar (1976: 62) to describe Ibn al-'Arabi's mystical interpretation of the Arabic letters as corresponding to Qur'ānic names of the Divine. Each letter represents a particular attribute and cosmic reality.

the same truth. If, as Sufis like Ibn al-'Arabi claim, reality is ultimately one, then it follows that direct encounters with this reality will foster philosophies that resemble one another. Hence, a resemblance between Neoplatonism and Sufism may indicate a shared encounter with reality rather than a historical transmission of ideas.

Whether one accepts the basic premises of the Perennial philosophy or not, it is historically evident that the Islamic tradition is a tradition of synthesis, coming of age as a religion and culture in the Near East, absorbing important elements of Graeco-Roman, Persian, Egyptian, and Mesopotamian law, philosophy, and mysticism. One notable place where this occurs is in the centre of the Qur'ān, the mysterious 18th chapter, *Surah al-Kaf*, the chapter of "the Cave". The centre of this chapter includes three stories rooted in older Near Eastern mythology – stories valued for their symbolism, mystery, and evocation of timeless themes of quest, wisdom, life and death. It is here that we find perhaps the most paradigmatic story of the Sufi path in the Qur'ān, the story of Moses' encounter "where the two seas meet" with a mysterious figure given knowledge directly "from the presence" of God, whose actions initially befuddle Moses. With echoes of the Epic of Gilgamesh, the story encapsulates ancient themes with overt mystical tones.

Figure 6.6: *Khidr.*[5]

5.   This Mughal miniature depicts Khidr on a fish, a Sufi symbol representing the "water of life" and the spiritual quest for immortality.

Khidr and Moses

Although he is not named in the Qur'ān, the mysterious figure that Moses encounters has been described in *hadith* as al-Khidr, literally "the Green One". Why green? Commentators have suggested that al-Khidr is an immortal, a being ever present to offer assistance to those travellers, physical or otherwise, in need of aid. Al-Khidr's immortality then is an abundance of life, so much so that greenery is said to grow under his feet wherever he goes, and hence his name. Al-Khidr is, of course, not the only figure with these qualities in the mythological archive of the Near East. The Bible's Elijah and Melchizedek are interesting precedents in this regard.

Sufis would develop a variety of themes from the story of Moses' encounter with Khidr, this unusual "servant of God" who has been endowed with direct knowledge from God's presence (*'ilm al-laduni*). As we will see in the story, taken verbatim from the Qur'ān in what follows, Moses is seeking knowledge from al-Khidr, but is warned that he will not be able to bear with al-Khidr. Indeed he is shocked by the mysterious green one's actions, which on the surface appear to flagrantly contradict the moral norms of sacred law and common sense. The story concludes with al-Khidr offering an interpretation (*ta'wil*) of these otherwise incomprehensible actions. Al-Khidr describes the unseen conditions that precipitate his acts. For Sufis, this story, found at the very heart of the Qur'ān, is a paradigm of the master-disciple relationship, which illustrates the importance of the disciple's patience in bearing with one whose actions are rooted in knowledge of the unseen:

Qur'ān 18:60–82:
Moses said to his attendant, "I will not give up until I reach the confluence of the two seas or else I will march on continually".

And when they reached the meeting of the seas, they found that they forgot to take their fish, which made its way to the sea through a hidden channel.

When they had proceeded further, he said to his squire: "Bring us breakfast. What we have found in this journey of ours is exhaustion".

He replied: "Did you notice that when we took refuge in the rock, I forgot the fish? It could only have been Satan that made me forget to remember it. In a marvellous fashion, it has made its way back to the sea".

He said: "That is what we have been seeking!" So they retraced their own tracks.

There they found one of our servants, to whom we have granted compassion and whom we had taught the special knowledge.

Moses said to him: "May I follow you in order to learn the integrity of action that you have been taught?"

He replied: "You will not be able to keep patience with me. How can you be patient in what your experience has not encompassed?"

He said: "You will find me patient, God willing. I will not cross your command".

He replied: "If you follow me, you must not ask me about anything until I mention the matter myself".

They set out. When they had boarded a ship, he gouged a hole in it. Moses said: "You've gouged a hole in order to drown the passengers. You've committed a terrible crime!"

He said: "Did I not say you would not be able to keep patience with me?"

Moses answered: "Do not hold me to account for my forgetfulness and do not be harsh with me".

They set out again until they met a young boy. He killed him. Moses said: "You've killed a person who was innocent of any killing. You've committed an atrocity!"

He said: "Did I not say you would not be able to be patient with me?"

Moses said: "If I ask you about anything else, cut me off from your company. You will be excused on my part".

They set out until they came to a town and asked its people for food, but they refused them hospitality. They came upon a wall on the point of collapsing. He repaired it. Moses said: "If you had wanted, you could have taken payment".

He said: "This is the parting of our ways. Now I will give you the inner interpretation (*ta'wil*) of what you couldn't bear with patience. As for the ship, it belonged to the poor who worked the sea. I wanted to cripple it, because just behind them was a king who was seizing by force every ship".

As for the boy, his parents were believers (*muslim*). I had reason to fear that he would oppress them with abuse and disbelief.

We wanted their lord to substitute for him one who was more pure of heart and compassionate.

And as for the wall – there were a pair of orphans in town who had a treasure under it. Their father had been a upright man and your lord wished that they should retrieve the treasure upon reaching maturity, as a mercy from your lord. I did not act by my own command. This is the inner interpretation of what you could not bear with patience.

For Sufis, a direct encounter with God or constant awareness of God's presence (*'ilm al-laduni*), is the innate nature of Islam and is a possibility for any devout Muslim. Indeed, such an awareness is intimately tied to the Sufi goal of becoming a complete or whole and perfected human being. For Muslims, this mysticism is derived from "the miracle of Islam", the Qur'ān, while the Messenger of the Qur'ān, the Prophet Muhammad, is the model of living its mystical message. For Sufis then, the historical origin of Sufism can be traced to the life of the Prophet Muhammad and the revelation he transmitted, the Qur'ān. "Sufi" becomes the label later Muslims would give to those who practised the intensive spirituality taught by Muhammad to his cousin and son-in-law 'Ali, and to his close companion and father-in-law, Abu Bakr. This intensive spirituality is most often understood as nothing less than the perfection of the Islamic faith and its very core, hence later Sufis could lay claim to being the true "Heirs of the Prophet", or inheritors of the fullness of prophetic knowledge, and the "Friends of God" preserving the purity of Islam and the spiritual integrity of the world itself.

While this narrative of Sufism's origin reflects the self-understanding and spiritual identity of most traditional Sufis, it is worth noting that Sufis were more often than not inclined to perceive continuity between Islam and prior religious and spiritual traditions, and were committed to affirming the presence of divine wisdom as manifested in diverse sources. We should not be surprised therefore, to find much evidence that the Sufi tradition developed in conversation with religious traditions already well established in the Middle East. In short, Sufism, like Islam and indeed other religions, did not emerge in a vacuum. Sufism's common forms of spiritual wisdom unfolded dynamically, taking a variety of forms within different times and contexts. Two consistent themes are found in this diversity: calling for stringent efforts to move toward transcendence of the lower ego and communion with the divine, and doing this in a manner that sought a broader harmony and unity (*tawhid*).

Though with origins in Arabia, Islam grew in the soil of the ancient Near East where there was a presence of Neoplatonic thinking, Judaism, Christianity, and Zoroastrianism, among other influences. Rather than as sources of possible corruption, Sufis engaged these legacies with an eye to what wisdom they might offer that was consistent with the core of Islamic revelation and prophetic history. Historically, these traditions all influenced the context within which Islam unfolded – legally, spiritually, culturally, and philosophically. Muslims did not passively adopt elements of pre-existing traditions, however, but creatively adapted them to fit within a new, emerging paradigm.

Historical evidence indicates that early Muslims were quite comfortable interacting with peoples of other religions, and embracing ideas from other cultures. This comfort arguably has roots in the Qur'ān itself. According to the Qur'ān, "Islam" is the name given to the message of all of the prophets sent to humanity – including the key figures of Judaism and Christianity such as Noah, Abraham, Moses, and Jesus. Muslims understand Muhammad, then, as simply the last prophet to bear this universal message, reviving it before the world's end. For Sufis, this universal Islam always consists of both an outward ethic and law, and an inward spiritual teaching. Just as Muslims have understood Judaism and Christianity to represent prior forms of Islam, so Sufis have understood elements of Jewish and Christian spirituality to represent prior forms of Sufism. Classical Sufi literature includes references to the "Sufism" of the Christians and Jews, for example. Hence, one can say that most Sufi Muslims understand Sufism as an ancient Near Eastern wisdom tradition that, on the one hand, pre-dates Islam but, on the other hand, was revived by the message and presence of Islam. Hence, it is important to understand some of the traditions that pre-date Islam in the Near East, as these certainly helped shape Sufism – although the degree to which they did (or did not) is impossible to prove decisively.

As Muslims came to rule lands that were predominantly Christian in the Mediterranean and Near East, they had an extended encounter with Christians and their spiritual practices. The Middle East was more thoroughly Christianized in the seventh century than Europe was at the time: the Middle East that Muslims first encountered was "a landscape of churches, monasteries and saintly shrines" (Green 2012: 19). Muslims not only gave legal protection to these sites, but in some cases co-opted them, with Christian tombs of saints and prophets becoming Muslim sites of pilgrimage, as well (Green 2012: 19).

With Islam's first dynastic capital in Damascus, it is not surprising that the practices and principles of Christian ascetics in Syria coincide with elements of early Muslim asceticism. This coincidence in and of itself does not offer us conclusive evidence that Sufi practices can be traced to Christian ones, although it does clearly show that Muslim ascetic and mystical movements took shape in a larger Middle Eastern context in which Christian asceticism and mysticism were already widespread. Christian ascetics and hermits who lived in Iraq, Syria, and Lebanon are mentioned frequently in Sufi stories. The "Christian ascetic" and "wise monk" became a popular figure in Sufi tales, often appearing in the role of a wise teacher giving advice to Sufi seekers. Also, the sayings from the Gospels and from the apocryphal sayings of Jesus are found in the oldest Sufi biographies (Nicholson 1989: 10).

Other scholars suggest that the woollen garment associated with Sufis may have been adopted from Christian ascetics, who themselves wore such garments. Like Sufis, Christian ascetics wore wool, engaged in voluntary poverty and repentance, and focused on the constant repetition of prayers thought to lead to a constant awareness of and closeness to God. Although not common, some Muslim ascetics had a preference for celibacy; according to one early Sufi personality, Abu Sulayman al-Darani (d. 830), "the sweetness of adoration and undisturbed surrender of the heart which the single man can feel the married man can never experience" (Schimmel 1975: 36). It then can be speculated that such tendencies towards celibacy may have been fostered by Muslim encounters with Christian monasticism. However, unlike Christianity, where monasticism became central to the religion's tradition of contemplation, Muslim contemplatives as a whole did not adopt celibacy, keeping instead with Muhammad's practice of marriage. Muhammad's famous companion, Ibn Mas'ud (d. 650), for example, is reported to have discouraged a group of Iraqi Muslims from living celibately in the desert to devote themselves solely to worship (Melchert 2015: 5).

The ascetic drive is not one that can be claimed by any particular religious expression, being an important strand of Middle Eastern culture for millennia. The famed Desert Fathers and Mothers of Egypt and Syria, so central to the formation of Christian monasticism and spiritual life, themselves replicated patterns found in the ascetic movement of the Essenes and before them the Cynics. The Cynics were often dismissed as vagrants, but they saw themselves as people who rejected the limitations of society's institutions to take a "short cut" to the philosopher's goal of enlightenment. They were unconventional and disruptive, but often respected as "holy fools". Their most famous representative, Diogenes of Sinope (d. 323 BCE), was reputed to have lived and slept outside or in a large clay wine jar. He was said to have carried a lamp during the day to find "one honest man". According to one tradition, Alexander the Great famously encounters Diogenes lying in the sun, and asks if there is anything he can do for the great philosopher, who simply replies to the world's most powerful ruler: "get out of my sunlight". Later antinomian Christian and Muslim mystics closely resemble Cynics (e.g. the *Qalandariyya* and Mulla Nasruddin).

Another pattern of connection between Sufism and Christianity is the influence of Neoplatonism. Neoplatonism is a modern term given to an elaboration on Plato's thought that developed into a system of mystical doctrines and practices between the third and sixth centuries CE, in cities such as Alexandria and Athens (Dickson 2015: 57). Neoplatonism was a significant intellectual and spiritual competitor with Christianity during the new religion's rise in the Mediterranean. Its demise as a living school of thought is usually associated with Emperor Justinian's closing of the Platonic Academy in Athens in 529. The key principle that Neoplatonists agreed on is that reality can be divided into (a) the sensible realm, that which is available to our senses, and (b) the intelligible realm, that which is available to our intellect. They further agreed that the intelligible realm is made up of a hierarchy of different levels. As one ascends the hierarchy of intelligibility, according to the Neoplatonists, one encounters levels of reality that are marked by increasing unity, wholeness, and integration, culminating in the first principle, that which Plato called "the Good", and Aristotle called "the One". As the principle of all life and existence, all beings desire to return to this One, and the Neoplatonists engaged in practices that were thought to facilitate the soul's return to its unitary origin.

Although a Christian emperor closed the Platonic Academy, Christian thinkers such as Augustine (d. 430) and Pseudo-Dionysius (d. late fifth–early sixth century) would synthesize Neoplatonism with Christian theology: "Neoplatonism had deeply permeated the Near East", and was hence "in the air" in the region, so it is not surprising that Muslims encountered Neoplatonic thought (Schimmel 1975: 10). Some examples of this encounter include the Arabic translation of Porphyry's commentary on Plotinus's *Enneads* as early as 840 – unfortunately under the wrong title of, "The Theology of Aristotle".

The numerous shared emphases of later Islamic philosophy with Neoplatonism, and the explicit reference of Sufi or Sufi-related writers to Greek and particularly Neoplatonic thought, make the connection between Neoplatonism and Sufism well established. However, as evidence of Neoplatonic influence comes later in the development of Sufism, this particular form of Greek mysticism was not likely a source of Sufism, though it clearly had a notable influence on how Sufism (particularly its unique ontology and cosmology) came to be articulated.

An example of Neoplatonism and Sufism's relationship is found in the many Sufi references to Plotinus as "The Greek Master" (Shaykh al-Yaunani), and further in that Ibn al-'Arabi is referred to as the "Son of Plato" (Ibn Flatun) due to the similarity between elements of his thought and the thought of Plato. Generally speaking, because of Neoplatonism's mystical orientation, its emphasis on the oneness of reality, and its permeation throughout the Near East, many scholars have drawn connections between it and Sufism.

Another spiritual tradition with which Sufis felt kinship was Hermeticism. Hermeticism can briefly be defined as a set of philosophical and religious beliefs or gnosis based primarily upon the Hellenistic Egyptian writings, known as the *Corpus Hermeticum*, attributed to Hermes Trismegistus (al-Haramisa in Arabic), who is the representation of the conflation of the ancient Egyptian god Thoth with the ancient Greek Hermes. Hermetic writings from the first to fourth centuries CE were translated into Arabic. Hermes is traditionally related to Enoch in the Old Testament and Hebrew Scriptures, and Muslims believe he appears in the Qur'ān as the Prophet Idris (Nasr 1967: 64).

Throughout the *Hermeticum*, Hermes is portrayed as an initiator into wisdom, summoning human beings to make themselves equal to the Absolute, so that they may know it (Dickson 2015: 57). The goal of Hermetic practice is to transform the lower, base, and material elements in people into something more refined, higher, and spiritual. Humanity is then called to re-integrate with the divine, or re-ascend to the divine. This ascent to higher planes of existence can be accomplished by using the inner faculty of spiritual knowing. Using this faculty, humans can connect with higher spiritual intelligences, represented by planetary spheres, which are encountered through ascent. Hermetical texts on theurgy, alchemy, and astrology are important for the Western mystical traditions as a whole including mystical Christianity, Jewish Kabbalah, Sufism, as well as Western esoteric traditions (e.g. Rosicrucianism) only loosely connected to the Abrahamic faiths.

One example of Hermeticism and Sufism coming together is found in the thought and practice of the Sufi teacher Shihab al-Din Yahya Suhrawardi (d. 1191). Suhrawardi has been described as "the great reviver of Hermetic Gnosticism in Islam" (Ephrat 2008: 75). In his work *Hikmat al-Ishraq*, or the "Wisdom of Illumination", Suhrawardi claims that the "science of light" or "wisdom of illumination", has always had its exponents, including Plato, Hermes, Empedocles, Pythagoras, Aristotle, and Zoroaster. All of these sages, according to Suhrawardi, despite their differences, "shared in a universal and perennial wisdom, originally revealed to Hermes" (Fakhry 2004: 307).

Another famous and controversial Muslim Hermeticist was Ibn Sab'in (1217–1269 CE), the Andalusian Sufi-philosopher who coined the term *wahdat al-wujud*, or the "oneness of being" (which later became associated with Ibn al-'Arabi). Ibn Sab'in's work, *Sharh Kitab Idris*, was a commentary on a scripture attributed to Idris, or Hermes. In the opening of the text Ibn Sab'in writes:

> I petitioned God to propagate through me the wisdom which Hermes Trimegistus revealed in the earliest times, the realities that prophetic guidance has made beneficial for mankind, the happiness that is sought by every person of guidance, the light by which every fully-actualized seeker wishes to be illuminated, the knowledge that will no longer be disseminated from Hermes in future ages, and the secret from which and through which and for the sake of which the prophets were sent (Cornell 1997: 54).

According to Ibn Sab'in, the function of the prophets is not to originate doctrine but to reaffirm a primordial wisdom that transcends all of the revealed religions. Also, Ibn Sab'in held that although Sufism was an important path to the truth, the highest truth could only be attained by following the way of Hermes. Cornell posits that Ibn Sab'in "is best summed up as a Muslim universalist, a Plotinian mystic, and a devotee of Hermes Trismegistus who drew from the wellsprings of both philosophy and Sufism without identifying himself completely with either one" (Cornell 1997: 61).

By the time of Ibn Sab'in, it appears that at least seven and as many as 18 tractates of the *Corpus Hermeticum* were available in Arabic: "Hermeticism was widespread in medieval Spain and claimed followers on both sides of the Muslim-Christian frontier" (1997: 56), and Arab historians named a number of important Sufi hermeticists in al-Andalus (Arab/Muslim Spain).

Zoroastrianism, the religion of ancient Iran (Persia), also informed the spiritual visions of some Sufis, particularly as Muslims established themselves in the Persian cultural sphere. Elements of Zoroastrian theologies of light and darkness, duality, and angels were incorporated into Sufi thought by Suhrawardi as well as Najm al-Din Kubra (d. 1220). According to Henry Corbin (d. 1968), "Sohravardi carried out the great project of reviving the wisdom or theosophy of ancient pre-Islamic Zoroastrian Iran" (Corbin 1994: 8).

Illustrating how numerous strands of doctrine and practice came to be woven together in Sufi mysticism, Corbin writes, "Sohravardi's [Suhrawardi] work made a link between Plato and Zarathustra, in a doctrine dominated by the name and wisdom of Hermes" (1994: 8). In particular, Zoroastrian angelology has been compared with elements of Sufi cosmology, with scholars such as Corbin drawing important comparative links (1994: 55).

While it is possible to identify particular lines of influence and affinity between Sufism and pre-existing spiritual and philosophical traditions, these connections are diverse – a diversity that does not thereby negate a broader coherence. Sufism developed in conversation, resonating with that which Sufis perceived to carry spiritual validity and depth. For many Sufis, the perennialism inherent in the Qur'ān – which affirms a single truth taught in different times and places by the messengers and prophets – opens up the Islamic tradition to recognizing the whole spiritual heritage of humanity as essentially one, if expressed in a multitude of ways. This does not erase the genuine differences of doctrine and practice, but argues that, at the deepest level, these differences are eclipsed by the deeper unity that underpins them – a unity premised on the transformation of the human self, a process that in its essence is timeless.

Discussion Questions:

1. What were some of the main differences between esoteric and exoteric interpretations of early Qur'ānic commentary?
2. How did these Qur'ānic debates shape the early formative period of Sufism (as discussed in Chapter 5)?
3. Describe three main Qur'ānic themes that would influence Sufi thought and practice.
4. What is letter mysticism, and how is it connected to the art of Qur'ānic calligraphy as practiced by many Sufi masters?

5. Describe the different ways in which Islam and Muslim may be defined, in relation to Sufism.

Further Reading:

Mayer, F. (trans.). (2011). *Spiritual Gems: The Mystical Qur'ān Commentary Ascribed to Jaf'ar al-Sadiq as Contained in Sulami's Haqa'iq al-Tafsir from the Text of Paul Nwyia.* Louisville, KY: Fons Vitae Publishers.

Nasr, S. H. (1987). *Islamic Art and Spirituality.* Albany, NY: State University of New York Press.

Nasr, S. H., Dagli, C. K., Dakake, M. M., Lumbard, J. E. B., & Rustom, M. (eds). (2015). *The Study Qur'ān: A New Translation and Commentary.* New York: Harper Collins.

Sands, K. Z. (2006). *Sufi Commentaries on the Qur'ān in Classical Islam.* London: Routledge.

Schimmel, A. (1984). *Calligraphy and Islamic Culture.* New York: New York University Press.

Schimmel, A. (1994). *Deciphering the Signs of God: A Phenomenological Approach to Islam.* Albany, NY: State University of New York Press.

CONCLUSION

Widely regarded as his masterwork, Rumi's *Mathnavi* is one of the most popular works in the Sufi literary canon and within Persian literature more generally. W. M. Thackston Jr. even goes so far as to suggest that, "It is probably safe to say that from the time of its completion, no book within the realm of Islam, with the exception of the Koran, has been so venerated and revered as Rumi's *Mathnavi*" (Thackston 1999: xiii), though Hafiz's *Diwan* may be a contender in this respect. The full title of the work is *Mathnavi-i ma'navi*, or the "Rhyming Couplets of Intrinsic Meaning". The title suggests something of the book's purpose, which is to use words to draw the reader to an underlying meaning. The *Mathnavi* is brimming with stories of seemingly mundane circumstances that communicate subtle truths. One of the more widely shared examples of this type of story in the *Mathnavi* is a tale of four travellers who are collectively given a single silver coin. They immediately begin to quarrel over what they are to do with their newfound wealth. The first traveller to speak, a Persian, suggests they buy *angur*, to which the second traveller, an Arab, objects that they should instead get *'inab*. The third traveller, a Turk, argues that they would be wiser to purchase *uzum*, while the fourth traveller, a Greek, protests that they are all wrong, and that they should buy *istafil*. The dispute intensifies, turning into an angry debate. A sage who knows the meaning of the various words they are fighting over then appears, and offers to solve the travellers' problem for them, granting each person what he seeks. Though sceptical the weary conflictants hand over their silver coin. The wise one returns with four bunches of grapes. They all erupt in jubilation, each exclaiming that this is the *angur* or the *'inab* which they were looking for. Although the names they invoked were different, the named they were seeking is one.

Despite the diverse names by which grapes are called, the grapes themselves are one thing. Like the grapes in Rumi's tale, Sufism itself can be described and defined in myriad ways, and yet in its essence the Sufi tradition has core elements which unify its diverse interpretations. This theme of a unity underlying diversity is central to Sufism as a whole, as we have explored throughout this book. The way we explored such themes central to Sufism in this book is a little unconventional. In contrast to most introductory texts on Sufism, we began not with the historical past, but with the contemporary present – specifically, lived Sufism in North America today. After commencing with Sufism in the twentieth and twenty-first centuries in North America, we proceeded, in each succeeding chapter, to unveil the complexities of Sufism as we moved deeper through time and space, journeying through a variety of historical, political, and cultural contexts, delving deeper into the past and closer to the origin of Sufism. In this manner, we have sought to understand the diverse expressions of Sufism in each era as well as patterns of connection between expressions of Sufism in different times. Throughout, we have attempted to offer a nuanced, multi-dimensional perspective, giving both a broad overview and specific case studies, for instance, from 'Abd al-Qadir al-Jaza'iri's spiritually-informed resistance to French invasion, to the place of the wandering dervish in medieval Muslim societies. While each case and period involved some features and debates that were unique, certain key themes resurfaced in different times and contexts, some of which we highlight below.

SUFISM AND POLITICS

Most introductions to the subject of Sufism offer both historical overview along with some explanation of Sufi philosophy. While both the history of Sufism and its philosophical developments are important to address, in this work we have sought to further consider the political contexts within which Sufism took shape historically and philosophically. The life of the mind and spirit, though in some sense transcending the rough and tumble of politics and power, remains within social formations conditioned by political circumstances; even ascetics and mystics had to contend with rulers and the highly political theological debates of their time. Further, as we have seen, many Sufis wanted not to retreat from the world, but to shape it, integrating spirituality with political activism ranging from advisory roles to taking positions of leadership in society or even organizing military campaigns.

The question of epistemology, for example, has proven to be one with profound political implications. Authoritative knowledge of the Qur'ān and *Sunnah* was foundational to Muslim societies, so determining *what* exactly this knowledge was, *how* it was to be applied at the individual and social levels, and *who* had the power to define and implement this knowledge, shaped Muslim normative behaviour, social order, governance, and culture. As we saw in Chapter 5, jurists like Ibn Hanbal, were sceptical and critical of Sufi claims to inner knowledge. Then in Chapter 4, we saw al-Ghazali attempting to secure the place of this knowledge within Islam, in breaking down authoritative Islamic knowledge into two categories: the "outward" sciences of theology, jurisprudence, *hadith* and Qur'ānic commentary, and sciences of the inner world. Al-Ghazali's articulation of the inner and outward sciences of Islam was the fruition of centuries of discourse, some traced back to al-Sadiq, among others, who suggested that the Qur'ān had both outward and inward meanings. Although al-Ghazali's efforts to synthesize the various epistemologies of the Islamic tradition were widely accepted after him among Sunni jurists and theologians, some of them either totally rejected the possibility of the inner sciences, or were highly sceptical of any who claimed to have this esoteric knowledge. Others like Ibn Tayimiyya had a highly restrictive sense of the ways in which inner knowledge could be expressed and lived. We find then a persistent tension between the rational and tradition-based claims to knowledge of these jurists (whom al-Ghazali called the *'ulama al-zahir*), and the Sufis (many of whom were themselves jurists), who claimed a direct, experiential knowledge from the very source of the texts. Those thought to have experienced an unveiling became renowned as saints and friends of God, by peasants and rulers alike. As the inner experiences of these individuals were acknowledged as genuine, they became exemplars of the Islamic life, heirs to prophetic forms of knowledge and authority, and a source of communal values: the private was inevitably political.

This tension between different understandings of knowledge has been a perennial one throughout Islamic history, as we saw in Chapter 2, as al-'Alawi defended Sufi ways of knowing and interpreting the Qur'ān against Salafi criticisms of these epistemologies as lacking grounding in Islamic tradition and rationality. Interestingly, Salafi and Orientalist analyses of Sufism coincided in many respects, in seeing Sufism as something un-Islamic. Then we saw in Chapter 1 that contemporary debates over what it means to be Muslim are rehashing much older debates over the legitimacy of an inner form of knowledge, and its implications for Muslim doctrine, identity, and practice. The increasingly common destruction of Sufi shrines throughout Muslim lands then is a contemporary manifestation of this recurrent debate over the legitimacy of Sufi ways of knowing and their role in Muslim selves and societies. The shrines stand as symbols of the integration of Sufism into the very fabric of Muslim life, space, geography, culture, and religious practice. Destroying them erases evidence of a historical synthesis, one now rejected by current anti-Sufi movements. This raises the question of the sustainability of Sufism in contexts where it historically flourished. However just as we see Sufism being purged from its traditional contexts, we find Sufism experiencing something of a renaissance globally. Students and scholars are hence asking whether or not the twenty-first century will be one in which Sufism will have an integral place within Muslim and non-Muslim societies? This book has highlighted some of the diverse ways in which Sufis understand their own tradition. The question remains as to how contemporary Sufis will reconcile their different perspectives in the twenty-first century, and how these will be understood by Muslims and non-Muslims alike.

On a deeper level, the destruction of Sufi shrines further represents the total rejection of an epistemology of *kashf*, flattening out the means of gaining and applying religious knowledge, to simply understanding the outward meaning of canonical texts and attempting to apply them in a decontextualized manner. It is further a rejection of pre-modern Muslim conceptions of beauty, which saw the sacred embodied in material form. Perhaps ironically then, this anti-Sufi approach is premised on a highly modern epistemology (at least one strand of modern thought), where the world and scripture cease to be perceived in a symbolic fashion. No longer signifying higher realities, the world and scripture instead are perceived as signs only of themselves, and hence knowledge is a simple apprehension of the apparent, forgoing a deeper exploration of the symbolic. This epistemology of *kashf* or unveiling, includes other terminology that Sufis have developed. If *kashf* can be thought of as the methodology whereby the Sufi aspirant accesses knowledge, the ontological nature of this knowledge is the self-disclosure of God's being, or *tajalli*. The knowledge itself is the *'ilm al-laduni*, the direct knowledge from God's presence. It is no surprise then that *kashf* was a controversial methodology. However, despite the disputes surrounding its legitimacy, as we have seen in this work, Sufi ways of knowing were ultimately integrated into holistic Islamic paradigms. This integration however could only take hold with the approval of political elites, and hence the role of political power in establishing this medieval Islamic synthesis of outward and inward ways of knowing as normative. Although broadly accepted, the Sufi claim to a direct mystical knowledge remained somewhat disputed, as we see reflected in contemporary debates.

Historical disputes took place not only over Sufi ways of knowing, but also among Sufis themselves, in terms of how Sufi ways of knowing were to be expressed in doctrine and practice. As we have illustrated in this book, all agreed that the essence of Sufism was the experience of existential unity fostered by spiritual practices and principles. And yet Sufis differed profoundly over how this essence was to be lived. What form should the practice of Sufism take? What sorts of daily rules and rituals should frame the Sufi path? How should Sufis relate to the social norms and institutions of Muslim and non-Muslim societies? From one perspective, we find more scrupulously *shari'a*-minded Sufis, who negated any intuitive insight that appeared to contradict the authoritative consensus of the learned, and whose understanding of what it meant to be "Muslim" was sharply bounded. For Sufis of this orientation, the essence of the Sufi path was contained, preserved, and protected by Islamic law and ritual life. This perspective often was found in the company of a sense of Islamic superiority, and the need to preserve or spread Islamic rule and power. With Sirhindi for example, we find a Sufi leader opposing the erasure of distinctions between Muslims and Hindus, arguing instead for the privileging of Muslims in government and society, and the establishment of Islamic norms over all others. Presenting an alternative to these perspectives, as we have seen throughout this book, was often dangerous. Figures like al-Hallaj, Shams of Tabriz, and Dara Shikoh all became martrys, in part due to their rejection of conventional ways of being, knowing, and behaving. Each would respond to discourses of orthodoxy in different ways, representing alternative streams of Sufi thought, ones that interpreted Islamic sources and practices in ways that challenged or overturned established understandings, dissolved boundaries between self and God, and erased distinctions between Muslim and non-Muslim.

We also find broader antinomian tendencies among dervishes, many who rejected the strictures of the law as inhibiting the free expression of spirit. There were the wild, wandering mendicants who consciously unsettled the status quo, who were less deferential to many established forms of custom and morality, and who understood terms such as "Muslim" in more existential (and, some might say, "socially deviant") terms. Mulla Nasruddin would become a fictional, humorous, icon of this social critique, a beloved figure shared across many Muslim cultures. Totally unpredictable, continually destabilizing the rational mind, Mulla Nasruddin represented the way in which dervishes opened up space for transformation through paradoxical behaviour. They would become living symbols, even in their dress and lifestyle, of spiritual renunciation, representing a total, uncompromising way of life, which most people could only aspire to, but were nonetheless inspired by. One of the ways in which Muslim societies have changed since the colonial period, is the gradual disappearance of the dervish way of life in Muslim societies, from Morocco, to Iran and India.

In general however, most Sufis were not anti-conformist, but neither were they strictly literalistic, legalistic or formalistic in their approach. Generally, we find Sufis valuing flexibility in approach, to adapt Sufism to particular contexts, as al-Junayd famously said, "water takes on the colour of its container". Sufis addressed the following questions in a variety of ways: How mutable are the forms within which Sufism is expressed and lived? What is the relationship between Sufism and *shari'a*? What must be preserved within Sufism and what changed to suit the context? What aspects of Sufism are universal, and what specifically religiously Islamic in nature? Providing different answers, Sufis tended to function within the diversity of possibility.

Regarding the last question over universality, Sufis differed in terms of understanding pluralistic realities of religions. For instance, Ibn al-'Arabi famously articulated an outlook of Islamic universalism, affirming the presence of God's continual self-manifestation in all forms, including those taken by different religious traditions. While still upholding a rigorous understanding of Islamic norms and ritual, he articulated a worldview that many generations of Muslims found to express the heart of Qur'ānic teachings concerning God's revelations to many peoples, and ever-present reality within and beyond the phenomenal world. As discussed in Chapter 3, his worldview would influence how Muslim dynasties would understand the nature of Islamic rule and the role of non-Muslims in Muslim-led societies. Then in Chapter 2, we saw how 'Abd al-Qadir al-Jaza'iri's profound respect for Christians and Christianity, was directly informed by his close study of Ibn al-'Arabi's religious pluralism.

This view did not go uncontested, with many, from his time to the present, invoking alternative authorities such as Ibn Taymiyya – himself professing an affinity for a much more formalistic approach to Sufism. Profoundly different conclusions emerged, with markedly divergent implications for how to engage the religious "other" or, indeed, an "other" who advocates a divergent reading of Islam. We learned that seeds of both contemporary Sufism and anti-Sufism are deeply planted. As long as there have been universalistic forms of Sufism, there have also been counter-currents.

These debates between Sufis and their theological opponents, and among Sufis over the best way to live a Muslim life, were far from strictly academic in nature; they would have far reaching social effects. For example, although Sufism for much of its history was practised in mountain caves, lodges, and homes, as we have seen Sufi practice was in various ways integrated into diverse professions, including military ones. One of the first Sufi "cloisters" established on the island of Abbadan, was mostly made up of soldiers renowned for combining military service with spiritual practice. Later the Janissaries, the elite troops of the Ottoman Empire, would be closely affiliated with the Bektashi Sufi order. Even later we see 'Abd al-Qadir al-Jaza'iri combining an intensive spiritual practice with organizing military resistance to the French invasion of Algeria.

Some early Sufis advocated keeping a distance from rulers, as sources of the corrupting influence of power and wealth. Others however, were more comfortable establishing relations with elite figures or seeking to influence them. Later Sufis would in many cases play close advisory roles to sultans and shahs, even steering government policy. Sultans and shahs were often disciples of Sufi masters, who despite their positions of great power, still sought spiritual transformation, advice, and blessing from living and departed "friends of God".

Within civil society, we saw that Sufis would create and support social institutions that would be essential to the structure of medieval Muslim societies. Notable here are the various Sufi-oriented guilds, which included professions as varied as butchers, bakers, tailors, goldsmiths, swordmakers, doctors, bookbinders, and night watchmen. Guild meetings began with Sufi rituals, and their leaders were themselves often Sufi masters. The various crafts engaged in were pursued in a manner that integrated the remembrance of God, fusing work and devotion. Sufism then infused commerce, trade, crafts, and the arts and sciences.

SUFI METAPHYSICS AND SPIRITUAL PRACTICES

As this work has illustrated, the metaphysical principles and spiritual practices of Sufism were integrated into Islamic doctrine, governance, culture, and social structure more broadly. These principles and practices are all rooted in the concept of a journey: most Sufis have been united in their central aspiration to know God and indeed to directly encounter the sacred source, both in seclusion and in the midst of everyday life. As in all mystical traditions, there is a seeker who sets out on a journey to God in order to awaken the higher faculties of the self and remove the veil which conceals the Divine.

> We begin the Quest by removing the veil, only to become aware that the veil and the Divine are one and the same thing. The veil is a theophany itself: the manifestation of the Divine through Its Names and Qualities. When we see the veil, we are seeing nothing but the Divine (Bakhtiar 1976: 32).

Although the journey is necessary, there is a sense in which it is illusory, as there is no place outside the Divine from which to journey to the Divine. The purpose of the journey is to realize that the sense of separateness from God is itself an illusion, to know the reality of unity beyond the appearance of multiplicity.

Whether through chanting, poetry, architecture, science, trade, calligraphy, philosophy, or even the imperial courtly debates (to name a few), remembering the Divine (*dhikr*) is a thread which unites different Sufi realities on a journey towards the One, orienting the one who remembers, to a path of knowledge and, ultimately, love. According to Plato, all knowledge is recollection, remembrance of what the soul already knows but has forgotten. For Sufis, the remembrance of God is the soul's recollection of its divine source, and the wayfarer's most important task. The Qur'ān asserts that, above all forms of worship, "the remembrance of God is greater" (29:45). In Chapter 1 we opened by describing Lex Hixon's leading of *dhikr* at the Jerrahi mosque in Manhattan, and later Fariha al-Jerrahi's continuation of this role as *shaykha* of the order. In Chapter 2, we saw 'Abd al-Qadir al-Jazai'iri weave the practice of *dhikr* into his daily life, while in Chapter 3 we explored the importance of shrines as sites where the remembrance of God is practised in culturally diverse ways, and how Islamic material culture, from shrines, to prayer beads, to even the dervish cloak, all functioned to facilitate *dhikr*. In Chapter 4, we saw how Sufis practised *dhikr* through forms of music, dance, and even serving the poor, travellers, or those in need. Sufi biographers recorded for later generations the foundational practices of remembrance transmitted by early Sufi figures, as we discussed in Chapter 5, while in Chapter 6 we explored the role of the Qur'ān as the original source of remembrance, and the Prophet Muhammad as the foremost exemplar of integrating *dhikr* into every aspect of life.

The practise of *dhikr* was something most often engaged in under the influence and direction of a guide, one who has personally taken the journey, traversing its various perils. Of course, as we have seen, the guide is not always physical: from the immortal Khidr, to the spiritual form of teachers who have passed long ago, Sufi aspirants experienced guidance from a variety of sources. Ibn al-'Arabi for example, had a series of encounters with Khidr, who is said to have invested him with his *khirqa* or cloak, transmitting his *baraka* with this "initiative mantle" (Addas 1993: 62). Often a first step on the path involved initiation, whereby the process of transmitting *baraka* begins, continuing the chain of transmission, the *silsila* going back through generations of practitioners to the saints and prophets, and ultimately God. The seeker experiences a reorientation of self toward divine remembrance, usually symbolized in the sacred objects, clothing, and practices of a particular Sufi order.

The path involves engaging with the lower, destructive aspects of oneself, ultimately integrating, transforming and transcending them. This transcendence is in a sense emptying, emptying the self so that it is in a state of receptivity to the Divine. The total emptiness of the self has, in the Islamic tradition, been described using the metaphors of both death and awakening. The Prophet Muhammad is reported to have said, "Men sleep and when they die they shall awake". He is also reported to have said, "Die before you die". These two sayings, beloved by Sufis, can be understood together as representing the inner journey, as one of dying to the limited self, to awaken to a deeper reality.

Ibn al-'Arabi wrote, in his famous work *The Meccan Revelations*, "There is not one single thing that cannot be known through revelation (*kashf*) or spiritual experience (*wujud*)" (Addas 1993: 105). Unveiling reveals the way in which all forms represent or symbolize the Divine. Hence through the experience of *kashf*, the aspirant begins to see how both the cosmos and self reflect the presence of God, as the Qur'ān suggests, describing the "signs on the horizons and in themselves" (41:53). The journey within God involves deciphering the signs of God, seeing their cosmological and psychological significance. All things of the world, the various elements that make it up, its directions and colours, shapes, the objects and subjects from stars, to animals, to letters, all are in a sense read as one reads a book. Each a letter or word transmitting meaning through form. The universe then is not simply a somewhat random collection of energy and matter, but a cosmos, a realm rich with hidden meanings and order. The symbolic nature of the universe is a subject found in the writings of many Sufis throughout history, including al-'Alawi, whose writings we considered in the second chapter. The mystic, in polishing and opening the eye of the heart, makes oneself available to the possibility of *kashf*, the unveiling of the hidden meanings found within the vast expanse of the cosmos, and the even vaster expanse of the self. Sufi meta-physicians like Ibn al-'Arabi and Rumi have pursued this symbolic vision of the universe to map the cosmos, describing the various levels of reality, often symbolized with Qur'ānic and pre-Islamic imagery, like the Pen, the Tablet, or the Throne, or various sorts of plants, animals, and birds.

Many Sufis focused in particular on the significance of letters, creating a whole mystical science of letters. In considering the significance of the Qur'ān, we noted in Chapter 6, that metaphysical reflections focused on the dot, the most basic written sign. The dot symbolized not only the origin of all of the letters, but of the whole universe. In particular, the dot underneath the second letter of the Arabic alphabet, *ba*, was associated with the "First Intellect" emerging from the unknown and unknowable Divine Essence. Letters were seen as part of a whole system of correspondences, whereby each letter was associated with particular Divine names and qualities, dif-ferent levels of reality and self, material elements, seasons, astrological signs, and colours.

These symbolic interperative frameworks were thought to emerge not out of speculative thought, but a direct, intuitive, experiential knowing. In Chapter 5, we explored how early Sufis like Dhu'l Nun distinguished between *'ilm* and *ma'rifa*. Whereas *'ilm* was discursive knowledge, *ma'rifa* was knowledge through being – a knowledge where the division between knower and known dissolves. It was this type of knowledge referred to in the famous saying of the Prophet Muhammad, "He who knows himself knows his Lord". The direct, experiential knowing of the self allows one to know the divine origin of the self.

The goal of the journey is to empty the self of lower inclinations and characteristics, so that more and more of God's qualities can be manifest and reflected into the world. This process of adopting the characteristics of God is known as *takhalluq bi-akhlaq Allah,* as discussed throughout this work. The comprehensive reflection of God's names is a state of perfection or *kamal*, and hence the figure of the *insan al-kamil* or perfected human being, as the exemplar of the journey's completion or fulfillment. Although it is an end, it is also a continual beginning, as Ibn al-'Arabi expressed, there is no repetition in God's self-disclosures, so the perfected soul con-tinues to journey through ever new manifestations of God's qualities, with-out end.

The perfected self exists in a sort of isthmus or *barzakh*, a "placeless place" or "station of no-station". It is here that the soul can simultaneously negate the relative while affirming the absolute in all things, recogniz-ing the perfection and limitation of every conceivable human perspective and belief. It was this perspective that is expressed by Ibn al-'Arabi in his famous poetry collection, *The Interpreter of Ardent Desires* or *Tarjuman al-Ashwaq*:

My heart is capable of every form:
For gazelles a meadow, a cloister for monks,
For the idols, sacred ground, Ka'aba for the circling pilgrim,
the tables of the Torah and the scrolls of the Qur'an.
I follow the religion of Love: wherever its caravan turns along the way,
that is my religion and my faith (Ibn al-'Arabi, in Nicholson 1911: 67).

In the "station of no station", not only are all perspectives seen in light of their prefections and limitations, but one exists in a state of perplexity and bewilderment. As Ibn al-'Arabi writes:

Tongues, by God, are too weak to express what hearts know, and hearts, by God, are too weak to understand the actual situation. They do not know if they are bewildered or not. Bewilderment exists, but no locus is known within which it abides. For whom does it exist and in whom does its property become manifest? For there is none but God (Ibn al-'Arabi, in Chittick 1998: 90).

Ibn al-'Arabi here describes the bewilderment that results from realizing the non-existence of the self. Indeed the realization of the self's illusory nature is the condition for genuine realization, for it is only when one is absent from oneself that one can be present with God, or alternatively, "When Allah is there, you are not" (Armstrong 1995: 54). We ourselves are the veil preventing the *'ilm al-ghayb*, or knowledge of the unseen. Ibn al-'Arabi suggests that the unseen is "All that the Real veils from you because of you, not because of Him" (Ibn al-'Arabi in Bayrak and Harris 1992: 108).

THE IMPACT OF SUFISM ON ISLAMIC ARTS AND CULTURE

As the conventional language of philosophy too often fails to prove an adequate means of communicating higher truths, Sufis have frequently sought more artistic means of expression, like poetry, art, and music. The arts embody metaphysical principles in visual and auditory forms, communicating these principles with an immediacy difficult if not impossible to achieve within the discursive confines of prose. The arts have further functioned as a means to express the simultaneous unity and diversity of Islamic civilization, as they communicate principles shared by all Muslims, and yet these principles are expressed through diverse cultural themes and motifs, illustrating the confounding array of cultural forms found within Islam.

Beyond specifically Muslim contexts however, the arts have acted as unrivalled bridges across cultural and civilizational divides. As we saw in Chapter 1, the thirteenth century Sufi poet Rumi has been embraced by a remarkable range of contemporary North American cultural creatives, ranging from poets and musicians to composers, choreographers, social activists, architects, and entrepreneurs. One of Islam's most revered mystics has proven to be a wellspring of inspiration for contemporary artists. This attraction to Sufi poetry did not begin in the twentieth century however. As we explored in the second chapter, it was during the colonial period that influential Western authors like Goethe and Emerson discovered the irresistible charm and hidden depth of Persian Sufi poetry, introducing Europeans and North Americans to the unique mix of satire and sacredness, sentiment and morality, found in the works of the famous Shirazi poets Hafiz and Sa'adi.

Moving further back through the centuries, in Chapter 3, we considered the way in which the sacred principles of Sufism took material form in structure, with the shrines of saints and Sufi lodges that came to architecturally define the great cities and expansive countrysides of Islamic lands. These structures were carefully constructed utilizing sacred geometrical principles, symbolic forms and ornamentation, colour theory, and sacred calligraphy, all brought together in a way that communicated higher realities and Sufi cosmologies.

The Sufi shrines and lodges and mosques of Muslim societies were pivotal sites around which Muslim culture revolved and evolved, where dervishes and sultans, devotees and those seeking healing, all came to participate in the presence of the sacred believed to be found at these sites. In many cases the structures of trade and residence would in a sense radiate outward from these sacred spaces, visually representing the concept of the *qutb*, the saint who watches over a particular region. Shrines and lodges integrated local cultural architectural forms, making African and Asian, Arab and Persian (to name just a few) architectural styles an integral part of Islamic architecture more broadly. These sites were also the places where one of Sufism's most iconic artistic forms took shape, the various sorts of chant and music developed by different Sufi orders. As illustrated in Chapter 4, each order would develop its own liturgy of chant, with particular formulas, breathing techniques, musical accompaniment, and even dance, reflecting the particular lineage and ethos of the order.

In Chapter 1, we encountered the profound influence of Persian Sufi poetry, and in Chapter 5, we looked at the early Sufi use of pre-Islamic Arab tribal poetry. In both cases of Persian and Arabic Sufi poetry, Sufis encountered pre-existing poetic forms, styles, and motifs, and in a sense sacralized them, or used them as symbols of the Sufi path. Pre-Islamic Persian court poetry celebrated wine, intoxication, and romance. Sufis would utilize these motifs as symbols of the love between the seeker and God. Pre-Islamic Arabic poetry mournfully eulogized the lost beloved, and the longing for the joy of the beloved's presence. Sufis saw this as an ideal metaphor for the seeker's longing for God, and the journey of the disciple, in longing for God, to return to the primordial day before creation, spoken of in the Qur'an, when all souls stood before their Creator and recognized their Beloved, their origin.

This deeply aesthetic orientation of Islamic culture more broadly is rooted in the Qur'ān itself, which expressed ethical and metaphysical principles with rhythm and rhyme. This divine beautification of the word would be emulated by Muslims, for whom the word was central to artistic expression. The Qur'ānic word then was beautified aurally in recitation, visually in architecture, calligraphy, and crafts. This beautific expression of the word further functioned to inspire divine remembrance, as the linguistic signs of God surrounded Muslim daily living. Hence calligraphy would have a pride of place in the Islamic arts, at least in terms of its ubiquity. For some Sufis calligraphy was a contemplative discipline, the practise of which was a form of *dhikr*, just as chanting was.

One of the purposes of this book is to highlight the ways in which different elements of Sufi tradition and culture were interwoven historically, so that ultimately metaphysics, politics, and the arts cannot be thought of as completely independent of one another, and ideally can only be understood in light of their mutual influence.

PARTING THOUGHTS: SEEKING THE ONE

In this book, both themes of unity and diversity have been woven throughout. According to a Sufi tradition, "There are as many paths to God as there are human hearts". Although the paths are potentially infinite in number, their goal is one. The image of a kaleidescope nicely represents both aspects of unity and diversity within Sufism – the light shining through the kaleidescope is one, unity, but the ever shifting patterns of interrelated colours are diverse. Sufis have conceived of the light of guidance as originating in a single source, Allah. This singular light however, is filtered through various cultural and political contexts, which then shape the expressions of Sufism, and the diversity of ways of relating to Islamic traditions and practices. The colours represent the diversity of expressions of Sufi metaphysics, art forms, ritual practices, symbolic sytems, cultural forms, as well as political orientations.

This book has offered an overview of Sufism, ranging from its contemporary practice in Manhattan, through its remarkable medieval florescence, to its hidden origins in Mecca. Although much can be and has been said about the nature of Sufism, its historical formation, intercultural influences, its many forms, philosophies, and practices, Sufis themselves have long held that in the end words are inadequate for expressing what Sufism truly is. Whatever might be said, there remains something else – something that words and concepts, histories and artifacts, buildings and poems, can never really communicate, but only ever hint at or point to, as these verses of Rabi'a suggest:

In love, nothing exists between heart and Heart.
Speech is born out of longing,
True description from the real taste.
The one who tastes, knows;
The one who explains, lies.
How can you describe the true form of Something
In whose presence you are blotted out?
And in whose being you still exist?
And who lives as a sign for your journey?

(Upton 1988: 36)

Paradoxically, words about Sufism must ultimately point beyond words. Sufis have long maintained that it is really only in silence that the truth of Sufism can be known – in insight that flashes in the heart lost in the presence of the moment, or immersed in the depths of prayer and meditation; in the unspoken knowing transmitted by the glance of the *shaykh*; or in the sweet intoxication that accompanies contemplation of profound beauty in any natural or artistic form: the wonder of nature, the grandeur of sacred architecture, the harmonious sounds of the *sema*, or the uplifting rhythms of poetry. It is ultimately here, the Sufis will say, in the presence of the present, and in receptivity to the gift of being, that the truth of the path can be known.

BIBLIOGRAPHY

Abdul Rauf, F. (2004). *What's Right with Islam is What's Right with America: A New Vision for Muslims and the West.* San Francisco, CA: HarperSanFrancisco.

Abdullah, T. (2003). *A Short History of Iraq.* Abingdon: Routledge.

Abou el Fadl, K. (2005). *The Great Theft: Wrestling Islam from the Extremists.* San Francisco, CA: HarperSanFrancisco.

Abrahamov, B. (2003). *Divine Love in Islamic Mysticism: The Teachings of al-Ghazali and al-Dabbagh.* New York: Routledge.

— (2014). *Ibn al-'Arabi and the Sufis.* Oxford: Anqa Publishers.

Abu Madyan. (1996). *The Way of Abu Madyan,* trans. Vincent J. Cornell. Cambridge: Islamic Texts Society.

Abu-Mannah, B. (1982). "The Naqshbandiyyah-Mujaddidiyah in the Ottoman Lands in the Early 19th Century". *Die Welt des Islams* 22: 1–36.

Abun-Nasr, J. M. (1987). *A History of the Maghreb in the Islamic Period.* New York: Cambridge University Press.

Adams Helminski, C. (2003). *Women of Sufism: A Hidden Treasure.* Boston, MA: Shambhala.

Addas, C. (1993). *Quest for the Red Sulpher: The Life of Ibn 'Arabi.* Cambridge: Islamic Texts Society.

Ahmed, A. (2007). *Journey into Islam: The Crisis of Globalization.* London: Viking.

Ahmed, S. (2016). *What is Islam? The Importance of Being Islamic.* Princeton, NJ: Princeton University Press.

Akkach, S. (2005). *Cosmology and Architecture in Premodern Islam: An Architectural Reading of Mystical Ideas.* Albany, NY: State University of New York Press.

al-Hassani, S. T. S. (ed.). (2012). *1001 Inventions: The Enduring Legacy of Muslim Civilization.* Washington, DC: National Geographic Society.

al-Huda, Q. (2003). "Khwaja Mu'in ud-Din Chishti's Death Festival: Competing Authorities over Sacred Space". *Journal of Ritual Studies* 17: 61–78.

al-Sadiq, Ja'far. (2011). *Spiritual Gems: The Mystical Qur'an Commentary Ascribed to Ja'far al-Sadiq as Contained in Sulami's Haqa'iq al-Tafsir from the Text of Paul Nwyia,* trans. F. Mayer. Louisville, KY: Fons Vitae Publishers.

al-Sulami, A. A. (1991). *The Way of Sufi Chivalry,* trans. Tosun Bayrak al-Jerrahi. Rochester, VT: Inner Traditions International.

— (1999). *Early Sufi Women: Dhikr an-Niswa al-Muta 'Abbidat as-Suffiyyat by Abu 'Abd ar-Rahman as-Sulami,* trans. Rkia E. Cornell. Louisville, KY: Fons Vitae Publishers.

— (2010). *Jawami Adab al-Sufiyya (A Collection of Sufi Rules of Conduct),* trans. Elena Biagi. Cambridge: Islamic Texts Society.

Aminrazavi, M. (ed.). (2014). *Sufism and American Literary Masters.* Albany, NY: State University of New York Press.

Anvar, I. (2002). *Divan-i Shams-i Tabriz: Forty-Eight Ghazals.* Den Haag, Netherlands: Semar.

Arberry, A. J. (1957). *The Seven Odes.* London: George Allen & Unwin Ltd.

— (1960). *Shiraz: Persian City of Saints and Poets*. Norman: University of Oklahoma Press.

Ardalan, N., & Bakhtiar, L. (1973). *The Sense of Unity: The Sufi Tradition in Persian Architecture*. Chicago, IL: University of Chicago Press.

Armstrong, A. (1995). *Sufi Terminology: The Mystical Language of Islam*. Kuala Lumpur: A.S. Noordeen.

Artiran, H. N. (2010). "Sertârik Mesnevîhân Sefik Can Dede'nin Mesnevî Üzerine Çalismalari". *SûfiArastirmalari/SufiStudies* 1, no. 2: 99.

Attar, F. (1966). *Muslim Saints and Mystics: Episodes from the Tadhkirat al-Auliya' (Memorial of the Saints') by Farid al-Din Attar*, trans. A. J. Arberry. London: Arkana Publishers.

Atwood, K. J. (2011). *Women Heroes of World War II: 26 Stories about Espionage, Sabotage, Resistance and Rescue*. Chicago, IL: Chicago Review Press.

Axworthy, M. (2010). *A History of Iran: Empire of the Mind*. New York: Basic Books.

Aymard, J.-B., & Laude, P. (2004). *Frithjof Schuon: Life and Teachings*. Albany, NY: State University of New York Press.

Bakhtiar, L. (1976). *Sufi: Expressions of the Mystic Quest*. New York: Thames and Hudson.

Barks, C. (2009). *Rumi: The Book of Love*. New York: HarperCollins.

Barret, P. M. (2007). *American Islam: The Struggle for the Soul of a Religion*. New York: Picador.

Basu, S. (2007). *Spy Princess: The Life of Noor Inayat Khan*. New York: Omega Publications, Inc.

Bayrak, T. (1992). *Secret of Secrets: Hadrat 'Abd al-Qadir al-Jilani*. Cambridge: Islamic Texts Society.

Beeston, A. F. L., Johnstone, T. M., Sergeant, R. B., & Smith, G. R. (eds.). (1982). *Arabic Literature to the End of the Umayyad Period*. Cambridge: Cambridge University Press.

Boyd, J., & Mack, B. (2013). *Educating Muslim Women: The West African Legacy of Nana Asma'u (1793–1864)*. Oxford: Interface.

Brait, E., & Gajanan, M. (2015). "Little Syria: New York Preservationists Fight for Remains of Historical Cultural Hub", *The Guardian*, December 28.

Buehler, A. F. (1998). *Sufi Heirs of the Prophet: The Indian Naqshbandiyya and the Rise of the Mediating Sufi Shaykh*. Columbia, SC: University of South Carolina Press.

Burckhardt, T. (1967). *Sacred Art in East and West*, trans. Lord Northbourne. Louisville, KY: Fons Vitae Publishers.

— (1977). *Mystical Astrology According to Ibn 'Arabi*, trans. Bulent Rauf. Gloucestershire: Beshara Publications.

Cadavid, L. (2007). *Two Who Attained: Twentieth-Century Sufi Saints: Fatima al-Yashrutiyya and Shaykh Ahmad al-'Alawi*. Louisville, KY: Fons Vitae.

California Institute of Earth Art and Architecture. Available at: http://calearth.org

Carette, J., & King, R. (2004). *Selling Spirituality: The Silent Takeover of Religion*. New York: Routledge.

Chittick, W. C. (1989). *The Sufi Path of Knowledge: Ibn al-'Arabi's Metaphysics of Imagination*. Albany, NY: State University of New York Press.

— (1994). *Imaginal Worlds: Ibn al-'Arabi and the Problem of Religious Diversity*. Albany, NY: State University of New York Press.

Chittick, W.C. (1998) *The Self-Disclosure of God: Principles of Ibn al-'Arabi's Cosmology*. Albany, NY: State University of New York Press.

— (2005). *Ibn 'Arabi: Heir to the Prophets*. Oxford: Oneworld.

Chittick, W. C., & Murata, S. (1994). *The Vision of Islam*. New York: Paragon House.

Chodkiewicz, M. (1993). *Seal of the Saints: Prophethood and Sainthood in the Doctrine of Ibn 'Arabi*, trans. Liadain Sherrard. Cambridge: The Islamic Texts Society.

— (1995). *The Spiritual Writings of Amir 'Abd al-Kader*. Albany, NY: State University of New York Press.

Henry Corbin. (1994). *The Man of Light in Iranian Sufism*, trans. Nancy Pearson. New Lebanon, NY: Omega Publications, Inc.

Corbin, H. (1993). *History of Islamic Philosophy*. London: Kegan Paul International.

Cornell, V. J. (1997). "The Way of the Axial Intellect: The Islamic Hermetism of Ibn Sab'in". *Journal of the Muhyiddin Ibn 'Arabi Society* 22: 41–79.

Cornell, R. E. (trans.). (1999). *Early Sufi Women: Dhikr an-Niswa al-Muta 'Abbidat as-Suffiyyat by Abu 'Abd ar-Rahman as-Sulami*. Louisville, KY: Fons Vitae Publishers.

Curtiss, R. H. (1999). "Dispute between US Muslim Groups Goes Public". *Washington Report on Middle East Affairs* 71: 101.

Damrel, D. W. (2006). "Aspects of the Naqshbandi-Haqqani Order in North America". In *Sufism in the West*, ed. Jamal Malik and John Hinnells, 115–26. New York: Routledge.

Dickson, W. R. (2014). "An American Sufism: The Naqshbandi-Haqqani Order as a Public Religion". *Studies in Religion* 43: 411–24.

— (2015). *Living Sufism in North America: From Tradition to Transformation*. Albany, NY: State University of New York Press.

Dyer, D. "A Day with Nur Atriran". Available at: http://sufism.org/articles/a-day-with-nur-artiran

Eickelman, D. F. "Shrine", *The Oxford Encyclopaedia of the Islamic World, Oxford Islamic Studies Online*. Available at: http://www.oxfordislamicstudies.com.lib-proxy.wlu.ca/article/opr/t236/e0739

Einboden, J. (2014). *Islam and Romanticism: Muslim Currents from Goethe to Emerson*. London: Oneworld.

Ekhtiyar, M. (2014). "The Chronological Development of Emerson's Interest in Persian Mysticism". In *Sufism and American Literary Masters*, ed. Mehdi Aminrazavi, 55–74. Albany, NY: State University of New York Press.

Emerson, R. W. "Saadi". *The Dial*, October 1842: 265–69.

— "Persian Poetry". *The Atlantic Monthly*, 1 April 1858: 724–34.

Ephrat, D. (2008). *Spiritual Wayfarers, Leaders in Piety: Sufis and the Dissemination of Islam in Medieval Palestine*. Cambridge: University of Harvard Press.

Ernst, C. W. (1997). *The Shambhala Guide to Sufism*. Boston, MA: Shambhala.

— (1999). *Teachings of Sufism*. Boston, MA: Shambhala.

— (2003). "The Islamization of Yoga in the *Amrtakunda* Translations". *Journal of the Royal Asiatic Society* 13: 199–226.

— (2005). "Situating Sufism and Yoga". *Journal of the Royal Asiatic Society* 15: 15–43.

— (2013). "Muslim Interpreters of Yoga". In *Yoga: The Art of Transformation*, ed. Debra Diamond, 59–68. New York; Washington, DC: Smithsonian.

Ernst, C.W., & Lawrence, B. (2002). *Sufi Martyrs of Love: Chishti Sufism in South Asia and Beyond*. New York: Palgrave-Macmillan.

Euben, R. E. (2006). *Journeys to the Other Shore: Muslim and Western Travelers in Search of Knowledge*. Princeton, NJ: Princeton University Press.

Fadiman, J., & Frager, R. (1997) *Essential Sufism*. San Francisco, CA: HarperSanFrancisco.

Fakhry, M. (2004). *A History of Islamic Philosophy*. 3rd edn. New York: Columbia University Press.

Farrin, R. (2011). *Abundance from the Desert: Classical Arabic Poetry*. Syracuse, NY: Syracuse University Press.

Fitzgerald, M. O. (2010). *Frithjof Schuon: Messenger of the Perennial Philosophy*. Bloomington, IN: World Wisdom.

Frembgen, J. W. (2008). *Journey to God: Sufis and Dervishes in Islam*. Karachi: Oxford University Press.

Friedlander, S. (1992). *The Whirling Dervishes*. Albany, NY: State of University of New York Press.

Genn, C. A. (2007). "The Development of a Modern Western Sufism". In *Sufism and the 'Modern' in Islam*, ed. Martin van Bruinessen and Julia Day Howell, 257–78. New York: I. B. Tauris.

GhaneaBassiri, K. (2010). *A History of Islam in America*. New York: Cambridge University Press.

Glasse, C. (1989). *The Concise Encyclopaedia of Islam*. New York: HarperCollins.

Gooch, B. (2002). *Godtalk: Travels in Spiritual America*. New York: Alfred A. Knopf.

Graham, D. A. S. (2001). "Spreading the Wisdom of Sufism: The Career of Pir-o-Murshid Inayat Khan in the West". In *A Pearl in Wine: Essays on the Life, Music and Sufism of Hazrat Inayat Khan*, ed. Zia Inayat Khan, 127–56. New Lebanon, NY: Omega Publications.

Granoff, J. Interview with William Rory Dickson, June 26, 2010, Philadelphia, PA.

Graves, R. (1964). "Introduction". In *The Sufis*, by Idries Shah, vii–xxii. New York: Doubleday.

Green, N. (2012). *Sufism: A Global History*. Chichester and Malden, MA: Wiley-Blackwell.

Griffel, F. (2009). *Al-Ghazali's Philosophical Theology*. New York: Oxford University Press.

Hahn, L. E., Auxier, R. E., & Stone, L. W., Jr. (eds.). (2001). *The Philosophy of Seyyed Hossein Nasr*. Peru, IL: Open Court.

Halman, T. (2003). *The Tales of Nasrettin Hoca (Told by Aziz Nesin)*, 3rd edn. Istanbul: Dost Yayinlari.

Halverson, J. R. (2010). *Theology and Creed in Sunni Islam: The Muslim Brotherhood, Ash'arism, and Political Sunnism*. New York: Palgrave Macmillan.

Helminski, K. E. (1999). *The Knowing Heart: A Sufi Path of Transformation*. Boston, MA: Shambhala.

Henry, G., & Marriott, S. (2008). *Beads of Faith*. Louisville, KY: Fons Vitae Publishers.

Herberg, W. (1955). *Protestant, Catholic, Jew*. New York: Doubleday.

Hermansen, M. (1996). "In the Garden of American Sufi Movements: Hybrids and Perennials". In *New Trends and Developments in the World of Islam*, ed. Peter B. Clarke, 155–78. London: Luzac.

— (2005). "Sufi Orders and Movements: Turkey, South Asia, Central Asia, Afghanistan, Iran, the Caucasus, and the Arab East". In *Encyclopaedia of Women and Islamic Cultures, Volume II: Family, Law and Politics*, ed. Suad Joseph. Leiden: Brill.

Hirtenstein, S. (1999). *The Unlimited Mercifier: The Spiritual Life and Thought of Ibn 'Arabi*. Oxford: Anqa Publishers.

Hixon, L. (1993). *Atom from the Sun of Knowledge*. Westport, CT: Pir Press.

Hodgson, M. G. S. (1974). *The Venture of Islam: Conscience and History in a World Civilization, Volumes 1–3*. Chicago, IL: University of Chicago Press.

Hujwiri, Ali bin 'Uthman al-Jullabi (1990). *Kashf al-Mahjub: The Oldest Persian Treatise on Sufism*, trans. R. A. Nicholson. Karachi: Darul Ishaat Publishers.

Ibn al-'Arabi, Muhyi al-Din. (1971). *Sufis of Andalusia: The Ruh al-Quds and al-Durrat al-fakhirah of Ibn 'Arabi*, trans. R. W. J. Austin. Berkeley, CA: University of California Press.

— (1980). *Ibn al-'Arabi: The Bezels of Wisdom*, trans. R.W. J. Austin. Mahwah, NJ: Paulist Press.

—. (1992). *What the Seeker Needs: Essays on Spiritual Practice; The One Alone; Majesty and Beauty*, trans. Tosun Bayrak & Rabia T. Harris. Putney, VT: Threshold Books.

Inayat Khan, H. (1979). *The Sufi Message of Hazrat Inayat Khan: The Inner Life*. Geneva: International Headquarters of the Sufi Movement.

— (1990). *The Complete Sayings of Hazrat Inayat Khan*. New Lebanon, NY: Omega Publications.

— (1999). *The Heart of Sufism: Essential Writings of Hazrat Inayat Khan*. Boston, MA: Shambhala.

Inayat Khan, P. V. (1978). *The Message in Our Time: The Life and Teaching of the Sufi Master, Pir-O-Murshid Inayat Khan*. New York: HarperCollins.

Inayat Khan, Z. (2006). "A Hybrid Sufi Order at the Crossroads of Modernity: The Sufi Order and Sufi Movement of Pir-o-Murshid Inayat Khan". PhD dissertation, Duke University, Durham, NC, USA.

Izutsu, T. (1971). "The Basic Structure of Metaphysical Thinking in Islam". In *Collected Papers on Islamic Philosophy and Mysticism*, ed. Mehdi Mohaghegh and Hermann Landolt. Tehran: Tehran Institute of McGill University and Tehran University.

— (1983). *Sufism and Taoism: A Comparative Study of Key Philosophical Concepts*. Berkeley, CA: University of California Press.

Jahanpour, F. (2014). "Emerson on Hafiz and Sa'di: The Narrative of Love and Wine". In *Sufism and American Literary Masters*, ed. Mehdi Aminrazavi, 117–51. Albany, NY: State University of New York Press.

Karamustafa, A. T. (2006). *God's Unruly Friends: Dervish Groups in the Islamic Middle Period 1200–1550*. Oxford: Oneworld.

— (2007). *Sufism: The Formative Period*. Los Angeles, CA: University of California Press.

Karamustafa, A. T. (2005). "Walayah According to al-Junayd." In *Reason and Inspiration in Islam: Theology, Philosophy, and Mysticism in Muslim Thought*, ed. Todd Lawson, 62–68. London: I.B. Tauris.

Keeler, A. (2006). *Sufi Hermeneutics: The Qur'an Commentary of Rashid al-Din Maybudi*. New York: Oxford University Press.

Kinney, J. (1994). "Introduction: The Sufi Conundrum". *Gnosis: A Journal of the Western Inner Traditions* 30: 10–13.

Kiser, J. W. (2008). *Commander of the Faithful: The Life and Times of Emir Abd el-Kader*. Rhinebeck, NY: Monkfish Book Publishing.

Knight, M. M. (2015). *Why I Am a Salafi*. Berkeley, CA: Soft Skull Press.

Knysh, A. (2000). *Islamic Mysticism: A Short History*. Leiden: Brill.

— (2011). *Islam in Historical Perspective*. Upper Saddler River, NJ: Prentice Hall.

Krepel, T., & Fong, J. "Who is Imam Feisal Abdul Rauf?". Available at: http://media-matters.org/research/2010/08/24/who-is-imam-feisal-abdul-rauf/169729

Lapidus, I. (2002). *A History of Islamic Societies*. 2nd edn. Cambridge: Cambridge University Press.

Lapidus, I. M. (2014). *A History of Islamic Societies*. 3rd edn. New York: Cambridge University Press.

Laude, P. D. (2003). "Seyyed Hossein Nasr in the Context of the Perennialist School". *Beacon of Knowledge: Essays in Honour of Seyyed Hossein Nasr*, ed. Mohammad H. Faghfoory, 245–60. Louisville, KY: Fons Vitae.

— (2011). "The God Conditioned by Belief". In *Universal Dimensions of Islam: Studies in Comparative Religion*, ed. Patrick Laude. Bloomington, IN: World Wisdom.

Le Gall, D. (2005). *A Culture of Sufism: Naqshbandis in the Ottoman World, 1450–1700*. Albany, NY: State University of New York Press.

Lewis, F. D. (2000). *Rumi: Past and Present, East and West*. Oxford: Oneworld.

Lewis, S. (2013). *Sufi Vision and Initiation: Meetings with Remarkable Beings*. San Francisco, CA: Sufi Ruhaniat International.

Lewisohn, L. (ed.). (2010). *Hafiz and the Religion of Love in Classical Persian Poetry*. New York: I.B. Tauris.

— (2014). "English Romantics and Persian Sufi Poets: A Wellspring of Inspiration for American Transcendentalists". In *Sufism and American Literary Masters*, ed. Mehdi Aminrazavi, 15–53. Albany, NY: State University of New York Press.

— (2015). "Sufism's Religion of Love, From Rabi'a to Ibn 'Arabi." In *The Cambridge Companion to Sufism*, ed. Lloyd Ridgeon, 150–80. New York: Cambridge University Press.

Lings, M. (1993). *A Sufi Saint of the Twentieth Century: Shayhk Ahmad al-'Alawi*. 3rd edn. Cambridge: The Islamic Texts Society.

— (2004). *Sufi Poems: A Mediaeval Anthology*. Cambridge: The Islamic Texts Society.

— (2005). *Symbol & Archetype: A Study of the Meaning of Existence*. Louisville, KY: Fons Vitae.

Lizzio, K. P. (2014). *Embattled Saints: My Year with the Sufis of Afghanistan*. Wheaton, IL: Quest Books.

Loloi, P. (2014). "Emerson and Aspects of Sa'di's Reception in Nineteenth-Century America". In *Sufism and American Literary Masters*, ed. Mehdi Aminrazavi, 91–116. Albany, NY: State University of New York Press.

Mack, B. (2015). "Nana Asma'u: Nineteenth Century West African Sufi". In *The Cambridge Companion to Sufism*, ed. Lloyd Ridgeon, 183–211. New York: Cambridge University Press.

Malik, J. (2006). "Introduction". In *Sufism in the West*, ed. Jamal Malik and John Hinnells, 1–27. New York: Routledge.

Malik, J., and Hinnells, J. (eds). (2006). *Sufism in the West*. New York: Routledge.

Massignon, L. (1982). *Hallaj: Mystic and Martyr*, trans. Herbert Mason. Princeton, NJ: Princeton University Press.

Masuzawa, T. (2005). *The Invention of World Religions, Or How European Universalism Was Preserved in the Language of Pluralism*. Chicago, IL: University of Chicago Press.

McCarthy, R. J. (2006). *Al-Ghazali's Path to Sufism*. Louisville, KY: Fons Vitae.

Melchert, C. (2015). "Origins and Early Sufism". In *The Cambridge Companion to Sufism*, ed. Lloyd Ridgeon, 3–23. New York: Cambridge University Press.

Merium. "Women and the Talibanization of Shrines in India". *Muslimah Media Watch*, December 11, 2012. Available at: http://www.patheos.com/blogs/mmw/2012/12/women-and-the-talibanization-of-shrines-in-india/

Meyer, W. A. (2001). "A Sunrise in the West: Hazrat Inayat Khan's Legacy in California". In *A Pearl in Wine: Essays on the Life, Music and Sufism of Hazrat Inayat Khan*, ed. Zia Inayat Khan, 395–436. New Lebanon, NY: Omega Publications.

Moosa, E. (2005). *Ghazali and the Poetics of Imagination*. Chapel Hill, NC: The University of North Carolina Press.

Nadeem, S. H. (1993). *A Critical Appreciation of Arabic Mystical Poetry*. Delhi: Adam Publishers & Distributors.

Nasr, S. H. (1967). *Islamic Studies*. Beirut: Librairie Du Liban.

— (1976). *Islamic Science: An Illustrated Study*. Westerham: The World of Islam Festival Publishing Co.

— (1987). *Islamic Art and Spirituality*. Albany, NY: State University of New York Press..

— (2007). *The Garden of Truth: The Vision and Promise of Sufism, Islam's Mystical Tradition*. New York: Harper Collins.

Nasr, S. H., Dagli, C. K., Dakake, M. M., Lumbard, J. E. B., & Rustom, M. (eds). (2015). *The Study Quran: A New Translation and Commentary*. New York: Harper Collins.

Nekbakht Foundation. (1979).*Biography of Pir-O-Murshid Knayat Khan.* London: East-West Publications.

Nurbakhsh. J. (1990). *Sufi Women*. New York: Khaniqahi-Nimatullahi Publications.

Ohlander, E. S. (2015). "Early Sufi Rituals, Beliefs, and Hermerneutics". In *The Cambridge Companion to Sufism*, ed. Lloyd Ridgeon, 53–73. New York: Cambridge University Press.

Özdemir, N. (2011). *The Philosopher's Philosopher: Nasreddin Hodja*. Ankara: Republic of Turkey Ministry of Culture and Tourism Publications.

Rabasa, A., Benard, C., Schwartz, L. H., & Sickle, P. (2007). *Building Moderate Muslim Networks*. Santa Monica: RAND Corporation.

Rahman, S. A. "Indian Women Enraged at Sufi Tomb Ban", *Deutsche Welle,* September 11, 2012. Available at: http://www.dw.de/indian-women-enraged-at-sufi-tomb-ban/a-16367871

Rausch, M. J. (2009). "Encountering Sufism on the Web: Two Halveti-Jerrahi Paths and Their Missions in the USA". In *Sufism Today: Heritage and Tradition in the Global Community*, eds. Catharina Raudvere and Leif Stenberg, 159–76. New York: I. B. Taurus.

Rawlinson, A. (1997). *The Book of Enlightened Masters: Western Teachers in Eastern Traditions*. Chicago, IL: Open Court.

Renard, J. (2005). *Historical Dictionary of Sufism*. Oxford: Scarecrow Press.

Ridgeon, L. (ed.). (2015). *The Cambridge Companion to Sufism*. New York: Cambridge University Press.

Rishmawi, G. K. (1995). "Emerson and the Sufis". *The Muslim World* 85: 147–55.

Rizvi, S. A. A. (1978). *A History of Sufism in India, Volume 1*. New Delhi: Munshiram Manoharlal.

Rogan, E. L. (2011). *The Arabs: A History*. New York: Basic Books.

Rosenthal, F. (2007). *Knowledge Triumphant: The Concept of Knowledge in Medieval Islam*. Boston, MA: Brill.

Safi, O. (2003). "Introduction". In *Progressive Muslims: On Justice, Gender, and Pluralism*, ed. Omid Safi, 1–29. Oxford: Oneworld.

— (2006). *The Politics of Knowledge in Premodern Islam: Negotiating Ideology and Religious Inquiry*. Chapel Hill, NC: The University of North Carolina Press.

Said, A. A. & Funk, N. C. (2003). "Peace in Islam: An Ecology of the Spirit". In *Islam and Ecology: A Bestowed Trust*, eds. Richard C. Foltz, Frederick M. Denny, & Azizan Baharuddin, 155–83. Cambridge, MA: Harvard University Press.

Said, E. W. (1978). *Orientalism*. New York: Random House.

Sands, K. Z. (2006). *Sufi Commentaries on the Qur'an in Classical Islam*. London: Routledge.

Schafer, M. (2012). *Program Notes: Music for the MorningWorld*, 38–39. Available at: http://www.patria.org/arcana/Programnotes.pdf

Schimmel, A. (1975). *Mystical Dimensions of Islam*. Chapel Hill, NC: University of North Carolina Press.

— (1984). *Calligraphy and Islamic Culture*. New York: New York University Press.

— (1987). *And Muhammad is His Messenger: The Veneration of the Prophet in Islamic Piety*. Lahore: Vanguard Books Ltd.

— (1992). *I am Wind You are Fire: The Life and Work of Rumi*. Boston, MA: Shambhala.

— (1994). *Deciphering the Signs of God: A Phenomenological Approach to Islam*. Albany, NY: State University of New York Press.

— (1997). *My Soul Is a Woman: The Feminine in Islam*. New York: The Continuum Publishing Company.

— (2001). *Rumi's World: The Life and Works of the Greatest Sufi Poet*. Boston, MA: Shambhala.

— (2004). *The Empire of the Great Mughals: History, Art and* Culture. London: Reaktion Books.

Schuon, F. (1984). *The Transcendent Unity of Religions*. Wheaton, IL: Quest Books.

Sedgwick, M. (2004). *Against the Modern World: Traditionalism and the Secret Intellectual History of the Twentieth Century*. New York: Oxford University Press.

Sells, M. A. (1989). *Desert Tracings: Six Classic Arabian Odes by 'Alqama, Shanfara, Labid, 'Antara, al-Asha and Dhu al-Rumma*. Hanover, NH: Wesleyan University Press.

— (1996). *Early Islamic Mysticism: Sufi, Qur'an, Miraj, Poetic, and Theological Writings*. New York: Paulist Press.

Shah, I. (1964). *The Sufis*. New York: Doubleday.

— (1971). *The Pleasantries of the Incredible Mulla Nasrudin*. New York: E. P. Dutton.

— (1983). *The Exploits of the Incomparable Mulla Nasrudin/The Subtleties of Inimitable Mulla Nasrudin*. London: Octagon Press.

— (1990 [1968]). *The Way of the Sufi: An Anthology of Sufi Writings*. New York: Penguin Compass.

Sharify-Funk. M. & Dickson, W. R. (2014). "Traces of Panentheism in Islam: Ibn al-'Arabi and the Kaleidoscope of Being". In *Panentheism Across the World's Religious Traditions*, eds. Loriliai Biernacki and Philip Clayton, 142–60. New York: Oxford University Press.

Sharify-Funk. M. & Said, A. A. (2003). *Cultural Diversity and Islam*. Oxford: University Press of America, Inc.

Simon, T. "Coleman Barks: Rumi, Grace, and Human Friendship", *Insights at the Edge*, syndicated from soundstrue.com, December 29, 2013. Available at: http://www.dailygood.org/story/468/coleman-barks-rumi-grace-and-human-friendship-tami-simon/

Sims, K. "Dancing to the Beat of Rumi's Poetry", *The Berkshire Eagle*, August 26, 2010.

Sirriyeh, E. (2013 [1999]). *Sufis and Anti-Sufis: The Defence, Rethinking and Rejection of Sufism in the Modern World*. New York: Routledge.

Smith, M. (2001). *Muslim Women Mystics: The Life and Work of Rabiʻa and Other Women Mystics in Islam*. Oxford: Oneworld Publications.

Snyder, B. H. (2003). "Heartspace: The Bawa Muhaiyaddeen Fellowship and the Culture of Unity". BA thesis, Haverford College, PA, USA.

Sperl, S. (1989). *Mannerism in Arabic Poetry: A Structural Analysis of Selected Texts (3rd Century AH – 9th Century AD – 5th Century AH – 11th Century AD)*. Cambridge: Cambridge University Press.

Stetkevych, J. (1993). *The Zephyrs of Najd: The Poetics of Nostalgia in the Classical Arabic Nasib*. Chicago, IL: University of Chicago Press.

Sutton, D. (2007). *Islamic Design: A Genius for Geometry*. Glastonbury, UK: Wooden Books.

Takim, L. N. (2006). *The Heirs of the Prophet: Charisma and Authority in Shiʻite Islam*. Albany, NY: State University of New York Press.

Thackston Jr., W. M. (1999). *Signs of the Unseen: The Discourses of Jalaluddin Rumi*. Boston: Shambhala.

Tharoor, I. "Can Sufism Diffuse Terrorism?", *Time Magazine*, July 22, 2009.

Tompkins, P. "Rumi Rules!", *Time Magazine*, October 29, 2002.

Toussulis, Y. (2010). *Sufism and the Way of Blame: Hidden Sources of a Sacred Psychology*. Wheaton, IL: Quest Books.

Tresham, S. "5 Ways to Discover 'Our' Murray Schafer", *CBC Music*, July 18, 2013. Available at: http://music.cbc.ca/#!/blogs/2013/7/5-ways-to-discover-our-Murray-Schafer

Trimingham, J. S. (1998). *The Sufi Orders in Islam*. Oxford: Oxford University Press.

Trix, F. (2009). *The Sufi Journey of Baba Rexheb*. Philadelphia, PA: University of Pennsylvania Press.

Twinch, C. (2010). "Created for Compassion: Ibn ʻArabi's Work on Dhu-l Nun the Egyptian". *Journal of the Muhyiddin Ibn ʻArabi Society* 47: 109–29.

Ullah, N. (1963). *Islamic Literature*. New York: Washington Square Press.

Upton, C. (1988). *Doorkeeper of the Heart: Versions of Rabiʻa*. Putney, VT: Threshold Books.

Vaughan-Lee, L. (1998). *Catching the Thread: Sufism, Dreamwork, and Jungian Psychology*. Inverness, CA: The Golden Sufi Center.

— Email Message to William Rory Dickson, November 11, 2014.

Vikor, K. (2015). "Sufism and Colonialism". In *The Cambridge Companion to Sufism*, ed. Lloyd Ridgeon, 212–32. New York: Cambridge University Press.

Voll, J. O. (1999). "Foundations for Renewal and Reform: Islamic Movements in the Eighteenth and Nineteenth Centuries". In *The Oxford History of Islam*, ed. John L. Esposito, 509–48. Oxford: Oxford University Press.

Von Schlegell, B.R. (1990). *Principles of Sufism by al-Qushayri*. Berkeley, CA: Mizan Press.

Webb, G. (2006). "Third-wave Sufism in America and the Bawa Muhaiyaddeen Fellowship". In *Sufism in the West*, eds. Jamal Malik & John Hinnells, 86–102. New York: Routledge.

Weismann, I. (2007). *The Naqshbandiyya: Orthodoxy and Activism in a Worldwide Sufi Tradition*. New York: Routledge.

Werbner, P. (2004). *Pilgrims of Love: The Anthropology of a Global Sufi Cult*. Bloomington, IN: Indiana University Press.

Wilkes, David. (2012). "Tribute to an Indian Princess who Died for Our Freedom: Sculpture Unveiled of Spy Tortured and Executed by Nazis after Refusing to betray Britain". Available at: http://tinyurl.com/article-2230082

Wink, A. (2009). *Akbar*. Oxford: Oneworld.

Witteveen, H. J. (2013). *Universal Sufism*. Humboldt County, CA: Wild Earth Press.

Wormholdt, A. (trans.). (1975). *Selections from Poems of Zuhair ibn Abi Sulma and Hussain ibn Mansur al-Hallaj*. Oskaloosa, IA: William Penn University.

— (trans.). (1977). *The Diwan of 'Ali ibn al-Abbas ibn al-Rumi*. Oskaloosa, IA: William Penn University.

Wuthnow, R. (1998). *After Heaven: Spirituality in America Since the 1950s*. Berkeley, CA: University of California Press.

Xavier, M. S., & Dickson, W. R. (2015). "Négociation du sacré à Philadelphie: soufismes concurrents au sanctuaire de Bawa Muhaiyaddeen". *Social Compass* 62(4): 584–97.

WEBSITES

Conscious Ink, http://consciousink.com

Cordoba Initiative, www.cordobainitiative.org

Hassan Massoudy, http://www.massoudy.net

Nuria Garcia Masip, http://www.nuriaart.com

Robin Becker Dance 2014, http://robinbeckerdance.org

INDEX

CPSIA information can be obtained
at www.ICGtesting.com
Printed in the USA
BVOW06s0210200917
495057BV00013B/4/P

9 781781 792445